[DEAR CARNAP, DEAR VAN]

Quine, at age twenty-seven.

Ina and Rudolf Carnap, Prague, 1933.

Dear Carnap,

Dear Van

The Quine–Carnap
Correspondence
and Related Work

**W.V. Quine and
Rudolf Carnap**

Edited, with an
Introduction by
Richard Creath

University of California Press
Berkeley · Los Angeles · London

Photographs of W. V. Quine and Ina and Rudolf Carnap courtesy
of the Archives of Scientific Philosophy, University of Pittsburgh

University of California Press
Berkeley and Los Angeles, California

University of California Press
Oxford, England

Library of Congress Cataloging-in-Publication Data

Carnap, Rudolf, 1891–1970.
Dear Carnap, dear Van : the Quine-Carnap correspondence and other
material / edited and with an introduction by Richard Creath.
p.   cm.
ISBN 0-520-06847-5
1. Analysis (Philosophy)   2. Logic.   3. Justification (Theory of
knowledge)   4. Carnap, Rudolf, 1891–1970—Correspondence.   5. Quine,
W. V. (Willard Van Orman)—Correspondence.   I. Quine, W.
V. (Willard Van Orman)   II. Creath, Richard.   III. Title.
B808.5.C38   1990
191—dc20   90-40111
                                                                      CIP

Printed in the United States of America

The paper used in this publication meets the minimum requirements of
ANSI/NISO Z39.48-1992 (R 1997) (*Permanence of Paper*). ∞

[CONTENTS]

[PREFACE]

THIS VOLUME is designed for two distinct audiences. The first of these includes a growing band of researchers who recognize that Quine and Carnap are historically very important and that the more we understand of their controversy the firmer our grasp will be of various central issues in the theory of knowledge and in philosophy more generally. This audience needs as much exact information about the manuscripts as can be provided to serve as a basis for its own research.

A second and equally important audience is made up of students (both undergraduate and graduate), interested laymen, and a good many professional philosophers for whom the issues and events of the Carnap-Quine controversy are not matters of regular study. What is essential for this audience is a clear, readable text, unburdened by massive scholarly paraphernalia, and an introduction that lays out the essential philosophic and biographical facts along with a guide to their interpretation.

Fortunately, it is possible to meet the needs of both audiences in a single volume. For the first group I have tried to reproduce as much of the character of the original manuscripts as possible: spellings, marginalia, corrections, and so on. For the second group, the information concerning marginalia, corrections, and so forth beyond the original text is reserved to footnotes. This allows a student, for example, to read and follow the basic text without drowning in the scholarly details. I have very occasionally intruded editorial notes and corrections into the text and set off such insertions by means of angle brackets ('⟨', '⟩'). This is to distinguish these insertions from Carnap's and Quine's material in parentheses or square brackets. That text will have the misspellings of the original, but that should not impair its readability. Besides, it often adds to the charm. Not only does this policy of preserving the "mistakes" conform to standard practice in the editing of scientific manuscripts, it is specifically endorsed by Quine for this project. Where it seemed to me that a reader might mistake an original error for a printer's error, I have inserted '⟨*sic*⟩' in the text. It was generally unnecessary to indicate what would be the corrected expression. I realize that the line is vague between those errors that require notation and those that do not. But vague distinctions are often valuable, and in this case the gain in utility seemed to outweigh the apparent loss of neatness. The text has been proofread repeatedly, so one should assume that residual errors were in the original.

The point of this, and of standard practice more generally, is to preserve as much of the character of and information about the original text as possible. It is the very features that editors tend to clean up that often provide evidence of the writer's mood, attentiveness to the issue, estimation of the recipient, or mastery of the language. For this reason it is often desirable to preserve every detail (short of photocopying), such as original pagination, information on whether the document is handwritten, the author's own corrections, and so on. All of this can be valuable in its place, but here the intended audience is wider than just advanced scholars seeking minute clues. Thus, where Carnap or Quine himself makes a correction in his own text, it is printed here in the corrected form with no notation. However, if the recipient makes a correction, this is noted. This becomes especially important in those letters resulting from the practice that Quine and Carnap adopted for a while of writing in each other's language, correcting the letters received for style and grammar, and returning the corrected copy to its author. The originals are still clear enough to be understood, so those are printed here intact, but the recipient's corrections are duly noted in the footnotes. Marginalia are also reported in the footnotes, and their location is indicated in the margin of the main text. Since Quine often composed his reply in the margins or on the back of Carnap's letters, the marginalia are sometimes cumbersome. In order to minimize the volume of footnotes, however, I have omitted information concerning the original pagination and the physical character of the documents. Moreover, as is customary, I have rendered underscored material in italics.

I have also translated those letters (and passages) which were written in German. This would not have been necessary in a purely scholarly text, but it is provided for students and others who need it. There might have been a question of whether to include both the English and German versions. Since the number of German letters is small, however, both parts of the intended audience could be accommodated without unreasonably compromising either part's needs simply by printing both versions. Thus, letters always appear in their original language first, followed if necessary by a translation into English. Both versions will have the same letter number, for example, 7. But the translation's number will be followed by an 'e', for example, 7.e.

It remains, finally, to say a few words about the sources of the documents: their provenance if you will. The "Lectures on Carnap" are taken from a carbon copy in the possession of Quine. Presumably it dates from when the lectures were delivered publicly in the fall of 1934. From that carbon copy, however, a number of pages were missing, removed, no doubt, for some more pressing philosophic business. Happily, a photocopy of the missing pages was supplied by Burton Dreben. There is another lecture entitled "Logical Positivism" which is part of the carbon copy and whose pages are numbered consecutively with the first three. It is not reprinted here for several reasons. First, it was not part of the original series of lectures but was instead given at Radcliffe College on December 17, 1934. In those days Radcliffe lectures were given separately from those at Harvard. Second, the lecture is of an entirely different kind because it is intended for an undergraduate audience. Third and last, the text is incomplete; what starts out as a full written text peters out into a series of lecture notes.

The sources for the correspondence are more complicated. Both Quine and Carnap tended to keep both sides of their correspondence. This means that there are often two copies of a letter from which to choose. Wherever possible I have used the original text, noting the changes in the copy. Carnap's letters—that is, those letters and copies in Carnap's possession—passed on his death to his daughter, Hanneliese Carnap Thost. She in turn sold the letters along with Carnap's library, manuscripts, and other material to the University of Pittsburgh in 1974. The Carnap Collection is enormous, including about ten thousand letters. While Carnap kept everything or seems to have tried to, most of his correspondence with Quine is absent from the material that was sold to the University of Pittsburgh. Why? We do not know. It could have been lost during one of Carnap's many moves; it could have been loaned to someone for some philosophic purpose; it could just unaccountably have been lost. Fortunately, the overwhelming bulk of this material appears in Quine's collection, so it has not been lost to posterity. While Quine has graciously provided copies of his correspondence with Carnap to the Carnap Collection, for this volume I worked directly from the originals which are still in the files in Quine's Emerson Hall office.

Are there letters between Carnap and Quine of which we have no copy? Of course. The letters we do have make that plain. Perhaps some of those missing letters may eventually turn up. I certainly hope they do. But in the meantime, we can be reasonably sure that we have the vast majority of the letters that were written, certainly enough to trace the development of their relationship both intellectual and personal.

The letters are interrupted in this volume by Carnap's reply to Quine: "Quine on Analyticity." This is transcribed and translated from a shorthand manuscript in the Rudolf Carnap Collection at the University of Pittsburgh. The transcription is by Richard Nollan. Unfortunately there is no entirely satisfactory place to print the paper within this volume. Placing it before or after the correspondence takes it far out of its natural chronological order. Including it within the correspondence would be misleading, for there is no evidence that Quine ever saw the paper. To avoid these difficulties, I have divided the correspondence into two (rather unequal) parts: (1) up through the publication of "Two Dogmas of Empiricism" and (2) thereafter. Thus, "Quine on Analyticity" appears in its correct chronological position (between letters 145 and 146) without thereby actually becoming part of the correspondence.

This volume is rounded out by Quine's "Homage to Carnap," which was delivered as part of the memorial to Carnap at the Philosophy of Science Association Meeting held in Boston in October of 1970. A number of philosophers spoke at the memorial session, and their remarks are printed in *PSA 1970: In Memory of Rudolf Carnap: Proceedings of the 1970 Biennial Meeting, Philosophy of Science Association.* The text of Quine's "Homage" in the present volume is taken directly and unchanged from that earlier printing.

The issues that Carnap and Quine struggled with, developed, and fought over have not gone away. Nor are they likely to become obsolete, for they are among the deepest questions in all philosophy. It is my hope that this collection, by preserving an important bit of philosophy's recent past, can help both students and scholars create a richer bit of philosophy's future.

Richard Creath

Tempe, Arizona
December 1988

[ACKNOWLEDGMENTS]

THE IDEA that the lectures and letters herein should be published has no doubt occurred to almost everyone who has had the opportunity to read them. The concrete plan that resulted in this volume, however, had a very definite beginning. Like so many other good ideas, it began in the philosophy department office of Professor Burton Dreben at Harvard University. I was there because I have an abiding interest in the issues that both united and divided Quine and Carnap and because Dreben has an unusually deep understanding of both the historical episodes and the philosophic ideas they embody. Dreben was there because it was, after all, his office, and he is unfailingly generous with his time to anyone, whatever age or persuasion, who wants to learn.

Dreben encouraged the idea that I should edit such a volume, as did Quine immediately thereafter. Since it seemed to me before the fact a much easier task than it now seems afterward, I readily agreed. In any case, I incurred along the way a number of debts that I am now happy to acknowledge even if I am not able to repay them. The first of these debts is, of course, to Quine and to Carnap for writing something so manifestly worthwhile.

I am grateful, as well, for the moral support that Quine provided throughout. He offered the necessary permissions and photocopies of the parts of this volume that were in his collection, several times honoring requests for ever clearer copies of the material. He also gave of his time and advice, and he generously provided access to other parts of his correspondence and manuscripts. All of this aided my understanding and, I trust, the volume enormously. For permission to publish the Carnap letters and "Quine on Analyticity" I am indebted both to the University of Pittsburgh, which houses the magnificent Rudolf Carnap Collection, and to the estate of Rudolf Carnap and Carnap's daughter Hanneliese Carnap Thost as trustee thereof. The only item in this book which has previously been published is the "Homage to Carnap," which appeared in *PSA 1970: In Memory of Rudolf Carnap: Proceedings of the 1970 Biennial Meeting, Philosophy of Science Association*, ed. Roger C. Buck and Robert S. Cohen, Boston Studies in the Philosophy of Science, vol. 8 (Dordrecht and Boston: D. Reidel Publishing Company, 1971), pp. xxii–xxv. Copyright © 1971 by D. Reidel Publishing Company, Dordrecht, Holland. Reprinted by permission of Kluwer Academic Publishers.

In addition to those who gave permissions there are many people who aided the project significantly. As indicated, I owe a special debt to Burton Dreben for his early and constant encouragement. I am glad also that he was able to supply the missing pages that had somehow disappeared from Quine's copy of the "Lectures."

At the University of Pittsburgh, special thanks go to Charles Aston, Coordinator of the Special Collections Department, to Richard Nollan, and to W. Gerald Heverly. Richard Nollan is a former curator of the Carnap Collection and of the Archive of Scientific Philosophy, of which it is a part. He assisted in the preparation of materials, checked and corrected my translations from the German, and transcribed Carnap's special German shorthand. Gerry Heverly is the current curator of these collections, and he provided valuable and timely assistance in the preparation and transcription of the materials.

I would also like to thank my research assistants, William Berge and Keith Korcz, both of whom helped with proofreading, and the staff (chiefly Bettyann Kevles and Elizabeth Knoll) and referees of the University of California Press. Their advice, their support, and their patience were enormously valuable. I'd also like to thank Diane Paul for being in the right place at the right time.

Very special thanks go to Joy Erickson, expert word processor for the Department of Philosophy, Arizona State University. She was and is far more than a typist. Not only did she rapidly produce clean, clear copy from illegible and complicated originals in both German and English, but her patience, good humor, and good sense have enriched the process and improved the product at every turn. She is truly a treasure.

[Acknowledgments]

There have been several sources of financial support for this project and other research. The National Endowment for the Humanities provided a fellowship for the academic year 1987–88 (NEH Grant #FB-24865-87), and the National Science Foundation provided financial support for the summers of 1987 and 1988 (NSF Grant #SES 19308). These were supplemented by grants from Arizona State University through the offices of both the Vice President for Research and the Dean of the College of Liberal Arts and Sciences. For all of these I am very grateful. There can be no doubt that without this time and support, this volume and other products of the research would have appeared only very much later if at all.

Finally, and most important, there is one person to whom more thanks are due than I can ever hope to offer. That is my wife and colleague, Jane Maienschein. Her help and support have literally made all the difference between the success and failure of this project. She offered substantive and stylistic advice, she read proof (lots of it), and she helped decode some of the more obscure marginalia. Far more than all of these, her warm encouragement and understanding helped the project go forward when otherwise it would surely have stopped.

[INTRODUCTION]

THE VOLUME that follows contains the complete correspondence over more than thirty-five years between Rudolf Carnap (1891–1970) and W. V. O. Quine (1908–). It also contains three very early (1934) lectures by Quine on Carnap as well as a short paper by Carnap and Quine's memorial tribute to Carnap of 1970. All but the last of these are hitherto unpublished. Together they provide a remarkable record of a major philosophic controversy and of an enduring friendship.

Carnap and Quine are undoubtedly two of the most important philosophers of the twentieth century. Carnap ranks with Russell and Wittgenstein as among the most influential philosophers of the last one hundred years. He made fundamental contributions to such diverse areas as epistemology, logic, philosophy of language, probability theory, philosophy of science, and even systematic metaphysics (though he would probably be aghast to think that he had aided metaphysics in any way). He was one of the leaders of the Logical Positivist movement from the late 1920s, and from the mid-1930s he was the unrivaled spokesman for the movement, which is today both honored and reviled. But even the latter reaction shows the power and durability of positivism's ideas, for its detractors so often concede in practice that it is the view to be overthrown.

Quine has dominated his generation of philosophers much as Carnap had done for his; indeed, Quine is probably the most influential philosopher alive today. For over fifty years his provocative and graceful writings have illuminated such areas as logic, philosophy of language, and epistemology. Quine began his career as an enthusiastic supporter of Carnap, but over the years their paths diverged. Quine became, in fact, Carnap's deepest, most persistent, yet most sympathetic critic.

The disagreement emerged only very slowly, but those differences proved to be fundamental. Even the principals did not initially suspect how much so. But the story of Carnap and Quine is no tale of a friendship gone sour. Alongside and through the controversy there remained an abundant affection and respect on both sides. Quite possibly the conflict even deepened their friendship and vice versa. This is not always the case among philosophers, but in the pages that follow I shall explore their relationship in more detail.

The initial task is to understand what the battle is all about. The first section of this Introduction, therefore, will be devoted to an examination of the fundamental features of Carnap's view and of Quine's alternative to it. As we shall see, though their differences are deep, so is their agreement. With the basic issue in mind, we can then turn in the second main section to the more historical task of tracing the development of these views. This will allow us not only to place the lectures and letters in historical context but also to see how the debate emerged and why it ended with no clear victor. In the process I shall examine the texts themselves and touch on related works in order to bring out their central themes and to tie them to our earlier discussion. Quine's three "Lectures on Carnap," for example, represent a very early stage in the association of the two men and, hence, a very useful point of comparison for their later work, especially for "Truth by Convention," to which the lectures are closely related. The correspondence raises a host of issues: English and German terminology, analyticity, and the method of intension and extension, to name only a few. The letters also teem with more personal matters, but it would be pointless to attempt any systematic treatment thereof. I do not mean to suggest, however, that there is or should be any decisive separation between the scientific work under study and the web of personal connections between Carnap and Quine. Quite the contrary! In any case it seems prudent to let these personal matters show themselves both in the letters and in Quine's "Homage to Carnap."

[THE BASIC ISSUE: ANALYTICITY]

To say that Carnap and Quine differed over analyticity is true enough but not very informative. This is, of course, because 'analyticity' is a bit of technical jargon unfamiliar to anyone except those philosophers who already believe they understand the disagreement between Carnap and Quine. The term will, however, prove useful in summarizing the issues once we have them in hand.

What lies behind the word 'analyticity' is the theory of knowledge. One of the central questions of this area of inquiry is: how can we justify our beliefs? Carnap and Quine have two quite different strategies for answering this question. So different are their strategies that the argument often seems to be about other topics altogether. It is not. At least in Carnap's case, his strategy is so deeply embedded in his whole approach to philosophy that he spends little time articulating either the question or his general plan for answering it, and he has some difficulty grasping or responding to questions or objections that are based on other strategies.

Fortunately for our purposes, Carnap's strategy can be stated briefly and nontechnically. Let us begin with our own practices. Generally, we justify our beliefs by citing our reasons. These reasons are, of course, other beliefs of ours, and in order for them to do the job they must have two features. First, they must stand in the right sort of logical relation to the belief whose justification is sought. Specifying what those relations are is the task of logicians and need not concern us here. The second feature that reasons must have is that they must themselves be justified. I can hardly justify a belief that my wife is the empress Josephine if my only reason is the completely unwarranted belief that I am Napoleon. If giving reasons were the only way to justify beliefs, however, the chain of reasons could never get started and all beliefs would be unwarranted. There must be some way to justify beliefs other than by inferring them from antecedently warranted beliefs.

Experience is one such way of justifying our beliefs. Philosophers disagree about which claims may be perceptually warranted, but in modern times there is unanimity that experience does justify some of our beliefs. Unfortunately, there is also pretty general agreement that experience is not enough. For some of our beliefs it has seemed irrelevant. In particular, it was thought irrelevant for mathematics. After all, what perceptual evidence could there be that zero is a number? More profoundly, experience has seemed irrelevant for logic and the theory of knowledge. Logic was presupposed in tying the experience to anything else, so it would be circular to use logic and experience to support logic. The theory of knowledge was likewise presupposed in taking those perceptual judgments as warranted at all.

There are also other "special" beliefs of ours (such as: Nothing is red and green all over at the same time) for which experience has seemed relevant but insufficient. Traditionally such claims have been called necessary or *a priori*, and this feature is contrasted with the contingency (or even fallibility) of perceptual claims. The same point can be made, but with less philosophic baggage, simply by noting that the degree of justification that we think we have for perceptual claims and the nature of their connection with the "special" beliefs seems to preclude experience providing as much justification for "special" beliefs as we think they in fact have.

Thus, if our usual convictions about how justified we are in our various beliefs are roughly correct, then there must be some *source* of justification other than experience. The philosophic tradition has, of course, obliged. There is an avenue, it was said, through which we can know the axioms of arithmetic, the fundamentals of logic, and many other things, and we can know them directly (not through inference) and certainly without any appeal to sensory experience. That avenue is *intuition*. Now the word 'intuition' has been used in many many ways throughout the history of philosophy. What I have in mind as intuition is a supposed direct metaphysical insight or grasp of objects or features of things independent of ourselves but inaccessible to ordinary sensory observation. It is then through intuition that the "special" beliefs lately noted can be justified. That there is such an intuitive means of justification is an idea characteristic of the whole Platonic tradition, but for our purposes especially of Frege and (usually) Russell, two of Carnap's most important philosophical forebears. Even the Kantian tradition (though it unraveled through the nineteenth century) relied on a form of intuition similar to the Platonic one and no less mysterious.

Unfortunately, when intuition in this sense is looked at with any care, it is not terribly attractive. Our intuitions notoriously contradict one another, and there is no way to separate the reliable intuitions from the unreliable. Importantly, no explanation can be given as to why any of them should be trusted. In this, intuition differs from perception. When I perceive that the book before me is red, in some way the book's being red brings about (causes) my perceptual judgment. This would account for the reliability of my judgment. It is, of course, difficult to spell out just how this process works, and at present psychologists have only a sketch. But we do have a sketch, and we are reasonably confident that we shall be able to fill it out more fully. This is not the case with, say, mathematical intuition. In fact, according to standard Platonic doctrine, numbers (the targets of this intuition) are not even in the causal order, and hence no such causal account of reliability is even possible. We are left with the sad conclusion that these intuitions are no more than prejudices in disguise, and any appeal to intuition is an act of desperation.

Carnap did not say all of this in just these words, but his verificationism and his antimetaphysical stance amount to the same thing. Given the difficulties with intuition, Carnap's suggestions on how to avoid reliance on intuition are both welcome and profound. Consider again those basic claims which together with experience are jointly sufficient to justify to the appropriate degree the rest of our beliefs, that is, the very ones previously thought to be grasped via intuition. These basic beliefs tell us a great deal about how the words therein are to be understood. In fact, why not treat them as definitions? This was precisely what Carnap proposed. The idea was an elaboration of an earlier proposal by Poincaré and by Hilbert for the special case of geometry. Carnap, however, was the first to suggest it for the full range of philosophic problems including the theory of knowledge.

Let us be clearer about what sort of definition is being suggested and what that involves for philosophy. These basic sentences (we can take the basic axioms of arithmetic as an example) certainly do not look like the familiar sort of definition that provides a word or phrase that has the same meaning as the word to be defined. These ordinary definitions are called explicit definitions, and the idea that they are all there is to learning the meaning of a word is problematic in the same way as the idea that having or giving reasons is all there is to justification. In the case of justification, the reasons had to be antecedently justified, and hence the chain of reasons had to begin with something justified in some other way. Similarly, if an explicit definition is to convey the meaning of a word, the word or words in the defining phrase must be antecedently understood, and hence the chain of explicit definitions must begin with words whose meaning is learned in some way other than explicit definition. But how? Again experience may provide some help through what used to be called ostensive definition, but this (again) seems insufficient for mathematics or logic among other things. What else is there, and what does one know when one understands a term? Concerning the latter, what one needs to know is whether using a given term in various circumstances is appropriate or not. In the case of arithmetic, what one needs to know about the word 'zero' is that it is the name of a number, and what one needs to know about the words 'number' and 'successor' includes that every number has a successor. In short, what one needs to understand of arithmetic words is that the axioms of arithmetic are true. Specifying such axioms as truths might therefore count as a kind of definition. Call it implicit definition to differentiate it from the explicit variety described earlier.

Carnap's proposal, then, is to treat the basic axioms of mathematics, of logic, and of the theory of knowledge itself, as well as the sundry other special sentences, as an implicit definition of the terms they contain. The upshot of this is that simultaneously the basic terms are understood with enough meaning for the purpose of mathematics, logic, and so on, and the basic claims thereof need no further justification, for we have so chosen our language as to make these particular claims true. The contrast here between this approach and the previously discussed approach of relying on intuition could not be clearer. Previously it was imagined that there was a domain of truths independent of ourselves to which we were gaining some mysterious access via intuition. Unfortunately there was no way to defend the idea that that access was genuine. On Carnap's proposal the basic claims are in some sense truths of our own making. It is not that we make objects and features thereof, rather we construct our language in such a way that those basic claims are true. No question of fidelity to independent fact arises in choosing a language. The basic claims and their logical consequences are true in virtue of their meaning. The claims can, therefore, become known through an *analysis* of the meanings of the terms they contain. Such claims as are true in virtue of their meaning Carnap calls *analytic*. The word 'analytic' here is obviously a technical term embedded in Carnap's theory of justification, and the question of whether there are analytic truths comes to no more and no less than the question of whether Carnap's general theory of knowledge is right, or at least nearly so.

One consequence of Carnap's theory is that the basic metaphysical commitments, logical rules, epistemic principles, and so on are language-dependent, that is, that they depend on what definitions are chosen. If you choose differently from me, we do not thereby disagree; we merely speak different languages. Now languages are neither true nor false. They are not that sort of thing. Sentences, or statements, or beliefs are true or false, but they are so only after their terms are endowed with enough meaning that the sentences or whatever say something. That is to say that truth arises only after the language is laid down. If languages are neither true nor false, the choice of a language is a matter of convention. To say that the choice is conventional is just to say that we could have chosen otherwise and that there can be no epistemic reasons for one choice over another (i.e., we can have no reason for thinking that one choice is more likely to be true than another). Certainly this accords well with our usual beliefs that grammar is conventional and that the choice of, say, metrical units is conventional.

While there may be no true or false in choosing a language, some choices are bound to be more convenient than others, though this may vary for differing purposes. This tie to interests, aims, or purposes makes choosing conventions a pragmatic matter. There may be no epistemic reasons for choosing one language over another, but there may be pragmatic reasons for doing so. Indeed Carnap was convinced that the primary task of philosophers should be to discover and evaluate the pragmatic consequences of this or that linguistic structure. Philosophy, on this model, becomes a kind of conceptual engineering, and a great deal depends on the linguistic structures we devise. Consider some of the defects that such a structure can have. One of the most serious pragmatic defects that can befall a language is inconsistency. In an inconsistent system every sentence and its negation is a logical consequence of the language alone and hence of every sentence within it. The language loses all hope of distinguishing between what is affirmed and what is denied. In brief, the whole language loses its point. There can be pragmatic defects short of inconsistency, too. If a language lacks inductive inference rules or has ones that are too weak, then we cannot make any prediction or not enough for the purposes of everyday life. If the inductive rules are too strong, the conclusions we draw will constantly conflict with one another and on pain of contradiction must constantly be revised, all of which is rather a costly nuisance. Similarly the only real test of a mathematical system is its utility for such work as physics or accounting. Metaphysics too becomes a pragmatic matter, as does the theory of knowledge itself.

These results are in fact enormously encouraging, for they seem to show both that many philosophical disputes can be resolved and how to do so. The history of philosophy has been marked by a wide variety of elaborate systems, none of which has been able to establish itself as uniquely correct. Nonphilosophers often complain that philosophy makes no progress at all, but that is perhaps too harsh a judgment. Part of the problem may be that good ideas that are both novel and fundamental are rare in any field. But that cannot be the whole story. Perhaps philosophers have also made their task unnecessarily difficult by attempting too much, that is, by attempting to prove that a given system is uniquely correct. If, however, as Carnap suggests, basic philosophic commitments are really definitions in disguise, then some philosophic disputes will turn out to be merely verbal. These, then, can be set aside. Second, Carnap's program firmly ties philosophy to the study of formal languages, that is, to symbolic logic. This area of study had been making astonishingly rapid progress from the 1870s through the 1930s, and this progress seemed durable in the sense that it would not be lost whenever metaphysical fashion changed. If any of this progressiveness could rub off on philosophy more generally, that would be all to the good. Third, Carnap's program provides a clearer sense of how to go about the evaluation of philosophic ideas; one tests their consequences for pragmatic utility. For example, we can finally jettison the sterile arguments over whether inductive inferences are justified and get down to the serious business of discovering which inductive rules are most useful. This provides a real sense of direction to the enterprise.

Carnap's work, however, represents far more than an exciting program for future research. After all, it could already number among its achievements an important triumph over the apparent need to rely on mysterious and suspect intuitions. Though ideas that are new, deep, and genuinely helpful are exceedingly rare in any discipline, Carnap's suggestion of treating the claims that are justificationally most basic as implicit definitions or linguistic conventions nonetheless seems to be just such an idea. I do not mean to say that it is thereby the last word in philosophy, only that it is a genuine step forward.

In relativizing metaphysical and epistemological truth to a language and by turning philosophical disputations into arguments over the pragmatic utility of language systems, Carnap strikes a very deep philosophical nerve. It is not surprising that the most vigorous opposition to Carnap's views comes from those who are horrified by just this outcome. Indeed, for each feature of Carnap's system that is attractive to some philosophers there are other philosophers who will be put off by just that feature. Philosophers who have invested their lives in various disputes are insulted and angered to be told that any of those disputes is merely verbal. Second, philosophy has often seemed to be the paradigmatically nontechnical field. When Carnap suggests that philosophy could and should become more like logic, those who are unsure of their own technical abilities are more than a little alarmed. It is all very well for physics or forensic pathology to become technical specialties but not for philosophy to do so. Besides, the more clearly and precisely philosophic doctrines are expected to be stated, the more readily their defects are exposed. There is real safety in vagueness. Third, there are those who object to Carnap's pragmatism itself. Philosophy and mathematics have often enjoyed a kind of aristocratic otherworldliness according to which Truth and Beauty have nothing to do with mere utility, and to be concerned with pragmatic matters is to reveal oneself a philistine or, worse yet, a member of the commercial rather than the intellectual class.

Just as Carnap's circumvention of intuition is the chief virtue of his system, there are those who find the loss of intuition unendurable or the relativism intrinsic to its replacement unacceptable. Some, attempting to make a virtue of necessity, hold that intuition is what makes philosophy (and mathematics) special. By providing a unique access to a domain of truths beyond experience, intuition makes philosophy higher and nobler than the empirical sciences. There is perhaps no point in Carnap's replying to those who find mysteriousness and ineffability as the objects of their veneration. But to the rest, Carnap need only say that while intuition may indeed have made earlier philosophies special, that is by itself no cause for rejoicing. Unless and until a satisfactory account can be given as to why we should trust intuition, that specialness must be reckoned a vice rather than a virtue.

The other half of this objection, that Carnap's proposals amount to a form of relativism, is more serious. Here the matter is less a rearguard action on behalf of intuition than a counteroffensive designed to show that Carnap's answer is unacceptable as well. The issue is large enough that it cannot be dealt with definitively here, but Carnap can defend himself. First, remember that the conventionality of language, even natural language, is not under attack. No one denies that we are free to introduce novel notation or grammatical structures at our convenience. It is equally hard to deny that we could lay down just those sentences which were heretofore thought to be intuited as conventions of language. Rather the worry is that we ought not think of such principles in Carnap's way because (it is supposed) every convention must be equally good, so on Carnap's strategy no rules of inference, for example, could be better than any other, and no set of arithmetic axioms could be better than any other. Such a relativism clashes squarely with our naive faith that we have reality by the throat, that we have latched onto the correct metaphysics and rules of reasoning, or at least that we can do so. Of course, this naive faith begs the question at issue; it is not an argument against Carnap but a flat rejection of his view. This idea that if the axioms of arithmetic or logic are treated as linguistic conventions, then all must be equally good should not be dismissed but answered, for it represents a fundamental misunderstanding of Carnap's philosophy. In the first place Carnap obviously does not believe that all systems are equally good. That is the whole point of pragmatic evaluation. Nor is one free to affirm in one system what one denies in another. After all, the meanings are not fixed until after the linguistic conventions are established. If different rules are laid down, then there is no one common claim with a single meaning that is variously asserted and denied. Of course, one sentence (as a string of letters and spaces) may occur in two languages and be true in one and false in the other. That, however, is not news, and

it is not alarming. Once a statement with a fixed meaning is specified, then the linguistic conventions that give it that meaning are
also fixed. Once meanings are fixed, the charge of relativism is
completely unfounded. Before they are fixed, there is no question
of truth to relativize.

I have spent some time in detailing why some philosophers
have found Carnap's system attractive and why various others
have found it distasteful for the selfsame reasons. While it is well
known that Quine disagreed vigorously with Carnap, it must be
noted that the reasons cited above attracted him to Carnap. When
the two met, Quine was too young to have had any significant
investment of time in the systems Carnap undermined. Second,
Quine was a new but justly confident logician who welcomed the
tie between logic and philosophy more generally. Third, Quine too
was initially hostile to the otherworldliness of much of the philosophic scene, and his own pragmatism was at least as robust as
Carnap's. Most important, Quine was also an enemy of intuition,
and Carnap's so-called relativism was to be extended by Quine to
include relativizing ontology and translation as well. As we shall
see, Quine began his career as an enthusiastic advocate for
Carnap. When disagreement did come, it was not because Quine
wanted to retreat to a theory of knowledge that relied on intuition.
Rather, Quine sought to forge a new epistemology that would
escape both from intuition and from Carnap's linguistic conventionalism. It is to this mature (non-Carnapian) Quine that we now
turn.

Before examining Quine's own system directly, however, let us
see what he objects to about Carnap's position. Quine's basic
claim is not that there are no analytic truths but rather that the
whole idea of analyticity is unintelligible. There are essentially
three (connected) arguments that Quine has for this. First, all attempts to clarify the notion are as yet unsuitable for the purpose of
science since each such attempt appeals at bottom to other notions
that are at least as suspect as analyticity itself. Second, Carnap's
attempts to clarify the notion for artificial languages fail. Third,
and by far most important, Quine favors an alternative theory of
knowledge in which there is no place for an analog of analyticity,
meaning, or synonymy. We shall look at each argument in turn.

Quine's first argument against analyticity is that no one has produced a satisfactory clarification of it yet. In order to appreciate the force of this argument, we need to examine some sample attempts to see what it is about them that Quine finds defective. Then we can understand more fully what Quine's standards of intelligibility are. In fact it is easy to define analyticity: analytic claims are just those which are true by virtue of their meaning, analytic claims are just those which result from logical truths by replacing expressions with others synonymous with them.[1] These informal definitions would provide sufficient clarity to the word 'analytic' only if all terms therein were themselves sufficiently clear. According to Quine they are not. In fact there is a whole family of terms, each of which can be defined using others from the family. This family includes: 'analytic', 'meaning', 'synonymy', 'necessity', 'self-contradictory', 'semantical rule', and 'is defined as'.

Quine thinks that the whole family is unintelligible. For those who think otherwise, Quine knows, the existence of dictionaries is a source of comfort and reassurance: surely there are synonymies, for lexicographers have found them. Quine is unfazed by this for two reasons: First, this view of dictionaries begs the question; it presupposes a working notion of synonymy rather than explaining it. It says nothing as to what the lexicographers are supposed to report. Second, Quine argues, lexicography is more varied than just reporting synonymies, if any. Any unfamiliar fact, or theory, or extensional equivalent might serve to instruct the unschooled in the verbal habits of the community, and such instruction is what the writers of dictionaries give us.

Quine has conceded that in "the explicitly conventional introduction of novel notation for the purposes of sheer abbreviation," the abbreviation really is synonymous with what it abbreviates. This has seemed to some to give the whole game away. It does not, for Quine denies that such explicit abbreviation results in a special kind of truth. Rather, the phrase 'true by definition' reminds us that the equivalence became true through the passing historical episode of an explicit act of defining. This is precisely what words from natural language typically lack.

There are two things that this discussion of definition reveals.

1. This works for some but not all the truths said to be analytic.

One, Quine's attention is focused on natural languages rather than the artificial languages that logicians construct, and, two, the intelligibility demands that Quine places on 'analytic' and other terms is that they be employable in empirical linguistics. Quine is often criticized on these two points, so it is worthwhile pausing to defend him. To take the second point first: Quine often suggests that what he demands of 'analytic' is that it be explicitly defined in behavioral terms. With the diminishing popularity of behaviorism, Quine's demands have come under increasing attack. But Quine's demands need not be tied to behaviorism. What demands ought one place on new terms in empirical science? For that matter, what demands did Carnap place on such terms? Carnap's answer, and it seems to be a good one, is that we must be able at least sometimes to confirm or disconfirm claims containing the term, and this involves tying the term back ultimately to terms that we can use observationally. Carnap called these ties back to observation 'correspondence rules'. This is precisely what Quine is demanding and what he fails to find for 'analytic', 'synonymy', and so on.

Quine's emphasis on natural languages perhaps needs no defense. Of course we want our terminology to be able to describe natural languages as well as artificial ones. But there are those, Carnap apparently among them, who think that the only problems to which Quine points are problems arising from the vagueness of ordinary language. The only way for Quine to achieve the clarity he craves is by looking at the results of appropriately clarifying ordinary language, that is, by examining the artificial languages that result from explicating ordinary language. For these constructed language systems no need for empirical test criteria arises.

Quine's response to this is, in essence, his second main objection to analyticity. He claims that constructed languages à la Carnap do not, in fact, clarify the term 'analytic'. Carnap was able to provide a completely precise specification of which sentences of a given artificial language are analytic. Quine agrees, but argues that we are none the wiser about what is being attributed to all those sentences. For all we know, all they have in common is appearing on a list under the heading 'analytic sentences'. What Carnap has succeeded in defining is 'analytic-in-L', where 'L' names the specific artificial language he has constructed, but that throws no light on the interesting word 'analytic'. What is needed is a definition of 'analytic in L' for variable 'L'.

Many have found this puzzling, and many others have found it just wrongheaded. How, they ask, can it be demanded that we have a definition for 'analytic in L' for variable 'L' where we have no definition for 'true in L' for variable 'L'? Certainly Quine has no intention of abandoning the notion of truth, nor does he think that the intelligibility of 'true' is even seriously in question. I am not sure that Quine's response to this has been entirely satisfactory, but there is something to Quine's second argument against analyticity that must not be dismissed out of hand. An analogy might bring out this something.

Consider for a moment the axioms of your favorite geometry as an implicit definition of the terms 'point', 'line', 'between', and so on contained therein. Construed purely as an implicit definition, the axioms will have in any sufficiently numerous domain of objects what logicians call a model. Thus, as pure implicit definition, there is no reason to suppose that the system is about *lines* rather than, say, tigers. But the use of such words as 'line', 'point', and so on is not gratuitous in this case: we know how to supplement the interpretation provided by the implicit definition and thereby turn what Carnap calls a pure geometry into what he calls a physical geometry. The latter is a theory that is genuinely about this familiar physical space and describes it whether truly or falsely. It is the availability of the additional interpretation, usually provided by methods of measurement, that legitimates the use of the word 'line' within the implicit definition. If no such correspondence rules, as Carnap calls them, are possible, then the pure geometries lose their point. What Quine is demanding from 'analytic' is the analog of those measurement methods; that is, he demands that there be available some additional interpretation that assures us that the purely formal construction is talking about what it is supposed to be. Such a demand on Quine's part is perfectly reasonable.

I happen to think that both of Quine's first two objections to analyticity can be answered. The answer would come from spelling out the role that analytic sentences play within a system of confirmation (I do not mean here that analytic sentences are confirmed come what may; as we saw, that is misleading). In fact the prior description of Carnap's theory of knowledge outlines the role of analytic sentences and thus goes several steps toward answering Quine's objection. The focus on confirmation or justification also suggests the required empirical criteria as well. We can watch people argue in order to discover what is taken as an argument and what the community practices are in evaluating the strengths of those arguments. There is neither space nor need to say more here.

Quine's third argument against analyticity, however, is of an entirely different sort. Rather than pointing to a specific defect in Carnap's system, Quine here offers an alternative to it. Quine must make his alternative internally acceptable, but the issue is broader than that. He needs to show that his system is importantly *better than* Carnap's. If he can do that, then analyticity must be rejected even if that notion is wholly intelligible. If he cannot, then his strongest argument against analyticity fails. This issue at hand, then, is essentially comparative, and it can be addressed only by laying out Quine's system in detail.

According to Quine, scientific reasoning begins with a body of beliefs, the beliefs that we do in fact have. Never mind how we came by those beliefs. Quine calls this the lore of our fathers, and perhaps there is nowhere else that we can begin. But experience does not always conform to these beliefs, so we must revise. This revision is governed by only two principles: simplicity and conservatism. We want to effect as simple and tidy a system as possible, and we want to preserve as much of our previous belief as possible. Note that these are global considerations dictating features of the overall system rather than any part of it. As a result there is much latitude in where to revise within the system; in fact any statement is open to revision, including the statements of logic and mathematics, and any statement may be retained come what may in the way of evidence, should we choose to retain it.

This is not to say that we are equally likely to revise everywhere. Some experiences will prompt only local changes, say, in the belief that there are brick houses on Elm Street. These experiences are thus "germane" to those beliefs, and conversely those beliefs may have a fairly narrow "empirical focus," that is, a fairly narrow range of experiences that might prompt their revision. Revising some beliefs may prompt the revision of others because of their logical connections, but the so-called logical laws are just further statements within the system and hence open to revision. Finally there are some beliefs which we would surrender last if at all. They are open to revision, but we would in fact always abandon other beliefs first. These beliefs might also be central in the sense that giving them up might require revising much else. For this reason the principle of conservatism urges us to avoid tampering with them. Logical and mathematical beliefs would presumably fit this description, so they are not different in kind from other beliefs but only in degree (in the degree of our reluctance to abandon them).

A system such as Quine's differs markedly from Carnap's. Gone are the intricate chains of reasons that justify beliefs bit by bit. Instead our beliefs are justified if they are part of a system that results from the revision procedures outlined above. Quine's approach seems to preclude confirming individual statements apart from confirming the system as a whole. Gone, too, is any talk of linguistic conventions leading to analytic truth. Of course language is still in some sense conventional, but there is no longer any attempt to locate the conventional elements. There is no distinction drawn between on one hand choosing a language and all that might follow from that choice and on the other hand saying something within that language. All sentences turn out on a par, differing at most in the degree of our intransigence with respect to them. Analyticity simply has no place within Quine's system.

It is an interesting question whether intuition has any place within this system. Certainly Quine nowhere suggests that we have any power directly to grasp truths that are independent of ourselves but beyond experience. Indeed, the whole thrust of his system is to make everything, logic and mathematics included, subject to a sort of empirical test. The only part of Quine's doctrine that raises questions in this regard is the role played by those initial beliefs that Quine calls the lore of our fathers. The suggestion is that it doesn't much matter which beliefs one starts with, but a suggestion is hardly a proof. In some theories of knowledge, overtly modeled on Quine's, it makes a great deal of difference what beliefs we start with. The required revisions are thought to be a kind of mutual adjustment of these starting points and to result in "reflective equilibrium." In effect this treats the initial beliefs as intuitions, albeit as fallible ones. As an alternative to this as an interpretation of Quine, there is the model of subjectivist theories of probability. Here it is explicitly argued that the initial beliefs about probabilities make only negligible differences in the end. One can choose those central beliefs in any way one wants, and, under the pressure of incoming data, the beliefs will converge toward a common value. Such an interpretation of Quine fares no better than the first, however, for he explicitly denies that there is any mechanism of convergence. In any case Quine places no weight on the lore of our fathers, so that is unlikely to serve as intuition would. Moreover, in his repeated assertions that there is no clairvoyance he limits our sources of news about the world to observation alone. There is, thus, no room for intuition.

There are three other themes in Quine's work that should be highlighted: pragmatism, holism, and naturalism, of which the most basic is the first. Quine embraces pragmatism by name, but he nowhere spells out what he means by that term. One might suppose that he intends to extend Carnap's attitude toward the choice of languages to the choice of scientific theories generally, but this cannot be what he has in mind. The choices that Carnap takes to be pragmatic are just those where no question of truth arises. But Quine has no intention of avoiding questions of truth for science generally, nor does he adopt a so-called pragmatic theory of truth. Instead of this, we may suppose, the chief consequence of Quine's pragmatism is to make plausible the reliance on simplicity and conservatism as the main pillars of his theory of knowledge. Simplicity is a pragmatic matter because simpler systems are easier to use. Conservatism, too, has its roots in practice because it is often convenient to avoid the effort of learning to use new (conceptual) tools.

Pragmatism also has its effect through holism and naturalism, and both of the latter have been recurrent themes over the history of pragmatism. In particular, Quine's brand of pragmatism changes the style of justification away from chains of reasons supporting each justified belief and toward a strategy of beginning in the middle of things with the beliefs we do have and then revising so as to maximize the utility of the overall system. Utility, in turn, is unpacked in terms of simplicity and conservatism. That what is at stake is *overall* utility makes the view a variety of holism as well. Holism here is the doctrine that our beliefs are justified (by experience or otherwise) together as a body rather than individually. Not unexpectedly, there are varieties of the holist doctrine. The most extreme of these might be called *radical holism*, which holds that it is only the totality of our beliefs which meets experiences or not at all. This is a very daring view because it seems to preclude that any of our beliefs are better justified than any others. One might therefore prefer a weaker version called *modest holism*, according to which what meets experience would be sufficiently large chunks of doctrine. These chunks would be larger than individual beliefs or even than individual theories as those are usually grouped, but smaller than the totality of our beliefs. This more modest version of holism faces difficulties of its own. Indeed, it is not clear when it is worked out in detail whether this holism differs appreciably from Carnap's doctrine. In any case, I need not review all the intricacies here. I might mention, however, that both versions of holism depend on the notions of simplicity and conservatism, and both of these notions are extremely vague. It is never made clear how the simplicity of a system is to be judged or which revisions are to be counted as more conservative.

Whatever difficulties these versions of holism may face, those difficulties might be blunted by reinterpreting the theory. A theory of justification might be either normative or naturalistic. That is to say, it may tell us how we *ought* to defend or revise or justify our beliefs, or else it may describe how we or others *actually* do these things. A theory that is problematic as a normative theory, perhaps because its advice is unclear or self-defeating, might nevertheless be perfectly correct as a naturalistic theory. Our practices, or those of others, might in fact be unclear or self-defeating. Quine may intend his holism to have normative force, but he also clearly intends it to be taken naturalistically as well. His discussions of evidential relevance and even conservatism are put in sociological terms, and in later years, especially in such papers as "Epistemology Naturalized," Quine speaks of epistemology as simply a branch of empirical psychology.

While a purely naturalistic theory can circumvent the difficulties of a normative theory (by addressing different issues), such a naturalistic theory faces special questions of its own. First, we must ask whether such a theory is complete. Suppose for a moment that we had a fully accurate description of how, within a certain community, beliefs arise and change. Is that enough? It is certainly enough for the purposes of empirical psychology, but does it finish the philosophic task? Philosophers have traditionally sought to make recommendations about how people ought to do things. Those who would defend the purely naturalistic interpretation of epistemology, therefore, must show either that an empirical psychology entails a suitable normative doctrine or that the quest for a normative doctrine is misguided. Either of these tasks is difficult.

For any particular epistemology, interpreted naturalistically, there is a second important question: Is it correct, even as a description of actual behavior? In Quine's case this amounts to the question of whether people do in fact always try, other things being equal, to make their theories as simple as possible while also always seeking, other things being equal, to change their minds as little as possible. Given the variety of human behavior, any generalization (including this one) is dangerous. What is perhaps worth emphasizing here is that descriptive or naturalistic theories cannot dismiss nonconforming behavior as irrelevant as readily as a normative theory can. What is, from the point of view of a normative theory, merely a sad lapse of propriety must be counted as disconfirming evidence for the corresponding naturalistic theory.

While we have dwelt in recent paragraphs on areas of possible objections to Quine's system, we must not lose sight of its enormous attractiveness as well. There are many sources of this attractiveness. First, Quine's theory of knowledge has the elegance and beauty of any good theory that explains much with little. Quine appeals to very few principles such as simplicity and conservatism, and with them he is able to give a very sophisticated and at least initially plausible treatment of a wide variety of scientific judgments. The same principles are at work in mathematics, in metaphysics, in chemistry, and in everyday life. This effects a powerful unification of our beliefs and of our theory of knowledge. The whole operation is so neat that one *wants* the theory to be true. In addition, though Quine himself is by no means eager for this result, the theory provides a promising line of approach for justifying ethical or aesthetic judgments. This promise attracts not only those whose interests lie primarily outside science, but many scientists as well.

The second attractive feature of Quine's system is perhaps more important, and that is that it renders logic, mathematics, and the theory of knowledge itself as objective as commonsense beliefs about tables and chairs. They are each judged by the same standard, and each has an equal right to be called part of the correct picture of the world. Certainly when each of us began reflecting on these matters of justification, we did believe that our own mathematical and epistemic commitments were the right ones. It is very reassuring to be told that these are not matters of convention after all but represent objective features of the world. At a later stage in unpacking the system, disturbing relativistic consequences may appear, but at least at the outset the objectivity of our various views is fully embraced.

Third, as we have already seen, the system seems to avoid relying on intuition. This accomplishment is nontrivial.

Fourth, there is something reassuring about Quine's naturalism. Even when the system is construed normatively, the naturalistic remarks that accompany it reassure us that in some sense we ourselves have been embracing these norms all along, and that scientific work thus far supports both the methods that Quine uses and the conclusion that he reaches. When the system is construed descriptively, we are reassured that interminable quarrels among philosophers can at last be surmounted by the very devices that have served so well in the sciences.

Finally, the fact that Quine leaves much unsaid (e.g., What are the measures of simplicity or of conservative revisions? How much depends on the initial beliefs? Is the system descriptive or normative?) provides a rich opportunity for other theorists. It offers them room to work and the prospect of interesting results. Not incidentally, it also allows Quine more room for defending himself than would a system that is completely worked out in every detail.

How, then, shall we compare the systems of Carnap and Quine? Not, I think, by saying which one of them is right or more nearly so. That, even if it could be done at all, would be out of place in an introduction such as this. Nor is it possible to say historically which of them has triumphed or will triumph. The situation is still too fluid. Rather than attempting either of these comparisons we must content ourselves with laying out the cores of the respective systems and indicating what kinds of objections might be raised against each, where the issues between Carnap and Quine lie, and why those issues matter.

The core of Carnap's system, as we have seen, is a thorough-going linguistic conventionalism, controlled and moderated by an underlying pragmatism. Carnap uses convention in order to avoid relying on intuition and then uses the notion of meaning to avoid the charge that anything goes. After all, the conventions endow our words with meaning so that apparently conflicting conventions need not disagree; they are just different languages. Thus, what has to be added to observation in order to get roughly our current scientific beliefs justified to roughly the expected levels is not a set of *a priori* truths known through the mysterious rites of intuition, but rather what Carnap calls analytic sentences, that is, claims that are true in virtue of their meaning or, equivalently, claims that can be completely justified on the basis of the linguistic conventions alone.

Quine rejects the very ideas of analyticity, meaning, and so forth, as unintelligible. But this is because he rejects the whole theory of justification in which these are embedded. In its stead Quine offers a form of pragmatism that involves holism and natu-ralism as well. He specifically denies that the justification of indi-vidual claims can be traced back to observation with or without intuition and/or convention. Rather, the system consists in rules of revision that tell us to maximize simplicity and to minimize change. In the end Quine treats the whole theory of knowledge as a branch of empirical psychology. It is itself to be tested and justi-fied like all other scientific claims, that is, by a proper comparison with experience. And its aims are likewise those of empirical psy-chology: a correct description of human behavior, in this case the behavior associated with belief acquisition and change.

Both Quine and Carnap reject intuition. Both are pragmatists; though how that pragmatism plays out is different in the two cases. There are other striking differences as well. Carnap holds that the chains of reasons by which individual claims are justified can be traced back to observation and linguistic conventions. Some-times individual claims can be tested only when they are consid-ered together with whole theories, but the basic idea is still one of tracing the chain of reasons back to original sources. In contrast

Quine considers only whole theories or belief systems and indicates for them only global features that are to be maximized or minimized. One doesn't keep track of the justification of individual sentences, and one doesn't trace that justification back to sources. Carnap's approach is clearly normative. There is important descriptive work for psychologists to do, but the philosopher's task is to consider alternative sets of norms (i.e., languages), to spell out the practical consequences of adapting these sets of norms, and to make proposals. Quine is less clearly normative. He embraces a form of naturalism that Carnap would not reject, but it is frankly not clear whether any fully normative theory is compatible with Quine's naturalism or, if so, what sort of norms those might be.

The issues of justification and its sources, of naturalism, and of holism still vex contemporary philosophers, as well they should. Where many current writers differ from Carnap or Quine is in being less clear that intuition must be rejected and in not having, as these two men did, novel strategies for doing so. Having thus sketched these two strategies, let us put them in historical context by indicating briefly the stages of their development and of the interaction between Carnap and Quine.

[THE HISTORICAL FRAMEWORK]

The pages that follow are intended to outline some of the major steps in the historical development of the two foregoing theories of knowledge and of the interaction between Carnap and Quine as well. They are not intended as a complete philosophic history, much less as complete biographies.

Rudolf Carnap was born on May 18, 1891, in a small village that has now been incorporated into Wuppertal in the Federal Republic of Germany. May 18, incidentally, is also the birthday of Bertrand Russell, who was Carnap's senior by nineteen years. The full name that appeared on Carnap's birth certificate is "Paul Rudolf Carnap," though by the time he moved to the U.S. the "Paul" and the "Rudolf" had changed places. It makes little difference, however, for he disliked both of his first names and went by the name "Carnap" even to his closest friends. Though Carnap's parents were deeply pious, they were less concerned with dogma than with a virtuous life. His father had begun as a poor, independent ribbon weaver, and rose to become the prosperous owner of a ribbon factory. Rudolf was the youngest of twelve children. His father died when the boy was seven. Carnap recalls that while his father had little formal education, the elder Carnap read widely and thought independently. Carnap's mother was from a more academically inclined family. Her father, Friedrich Wilhelm Dörpfeld, had been a well-known educational reformer, and her oldest brother, also Wilhelm Dörpfeld, was a distinguished archaeologist active in discovering the remains of Troy. At the age of ten, Carnap even joined his famous uncle on an archaeological expedition in Greece. Carnap himself was a voracious reader, and he kept detailed records of his reading. (The reading lists still exist.) The surviving record also indicates that his interests as a young man were at least as much romantic and political as they were academic.

From 1910 to 1914 Carnap studied at the universities of Jena and Freiburg. Among his instructors in Jena was Gottlob Frege, one of the founders of modern logic. In 1914 World War I broke out. Though opposed to war on moral and political grounds, Carnap felt it his duty to defend the fatherland, at first on the front and then later in Berlin. While in Berlin he became more active politically, but his scientific interests were not abandoned. In fact, at this time he read and became an enthusiastic supporter of Einstein's theory of relativity.

Also during the war Carnap married Elizabeth Schöndube. They had four children, but the marriage ended in divorce in 1929. In 1933 he married Elizabeth Ina Stögner. Ina generally went by her middle name (apparently an abbreviation of "Ignatia") and preferred not to capitalize it. This marriage flourished until Ina's death in 1964.

Carnap returned to the University of Jena after the war, completing a dissertation (*Der Raum*) in 1921 on conceptions of mathematical, visual, and physical spaces. Initiating a theme that he would develop over the coming years, Carnap argued that the alternatives involve different concepts but not conflicting ones.

Carnap read Whitehead and Russell's *Principia Mathematica* in 1919 and was deeply impressed with its power and promise. When he read Russell's *Our Knowledge of the External World*, Carnap was even more impressed. Despite Russell's reliance on intuition elsewhere in his writing, in this book he attacked it vigorously. Not only that, Russell called for the rational reconstruction of our knowledge on the basis of sense experience and urged the narrowest and deepest selection of basic concepts. It seemed to speak directly to Carnap. In fact he penciled in the margin of his copy: "This narrowing and deepening of *the fundamental* postulates is my task!" And so it proved to be. Carnap took up the challenge, and the result was the *Aufbau* (1928), where what in effect had been the first stages of Russell's program is worked out in detail rather than just talked about as previous philosophers including Russell had done.

In the years immediately after the dissertation Carnap lived in Buchenbach, Germany, without benefit of an academic post. During this time he worked not only on the *Aufbau* but also on the *Abriss der Logistik,* which in textbook form made symbolic logic and its applications available to the German-speaking world. He also produced a series of articles, largely in philosophy of science. These emphasized a form of conventionalism that would, perhaps, better be called a thesis of the underdetermination of physical theory by empirical fact.

In 1926 Carnap was called to the University of Vienna to join the circle of philosophers, mathematicians, and scientists emerging around Moritz Schlick, the so-called Vienna Circle. Carnap came in time to be perhaps the dominant force within the Circle. Along with Otto Neurath, Carnap led what might be called the Circle's "left wing." In urging ever more liberal and inclusive formulations of criteria for meaningfulness, testing, and the language of science, Carnap and Neurath also proposed that even observation reports be couched in the physical language rather than a private sensory language and that absolute certainty was not a prerequisite of science, neither at the observational nor at the theoretical level. The "right wing" of the Circle, led by Schlick and Friedrich Waissmann, was more strongly influenced by direct contact with Wittgenstein and resisted the Carnap/Neurath innovations.

Carnap's *Aufbau* is sometimes seen as the quintessential statement of Viennese positivism. That its project was later abandoned is correspondingly viewed as an admission that the whole movement was fundamentally misguided and that each subsequent position was only a vain attempt to salvage as much of the *Aufbau* as possible. This picture of the relation between the *Aufbau* and the Circle could have been generated only by ignorance or malice or both.

In the first place the view ignores the enormous variety of views within the Circle. There is no possibility even of outlining them all here, but the Circle plainly held no monolithic doctrines. Second, the suggestion that change of opinion reveals deep-seated confusion is just foolish. If one's deepest convictions prohibit progressive change of opinion, then there is indeed something very wrong.

Moreover, the above picture of the *Aufbau* exaggerates both its defects and its importance within the Circle or even within Carnap's own work. A close look at the *Aufbau* shows that it does not have some of the defects often urged against it. Others of its faults, such as those uncovered by Nelson Goodman, are real enough, but it may well turn out that to a large extent they can be avoided (perhaps by devices offered by Quine or David Lewis) while staying broadly within Carnap's own program. Moreover, Michael Friedman has convincingly argued[2] that while the *Aufbau* embodies (among other things) a program of phenomenalistic reduction, that program *is not the main point* of the *Aufbau*. The book is interesting and important in its own right, and it does represent some hard thinking about some difficult issues. But there is simply no evidence that Carnap pined for it after he had set it aside. The work from the years which followed the *Aufbau* is even more intrinsically interesting and more important to Carnap's subsequent development.

Though they are by no means original to the *Aufbau* or to Carnap for that matter, a number of themes that get expressed there had wide currency within the Circle. One of these is a rejection of psychologism, that is, the view that logic or other branches of philosophy *describe* how people think. Carnap saw the enterprise of philosophy as normative rather than descriptive. Second, there is a very strong empiricism, not only in the *Aufbau* but throughout the Circle. The decision to rely only on experience became a standard of what

2. Michael Friedman, "Carnap's *Aufbau* Reconsidered," *Nous* 21 (December 1987): 521–545.

could be known and also of what was even intelligible. Consequently, metaphysical claims about a transempirical domain of reality were rejected, not as false or even as unknowable, but as utterly without meaningful content. Finally, there was the widely accepted slogan that there is no synthetic *a priori*. The phrase refers back to Kant, who had distinguished analytic from synthetic claims on the ground that there was a special connection between the concepts involved in the former but not in the latter. Claims exhibiting this special connection were analytic, and they were also *a priori*; that is, they could be known to be true without observational justification. So far everyone agreed, but Kant also held that some claims lacking this special connection among concepts (synthetic claims) could also be known *a priori*. Thus some claims that seemed to convey news either about the world or about our way of conceiving it could be known without experience owing to our mysterious power of pure intuition (whatever that is). Included in the synthetic *a priori* by Kant were geometry and arithmetic, as well as much of the rest of philosophy. Throughout the nineteenth century various writers had chipped away at Kant's doctrine of the synthetic *a priori*; with the Vienna Circle it was formally and finally rejected (at least as finally as things are ever rejected in philosophy).

Having a slogan that rules out the synthetic *a priori* is one thing; having well-worked-out conceptions of analyticity and of knowledge that do justice to geometry, arithmetic, and logic is quite another. This was in fact the project through the nineteenth century, and this project culminated in Carnap's work of the early 1930s; that is, it culminated in the doctrines described in the opening section of this Introduction. The first full and certainly the deepest statement of Carnap's linguistic and pragmatic conventionalism is to be found in *The Logical Syntax of Language* (1934). It was precisely at the time when this book was being drafted that Quine met Carnap.

Willard Van Orman Quine was born June 25, 1908, in Akron, Ohio, the younger of two sons. The full name is rather a mouthful, a bit much even for signing one's published work. In fact no version of it became standard on publications, but in time "Van" became the preferred form to friends and associates. Quine's paternal grandfather had come from the Isle of Man, and his pride in being Manx endured. Quine's mother, née van Orman, was of

Dutch heritage. Quine's father, though born to modest means, entered the tire business and prospered, coming finally to own a tire-manufacturing firm. Quine himself seems to have developed the spirit of enterprise, for as a youth he started a small but international stamp newsletter and sales business as well as a minor cartographic concern. In school he reports interests primarily in mathematics, philosophy, and language, especially word origins (which is not far from Carnap's early interests in mathematics and languages, especially Latin).

At the canonical age Quine went off to nearby Oberlin College, graduating after four years in 1930. While there, he looked for a way of combining his various interests. He had read a little of Russell, and so he concluded that mathematical logic might offer the widest scope. There was on the faculty no one to teach the subject, but it still might be possible to study it by majoring in mathematics with an honors project on logic. As with Carnap, one of his primary inspirations was Whitehead and Russell's *Principia Mathematica*. It seemed natural, therefore, to do his graduate work with Whitehead who was then at Harvard. So he did.

Whitehead was by then more interested in metaphysics than logic. Thus, Quine got little direction from his dissertation director, but this facilitated speed of completion. Speed was needed, too, for the costs of graduate school and not having a job could be ill afforded in those depression years. Also Quine had married Naomi Clayton at the start of his graduate work and needed to think of her support as well. So Quine finished his Ph.D. in two years.

That was a misfortune, but he made up for it handsomely. The time for reflection was supplied first by a Sheldon Travelling Fellowship and then by something even better. Quine had heard of Carnap both from Herbert Feigl, a friend of Carnap's and also a member of the Vienna Circle, who was visiting at Harvard, and from John Cooley, a fellow graduate student of Quine's who was much interested in the *Aufbau*. So Quine went to Vienna in the fall of 1932, but Carnap was no longer there. He had just been named professor at the German University at Prague. Vienna was not empty, though, so Quine stayed on to attend Schlick's lectures, from which he gained primarily greater fluency in German. Finally a meeting with Carnap was arranged for early 1933 in Prague.

Quine's recollection of that meeting, contained in his "Homage to Carnap" reprinted here, is moving indeed.

Quine does not say so in his memoir, but it was in the same month that he met Carnap (March 1933) that Carnap and Ina were married. Quine does recount that in these first days he read the pages of the *Logical Syntax of Language* as they poured out of Ina's typewriter. Astonishingly, Quine's very first reaction (preserved in a brief shorthand note by Carnap) contains in embryonic form his whole view of the matter: Might not, he wondered, the difference between the (analytic) axioms of arithmetic and (synthetic) empirical claims about physical bodies be a difference of degree? Might not these degrees reflect our relative willingness to abandon the various beliefs under consideration?

From Prague, Quine went on to Warsaw, where he learned of the recent technical developments being made by such figures as Tarski, Lesniewski, and Lukasiewicz. Also while still in Europe Quine heard of his second piece of good fortune. Along with B. F. Skinner, the psychologist, and Garrett Birkhoff, the mathematician, and three other young men, Quine had been chosen for the very first class of Junior Fellows in Harvard's Society of Fellows. This would afford him three years of research and writing uninterrupted by teaching or lecture duties, to use as he saw fit. And use it he did. During those three years Quine produced one book, *A System of Logistic,* and a stream of articles of which probably the most important has been "Truth by Convention."

Within the Society of Fellows Quine remained enthusiastic about Carnap, so clearly so that the Society asked Quine to give a series of three public lectures that would set forth Carnap's most recent views. Thus on Thursday, November 8, 1934, and on the two succeeding Thursdays, Quine delivered his three "Lectures on Carnap," which gave essentially a prepublication report on Carnap's *Logical Syntax of Language.* They are reprinted in this volume.

Let us take a moment to see what Quine is doing in these lectures. Lecture I contains Quine's substantive argument *in favor* of making logic and mathematics true by convention. That Quine here endorses Carnap's results is important. This is because Quine went on very quickly to rewrite this lecture into "Truth by Convention," which expresses some reservations about analyticity. These initial reservations can be and have been seriously misunderstood in large part because until now it has not been possible to compare "Truth by Convention" with the lectures from which it sprang. Lecture I (like its offspring) is divided into three parts: The first concerns definition, implicit as well as explicit. The second shows how to frame definitions so as to render logic and mathematics true by convention. The third part asks (and answers) the question of how far this conventionality is to go. Plainly we could so construct our definitions as to render true by convention far more than we typically do, perhaps as much as the totality of our belief. Why stop at some middling point? Quine embraces Carnap's answer: Conventionalizing logic and mathematics helpfully forestalls awkward epistemological questions; yet going too much further might have the impractical result of forcing us as science progresses to revise the conventions continuously.

In reaching this Carnapian result, however, Quine reveals a set of commitments that would eventually force him to reject the Carnapian doctrines that he here embraces. In talking about definition Quine explicitly sets aside all questions of justification. But justification, as I argued above, is the very core of Carnap's conception of meaning. Moreover, Quine plainly focuses on natural as opposed to constructed languages, and he plainly expects there to be behavioral or other empirical criteria (correspondence rules, if you like) for any concept used to describe language. Quine's view here is not strictly un-Carnapian, but it is, nonetheless, the framework around which Quine was to fashion his sharpest attacks on analyticity. Finally, Quine reveals in embryonic form a theory of knowledge that is both holistic and naturalistic. This was to be the core of Quine's alternative to Carnap.

Lectures II and III can be noted more briefly. The former gives an exposition of some important notions from *Logical Syntax of Language*. Specifically we learn that syntax is a much broader notion for Carnap than it was later to become, for it here includes not only rules of grammar but also rules of inference (logic). Carnap calls these rules of inference transformative rules, and they can be used in turn to define 'analytic'. In this lecture, Quine seems completely unruffled by the result. In the process Quine provides an informal but masterly exposition of arithmetization. This last is a method devised by Kurt Gödel for assigning numbers to expressions and hence to sentences and proofs. This in turn allows one to use the powerful tools of arithmetic in describing the syntax of a language including its logic.

As its title indicates, the third lecture discusses Carnap's thesis that philosophy is the syntax of language. Here, especially in his closing paragraphs, Quine shows himself not only Carnap's expositor but also his champion. Curiously, the feature of Carnap's work that most attracts Quine is one that was almost wholly unintended by Carnap. Carnap had argued that talk that appears to be about, say, possibilities, properties, relations, numbers, and so on can be reconstrued most perspicuously as being about sentences, predicates, and so on. This led many, including Quine, to think that Carnap thereby denied that there were such metaphysical entities. Quine thus not implausibly interprets the thesis that philosophy is syntax as a program of ontological reduction. As such, he embraces it. In fact, however, Carnap rejected *both* the assertion that there are such entities *and the denial* of their existence; both were metaphysical nonsense. Carnap never wavered in his conviction that questions of metaphysical existence were purely verbal. But, he came increasingly to think, if one recognizes it as merely verbal, one is free to go on using a language that employs such words as 'possible', 'property', and 'relation'. To Quine, this apparent change of view was heresy and Carnap a turncoat. Perhaps this judgment was not fair to Carnap, but perhaps it was also inevitable given Quine's not implausible interpretation of Carnap's *Logical Syntax*.

Given this analysis of the "Lectures on Carnap" it is hard to see "Truth by Convention" as an attack on Carnap either, though many have done so. The latter paper was published by Quine in 1936, that is to say shortly after the "Lectures" but while he was still a Harvard Junior Fellow. As indicated, "Truth by Convention" is a revision of "Lecture I" so it is unlikely that what is taken over from that lecture was intended as hostile to Carnap. Nor does what is new amount to an attack on Carnap's doctrine. There are some new arguments that are sometimes viewed as such an attack, but Quine himself answers these arguments. At the beginning and end of the paper Quine does wonder just what 'analytic' is supposed to mean, but this is best viewed as a request for further clarification rather than as an attack. Finally, even after 1936, Quine freely used the notion of analyticity, and tried in public presentations to extend Carnap's doctrines. It was not until 1947, and then in private correspondence, that Quine came fully and finally to reject Carnap's doctrine that there are analytic truths. Quine arrived at that break of 1947 only by stages, and it is to the stages of the developing views of Carnap and Quine just after the "Lectures" that we now turn.

In the *Logical Syntax of Language* Carnap had thought that the concept of truth was riddled with paradox (the so-called semantic paradoxes). Thus, he eschewed the concept of truth. By the time *Logical Syntax* actually appeared in print, however, Tarski had already showed that a concept of truth could be defined for formal languages which appeared to avoid the semantical paradoxes. Characteristically, Carnap was among the first to accept Tarski's results. Throughout the late 1930s Carnap progressively assimilated Tarski's work and then elaborated it to produce *Introduction to Semantics* in 1940.

Because we have a narrower notion of syntax, it is nowadays generally thought that the new semantical methods showed the insufficiency of syntax, but at that time things looked quite different. At the time both Carnap and Tarski saw the new definition of truth as an illustration of syntactical procedures and as well within Carnap's program. After all, what was added? Just a new definition. True, the object languages and metalanguages had to be rigorously separated, but this was a result that even from within syntax Carnap could contemplate with equanimity. However, I have no wish to downplay the importance of Carnap's move to semantics. The newfound freedom to discuss the relation between bits of language and other objects described by science is crucial to a whole range of issues. But it is a mistake to think that this renders all of Carnap's earlier work obsolete.

More specifically, it is important to see that Carnap's move to semantics affected his doctrine of analyticity almost not at all. Carnap still accepted the linguistic and pragmatic conventionalism that generated the notion of analyticity. He still held that philosophy is a form of conceptual engineering, and he was still a thoroughgoing verificationist (confirmationist) about linguistic matters. Though he became increasingly willing to speak of properties, propositions, and the like, his antimetaphysical fervor never really declined. Nor is there any reason why Carnap should have changed any of this just because he was now prepared to employ a mutually interdefinable set of semantical predicates.

Carnap's move to semantics coincided more or less with his move to America. The latter, at least, was fully complete by 1936 when he joined the faculty at the University of Chicago. At Chicago, Carnap had good teaching loads and abundant leaves for research, but even so his time there was unhappy. This was because some of his colleagues were, well, difficult. Since Carnap was never a combative man, he chose to spend as much time away as possible. I suppose we should be grateful for Carnap's unhappiness, for his output while on leave was prodigious. All told, Carnap spent eighteen years on the faculty at Chicago, but the last two of these eighteen were really spent at the Institute for Advanced Study at Princeton. In 1954 Carnap moved to UCLA to replace his old friend Hans Reichenbach, who had died shortly before. Carnap stayed (happily) at UCLA until his death in 1970.

When he first came to the United States and even into the 1940s Carnap worried a lot initially about how to translate various technical terms into English and then about what English words to use for various technical notions. He therefore sent questionnaires to his various associates, including Quine, and these have been preserved within their correspondence. There are those who will find these matters tedious, but we must not suppose that the issues are unimportant or of narrowly philological interest. What Carnap was doing, alongside other emigrés, was transporting a well-developed European tradition in logic and philosophy into the American idiom. In addition Carnap was trying to minimize merely verbal differences whenever it was possible to do so. Outside philosophy he was keenly interested in such international languages as Esperanto and Basic English for essentially the same reason.

The attempt to achieve a common vocabulary, and the right one at that, is both difficult and important. However precisely or technically defined, words hold on tenaciously to the reverberations of their ordinary senses and thus guide our thought. Besides, as every writer knows (and as Mark Twain had the wit to say), the difference between the right word and the almost right word is the difference between lightning and the lightning bug. Which words are right and which reverberations we want, however, depends on which theories we seek to advance. Since Carnap, Quine, Church, and others differed sharply in their views of logic, it should come as no surprise that agreement over vocabulary was hard to come by.

The issues of the period were by no means all terminological. In 1939 there was a large international congress held at Harvard. In many ways it was the whole positivist movement in exile, with the addition, of course, of many who would not have considered themselves positivists. After much persuasion even Tarski came, thereby narrowly escaping the German invasion of Poland. While at Harvard, Carnap held a seminar in which he presented the material from his forthcoming *Introduction to Semantics*. Almost from the very beginning Quine, joined now by Tarski, demanded a fuller clarification of the notion of analyticity. Too little in the way of documentary evidence remains for us to judge just what was said on either side, but it is fair to say that neither Carnap nor his questioners were persuaded by the discussion. So far as we know, however, this was the first time that Quine's doubts were voiced in a public forum.

The debate might have developed more rapidly, but World War II intervened. Quine joined the Navy, and spent much of the war in Washington, D.C., and in Brazil. He was gone from Harvard, but he plainly did not leave philosophy behind. While in the Navy in the early 1940s Quine tried to formulate more clearly his worries about analyticity, meaning, synonymy, and the like, first in *O Sentido da Nova Logica* and then in "Notes on Existence and Necessity," which is a translation of part of the former. The attempt thus to clarify these worries resulted in an intense correspondence with Carnap, culminating in 1943. There are far more letters between the two during 1943 than in any other year. But the volume of letters is hardly the most salient feature of the correspondence at this point. Each man struggled valiantly to make himself understood and to understand the other. Both failed. Why? It would be easy, but I think wrong, to put the blame on one side only, to assume, say, that Carnap was just obtuse or that Quine's worries were just insubstantial or unreasonable. Nevertheless, Carnap is certainly inarticulate about his underlying epistemology and about the extent to which the notion of analyticity flows out of that. Perhaps the reason why Carnap is so inarticulate is that he is deeply ambivalent about normative notions, including normative epistemology, but this is not the place to pursue such conjectures. On the other side, Quine is also unable to say (perhaps because he is not yet clear himself) that he tacitly presupposes an *alternative* epistemic strategy and that it is within this alternative epistemology that analyticity makes no sense.

What does emerge from the discussion is that both men still hope for a reconciliation or at least that their differences will prove to be superficial and that they could agree to disagree. This, of course, was not to be, but there were reasons for hope. Certainly they did clear away some of the philosophical underbrush. Certainly they did find formulations that were more nearly mutually acceptable. Why should they not suppose that with enough effort this progress would continue until they had reached full agreement? The answer, I think, is that from Quine's point of view even the progress to date left what was to become the central disagreement untouched. Even the phrase 'the central disagreement' can be misleading. It is a misdiagnosis to see the letters of 1943 as between two philosophers with clearly different theories who are nevertheless inching toward one another. Those letters are, rather, between philosophers who believe that they are in fundamental agreement who are slowly and unwillingly discovering that what they thought was a minor disagreement is turning out to be more fundamental than either had supposed. By the end of 1943 Quine had not quite yet given up hope on analyticity, but he had largely abandoned hope that further correspondence with Carnap would resolve his worries. As a consequence the volume of letters declined sharply.

One can also learn from this part of the correspondence how intensely Carnap disliked polemics, especially with persons such as Quine whom he liked and admired. Carnap was perfectly capable of turning a persuasive phrase. Consider, for example, his line in the letter of February 11, 1938, in reply to Quine's objection to any treatment of intensional languages. "Although we usually do not like to apply intensional languages, nevertheless I think we cannot help analyzing them. What would you think of an entomologist who refuses to investigate fleas and lice because he dislikes them?" Still this was not, in general, Carnap's style. Rather than level a direct criticism at Quine, he preferred to lay out his positive views in a systematic way. Thus, instead of replying in the compass of a letter, Carnap wrote a paper, which became a long paper, which became a monograph, which became a book. That book is called Extension and Intension in the letters, but we know it as *Meaning and Necessity*. This is still Carnap's most popular work, at least among professional philosophers, though it is not widely known that it developed directly out of the Quine-Carnap correspondence.

Through the late 1940s Carnap worked intensively to develop the ideas that were to appear in a now neglected masterwork, *Logical Foundations of Probability*. The book is still a gold mine of epistemological insight and argument. In it Carnap developed a conception of probability as a measure of the relation between premises and conclusion in inductive arguments, that is, in arguments where the premises provide some good reason (but not conclusive reasons) to believe the conclusion. On this conception, probability thus becomes a generalization of ordinary deductive logic and absorbs the latter into an overarching epistemic structure.

Also in the mid and late 1940s Quine's domestic situation changed. As Quine describes in his autobiography, his first marriage had been deteriorating for some time and in 1944 Naomi deserted him. (Hence the cryptic opening of Carnap's letter of May 23, 1944.) A divorce came in 1947, and in 1948 Quine married Marjorie Boynton.

There were intellectual changes as well. I said a few paragraphs back that in 1943 Quine had not yet given up on analyticity. Plainly, he did thereafter. The most likely date that he did so would be the summer of 1947. At that time Quine engaged in a triangular correspondence with Nelson Goodman and Morton White. Even then Quine was cautious, almost reluctant. But over the course of that summer he clearly came firmly and finally to reject the notion of analyticity as unintelligible and to eschew it in his own discussions of language. One result of those 1947 discussions was Morton White's 1950 paper "The Analytic and Synthetic: An Untenable Dualism." Quine could hardly let others speak for him, however, so when he was asked to give an address to the American Philosophical Association, the product was "Two Dogmas of Empiricism."

"Two Dogmas" is one of the landmarks of twentieth-century philosophy. It is Quine's decisive public break with Carnap. Its arguments against analyticity are those I have sketched in the opening section of this Introduction, and Quine's paper also contains in outline form the alternative epistemological structure in which analyticity has no place. Carnap did not hear Quine's address before the A.P.A., so shortly thereafter Quine went to Chicago to give a shortened version of "Two Dogmas." Apparently Carnap did not wilt. In fact, after the seminar Quine wrote to Carnap (March 29, 1951) saying that until the discussion in the seminar he had not fully understood Carnap's position. But rather than his (Quine's) publishing a retraction, perhaps Carnap should write a reply that would set the matter straight. Carnap did indeed write such a reply, and it is published here for the first time as "Quine on Analyticity." It discusses the role of explication (the clarification and further specification of words already in use) in answering Quine's questions about analyticity. When combined with some of Carnap's other contemporaneous writing, the reply forms a powerful rejoinder to Quine.

One reason that the reply remained unpublished is that about that time it became clear that there would be an opportunity for another complete exchange of papers with Quine, this time in the context of a thorough examination of Carnap's philosophy. This examination was to be *The Philosophy of Rudolf Carnap*, a volume in a series edited by P. A. Schilpp, so I shall call it the Schilpp volume. These books were each to contain an autobiography by the subject, a series of articles about the subject by other prominent philosophers, replies to each of these articles by the subject, and a complete bibliography of the subject's work. Of course, Quine was to write one of the articles in Carnap's Schilpp volume, and the reply there could be much more complete, so there was no need to publish something now.

Planning for the volume began in the early 1950s, and as the correspondence shows, Carnap had Quine's contribution by mid-1954. As the letters show, even at this time Carnap wanted rigidly to separate natural from artificial languages and to insist that Quine's worries arose solely from the vagueness of natural languages and did not apply to artificial languages. This is because those artificial languages amount to explications or clarifications of natural language in precisely those respects which bred Quine's worries. Since the concept of analyticity was intended by Carnap to apply only to artificial languages, he thought he could dismiss Quine's arguments as inapplicable.

Quine, of course, was not to be put off so easily. First, he stoutly resists dividing the problem into natural and artificial cases. If analyticity is to be intelligible in artificial languages, it must likewise be so in natural ones. Those correspondence rules, the ones mentioned in our initial presentation of Quine's argument, are still needed. Quine did not actually use the expression 'correspondence rules', which is unfortunate, for if he had phrased his point thus in Carnap's own vocabulary, Carnap could have understood it more directly. Certainly, Carnap would not have been able to sidestep the issue, and he might have been able to provide a more forceful answer. Quine also makes plain in his essay that he rejects, not only Carnap's account of those so-called analytic claims which were not logical truths, but also Carnap's whole linguistic and pragmatic conventionalism, specifically including its account of logic and mathematics as well. Quine did not, however, set up the issue as one between rival epistemologies. Quine does not deny that language is in some sense conventional but only that there is any hope of separating out that conventional element.

Carnap's reply must be seen to have two parts: the portion that actually appears in the Schilpp volume and the part that appears as a separate paper, "Meaning and Synonymy in Natural Languages," because it was too long even for the massive Schilpp volume. In the first part of this reply Carnap insists on the crucial importance of explication, just as he had done in the unpublished reply to "Two Dogmas." It is obvious, he thinks, that natural languages are vague and unclear and that we can thus hope for a clear notion of analyticity only in the case of artificial languages that are the results of explication. Since no one as perceptive as Quine would deny a truth so obvious, Carnap thinks, the chief task is to give an account of Quine's view which renders it plausible though mistaken. Quine, Carnap concludes, simply believes that ordinary language is so vague that the enterprise of explication is hopeless. Carnap can appreciate the difficulties involved, but he assures us that the intensional aspects of language (meaning, synonymy, analyticity, and the like) are no worse than its extensional aspects (reference, extension, truth, etc.).

Carnap's chief argument for this last is reserved for "Meaning and Synonymy in Natural Language." Here he tries to provide a method for determining, out in the field, so to speak, what are the intensions or meanings of a speaker's general terms. For example, the words 'griffin' and 'unicorn' presumably have the same extension, that is, they are true of or apply to the same objects, namely to none whatsoever. But commonly we take these words not to be the same in meaning, and Carnap hopes to provide some empirical sense to this notion of meaning such that the two words do not have the same meaning. Carnap admits that there will be all of the usual inductive difficulties, but these can be dismissed. Applying any theoretical terms encounters such problems, and specifically so would applying such terms as 'extension', 'reference', and 'truth'. If Carnap is successful, his method for determining intensions will be at least a giant first step toward providing the correspondence rules that Quine was demanding.

Very roughly, Carnap's suggested method was to display pictures of various actual and imaginary animals and for each picture ask the native speaker what he or she would call such a creature. Presumably the native's words are not our own, but suppose the native says that he or she would use the word 'Einhorn' to describe the creatures depicted in what we call pictures of unicorns but not those in what we call pictures of griffins, and that conversely he or she would use the word 'Kobald' in connection with our griffin pictures but not our unicorn pictures. If so, we have a bit of news about the native's speech more fine-grained than just the extensions of his general terms. This is hardly a general method, but the hint that it gives is sufficient for the purposes at hand. Note that the method is interestingly similar to Nelson Goodman's talk of primary and secondary extensions. Goodman strives for a more fine-grained analysis of language by appealing not only to the (primary) extensions of our general terms but also to their secondary extensions, that is, to the primary extensions of compound expressions involving the terms. For example, 'unicorn' and 'griffin' may have the same primary extensions (namely the empty set), but 'unicorn-picture' and 'griffin-picture' do not, so those two initial words differ in their secondary though not in their primary extensions.

Though similar in this way to Goodman's approach, Carnap's method for determining intensions is totally unacceptable to

Quine. The method trades on subjunctive conditionals (would you call this a . . .), and any use thereof is so problematic as to be unintelligible. It is bad enough for the linguist to frame his or her results in such a vocabulary, but to suppose that the native has an unproblematic command of subjunctive conditionals and can communicate that to us is beyond consideration. Carnap, himself, has no such qualms about subjunctives, but he should have known better than to suppose that such a method would have satisfied Quine. Ironically, Carnap has at his disposal and already in print (scattered through *Logical Foundations of Probability*) another and better answer. In brief one watches how the native speaker argues and notices that an argument that such and such is an "Einhorn" is not an argument that it is, say, a "Kobald." Thus, 'Einhorn' and 'Kobald' must have different meanings even if they have the same extension. Note that whatever one thinks of either of these methods for determining the intension of a term, the point that Carnap is trying fundamentally to make is that intension is no worse than extension in empirical linguistics.

The appearance of Carnap's Schilpp volume also marks a quite different and sadder event. On May 26, 1964, Ina Carnap committed suicide. For many years she had suffered bouts of severe depression. She had been under careful medical and psychological care for this condition, but obviously these efforts proved unsuccessful. Thereafter Carnap's daughter, Hanneliese, came from Europe to Los Angeles to care for her father during his last six years.

With the Schilpp volume, the public exchange of papers as well as the private exchange of letters on the issue of analyticity came to an end between Carnap and Quine. That the debate should thus end, so to speak with neither a bang nor a whimper, is remarkable and needs to be explained. As is so often the case with historical episodes, a number of factors contributed to the discontinuance of the debate. Some of these are connected directly with the Schilpp volume. The Quine-Carnap exchange was written in the mid-1950s, but the volume itself did not appear until 1964 (its copyright date of 1963 notwithstanding). This gap is due to delays on the part of contributors, on the part of Carnap, and above all on the part of Schilpp and the publisher. As the letters of early 1959 make clear, Carnap and especially Quine were most unhappy about the delay. (Sadly, Quine's own Schilpp volume was delayed even longer than Carnap's.) In any case, once they had written their essays, both Carnap and Quine thought it best to postpone further public discussion until after publication so as not to confuse the public. Ultimately, the delay was so long as to render the issue somewhat stale.

In addition, during the interval both men had gone on to other topics. Carnap was deeply involved in a major revision of his probability theory. His most pressing concern was to finish that revision before he died. This probability theory *was* his theory of confirmation and, indeed, the detailed working out of his theory of knowledge. Carnap did succeed in producing a significant revision and improvement of the theory, but even so the result (published in part posthumously) fell short of Carnap's desires. If he had been able to provide the sort of theory that he sought, it would have been a powerful step forward even with respect to the analyticity debate, for it would have provided a detailed workable account of confirmation in which analyticity played a crucial role. Nothing carries conviction quite like a concrete example, so Carnap would have been in a strong position to demand that Quine provide an equally detailed and workable confirmation theory in which intensional notions such as analyticity did not appear.

Quine, too, had turned to other topics before the Schilpp volume appeared in print. During the late 1950s Quine wrote what is perhaps his most important work, *Word and Object*, a work which he dedicated: "To Rudolf Carnap, teacher and friend." In the first two chapters of this book he argued that translation is in important respects indeterminate, that is, that there are many perfectly satisfactory translations of a foreign sentence into our own language, that the various results of these translations are not even about the same objects, and that as a consequence there is no fact of the matter about what the foreign speaker intends by his sentence or is even talking about. Because we have no more access to our own language than we have to the foreigner's, there are no such facts of the matter about our own speech either. This is or at least was a staggering thesis. Naturally, it provoked a firestorm of controversy. In the remainder of *Word and Object* Quine developed a general theory of language in which meaning, analyticity, and so on are absent, but plainly what captured the imagination of the philosophical public was the indeterminacy thesis. In the 1960s

Quine defended and extended this thesis into a thesis of ontological relativity, which I need not discuss here. Also in the 1960s he made explicit in his paper "Epistemology Naturalized" a view that had long been implicit in his writings on analyticity, namely that he conceives of epistemology as a branch of empirical psychology and hence as a descriptive enterprise rather than as a normative one.

In the last two paragraphs I have been discussing the projects that Carnap and Quine turned to while the Schilpp volume was still forthcoming. Plainly these projects had a momentum of their own that would divert the two men from resuming the analyticity debate directly. There is, however, another factor that conspired with the foregoing to block resumption of the debate. This factor is that Quine's *Word and Object* is itself open to alternative interpretations such that each side could view itself as vindicated by the book. There would, therefore, be no need to resume the debate. As indicated above, Quine can view the book as a systematic presentation of a philosophy of language that makes no appeal to analyticity or other intensional notions. Moreover, since not even reference or extension is shared across the available translations, Quine reasonably believes that the indeterminacy thesis stands in the way of the idea that our words have meanings one by one.

Carnap, however, could look at the book in a quite different way. There is reason to suppose that he did. Carnap filled the margins of much of his personal copy of *Word and Object* with protests and various other comments. But there are no protests in the margins of the first two chapters, where the indeterminacy thesis is advanced and defended. Apparently Carnap did not bat an eye. Why should he? He can view Quine as revealing the enormous difficulties inhering in any attempt to discover the extension of the expressions of some natural language, and this he can see as reinforcing his previous argument that intension is no worse than extension in this regard. Quine has no desire to abandon notions from the theory of reference even in the face of indeterminacy; why should Carnap give up something that is no worse? Moreover, it is instructive to see how Quine proposes to salvage reference. The linguist, he says, must lay down a set of "analytical hypotheses" in order to proceed with the translation. There are alternative sets of such analytical hypotheses which are equally acceptable, but the linguist must select one. Carnap could reply that this is exactly right: the analytical hypotheses have the status of conventions in that alternative sets are available and there is no fact of the matter as to which set is the correct one. Even Quine's use of the word 'analytical' is suggestive, for Carnap had long argued that every scientific inquiry must presuppose a set of analytic hypotheses (meaning postulates) without which it could not proceed.

It is indeed ironic and instructive that there are these two interpretations of *Word and Object*, that what Quine could view as the ultimate refutation Carnap could view as the ultimate concession. Neither side needed to continue the debate. This factor added to their other reasons for discontinuing their debate: they wished to avoid undermining the Schilpp volume and confusing the public before that volume came out, and in the interim they had both turned to other topics.

Carnap died on September 14, 1970, and to the very end there was between the two a deep mutual respect and affection. This is beautifully illustrated by Quine's "Homage to Carnap" reprinted in this volume. The essay was delivered as part of a memorial session held at the Philosophy of Science Association meeting and it amounts to a funeral oration for Carnap.

In an important sense, nonetheless, even with Carnap's death his debate with Quine did not end. This is because each represented deep epistemic strategies, and the issue between these is unresolved. During their exchange of papers the contrast between and the consequences of these strategies were never brought sufficiently into the foreground. We are still discovering the extent to which their semantical claims hinge on prior epistemic commitments. In addition the issues are too broad and too important ever to be settled with finality. It is hard either to prove or to refute a strategy. Finality aside, the issues that Carnap and Quine raised about the source of our knowledge and about the character of our reasons are unavoidably at the center of our ongoing philosophic concerns.

In speaking of their debate we must not lose sight of the important similarities between them. They did indeed have similar economic and social backgrounds: In each case the fathers established the family economically, rising ultimately to direct manufacturing enterprises. Quine and Carnap were both younger sons; they had similar youthful interests; both remarried after divorces and both became extremely and justly influential academic philosophers. But all of this does very little to explain the extraordinary personal friendship between them or the close kinship between their ideas.

In order to understand this last, one would have to look at the content of their theories. Here more important similarities abound. Both were logicians and semanticists who sought to develop their views within the context of a broader philosophic program. Within those programs epistemic matters were in each case central. Even their epistemic allegiances were close. Both defended a strong empiricism that insisted that observation is the only source of news about the world; whatever is not provided by experience is generated by ourselves. Thus, both rejected intuition. Even their resultant doctrines were kin, for there is a family resemblance between Quine's doctrine of translational indeterminacy and ontological relativity and Carnap's sweeping rejection of metaphysics and especially of ontology. Even their theories of observation are similar, for both held that our observational judgments are directly about physical objects and that those judgments are far from incorrigible. Finally, both held that modality (necessity, possibility, etc.) arises at best from our own contribution to science and represents no extralinguistic fact. Of course, they still had their differences over modality and over a wide variety of other topics, but this should not obscure the wide range of their agreement.

The debate over strategy, these agreements both large and small, and a remarkable friendship are all documented in the pages that follow. Of these it is the friendship that shines through most persistently. Certainly there is no need for us to dissect that part of their relationship here; some things may be shown better than said.

[LECTURES ON CARNAP]

AT
HARVARD UNIVERSITY
NOVEMBER 8–22, 1934

BY
WILLARD VAN ORMAN QUINE

[LECTURE I]
THE *A PRIORI*

THESE THREE lectures are to be concerned with Carnap's very recent work only. His earlier book, *Der Logische Aufban der Welt*, must be excluded entirely, because, although a very important piece of work, it lies outside the direction of Carnap's latest book and articles; these lectures must, for lack of time, be confined to the new Carnap.

Carnap's central doctrine, which is the main concern of these lectures, is the doctrine that philosophy is syntax. In this hour I shall lead up to that doctrine by discussing the analytic character of the *a priori*. I will present none of Carnap's actual work this time, but will attempt only to put the mentioned doctrine in a suitable setting. In the remaining two lectures we can get into the details of Carnap's own developments.

The efforts of Carnap and his associates in the Viennese Circle have been directed in large part to showing us how to *avoid* metaphysics. Perhaps it will bear poor testimony to their success if I start out by discussing Kant. But a discussion of the analytic and the *a priori* starts us off with Kant.

According to Kant, *a priori* judgments and *analytic* judgments do not entirely coincide; for him all analytic judgments are of course *a priori*, but not all *a priori* judgments are analytic. A judgment is *a priori* if it has "the character of an inward necessity," as Kant says, and holds independently of any possible experience.

An analytic judgment is a judgment the truth of which may be established directly by analysis of the concepts involved. An analytic judgment can do no more than call our attention to something already contained in the definitions of our terms. Analytic judgments are consequences of definitions, conventions as to the uses of words. They are consequences of linguistic fiat. Clearly they are *a priori*; their truth does not depend upon experience, but upon vocabulary. Among analytic judgments are to be reckoned logic and the bulk, at least, of mathematics.

Analytic judgments are *a priori*; but the converse, according to Kant, does not obtain. He holds that there are *a priori* truths, not dependent upon experience, which yet do not follow merely from the definitions of terms. He thus recognizes *synthetic*, or non-analytic, *a priori* judgments. Among these *a priori* synthetic judgments he reckons the propositions of geometry.

But the development of foundational studies in mathematics during the past century has made it clear that none of mathematics, not even geometry, need rest on anything but linguistic conventions of a definitional kind. In this way it becomes possible to relegate geometry to the analytic realm, along with the rest of mathematics. This empties out the *a priori* synthetic. The analytic and the *a priori* become coëxtensive. Thus Professor Lewis writes: "The a priori is not a material truth, delimiting or delineating the content of experience as such, but is definitive or analytic in its nature."[1]

It will be worth while, by way of examining this doctrine, to consider in detail the nature of the analytic. To begin with, let us distinguish two kinds of definition. First there is *explicit* definition, which is merely a convention of abbreviation. For example the definition of momentum as mass times velocity is an explicit definition: it is a linguistic convention whereby the word "momentum" is introduced as an arbitrary abbreviation for the compound expression "mass times velocity." The explicit definition is perhaps what we ordinarily think of as a definition.

An *implicit* definition is of an entirely different form. An implicit definition of a notion K is a set of one or more rules specifying that all sentences containing the word K in such and such a way are to be accepted, by convention, as true; their truth constitutes the meaning of K. For example, a set of postulates containing an undefined word K can be construed as an implicit definition of K: the postulates are adopted as true by convention, and the sign K is

1. ⟨Clarence Irving Lewis,⟩ *Mind and the World Order* ⟨New York: Charles Scribner's Sons, 1929⟩, p. 231.

thereby partially or completely defined. An implicit definition, like an explicit definition, is a convention as to how the word in question is to be used. An explicit definition stipulates our use of the word, say "momentum", by referring us to our uses of certain other words, in this case "mass", "times" and "velocity", where the use of these words has presumably been already stipulated in the past. An explicit definition, unlike an implicit definition, is thus necessarily relative.

Often the word "definition" is restricted to explicit definition, and that has been my procedure elsewhere. But it will be convenient at present to use the word in the broader sense, covering both implicit and explicit definitions. This usage also has precedent; for the phrase "implicit definition" is not my own.

The analytic depends upon nothing more than definition, or conventions as to the uses of words. But in the ordinary uncriticized language of common sense we have little to do with deliberate definition. We learn our vocabulary through the usual process of psychological conditioning. We proceed glibly to use our vocabulary, and so long as we move among compatriots we get on without much difficulty: for their conditioning has been substantially the same as ours. At this level we feel no need of defining our terms, or introducing deliberate conventions as to the use of language. This comes only at a more sophisticated stage—for example in mathematics and in science.

Suppose now we start at a common-sense level, or an ultra-common-sense level, at which no conscious or deliberate definition has taken place. Then suppose we schematically run through the whole process of thoroughly defining the terms which we had been using without definition all along.

Let K be any word mathematical, logical or otherwise—perhaps the word "if", or perhaps "two", or "cat". Now let us consider the whole range of admittedly true sentences in which K occurs: true sentences, I mean, under the usual implicit, common-sense use of the word K, and true according to the given stage in the progress of science. The distinction between *a priori* and empirical does not concern me here. Let us call these accepted sentences the *accepted K-sentences*.

Now suppose we are confronted with the job of defining K. If we can frame a definition which fulfills all the accepted K-sentences, then obviously we shall have done a perfectly satisfactory job. Nobody who was inclined to dispute the definition could point to a single respect in which the definition diverged from the accepted usage of the word K: for all accepted K-sentences would be verified.

Such a definition of K would be easily accomplished if there were only say three dozen accepted K-sentences. K could be given implicit definition by setting down those three dozen sentences, by fiat, and declaring that this was how you proposed to use the word K. Of course the definition might not be completely determinate; there might be several distinct notions all of which satisfied all thirty-six sentences, and the definition would not tell us which of these notions the word K was intended to represent. To that extent the definition would be only a partial definition, and to that extent the word K would retain ambiguity. But nobody could object to this ambiguity, since, by hypothesis, the definition is near enough to being complete so that it satisfies all accepted K-sentences.

But as a matter of fact this easy method is closed to us, since, for any word K, there will be an indefinite multitude of accepted K-sentences. If we are to find a definition of K which will satisfy even a fair representation of the accepted K-sentences, we must first develop a technique for organizing the accepted K-sentences and providing for them with finite means.

For one thing, we shall not be called upon to define any one word K in a vacuum. In defining K we must take into consideration the accepted K-sentences, and in defining another word H we must take into consideration the accepted H-sentences; but these sentences will overlap to some extent, and there is no need to consider the overlapping sentences twice. Namely, among the accepted K-sentences there will be some which are at the same time H-sentences: sentences involving both the word K and the word H. In defining K we might ignore some of the accepted K-sentences which are at the same time H-sentences; these can be picked up later when we come to define H.

For example, suppose that K is the word "two", and that H is the word "apple". Then these accepted sentences are at once K-sentences and H-sentences.

a) Within any class of *two apples* there is at least one *apple*.

b) Every *apple* weighs at least *two* grams.

Each of these is both an accepted "two"-sentence and an accepted "apple"-sentence. In defining the word "two" and the word "apple" there is no need to consider these sentences twice. We may apportion these one way or the other: we may take them into consideration in defining "apple", or we may take them into consideration in defining "two". Or, third, we might provide for the first one in defining "two", and provide for the second one later in defining "apple".

There is an important distinction between a) and b). Note that a) is just one case of a general form *all* cases of which are true. All sentences of the form of a) will be accepted two-sentences, regardless of what noun may occur in sixth and last place instead of "apple". "Within any class of two so-&-so's there is at least one so-&-so": any sentence of this form is true, no matter what "so-&-so" may be. Let us describe such a sentence as a) by saying that it involves "apple" *vacuously.* Any sentence which contains a word H (say "apple"), and which remains unaffected in point of truth or falsity by all possible substitutions upon the word H (as a) does), will be said to involve H vacuously.

Unlike a), b) involves "apple" *materially,* or non-vacuously: for there are substitutions for "apple" which would turn b) false—for example "mustard-seed".

Now in defining "two" we might provide at one stroke for all sentences of the general form of which a) is a special case: we might provide once and for all, in our definition of "two", for the truth of all sentences of the form "In any class of two so-&-so's there is at least one so-&-so". If on the other hand we were to provide for a) rather under the definition of "apple", we would thereby succeed in providing for a) alone, while all the other sentences of the same form would remain to be provided for. It therefore behooves us in the interests of economy and simplicity not to handle a) under the definition of "apple", but to provide for it rather under the definition of "two", by providing there for the more general form of which a) is a special case.

This same reasoning applies in the case of any sentence involving a given word vacuously. Given any accepted sentence which involves both the word K and the word H, but involves K materially and H only vacuously, it will be simplest to provide for the sentence when defining K rather than when defining H.

But there remains the case of sentences involving both K and H materially. Whereas, for example, it is decided that a) is to be awarded to "two", it remains to be decided whether b) is to be awarded to "two" or to "apple". This is a question to be decided by arbitrary choice. It is the question of whether to define the word "two" first, independently of the word "apple", and then to define the word "apple" later, or *vice versa*.

Let us suppose that the word K is to be defined prior to defining a word H. At this stage then we need consider only such accepted K-sentences as involve K materially without involving H materially. Subsequently, when we come to define H, we shall have to pick up the sentences involving H and K together materially, as well as others involving H materially.

K, we suppose, is given precedence over H. Now here is another word G. The question repeats itself—should K be given precedence over G, or *vice versa*? If it be decided that K is to be given precedence over G, then in defining K we need look only to accepted sentences which involve K materially but involve neither G nor H materially.

Relatively to every concept, either individually or at wholesale, the priority of every concept must be favorably or unfavorably decided upon. In each case the choice of priority is conventional and arbitrary, and presumably to be guided by considerations of simplicity in the result. Such considerations seem to point in any case to giving general or abstract notions priority over special or concrete notions, and to giving so-called logical and mathematical notions priority over so-called empirical notions. Thus for example "two" may be expected to be given precedence over "apple". Hence the accepted sentences to be dealt with in defining "two" will comprise none which materially involve "apple". The sentence b) will therefore not be taken into consideration in defining "two", but will have to wait until we come to define "apple".

If we decide then to give the word "two" precedence over all so-called empirical notions, then the accepted "two"-sentences which we shall have to consider in defining "two" will involve no empirical words whatever, unless vacuously. All accepted "two"-sentences which, like b), materially involve empirical notions, will thus be set aside until the time when we are ready to define those empirical notions; none of those sentences will be dealt with in defining "two". The only "two"-sentences to be provided for in defining "two" will thus be the accepted logico-mathematical "two"-sentences (including those applied forms which mention empirical notions vacuously). What is thus true of the word "two" will be equally true of any other word from the vocabulary of logic and mathematics. Since all such notions will be given precedence over empirical notions, the definitions of all logico-mathematical notions need be so framed only as to provide for accepted logico-mathematical sentences.

Within the logico-mathematical realm the considerations of priority between concepts run as before. They are arbitrary, and to a great extent it is in different choices in this respect that differences in alternative systematizations of logic and mathematics reside. It has been the procedure in Whitehead and Russell's *Principia Mathematica* to give all of the so-called logical concepts priority over the so-called mathematical ones—although the distinction between these categories is somewhat vague and corresponds to no sharp structural cleavage. For example, the logical notion "if-then" will be given priority over the mathematical notion "two", and priority likewise over all other mathematical notions. Thus we shall be confined, in defining "if-then", to a consideration of only such accepted "if-then" sentences as involve no extra-logical words materially.

Suppose then that logical notions thus be given priority over *all* non-logical notions, mathematical and otherwise. Then there remains the question of priority among purely logical notions—"if-then", "and", "not", "neither-nor", "some", "all", etc. Suppose "neither-nor" be given priority over *all* other logical words, and hence over all other words of *whatever* kind. Then, in framing a definition of "neither-nor", we have only to provide for such accepted "neither-nor"-sentences as involve absolutely no other words materially. These sentences may contain any words we like—"temperature", "cat", "two", and so on, but they must involve these words vacuously.

Here is an example of such a sentence:

Neither 'neither "today is Sunday" nor "neither 'today is Sunday' nor 'today is Sunday' " ' nor 'neither "Paris is in France" nor "neither 'Paris is France' nor 'Paris is in France' " '.

This sounds like Gertrude Stein, but the quotation marks may help somewhat; they are there merely to indicate grouping. This sentence will be accepted by everyone as true, once it has been studied long enough to be understood. Let us take this section first: "neither 'today is Sunday' nor 'today is Sunday'." This, obviously, is merely a clumsy way of saying that today is not Sunday. Then let us write that in instead. Now this whole segment becomes: 'neither "today is Sunday" nor "today is not Sunday".' This much is obviously false. "Today is neither Sunday nor not Sunday." Similarly the last half of the sentence turns out to mean that Paris is neither in France nor not in France. This again is false. But the whole sentence denies both of these falsehoods; it says, "Neither the one nor the other". Therefore the whole sentence is true; it is an accepted "nor"-sentence. Furthermore, this whole true sentence involves the words "today", "Sunday", "Paris", "France", "is" and "in" vacuously. It would continue to be true, by the same argument, no matter what clauses we might introduce in place of "today is Sunday" and "Paris is in France". Thus the only word which this sentence does involve non-vacuously, or materially, is "neither-nor". All such sentences will consist, like this one, of a "neither-nor" combining two sentences each of which is antilogical, and each of which is built up out of "neither-nor" in turn.

Now the class of such sentences is infinite; they can be built up in more and more complex forms, without end. But there is a perfectly finite way of providing for all of them.

Instead of the words "neither-nor" let us use the device of merely drawing a line over the affected clauses. Thus instead of "Neither so-and-so nor such-and-such" let us write $\overline{\text{so-\&-so such-\&-such}}$. Now it can be proved that all accepted sentences involving only "neither-nor" materially can be generated by these two rules:

A) Accept any sentence of the form $\overline{\overline{\overline{pq}\ \overline{pq}\ \overline{rp}\ \overline{pp}}\ \overline{p}\ \overline{\overline{sr}\ q\ \overline{pp}\ p}}$.

[By a sentence of the *form* $\overline{\overline{pq}\ \overline{pq}\ \overline{rp}\ \overline{pp}\ p\ \overline{sr}\ q\ \overline{pp}\ p}$ I mean a sentence which results when we write some sentence instead of the letter "p" in that form, and some sentence for "q", some sentence for "r", and some sentence for "s".]

B) Having accepted sentences of the forms "$\overline{\overline{pq}\,r}$" and "$\overline{qs}$", accept "p" likewise.

I shall not present the proof here, but it has been proved that all sentences involving only "neither-nor" materially can be generated by A) and B). Hence we may merely adopt A) and B) by fiat: they constitute an *implicit definition* of "neither-nor". A) and B) are a statement of the conventions according to which we propose to use the words "neither-nor". The implicit definition A)-B) is a finite scheme for generating an infinite series of sentences the truth of which constitutes the meaning of "neither-nor". And since it is demonstrable that *all* those accepted sentences of common-sense which involve only "neither-nor" materially are generable by A) and B), while *no* other sentences are generable by A) and B), we are assured that this implicit definition of "neither-nor" is *successful:* successful in the sense that it guarantees the customary usage of "neither-nor".

All accepted sentences materially involving only "neither-nor" become *analytic:* they become consequences merely of the linguistic conventions A) and B) governing the use of "neither-nor".

Now it will be possible to define a good many words in terms of "neither-nor" by *explicit* definition, or direct convention of notational abbreviation. Such an explicit definition is possible, for example, in the case of the logical notion "not". "Not" can be defined explicitly in terms of "neither-nor" by defining "not so-and-so" in every case as an abbreviation for "so-and-so so-and-so." Officially, this is a mere arbitrary abbreviation; but it obviously sqaures ⟨*sic*⟩ with the ordinary usage of the word "not".

Again, having thus defined "not" we can present an explicit definition of "or": namely, "so-and-so *or* such-and-such" can be introduced in every case as an abbreviation for "not so-&-so such-&-such." Again, "and" can be given an explicit definition in terms of "not" and "neither-nor", by defining "so-&-so *and* such-&-such" as an abbreviation for "not so-&-so not such-&-such." By "and" and "or" here I mean the clause-connecting kind of "and" and "or", not the noun-connecting kind of "and" and "or"; I mean "and" as in "Today is Sunday and tomorrow is Monday", not "and" as in "ham and eggs"; similarly for "or". The noun-connecting "and" and "or" would be handled as different words at some later stage of logic. They might be distinguished from these perhaps by an accent over the vowel.

Again, "if-then" can be defined in terms of "not" and "and" by introducing "if so-&-so then such-&-such" as an abbreviation for "not (so-&-so and not such-&-such)".

Thus "not", "or", "and" and "if" all admit of explicit definition in terms ultimately of "neither-nor". With these explicit definitions, the totality of sentences generable by A) and B) comes to include all accepted sentences involving *any* of the words "neither-nor", "not", "or", "and", and "if" materially (and other words vacuously). All these are generable by A) and B).

Let us see how the thing works. For brevity let us write "T" instead of "Today is Sunday", "W" instead of "Washington was a Spaniard", "M" instead of "All men are mortal", and "E" instead of "Eleven is prime". Now the sentence

1) $\overline{TE}$ $\overline{TC}$ $\overline{WT}$ $\overline{TT}$ T $\overline{MW}$ E $\overline{TT}$ T is generated directly by A). For, this sentence is of the *form* of the expression in A); it is had from the latter by putting "T" for "p", "E" for "q", "W" for "r" and "M" for "s". Here already is a simple example of the derivation, through A), of an accepted sentence involving only "neither-nor" materially. We need not stop to try to understand the actual meaning of 1); it could be done, of course.

Now let us derive another such sentence through A), namely this one:

2) T $\overline{MW}$ E T $\overline{MW}$ E $\overline{TT}$ T T $\overline{TT}$ T $\overline{TE}$ $\overline{TE}$ $\overline{WT}$ $\overline{TT}$ T $\overline{MW}$ E $\overline{TT}$ T
This is of the form of the formula in A), as is seen by the fact that 2) is had by putting "T" for "p", "$\overline{MW}$ E" for "q", "$\overline{TT}$ T" for "r", and "$\overline{TE}$ $\overline{TE}$ $\overline{WT}$" for "s".

Now 2) is of the form "$\overline{pq}$ r", and 1) is of the form "$\overline{q}s$", where the "q" is the same in both cases. Hence, B) tells us that we may infer "p", namely

3) T MW E T MW E TT T T TT T

Here then is a sentence derived through A) and B) together.

By a continuation of these processes, through ten more steps, we finally reach this sentence:

4) T TT T TT

Now we agreed to abbreviate "so-&-so so-&-so" as "not so-&-so". Hence 4) becomes

5) not T TT.

But we agreed to abbreviate "not so-&-so such-&-such" as "so-&-so *or* such-&-such". Hence 5) becomes

6) T or TT

Again, "TT" is abbreviated as "not T". 6) thus becomes

7) T or not T.

"Today is Sunday or not today is Sunday"; that is, either today is Sunday or it is not.

This sentence involves "or" and "not" materially, anything else vacuously. Instead of the words "today", "is" and "Sunday" in 7) we might have had any other words without falsifying the result; "today", "is" and "Sunday" occur vacuously in 7).

7), as we ordinarily say, is a truth of logic; although it mentions such non-logical notions as "today" and "Sunday", yet the truth of 7) depends upon logic alone: indeed, 7) is merely an application of the law of the excluded middle.

Any other identically true propositions, involving "neither-nor", "not", "or", "and", or "if", can be derived through A) and B) just as 1)–7) was derived. This class of propositions comprises the fundamental and most familiar part of modern logic. It will be worth while to digress for a moment on this point. The connectives "if-then", "and", "or", "not", and "neither-nor" are called *truth-functions*. They are characterized by the fact that the truth or falsity of a sentence compounded by such a connective is determined solely by the truth or falsity of the ingredient sentences. For example, consider the sentence "so-and-so or such-&-such". There are four possible cases: perhaps "so-&-so" and "such-&-such" are both true; perhaps the first is true and the second false; perhaps the second is true and the first false; or perhaps they are both false. Now the truth or falsity of the compound, "so-&-so or such-&-such" is determinate for each of these four cases; namely, the compound is true in the first three cases, false in the fourth case.

so-&-so	such-&-such	so-&-so *or* such-&-such
t	t	t
t	f	t
f	t	t
f	f	f

so-&-so *and* such-&-such
t
f
f
f

Again, the truth or falsity of the compound "so-and-so *and* such-&-such" is determined for the respective cases this way: true in the first case, false in the rest. Like "or" and "and", each of the truth-functions has its definite table of this kind. "Neither-nor", for example, would be "ffft". The truth-function "not" of course has a very simple table: "not so-&-so" is false when "so-&-so" is true, and true when "so-&-so" is false.

Such, then, is what is meant by a truth-function. Obviously "and", "or", "not", "if-then", and "neither-nor" are not the only truth-functions; there are also "if and only if", "not unless", "but not", and others for which ordinary language happens to have no simple idiom; there are infinitely many truth-functions, some combining sentences three at a time, some four at a time, and so on.

It was Professor Sheffer who discovered that every truth-function can be defined explicitly in terms solely of "neither-nor".

Each can be defined in terms of "neither-nor" in the manner in which I have already defined "not", "or", "and" and "if-then".

All of truth-function logic, in other words *all* truths involving nothing but truth-functions materially, can be derived through A) and B) alone—just as 1)–7) are derived. A) and B) are my own—discovered only a week ago. But my discovery of them was facilitated by some work done in a different connection, namely in terms of a different notion from "neither-nor", by Jean Nicod and Jan Łukasiewicz.

All truths involving only truth-functions materially are derivable through A) and B). These truths are infinite in number, so it is remarkable to be able to *prove* that we can get them all. The proof, a very ingenious one, is due to Łukasiewicz. His proof was concerned with a different starting-point than A) and B) and "neither-nor", but it is possible to turn his proof to these purposes.

So far, then, we have provided for all the truth-functions. "Neither-nor" was defined implicite, and the rest have been defined or can be defined explicite in terms of "neither-nor". From the definitions we are in position to derive any truths we like within a broad field: namely, we are in position to derive all accepted sentences materially involving the words "neither-nor", "not", "or", "and", "if-then", or any other truth-functions (and other words vacuously). All such sentences become *analytic*—direct consequences of our conventions as to the use of words.

Now we are ready to introduce some further logical notion, say L, which is *not* to be had by explicit definition in terms of "neither-nor". L might be the logical notion "all", or it might be some other logical notion. For this purpose we shall need to supplement A)–B) by another rule or two, say C) and D), by way of an implicit definition of L. Since "neither-nor" was the first notion to be defined, the schematic formulae occurring in analogous fashion in C) and D) need not be confined to involving only the new notion L, but may also depend upon any of the notions already defined, namely "neither-nor", "not", "or", "and" and so on.

C) and D) will be so framed that by them along with A) and B) we can generate all accepted sentences which materially involve L and "neither-nor" and the derivative notions explicitly defined in terms of "neither-nor", but involving other notions vacuously. Furthermore, we will be able to present explicit definitions of a new string of notions in terms of L and two preceding notions. Accepted sentences involving these new notions become generable likewise from A)B)C)D).

Next we may introduce some further logical notion through implicit definition, by adding say one more rule E). Analogously to the formula in A), E) will involve some formula using this newly defined notion; but the formula in E) may use also "neither-nor", L, and any of the other notions higherto ⟨sic; hitherto⟩ introduced.

About this much of a basis will prove to be enough, in the way of rules or implicit definitions, to provide for the whole of logic. All further notions of pure logic will admit of *explicit* or purely abbreviative definitions in terms ⟨of⟩ the words already defined. By A)B)C)D)E), and the explicit definitions depending upon A)B)C)D)E), we shall have defined every word of the kind which we ordinarily characterize as purely logical; and from these definitions all logic will follow analytically. In other words, the rules A)–E), and the subsidiary conventions of abbreviation or explicit definition, will be enough to provide for *all* accepted sentences which materially involve none but logical notions.

Next we start in on the vocabulary of ordinary mathematics. Whitehead and Russell, in their *Principia Mathematica*, established the important fact that, given logic, all pure mathematics, ordinarily so-called, can be developed without any more implicit definitions whatever! The logical rules or implicit definitions A) to E) are enough not only for all logic but for all mathematics; nothing more is needed beyond pure conventions of abbreviation, that is, explicit definitions. All mathematical notions can be introduced in that way on the given basis of logic, and *all* theorems of mathematics can be derived through the rules A) to E) alone, along with the explicit or purely abbreviative definitions.

So the rules of implicit definition A)–E) brought us farther along than we expected. We have now provided for the entire vocabulary of logic and mathematics, and therewith we have made it possible to derive all accepted sentences involving any mathematical or logical notions materially and other notions vacuously. [a) is one of these sentences: it involves only logical and mathematical words materially, "apple" vacuously.] All such sentences, in other words all mathematics and logic, become analytic: direct consequences of our definitions, or conventions as to the use of words.

But why stop here? I started out earlier in the hour, on the program of defining words in general, indiscriminately. Next it was found that we have to define words in order, and thus establish some order of priority, arbitrary but guided by convenience. The order of priority adopted involved disposing of so-called logical words first, then so-called mathematical ones. We have yet to deal with the so-called empirical words.

Suppose the first of these so-called empirical words that we decide to define is "event". We shall need an implicit definition for this word; that is, we shall need to supplement the rules A)–E) with say one more rule F). This rule will be so fashioned that from A)–F) we can derive all accepted sentences materially involving only the word "event" plus any mathematical or logical notions, but involving other words only vacuously. The sentences thus provided for will express only the completed general properties of events: only the sentences about "event" which, except for the word "event" are entirely logico-mathematical. All such sentences become *analytic:* they are immediately derivable from our definitions or conventions as to the use of words.

Now there will be words which can be defined explicitly, by pure abbreviative convention, in terms of the logico-mathematical words plus "event". Given these explicit definitions, the rules A)–F) provide for all accepted sentences which involve any of those words materially and other words only vacuously. All these sentences become analytic.

Then we may move to another so-called empirical word, say "energy" or "time", which is, let us suppose, not definable by explicit definitions in terms of notions thus far at hand. We then become ⟨*sic*⟩ an implicit definition for this word, and proceed as before. We may continue thus as far as we like, providing for one so-called empirical word after another, by explicit definition as far as possible, then by implicit definition. Each definition will be so framed as to provide for all accepted sentences materially involving only the notion in question and preceding notions, while vacuously involving any other notions.

But where should we stop in this process? Obviously we could go on indefinitely in the same way, introducing one word after another, and providing in each definition for the derivation of all accepted sentences which materially involve the word there defined and preceding words but no others. Suppose we were to keep this up until we have defined, implicitly or explicitly, and one after another, every word in the English language. Then *every* accepted sentence, no matter in what words, would be provided for by the implicit or explicit definitions; every accepted sentence would become analytic, that is, directly derivable from our conventions as to the use of words.

Now for some practical considerations. To carry this out down to the last word and provide for the most minute accepted sentence would be somewhat of an undertaking. Here is one accepted sentence: "In 1934 a picture of Immanuel Kant was hanging in Emerson Hall." Suppose all the other words in the sentence be given priority over "Immanuel Kant" and "Emerson Hall". Then this sentence, which involves "Immanuel Kant" and "Emerson Hall" materially, will not have been provided for in the definitions of any of those prior words. We shall then have to provide for the sentence within the implicit definition of "Immanuel Kant" or else within the implicit definition of "Emerson Hall"—whichever one happens to come last. Now obviously we do not want to deal with this sort of thing.

The absurdity of this case does not arise from the mere fact that the sentence "In 1934 a picture of Kant was hanging in Emerson Hall" is a so-called empirical sentence. The law of freely falling bodies is likewise ordinarily classed as an empirical sentence, yet there would be no such aversion to our making the law of freely falling bodies analytic instead of empirical by incorporating the law into the definition of "free fall". We may or may not incorporate the law of falling bodies into the definition of "free fall", as we choose; either one choice or the other might be preferable. But there is no chance of our choosing to incorporate the sentence about the picture into a definition of "Emerson Hall"—even under the absurd supposition that we should choose to *define* "Emerson Hall" at all!

There is a vast range of sentences which, because of their lack of generality or lack of importance, we simply would not bother to render analytic by deliberate definition. This is one of them.

Also there are accepted sentences which are both general and important, which however we hesitate to make analytic for another reason. Namely, the accommodation of new discoveries in science is constantly occasioning revision of old hypotheses, old empirical laws. In general we can choose, to *some* extent, where to revise, what principle to dislodge. Our choice is guided largely by the tendency to dislodge as little of previous doctrine as we can compatibly with the ideal of unity and simplicity in the resulting doctrine. Hence we may propose, by and large, to disturb first only such principles as support or underly, in a logical way, a minimum of other principles. It is therefore convenient to maintain a merely provisional, non-analytic status for such principles as we shall be most willing to sacrifice when need of revision at one point or another arises. If *all* empirical generalities are transformed into analytic propositions by redefinition of terms, we shall find ourselves continually redefining and then retrodefining; our definitions will not only be in an unnecessarily extreme state of flux, but there will be no immediate criterion for revising one definition rather than another. At every stage the entire conceptual scheme would be crystallized.

Yet we must define—and we must define sufficiently to make verbal usage specific in matters at least which are subject to rigorous treatment, as in the rigorous sciences. And we cannot define without making *some* of our accepted sentences analytic; it is a matter merely of choosing which. We saw just now that we will do best to render only such sentences analytic as we shall be most reluctant to revise when the demand arises for revision in one quarter or another. These include all the truths of logic and mathematics; we plan to stick to these in any case, and to make any revisions elsewhere. If psychological findings conflict intolerably with the Weber-Fechner law, namely that the intensity of sensation is proportional to the logarithm of the intensity of the stimulus, we shall of course adjust our doctrine by abandoning the Weber-Fechner law rather than by redefining "logarithm". Hence we may as well make the accepted sentences of mathematics and logic analytic.

But the language of so-called pure mathematics and logic does not embrace *all* the notions which have to be unambiguously defined in order to keep rigorous sciences rigorous. In defining these further terms, terms say of physics, we may follow the same principle; the definitions will be bound to make some of the accepted sentences of physics analytic, but we can so proceed as to render only those sentences analytic which, because of the key position which they occupy, we should be most inclined to preserve when called upon to make future revisions of the science.

For example, Einstein found it important, in enhancing the rigor of physics, to *define* "simultaneity"—rather than simply using the word, like "Emerson Hall" or "apple", on the assumption that everyone concerned knew well enough what it meant. Then which of the accepted sentences of physics was he to allow to be rendered analytic by the definition? He chose the sentence whose acceptance arose from the Michelson-Morley experiment: namely, the sentence to the effect that light travels at the same velocity in all directions: in others words, that simultaneously emitted flashes of light will meet at a midpoint between the two sources. Einstein based his definition of simultaneity upon this, by *defining* the simultaneity of light-emissions as *meaning* the collision of the light at the midpoint. He thereby rendered the Michelson-Morley law analytic; erected it, as Poincare would say, into a principle.

Such choices being made, and terminology being rendered sufficiently determinate for our purposes through implicit or explicit definition, we may as well stop defining, and let our remaining empirical laws keep their provisional status of synthetic propositions. In the face of future recalcitrant data, we shall in general confine our revision activity to these provisional laws, rather than saving them at the expense of changing our definitions.

Analytic propositions are true by linguistic convention. But it now appears further that it is likewise a matter of linguistic convention *which* propositions we are to make analytic and which not. How we choose to frame our definitions is a matter of choice. Of our pre-definitionally accepted propositions, we may make certain ones analytic, or other ones instead, depending upon the course of definition adopted.

So much for the analytic. What now of its relation to the *a priori?* Kant said that a judgment is *a priori* if it "has the character of an inward necessity." Now a problem appears which is much a question of which came first, the hen or the egg. When it is claimed that the *a priori* is analytic, the usual procedure is to suggest that the *a priori* has its character of an inward necessity only *because* it is analytic: first we have definitions, and thence we get the *a priori*. During this hour I have adopted the opposite fiction, that we first

have our whole range of accepted sentences, without any definitions, and then frame our definitions to fit these sentences. Historically, psychologically, the truth lies between these two extremes.
On the one hand, it is certain that there are words, technical
words, which we never had, prior to their definition, but have
deliberately coined and introduced through their definitions. On
the other hand it is likewise true that mathematics itself has not,
traditionally, developed through the sole process of deliberately
presenting implicit and explicit definitions, but has merely system-
atized and generated firmly accepted sentences of an abstract
kind.

But in any case there are more and less firmly accepted sentences prior to any sophisticated system of thoroughgoing definition. The more firmly accepted sentences we choose to modify
last, if at all, in the course of evolving and revamping our sciences
in the face of new discoveries. And among these accepted sentences which we choose to give up last, if at all, there are those
which we are not going to give up at all, so basic are they to our
whole conceptual scheme. These, if any, are the sentences to
which the epithet "a priori" would have to apply. And we have
seen during this hour that it is *convenient* so to frame our definitions as to make all these sentences analytic, along with others,
even, which were not quite so firmly accepted before being raised
to the analytic status.

But all this is a question only of how we choose to systematize
on language. We are equally free to leave some of our firmly accepted sentences outside the analytic realm, and yet to continue to
hold to them by what we may call deliberate dogma, or mystic
intuition, or divine revelation: but what's the use, since suitable
definition *can* be made to do the trick without any such trouble-
some assumptions? If we disapprove of the gratuitous creation of
metaphysical problems, we will provide for such firmly accepted
sentences within our definitions, or else cease to accept them so
firmly.

Kant's recognition of *a priori* synthetic propositions, and the
modern denial of such, are thus to be construed as statements of
conventions as to linguistic procedure. The modern convention
has the advantage of great theoretical economy; but the doctrine
that the *a priori* is analytic remains only a syntactic decision. It is

however no less important for *that* reason: as a syntactic decision it has the importance of enabling us to pursue foundations of mathematics and the logic of science without encountering extra-logical questions as to the source of the validity of our *a priori* judgments. The possibility of such a syntactic procedure has furthermore this important relevance to metaphysics: it shows that all metaphysical problems as to an *a priori* synthetic are gratuitous, and let in only by ill-advised syntactic procedures. Finally, the doctrine that the *a priori* is analytic *gains* in force by thus turning out to be a matter of syntactic convention; for the objection is thereby forestalled that our exclusion of the metaphysical difficulties of the *a priori* synthetic depends upon our adoption of a gratuitous metaphysical point of view in turn. Thus the province of this hour's talk has been syntax rather than metaphysics: I have been suggesting what syntax can accomplish without recourse to metaphysics.

When we adopt such a syntax, in which the *a priori* is confined to the analytic, every true proposition then falls into one of two classes: either it is a synthetic empirical proposition, belonging within one or another of the natural sciences, or it is an *a priori* analytic proposition, in which case it derives its validity from the conventional structure, or *syntax*, of the language itself—"syntax" being broadly enough construed to cover all linguistic conventions. Syntax must therefore provide for everything outside the natural sciences themselves: hence syntax must provide not only for logic and mathematics but also for whatever is valid in philosophy itself, when philosophy is purged of ingredients proper to natural science.

Carnap's thesis that philosophy is syntax is thus seen to follow from the principle that everything is analytic except the contingent propositions of empirical science. But like the principle that the *a priori* is analytic, Carnap's thesis is to be regarded not as a metaphysical conclusion, but as a syntactic decision. This conclusion should be gratifying to Carnap himself: for if philosophy is syntax, the philosophical view that philosophy is syntax should be syntax in turn; and this we see it to be.

We have seen that under the manifestly advantageous linguistic procedure under consideration all principles spring from syntax or experiment. Syntax is the tool for handling, organizing, empirical data. Syntax comes to constitute the basis not only for logic and mathematics but for the entire logic of science, philosophy itself. Hence the importance of a rigorous study of formal syntax. This task Carnap sets himself in his new book *Die logische Syntax der Sprache*, with which I shall be concerned next Thursday.

[LECTURE II]
SYNTAX

THE WORD *semantic* has been used in two very different senses. As used by C. S. Peirce "semantic" is the study of the modes of denotation of signs: whether a sign denotes its object through causal or symptomatic connection, or through imagery, or through arbitrary convention, and so on. This sense of semantic, namely a theory of *meaning*, is used also in empirical philology: *empirical semantic* is the study of historical changes of meanings of words. But "semantic" is used in a different sense by Chwistek, as meaning namely the study of signs themselves and the formal rules of their manipulation, without regard to their denotation. It is semantic in this sense that Carnap, avoiding the ambiguity of the word *semantic,* calls *syntax.*

Carnap finds it convenient to divide the syntactical rules of a language into two classes, which he calls *formative rules* and *transformative rules* (*Formregeln* and *Umformungsregeln*). The formative rules tell us how *sentences* may be built up. Suppose we have before us all the single signs of a language, and all possible results of stringing these out into complexes at random. Some of these combinations will "make sense," as we say, and will be sentences of the language, while others will not. Which of the expressions, or sign-complexes, are to rank as sentences and which are not is a syntactical question to be decided by the syntax of the language. The conventions whereby this is determined are called the *formative rules* of the language.

The traditional expositions of the grammar of the various natural languages are concerned with the formative rules. Thus we are told in an English grammar, in effect, that the sentence "Boston is a city" is grammatical while "Boston are a city" is not. In other words, the first string of signs is a sentence, the second is not. The first string of signs conforms to the various formative rules of English syntax, while the second string of signs violates one of the formative rules—the rule that the subject and predicate of a sentence must agree in grammatical number.

The formative rules of the natural languages are of course enormously complex. Their complete formulation involves a very extensive grammatical terminology, such as *number, case, gender, mood,* the parts of speech, and so on. These various notions must of course be formulated in turn. And when all this is done, and all the formative rules contained in an English grammar book are provided for, the job still is not done. There are further formative rules in English which the standard grammars do not include: miscellaneous specific rules according to which, for example, "He laid claim to that" and "He took cognizance of that" are sentences while "He laid cognizance to that" and "He took claim of that" are not sentences but meaningless or anti-syntactical strings of signs. Every unique idiom calls for some special formative rule.

Because of these complexities Carnap introduces an artificial symbolic language as object for syntactical study, rather than choosing a natural language. The irregularities of natural languages are historically interesting but from the logical standpoint they merely complicate the procedure gratuitously. The formative rules of Carnap's artificial language are few and simple, but to a certain extent they constitute a paradigm for the formative rules of more complex languages as well.

This artificial *specimen language* of Carnap's contains, for the most part, the customary signs of mathematical logic and mathematics. On the mathematical side there is just one peculiarity of notation which we need observe, namely the use of groups of letters for arithmetical operators. For example, instead of writing "$x + y$" for the sum of x and y, we write "sum (x, y)" in the specimen language, instead of writing "$x-y$", we write "dif (x, y)". Instead of writing "$x!$", we write "fac (x)". I find it convenient to regard the operators, not as the groups of letters "sum", "dif", "fac", etc., but rather as the notational molds or matrices "sum $(,)$", "dif $(,)$", "fac $( )$", etc., containing blanks whose purpose is to be filled in.

These operators are all *numerical* operators, in the sense that they are applied only to numerical expressions, and yield only numerical expressions in turn. Thus we use "sum (x, y)" only where "x" and "y" represent numbers; the whole complex in turn represents a number, namely the sum of the numbers x and y. The same holds for "dif" and "fac".

Aside from the use of these operators, which diverges from the usual mathematical notation, we may suppose that the logico-mathematical parts of the specimen language involve the usual notation.

Now the specimen language requires more than the logico-mathematical vocabulary, for it must enable us to construct descriptive sentences about the world. Instead of proper names, the specimen language uses a system of coördinates. Thus a given point-event might be represented by an ordered quadruple of numbers x, y, z, t, where the respective numbers x, y, z, and t measure, in arbitrary units, the longitude, latitude, altitude and tarditude (date) of the given point-event. Extended regions in space-time can be expressed through application of analytic geometry, namely by equations in four variables.

Not to cumber his specimen language with complexities irrelevant to his purpose, Carnap confines his developments to the case where we have only a one-dimensional series of discrete locations. These successive places are designated by the successive integers.

Carnap supposes further an arithmetization of such empirical properties as color, temperature, etc.: a gradation of empirical properties is, so to say, *calibrated*, perhaps according to a principle, perhaps only arbitrarily. In the case of temperature a calibration relatively to the expansion of mercury will do—say the centigrade calibration. In the case of color we can assign numbers to positions on the color pyramid. In this way, let us suppose, all empirical properties can be calibrated; some of the calibration may proceed systematically, and some of it by purely arbitrary assignment of numbers.

The specimen language contains an indefinite multitude of *descriptive operators*, as Carnap calls them. It is with the help of these that empirical sentences can be constructed. One such operator is the matrix "temp ( )", and may be translated to read "temperature of, in degrees centigrade". Thus "temp (7)" denotes the temperature, in degrees, of the place whose coördinate is 7. "temp (7) =

19″ is thus an empirical or synthetic sentence to the effect that the temperature of place No. 7 is 19°. The operator "temp" is a numerical operator, like the "sum", "dif", etc., considered earlier. Like the other numerical operators, "temp" applies only to numbers: "temp (x)" is used only where x is a number. Like the other numerical operators, moreover, "temp" yields a number in turn; "temp (x)" denotes a number, say 19. But the numerical operator "temp" differs from the numerical operators "sum" and "dif" in that it does not belong to pure mathematics. Although "temp", like "sum" and "dif", applies only to numbers and yields only numbers, yet the number which "temp" will yield in a given case is not determinable by the laws of pure mathematics, whereas the number which "sum" or "dif" will yield in any given case is determinable by the laws of pure mathematics. Such, in vague terms, is the respect in which "temp" is an empirical or *descriptive* operator.

Except for the operator "temp", the sentence "temp (7) = 19" is made up solely of the vocabulary of pure mathematics. The sentence is an empirical or synthetic sentence, but only because of the operator "temp". The syllable "temp" might be paraphrased to read: "Temperature, in degrees, of the place whose number is". Thus the sentence "temp (7) = 19" may be read "Temperature, in degrees, of the place whose number is 7, equals 19". The non-mathematical matter of this sentence is concentrated in the phrase "Temperature, in degrees, of the place whose number is"; for short, "temp".

Another descriptive operator of the specimen language is the matrix "co ( )", which may be read "color of", or more exactly "color, in terms of the calibration of the color pyramid, of the place whose number is". Thus "co (5) = 3" means that the color of the fifth place is Color Number 3, say ultramarine.

Now these descriptive operators, "temp", "co" and indefinitely many more, are the only special devices contained in the specimen language for purposes of dealing with empirical fact; over and above these descriptive operators there is only the logico-mathematical vocabulary. Sentences about empirical fact are constructed out of these operators along with the devices of logic and mathematics; such sentences as "temp (7) = 19" and "co (5) = 3", also more complicated sentences such as that every place from Place No. 10 to Place No. 30 has a temperature between 25 and 40, also perhaps a general sentence expressing some arithmetical functionality between the temperature of every place and that of the next neighboring place, also functional dependences between temperature and pressure, and so on. Within the specimen language, by means of logico-mathematical notions plus the descriptive operators, all empirical matters can be expressed, insofar as the properties involved have been fitted to some scheme of measurement, some manner of systematic or arbitrary calibration.

The formative rules of the specimen language presuppose a consideration of the so-called *primitive* signs of the language: that is, the signs which are used in the language without being defined by explicit definition as abbreviations of complexes of other signs. Whether or not the primitive signs be said to be defined by *implicit* definition, still they are not explicitly defined, which is what is frequently meant by definition.

By way of saving explanations I shall not give the primitives actually used by Carnap; it will be sufficient merely to consider a set of hypothetical primitive signs. Suppose then that the following signs are primitive for the specimen language. First, the "neither-nor" bar. Further, the italic letters "x", "y" etc., used as numerical variables as in algebra. Third, the sign "=" of numerical equality. Also the arithmetical operator of subtraction, namely the matrix "diff (,)". Actually, these primitives do *not* suffice for all logic and mathematics; we cannot define all other logico-mathematical notions by explicit definition in terms of these. A slightly different selection, no more elaborate than this one, would have been really sufficient, as is shown in my book *A System of Logistic*; but these notions would have taken much longer to expound. Let us suppose then, for simplicity but contrary to fact, that the primitive signs just now listed are enough for logic and mathematics, and that all other logico-mathematical notions can be introduced on this basis by explicit definitions, that is, conventions of mere abbreviation.

Now in addition to these logical primitives the specimen language contains an unspecified number of descriptive operators, such as "temp", "co", etc. Like the arithmetical difference-operator, there are groups of lower case letters followed by parentheses containing blanks: possibly a single blank, possibly several blanks sepa-

rated by commas. These descriptive operators, together with "diff
(,)", constitute the *primitive matrices*.

Framed relatively to this hypothetical set of primitives, the *formative* rules of the specimen language might be the following four:

1) "x = y" is a sentence.
2) If in a sentence an italic letter be replaced by another italic letter,
   or by a primitive matrix with its blanks filled with italic letters,
   the result is a sentence.
3) If ". . ." and "---" are sentences, "$\overline{. . . ---}$" is a sentence.
4) When a sentence is abbreviated through application of definitions, the result is a sentence.

For example, "temp (w) = y" is a sentence: for, by 1), "x = y" is
a sentence, and, by 2), the result of putting "temp (w)" for "x" in a
sentence is in turn a sentence. Again, since this is a sentence, 2)
tells us that "temp (w) = diff (x, x)" is a sentence. Now suppose
the sign "O" be introduced as an abbreviation for the expression
"diff (x, x)". Then, since "temp (w) = diff (x, x)" is a sentence, b)
tells us that "temp (w) = O" is a sentence. Again, this being a
sentence, 3) tells us that "$\overline{\text{temp (w)} = \text{O temp (w)} = \text{O}}$" is a
sentence. Now suppose a convention of abbreviation be intro-
duced whereby "$\overline{. . . = --- . . . = ---}$" is abbreviated in every case as
". . . ≠ ---". According to 4), then, since "$\overline{\text{temp (w)} = \text{O temp (w)}}$
$= \text{O}}$" is a sentence, "temp (w) ≠ O" is likewise a sentence.

All sentences expressible in the specimen language are provided for in this way by the formative rules. Rules 1)–3) tell us
how sentences can be built up in terms of the primitive signs, and
4) then allows us to bring in any explicitly defined signs as well.
Thus a sign which is neither explicitly defined in the specimen
language nor to be found among the given primitive signs cannot
occur in a sentence of the specimen language. Again, even expressions built up only of legitimate signs, primitive signs and explicitly defined signs, must be built up in the conventional fashion in
order to be sentences. For example, "=y" is not a sentence; neither
is "$\overline{\text{STU}}$", even though "S", "T" and "U" be sentences. These so-
called meaningless combinations of signs are excluded from the
realm of sentences, since they are not covered by 1)–4).

The formative rules 1)–4) are the rules of grammar of the specimen language, in the ordinary sense of grammar: they tell us that the ingredients of our vocabulary are to be combined just thus and so. And these rules of grammar take the form of a description of what a *sentence* is, for the language in question.

You have perhaps been wondering why "x = y" is classified as a *sentence;* since it contains variables, it would seem to be at most a *form* for sentences rather than a sentence itself. The same would apply to all the so-called sentences subsequently considered.

The answer to this question involves a certain feature of Carnap's model language which is not common to all languages. Namely, when in the model language we assert a sentence containing variables, we are asserting the sentence as true for all values of the variables, barring explicit indication to the contrary. The sentence "x = y" thus means "any number, x, is equal to any number, y"; in other words, that there are no unequal numbers. Thus interpreted, "x = y" is obviously an ordinary sentence, either true or false. As a matter of fact it is false—for there *are* unequal numbers. But it is none the less a sentence. On the other hand the sentence "x = x" is true; it means that every number is equal to itself.

So much for the formative rules. The other class into which Carnap divides the rules of syntax embraces the *transformative rules.* Whereas the formative rules specify the conditions under which signs may be combined, the transformative rules specify the conditions under which sentences may be *inferred.*

The transformative rules answer, in fact, to what I described last Thursday as *implicit definitions.* I explained last Thursday that all logic and mathematics, ordinarily so-called, could be generated by some such five rules as these:

A) Accept any sentence of the form "$\overline{pq}$ $\overline{pq}$ $\overline{rp}$ $\overline{pp}$ p $\overline{sr}$ q $\overline{pp}$ p".

B) Having accepted "$\overline{pq}$ r" and "$\overline{qs}$", accept "p" likewise.

C) ------------

D) ------------

E) Having accepted a sentence containing an italic letter, accept also the sentence obtained by replacing all occurrences of that letter by another letter or by a matrix filled with italic letters.

The rules A)B), governing the notion "neither-nor", I called an "implicit definition" of "neither-nor". C)D) similarly constituted an implicit definition of some further logical notion, which I did not stop to specify. The transformative rule E), left blank last time, I have here filled in arbitrarily. This rule might be regarded, in terms of implicit definitions, as implicitly defining the numerical variables, or italic letters. In another sense E) might be regarded as in effect an implicit definition of *all*, since, as I have explained, a sentence containing numerical variables is to be regarded in the model language as asserted for *all* values of those variables.

I explained also how we could go on and add more rules F), G) and so on, as far as we pleased; and that these could stand as implicit definitions of so-called empirical notions such as "event", "energy", "time" and so on. Where we stop in this process is an arbitrary matter, to be decided by pragmatic considerations.

Now Carnap, in his specimen language, stops his transformative rules, or implicit definitions in effect, with E): in other words, he introduces implicit definitions only for the ordinarily so-called logico-mathematical part of his language, and does not encroach upon concepts such as "event", "time", etc., which we ordinarily refer to as empirical. In this respect Carnap's language agrees with our usual procedure in ordinary language: namely, we are not in the habit of framing *postulate systems,* that is implicit definitions, for any of our so-called empirical notions, but only for the notions of so-called pure logic, pure arithmetic, pure geometry and pure analysis.

In Carnap's specimen language, then, there are just the five transformative rules, A)–E). These are, in other words, the extent of the *implicit definitions.* Carnap prefers to render his transformative rules in a slightly different way. Namely, he would render B) thus:

B') Where "p", "q", "r" and "s" stand for any sentences, "p" is an *immediate consequence* of the pair of sentences "$\overline{pq}$ r" and "$\overline{qs}$".

He would render A) thus:

A') Where "p", "q", "r" and "s" stand for sentences,

$$\overline{\overline{\overline{pq\ pq\ rp\ pp}}}\ \overline{\overline{\overline{p}\ \overline{sr}\ \overline{q}\ \overline{pp}}}\ p$$

"pq pq rp pp p sr q pp p"
is an *immediate consequence* of every sentence.

Phrased in this form, the transformative rules bear a certain analogy to the formative rules. Whereas the formative rules describe what expressions are *sentences,* within the given language, the transformative rules describe what *sentences* are *immediate consequences* of given sentences within the given language. Whereas the formative rules correspond roughly to what is traditionally included under *grammar,* the transformative rules correspond to what is traditionally included under *logic.*

Mr. T. P. Palmer of the Harvard mathematics department is working now at researches in mathematical logic, one aspect of which is interesting in the present connection. His results point the way, namely, to a possible elimination of formative rules in favor of transformative rules only. But I am of course not entering upon this pending his publication.

Sentence and *immediate consequence* are two key notions of syntax. Like syntax itself, the notions "sentence" and "immediate consequence" are relative to one or another specific language. A string of signs which is a sentence of one language may be only a meaningless string of signs for another language, even though the constituent signs occur in both languages. Whether a given string of signs is a sentence for a given language depends upon the formative rules of the language; whether a given string of signs is a sentence for the specimen language, for example, depends upon whether it is compelled to be by 1)–4).

Similarly one sentence may be an immediate consequence of another sentence within a given language, while this is not the case in another language—even though the expressions in question be *sentences* for both languages. Whether a given sentence is an immediate consequence of another, for a given language, depends upon the transformative rules of that language.

The application of "sentence" and "immediate consequence" thus varies from language to language. What these notions cover within a given language is specified by the rules, formative and transformative, of that language.

But conversely, the entire syntactic structure of a language is determined once we *do* know what passes for a sentence and what passes for an immediate consequence within that language. The formative and transformative rules of a language, in specifying sentences and immediate consequences for that language, sum up or epitomize the syntax of the language. It is in this sense that *sentence* and *immediate consequence* are concepts of syntax. They are strategic *syntactic functions* of a language.

In terms of *sentence* and *immediate consequence* a variety of further important syntactic notions can be explained. Like sentence and immediate consequence, these further notions are syntactic functions of languages; they vary from language to language, but are determinate for a given language once "sentence" and "immediate consequence" are determinate for that language.

One of these derivative notions is *consequence*—without the qualifier "immediate". Roughly: one sentence S is a consequence of another sentence T if there is a chain of sentences, beginning with T and ending with S, such that each sentence is an *immediate consequence* of its predecessor. This definition is not quite adequate, for it does not take into consideration the fact that one sentence is sometimes an immediate consequence only of a *set* of sentences— as in B'). Put it rather this way: a sentence S is a consequence of a sentence *or set of sentences* T if there is a chain of sentences *or sets of sentences* beginning with T and ending with S, such that every sentence of the chain is an immediate consequence of the preceding sentence *or set of sentences*.

Like "immediate consequence", "consequence" is a function of the language, and varies from one language to another according to the transformative rules of the respective languages. Now let us apply the notion of "consequence", in particular, to the model language. Suppose T is a sentence containing the italic letter "x". Suppose S is a sentence which matches T exactly except for exhibiting the expression "sum(y,z)" wherever S exhibits "x". Then, by E'), S is an immediate consequence of T. Now let L, M and N be any sentences. According to B'), T is an immediate consequence of

the pair of sentences "$\overline{TL}$ M" and "$\overline{LN}$". Hence S, being an immedi-

ate consequence of T, is a *consequence* of the pair "$\overline{TL}$ M" and "$\overline{LN}$": not an immediate consequence, but a consequence.

To avoid confusing those who are reading Carnap's book, I should mention that Carnap draws a distinction between "*Folge von*" and "*ableitbar aus*"—"consequence of" and "deducible from"— which is out of consideration only for a recent technical discovery by Gödel in foundations of mathematics. This and related dualities set up by Carnap are irrelevant to a brief survey, and I am deliberately blurring them in this lecture. My "consequence of" answers, strictly speaking, to Carnap's "ableitbar aus".

I should also warn readers of Carnap that his distinction between a *recursive* and an *explicit* definition has nothing to do with my distinction between an *implicit* and an *explicit* definition. Carnap would have done better to use *direct* instead of *explicit*.

The property of being *analytic* is another genuine syntactic property, a syntactic function, describable in terms of consequence. Namely, a sentence is *analytic* if it is a consequence of every sentence. In particular, let us apply this notion to the specimen language. We have seen that "S", under the given conditions, is a consequence of the pair "$\overline{\overline{TL}}$ M" and "$\overline{LN}$". Now suppose further that "$\overline{\overline{TL}}$ M" and "$\overline{LN}$" are both of the form of the expression in A).

Then, according to transformative rule A'), "$\overline{\overline{TL}}$ M" and "$\overline{LN}$" are each immediate consequences of every sentence. Hence "S", being a consequence in turn of "$\overline{\overline{TL}}$ M" and "$\overline{LN}$", is likewise a consequence of every sentence: "S" is, in other words, *analytic*.

In the same way any sentence generable by the rules A)–E) will be analytic for the specimen language. Now we saw last Thursday that *all* logic and mathematics is generable through A)B)C)D)E)—assuming C) and D) to be properly fashioned. In other words, we saw that all accepted sentences involving logico-mathematical words materially, other words vacuously, are generable by A)B)C)D)E). Hence all those sentences are *analytic* for the specimen language—insofar, of course, as they are sentences at all from the standpoint of the specimen language, while it is to be decided in each case by the *formative* rules.

"Analytic" is a function of the language, and varies from one language to another, as does the "consequence" relation upon which the property of being analytic depends. What is analytic and what is not analytic depends upon the transformative rules of the language in question. What is analytic for one language may not be analytic for another language. This is now seen from the formal definitions or explanations of the syntactic notion "analytic". But it is exactly the result which I came to last Thursday by an entirely different chain of reasoning: namely, that it is a matter of linguistic convention what truths turn out to be analytic and what ones do not: it depends upon how we frame our definitions (implicit definitions being, in Carnap's terminology, transformative rules). For one way of framing a language a given sentence will be analytic, for another way of framing a language it will not.

Another syntactic property is the property of being a *contradiction,* or of being *contradictory.* The contradictory is at the opposite extreme from the analytic, and its definition is analogous. A sentence or set of sentences is *contradictory* if every sentence is a consequence of it.

In other terms a contradictory sentence might be described as one whose *denial* is analytic. But "denial" has not been introduced, like "analytic", as a general syntactic notion; it has not been explained in terms say of "sentence" and "consequence", in abstraction from any one specific language. The other definition of the contradictory avoids this dependence upon denial, so that "contradictory" is put on a par with "analytic", "consequence" and "sentence". But it could be shown that in any non-trivial language the contradictory in this sense will agree exactly with the contradictory as defined in terms of denial.

In terms of "analytic" and "contradictory", now, we can describe the *synthetic:* namely, a sentence is *synthetic* which is neither analytic nor contradictory.

Last Thursday, confining my consideration to *true* sentences, or *accepted* sentences, I described a synthetic sentence merely as a non-analytic one; the contradictory did not enter at all. On the other hand this definition of a synthetic sentence, as one which is neither analytic nor contradictory, is a definition of synthetic sentences in general, true and false.

In fact, the separation of synthetic propositions into true and false cannot be carried out at all, within a more formally syntactical approach such as I am now engaged in. "Truth" *cannot* be given a general syntactic definition in terms of the formative and transformative rules of any random language, such as has been given for a "consequence" and "analytic". The truth of a sentence is not determined, in the general case, by the mere syntax of the language to which the sentence belongs. Although all known and unknown empirical truths are presumably expressible as sentences in the English language, we cannot discover these truths by studying English syntax. In the special case of analytic and contradictory sentences we *can* determine truth and falsity by means merely of the transformative rules, for the analytic ones are true and the contradictory ones false. But among synthetic propositions the case is otherwise; we can only describe synthetic sentences *in general*, namely as the sentences which are neither analytic nor contradictory.

An analytic sentence was defined as a sentence which is a consequence of all sentences, and a contradictory sentence as one of which all sentences are consequences. A synthetic sentence, then, being neither analytic nor contradictory, will be a sentence which neither is a consequence of all sentences nor has all sentences as its consequences. Like the analytic and the contradictory, the synthetic varies from language to language; its bounds depend upon the formative and transformative rules of the language in question.

These are by no means all the important syntactic notions that can be defined relatively to the formative and transformative rules of languages. Another important notion is *syntactic category:* two expressions are said to belong to the same *category* when every sentence containing either expression continues to be a sentence when the other expression is substituted. In other words, expressions belong to the same category when they are interchangeable so far as the *formative* rules are concerned.

Another important notion is *synonymity.* Two signs are *synonymous* if, when we replace either sign by the other in any given sentence, the resulting sentence is a consequence of the given sentence. Synonymity is ordinarily explained as sameness of *meaning,* which leaves us with a more difficult notion on our hands than synonymity itself. The definition just now given, on the other hand, makes no reference to meaning; it is a purely syntactic definition, depending only on the notion of consequence, or ultimately on the transformative rules of the language in question.

Another notion which is ordinarily handled still more vaguely than synonymity is the notion of the *content* of a proposition: ordinarily described perhaps as the total fact which the proposition communicates, or something of the sort. Carnap gives "content" a purely syntactic definition in terms of deducibility: namely, the *content* of a sentence is the class of all its non-analytic consequences. Note that according to this definition an analytic sentence is *empty* in point of content: for an analytic sentence has no non-analytic consequences. This result of course fits ordinary us-age: it is often said in describing analytic sentences that they are void of content. But here with Carnap, for the first time, the phrase receives a definite technical meaning.

These samples are already sufficient to suggest the gain af-forded by rigorous methods in syntax. Such concepts as "content" and "synonymity" are usually couched in hopelessly vague terms; such is to a lesser extent the case also with "consequence", "ana-lytic" and "synthetic". The problems associated with these notions are vaguely handled in epistemological logic or intensional logic or theory of meaning. Such matters here become sharply formulated for the first time and put on a basis where we have full command of what we are talking about: the basis, namely, of formal syntax.

Thus far I have used the English language as a medium for ex-pounding the syntax of Carnap's specimen language. But Carnap goes on to show that the syntax of the specimen language can be expressed within the specimen language itself—just as, indeed, we are accustomed to write grammars of the English language within the English language. I shall sketch the method.

A sign is itself of course an empirical notion: say an ink mark, or a general type of ink marks, or a rule for constructing such marks. In what we might call empirical or descriptive syntax, we describe certain signs or ink marks occurring at this or that place in the world: for example, we describe the inscriptions on the Rosetta Stone; or, on the basis of the study of manuscripts, we make empirical generalizations regarding Old French. Such matters may be called empirical syntax, a branch of anthropology.

Now insofar as these empirical matters are to be handled within the specimen language, they must, like any empirical matters, be handled by means solely of the logico-mathematical vocabulary plus descriptive operators. In the specimen language we describe the temperature of a given place by an equation of the form "temp $(x) = n$", where the number x is the coördinate of the place in question, and n is a number measuring the temperature of that place, according to the adopted numeration of temperatures—namely, the centigrade calibration of the mercury tube. In order to describe the *sign* occupying a given place, say the lower left-hand corner of the Rosetta Stone, we need some descriptive operator analogous to "temp": say the operator "sig". Just as "temp $(x) = n$"

means that Place No. x has Temperature No. n, so "sig (x) = n" will mean that Place No. x is occupied by Sign No. n. Perhaps Place No. x turns out to be the lower left-hand corner of the Rosetta Stone, and Sign No. n. turns out to be the cuneiform character " ⊨⊴ ".

The use of the descriptive operators "temp", "∞", etc. in the specimen language depends upon a systematic or arbitrary assignment of numbers to temperatures, colors, etc.; in the same way the use of the descriptive operator "sig" depends upon the systematic or arbitrary assignment of numbers to the various simple and complex typographical shapes.

This calibration of the typographical realm might, for example, be carried out as follows. We might take this year's catalogue of a large type-foundry, and confine our consideration to the typographical varieties offered for sale in that catalogue, together with complex expressions built up of rows of such individual characters. Now we might calibrate the individual characters by assigning these catalogue numbers according to some arbitrary scheme. Next we might assign numbers to complex expressions, namely rows of these simple signs, in the following manner. Consider the complex expression consisting of a row of simple signs, whose respective catalogue numbers are $x_1, x_2, x_3, ----, x_4$. Now the complex expression might be assigned the number $\prod_{i=1}^{n} P_i^{x_i}$, where P_i is the i-th prime number (not counting 1). For example, consider the expression made up of a row of five simple signs S_1, S_2, S_3, S_4 and S_5. Suppose the respective catalogue numbers of these five simple signs are x_1, x_2, x_3, x_4 and x_5. Then the number to be assigned to the complex expression will be $\prod_{i=1}^{5} P_i^{x_i}$, that is, $P_1^{x_1}, P_2^{x_2}, P_3^{x_3}, P_4^{x_4}, P_5^{x_5}$, where P_1 to P_5 are the first five prime numbers not counting 1, namely 2, 3, 5, 7 and 11. Thus the number assigned to the complex expression is the product $2^{x_1}, 3^{x_2}, 5^{x_3}, 7^{x_4}, 11^{x_5}$, where x_1 to x_5 are the prime numbers assigned by the catalogue method to the successive simple characters making up the complex expression in question.

This arithmetical function was adopted first for this purpose by Gödel. It worked backward: given a number assigned to some complex expression, we can determine that expression by analyzing the number into its prime factors. For non-ambiguity it is of course important that none of these derivative numbers correlated with complex expressions shall have occurred also as catalogue numbers of the simple signs. Our adoption of catalogue numbers must be confined to such numbers as will avoid any overlapping with the derivation numbers. One way of doing this would be to use as catalogue numbers only prime numbers greater than 1.

It is well also, in assigning the catalogue numbers, to reserve special categories of numbers for important special categories of signs. We may, for example, reserve for the italic letters "x", "y", etc., such of the prime numbers as are greater by one than squares: that is, prime numbers of the form $n^2 - 1$ ⟨*sic*; for '$-$' read '$+$'⟩.

Now the scheme just now outlined provides a complete calibration for all the expressions which we care to consider, namely simple characters occurring in our printer's catalogue, and linear complexes of them. It now becomes possible in the specimen language to use the descriptive operator "sig" just as we use the descriptive operator "temp". The sentence "sig (x) = n" means that the place x bears a mark of the kind, simple or complex, whose correlated number is n. Just as "temp (x) = n" means that the place x exhibits Temperature No. n, under the centigrade scheme of numbering temperatures, so "sig (x) = n" means that the place x exhibits Expression No. n according to the presented scheme of numbering expressions.

Perhaps this can be made clearer by some temporary coining of words. Let "signitude" mean typographical condition. Now just as we read "temp (x) = n" as "The Temperature of Place No. x is n degrees", suppose we read "sig (x) = n" as "The signitude of Place No. x is n points". A *degree of temperature* is a difference of one in the numbers assigned to the various temperatures; analogously we may say that a *point of signitude* is a difference of one in the numbers assigned to the various signitudes.

It is to be noted next that various syntactic notions can in effect be given purely arithmetical definitions in the specimen language, without use even of the descriptive operator "sig". Consider for example the syntactic notion "variable", which is to say "italic letter". "Var (n)" can be introduced in the specimen language by explicit definition as an abbreviation for this sentence: "n is prime, and there is an integer K such that $n = k^2 - 1$"—where this last would actually be expressed in the symbolic logic of the specimen language. This, as thus defined, "Var (n)" means, strictly speaking, not that n is an italic letter, a variable, but that n is the correlated number of an italic letter; in other words, that any place whose signitude, in points, is n, is occupied by some italic letter. But the definition of "Var (n)" is pure logic and arithmetic; the descriptive functor "sig" does not appear.

The same thing can be done with other syntactic notions, for example, *substitution:* we can present a purely logico-arithmetical definition, within the specimen language, for the ternary numerical operator "sub". Roughly, "sub (h, k, n)" denotes the expression resulting from substituting h for k throughout n; more exactly, "sub (h, k, n)" denotes the number *correlated* with the expression resulting from substituting the expression whose correlated number is h for the expression whose correlated number is k throughout the expression whose correlated number is n. "sub (h, k, n)" in this sense can be defined, of course, in terms solely of logic and arithmetic; more specifically, in terms of the multiplication and division of powers of prime numbers. The definition is complicated, but Carnap presents it.

In the same way we can handle the *sentence*. In terms of the arithmetical formulation of "variable", "substitution", and other preliminary syntactical notions, it is possible to run through the old formative rules in a purely arithmetical way. We can thus frame a purely arithmetical definition of "Sen (n)", where "Sen (n)" means, roughly, "n is a sentence"; more precisely, that n is the correlated number of a sentence.

By arithmetizing the old *transformative* rules in the same way, we can formulate a purely arithmetical definition of immediate consequence: we can thus define "Imc (m, n)", which may be interpreted roughly as meaning that m is immediately deducible from n, but more strictly as meaning that the sentence whose correlated number is m is an immediate consequence of the sentence whose correlated number is n. Then we can proceed in the same arithmetical fashion to the various derivative syntactic notions, such as "consequence", "analytic", "synthetic", "synonymity", "content", and so on; all of these, or rather the numbers correlated with these, admit of purely arithmetical definition in terms of prime numbers and so on. The whole of syntax becomes, in effect, a branch of pure arithmetic.

Now I entered upon this latter discussion with the thesis that the specimen language could describe its own syntax; I have ended up

John Smith & Son Bookshop
Glasgow University
Tel: +44 141 339 1463
Fax: +44 141 339 3690
Email: gu@johnsmith.co.uk

Description	Qty	Cost

9780520068476

DEPOSIT
Dear Carnap, Dear Van   1   31.16 D
Deposit - Do NOT Delete   -1   -31.16

Total To Pay: 0.00
Payment: Cash   0.00
Discount Total: 7.79

Refunds:A credit note will be issued
for any goods returned within 14 days
if stock is in perfect condition with
Exceptions apply.Thank you
VAT: GB 887 136 584
Receipt No:106270:12/01/09:1637:0015:04

with the arithmetization of syntax. These two features must be considered separately. Let us first consider the former point.

There is nothing in principle paradoxical about a language describing its own syntax, for there is nothing paradoxical about writing English grammars in English. This is not a case of vicious circularity, since the use of a language does not presuppose an explicit *account* of its syntax. In using a language we *conform* to its syntactic rules, but do not necessarily begin by *uttering* its syntactic rules in that language or any language. On the other hand we can use the language for discussing any matters we like, physics, or zoölogy, or, in particular, syntax; and there is nothing to prevent us from describing, among other things, the very syntactical rules to which we have been conforming all along. All that is required is that the vocabulary of the language be rich enough to deal with the matters in question; and this is true of discussion of syntax in just the sense that it is true of discussion of zoölogy; it is immaterial that the subject-matter of the one happens to be animals while the subject-matter of the other happens to be signs.

The specimen language is in a somewhat special situation only in that it does not have as rich a vocabulary as other general languages. All empirical matters, whether discussions of animals or of temperatures or of typographical shapes, happen to be expressed in the specimen language, if at all, only by means of descriptive *operators* together with the logico-mathematical vocabulary; there are no empirical *predicates* or *names* in the language, but only the empirical *operators* plus mathematics. It is for this reason that signs, like temperatures, can be handled in the specimen language only under a scheme of calibration. This calibration of signs, and consequent arithmetization of syntax, is not essential in general in order that a language describe its own syntax. But it is necessary in the specimen language because, insofar as the specimen language goes beyond pure logic and mathematics, it happens to be a measurement language or calibration language exclusively.

As a by-product of this peculiar limitation of the specimen language, we arrive at the arithmetization of syntax. We find ourselves in position to manipulate merely the established numerical correlates or *measures* of the signs—just as, in mathematical physics, one manipulates merely the numerical correlates or *measures* of the various physical entities under review.

Although I have not carried out enough technical details here to make it apparent, it happens to be true that the arithmetization of syntax greatly increases our powers of syntactic investigation. The applicability of the method of course is not confined to the syntax of the specimen language; the same method can be applied to any other language, merely by revising the catalogue-numbers of signs, as I called them, to fit the language in question, and revamping the arithmetical definitions of "sentence" and "immediate consequence" to match the formative and transformative rules of the language in question. The arithmetical definitions of the other syntactic notions, in terms of "sentence" and "immediate consequence", remain the same no matter what language is being studied, or even if no one specific language is specified.

The technical topics which fall properly under formal syntax, and can be investigated advantageously by arithmetized syntax, are numerous and important: questions of the isomorphism of systems, the completeness or incompleteness of postulates, and the consistency and independence of postulates, questions also as to general criteria of deducibility or non-deducibility of problematical theorems—such problems, so-called mathematical problems, are the core of foundational studies in mathematics. These matters are properly handled under syntax, and their investigation is enormously facilitated by the method of arithmetized syntax, as has been borne out by the results of Gödel and Tarski. Gödel, for example, made the epoch-making discovery that no deductive system containing within itself the entire language of arithmetic can possibly be complete: that is, no matter how many postulates be adopted, there will always remain would-be theorems which can neither be proved nor disproved within the system. This is the most famous recent discovery in foundations of mathematics; and it would never have been made if Gödel had not availed himself of the method of arithmetized syntax.

But I shall have no more to say about these technical applications, nor about arithmetized syntax itself. Next Thursday I shall sketch rather the manner in which Carnap applies his syntactic concepts and his syntactic point of view to general questions of philosophy and the logic of science. But for this purpose it will be sufficient to use the syntactic notions in their non-arithmetical formulation, as I developed them earlier in this hour.

[LECTURE III]
PHILOSOPHY AS SYNTAX

TWO WEEKS ago I sketched a general background for Carnap's doctrine that philosophy is syntax. It will be useful to recapitulate one result of that discussion. I began with the expository fiction that we have at hand all those sentences which, in 1934, we find ourselves accepting as true; and that up to this point we have done nothing in the way of definition, nothing in the way of conscious systematization of our language. I then set the problem of constructing an explicit formulation of the language which we had hitherto been using thus uncritically. The problem was to frame a set of implicit and explicit definitions which would square with our past use of the language, to the extent at least of providing for the truth of many of those hitherto accepted sentences and conflicting with the truth of none of them. The further we choose to carry this construction of definitions, the more of our old accepted sentences become analytic, or true by definition, and the fewer of our old accepted sentences remain synthetic. How far this is to be carried, and to what extent the analytic is to be extended at the expense of the synthetic, was, we saw, a matter of choice, to be guided by considerations of convenience.

We saw in particular that such considerations call upon us in any case to provide for all so-called *a priori* judgments on the analytic side so that nothing remains synthetic except some of the propositions of the empirical sciences. This being done, we saw that every true proposition thereby becomes *either* a consequence of our linguistic conventions *or* a synthetic empirical proposition. In consequence it becomes necessary for syntax to provide the entire basis not only for logic and mathematics but also for whatever is valid in philosophy itself, when philosophy is purged of matters belonging properly to natural or empirical science.

In all our general thinking, whether within metaphysics itself or in the natural sciences or in mathematics, we seem invariably to come up finally against some philosophic, non-empirical problem which cannot permanently be swept aside. If philosophy depends only upon syntax, we are faced with the choice of attacking these problems by the methods of syntax or throwing them out as illusory, meaningless questions. The extent to which problems of this kind turn out to submit fruitfully to the syntactic approach will determine the extent to which Carnap's point of view represents a constructive and not merely negative doctrine. It will be my concern in this concluding lecture to show in detail the form assumed by certain representative philosophic matters when approached from the syntactic standpoint. By so doing I hope to suggest, better than I could by any dialectic, the constructive quality and importance of Carnap's method.

In order to understand what is to follow we must keep strictly in mind the important distinction between a sign and the thing it denotes: the distinction between the geometrical pattern "BOSTON" and the region stretching from Orient Heights to Hyde Park. Alice was impatient with the White Knight's distinctions between the *name* of his song, and what the name of his song was *called*, and what the song itself was called, and what the song really was. But my sympathies are with the White Knight rather than with Alice. Carnap offers by way of example the pair of sentences "Omega is a letter" and " 'Omega' is not a letter but a five-letter word." These sentences are not in contradiction, but are both true—provided that we quote the second occurrence of "Omega".

Bound up with this distinction is the distinction between *sign-properties*, that is, properties of signs, and other properties. Suppose we write "F (x)" to mean that the object x has the property F. In particular, "Populous (Boston)" will mean that the object Boston is populous. Of course this sentence, which happens to be true, contains the *sign* "Boston"; indeed, every sentence contains signs. But this does not mean that the property of being populous is a sign-property, a property of the sign "Boston"; populousness is a property rather of the object Boston, the object denoted by the sign "Boston". On the other hand "Disyl ("Boston")", "The word 'Boston' is disyllabic", does not merely contain the sign "Boston", which *denotes* the city of that name; this sentence contains rather the sign ""Boston"", which *denotes* the *sign* "Boston". Unlike the property of populousness, which is a property of communities and not signs, the property of being disyllabic is a sign-property.

To sum up: The sentence "Populous (Boston)" *contains* the sign "Boston", thus *mentions* the city of Boston, and attributes the property of populousness to that city. On the other hand the sentence "Disyl ("Boston")" *contains* the sign ""Boston"", thus *mentions* the sign "Boston", and attributes the property of disyllabism to that *sign*. Disyllabism is thereby a sign-property, while populousness is not. Whereas any sentence *contains* signs, sentences attributing sign-properties have the peculiarity of *containing* signs *of* signs, and thus *mentioning* signs.

Now among sign-properties, or properties of signs, there is a certain kind which Carnap calls *syntactic properties*. A sign-property is called a *syntactic property* if, in order to determine whether or not a given sign x has the property, we never need go beyond the sign x and investigate properties of the object or objects, if any, which x denotes. [Repeat] This definition is not rigorous, but it will serve.

For example, disyllabism is a syntactic property. In attributing this property to the sign "Boston" we have no occasion to go beyond that sign and study properties of the city of Boston; likewise, in attributing disyllabism to any other word we are never called upon to consider properties of the object, if any, denoted by the word.

On the other hand, consider the sign-property *nomino-populousness*, by which I shall mean the property of being the name of a populous community. Thus "Nompop ("Boston")" means that the sign "Boston" is the name of a populous community. This sentence, like "Disyl ("Boston")", *contains* the sign ""Boston"" and thus *mentions* the sign "Boston". Nompop, like disyl, is a sign-property. Yet nompop is not, like disyl, a *syntactic* property: for in order to find out whether the sign "Boston" has the property nompop, we have to go beyond the sign and investigate the population of the city denoted by the sign.

We see therefore that whereas all syntactic properties are sign-properties, not all sign-properties are syntactic properties.

All that I have said about sign-properties, or properties of signs, can be applied analogously to sign-relations, that is, relations between signs or among signs. Among sign-relations, as in the case of sign-properties, we have *syntactic relations*, that is, relations which do not involve us in any investigation of the objects denoted by the related signs. An example of a syntactic relation is *synonymity*. It might be objected that *synonymous* means *having the same meaning, denoting the same thing,* and consequently that to speak of two signs as synonymous is to depend upon the denotation of the signs. But I disposed of this objection last Thursday, by showing how *synonymity* could be defined without reference to denotations: namely, if the replacement of the one sign by the other in every sentence yields a consequence of that sentence, then the two words are synonymous. "Consequence" here is *logical* consequence, consequence as determined by the transformative rules and explicit definitions of the language; there is no reference to meaning, denotation.

Let us now turn away from sign-properties and sign-relations, and consider other properties and relations. Among non-sign-properties there is one kind which Carnap calls a *quasi-syntactic* property. Let φ be a property, and let ψ be a syntactic property. Consider all the pairs of sentences that can be had by writing one expression or another in the matrix "$\varphi(\ )$", and writing the same expression in the matrix "$\psi("\ ")$". Thus in each case we have a ψ-sentence mentioning an expression which the corresponding φ-sentence contains. Now suppose each φ-sentence is a *consequence* of the corresponding ψ-sentence, and *vice versa:* consequence, that is, as defined syntactically last Thursday in terms of the transformative rules of the language in question. Then the syntactic property ψ is called a *syntactic correlate* of the property φ. A property which has such a syntactic correlate is called *quasi-syntactic*.

$$\varphi \text{ (cat)} \qquad \psi \text{ ("cat")}$$
$$\varphi \text{ (dog)} \qquad \psi \text{ ("dog")}$$
$$\varphi \text{ (Boston)} \qquad \psi \text{ ("Boston")}$$
$$\vdots \qquad\qquad\quad \vdots$$

One example of a quasi-syntactic property is the property of being mentioned, or referred to, by Roosevelt. For, let φ be the property of being mentioned by Roosevelt, and let the syntactic property ψ be the property of being synonymous with an expression uttered by Roosevelt. Then "φ (cat)" means "Roosevelt mentioned cat" or more idiomatically "Roosevelt mentioned the species *cat*", "Roosevelt mentioned cats". "ψ ("cat")", similarly, comes to mean "Roosevelt uttered a synonym of "cat"." These two sentences will clearly be consequences each of the other. Again, "Roosevelt mentioned Boston" and "Roosevelt uttered a synonym of "Boston" " are mutual consequences; and so on for the rest. Thus the property of being mentioned by Roosevelt is a quasi-syntactic property, and has as a syntactic correlate the property of being synonymous with an expression uttered by Roosevelt.

On the other hand the property of populousness is not quasi-syntactic. It is true, populousness has the correlated sign-property nompop; the sentence "Populous (Boston)" and "Nompop ("Boston")" are consequences each of the other, and the same holds when any other name is substituted. But a quasi-syntactic property must have a *syntactic* correlate; the correlate nompop is not syntactic.

I have explained "quasi-syntactic" as applied to *properties*. Obviously it can be applied in like fashion to *relations*. Where φ is a *quasi-syntactic relation*, and ψ the correlated syntactic relation, the sentence "φ (cat, dog)" must be a consequence of the sentence "ψ ("cat", "dog")", and *vice versa*, similarly for "φ (Boston, moon)", and so on.

By extension we may speak also of *syntactic* and *quasi-syntactic sentences*. A sentence is syntactic or quasi-syntactic according as it predicates a syntactic or quasi-syntactic property or relation. Thus the sentence "Roosevelt mentioned Boston" is a quasi-syntactic sentence, for it predicates the quasi-syntactic property of having been mentioned by Roosevelt; on the other hand "Roosevelt uttered something synonymous with 'Boston' " is a syntactic sentence. The sentence "Boston is populous", finally, is neither quasi-syntactic nor syntactic.

The sentence "Roosevelt uttered something synonymous with 'Boston' " may be called a *syntactic translation* of the quasi-syntactic sentence "Roosevelt mentioned Boston". In general, where a syntactic predicate ψ is a syntactic correlate of a quasi-syntactic predicate φ, the sentence "ψ ("----")" is called a *syntactic translation* of the sentence "φ (----)".

A syntactic sentence is, in a broad way, a sentence of syntax; but it may be a sentence of *empirical* syntax, that is, the history of the use of words, or it may be a sentence of *formal* syntax. A sentence of pure syntax will be either analytic or contradictory, for a given language, while a sentence of empirical syntax may be synthetic, like any other empirical sentence. The syntactic sentence "Roosevelt uttered something synonymous with Boston" is of course a sentence of empirical syntax, exactly analogous to the sentence, mentioned last week, to the effect that such-and-such a character occupies the lower left-hand corner of the Rosetta Stone. Both of these sentences are of course synthetic. On the other hand the sentence "Analytic and contradictory sentences are equal in number" is a sentence of formal syntax; with reference to any but trivial languages, this sentence will in fact be analytic.

Roughly, a syntactic sentence may be characterized as a sentence which treats both ostensibly and actually of a sign, while a quasi-syntactic sentence treats actually of the sign but ostensibly of the object of the sign. Clearly the quasi-syntactic is an indirect idiom, and should be eliminated in favor of the syntactic translation when we are concerned with a logical analysis of what is being said.

It is clear from the Roosevelt example that the word *mention* always involves the quasi-syntactic. The sentence "x mentioned so-&-so" has in every case the syntactic translation "x uttered something synonymous with 'so-&-so'." In view of the definition of synonymity, which makes no reference to denotations, the sentence "x uttered something synonymous with 'so-&-so' " depends only upon the expression "so-&-so" and not upon the object, if any, which that expression denotes.

The acceptance or rejection of the sentence "Roosevelt mentioned Boston" will involve us, not in a study of the city of Boston, but only in a study of the syntactic relations, synonymity or otherwise, borne by the *word* "Boston" to words uttered by Roosevelt. The sentence is in effect a sentence about the *word* "Boston"; and this situation is made explicit when we give the sentence its syntactic translation "Roosevelt uttered something synonymous with 'Boston'." The same applies to any occurrence of the word "mention".

Again, the relation of *meaning*, or *denoting*, can itself be avoided through abandoning the quasi-syntactic.

Consider the sentence "The letters 'C.C.C.' denote the Civilian Conservation Corps." This is quasi-syntactic, for it has as a syntactic translation the sentence "The expressions 'C.C.C.' and 'Civilian Conservation Corps' are synonymous." This syntactic translation makes explicit the fact that what is relevant here is not the Civilian Conservation Corps, but only the *expression* "Civilian Conservation Corps".

In the analysis of concepts and doctrines, both in the logic of science and in other branches of philosophy, we are continually encountering or seeming to encounter the problem of *meaning*. But these examples are sufficient to suggest that such problems arise only through careless formulation; we are brought to problems of meaning through use of such relations as *mentioning, denoting,* etc., and these relations come in only through use of the quasi-syntactic idiom. When the quasi-syntactic idiom is eliminated we find ourselves working within the syntactic level quite independently of the meaning-relation.

The empirical psychologist, a natural scientist, is concerned with the empirical relations or interaction between certain objects, say men, and other objects, called, collectively, the environment. One aspect of the behavior of the objects of the first part consists in the uttering of sounds or the writing of marks. This so-called *linguistic* behavior on the part of men stands in certain empirical correlations or cause-and-effect relations with the objects of the second part, the environment. Among these empirical correlations it may or may not prove to be experimentally useful to single out and define a certain complex relation which may be called the relation of *denotation:* a relation of certain ingredients of man's colloquial and literary behavior to certain ingredients of the environment. But all this belongs to empirical psychology, and is no different in principle from the procedure in any other empirical science. Psychologically the denotation-relation is a relation between experimental phenomena of the empirical world—on the one hand a class of physical events describable collectively as utterance of the syllables "Emerson Hall", and on the other hand a certain hollow mass of brick and mortar.

But beyond this there is no need to go; we are not called upon to give a metaphysical, non-empirical account—whatever that might be—of the relation of denotation or meaning. Our non-empirical analysis of concepts can be carried out entirely within syntax, in terms of "sentence", "immediate consequence", and derivative notions such as "synonymity". That this has not appeared to be the case is due to use of the quasi-syntactic idiom, in which objects of signs are gratuitously invoked where only the sign is concerned. That it *is* the case that the meaning-relation can thus be sidestepped is shown by the translatability of the quasi-syntactic into the syntactic, whereat the relations of "denotation", "mentioning", etc., drop out.

Having thus berated the words "meaning" and "denotation", I shall continue to use them as before. We are so accustomed to the quasi-syntactic idiom that its use simplifies exposition; to that extent it is a great convenience, provided that we do not let it mislead us, and that we stand ready to translate it into the syntactic idiom in all emergencies.

A more dangerous source of confusion than the words "mention", "meaning" and "denotation" is the word "impossible". What do we mean when we say that so-and-so is impossible? Perhaps that so-and-so is *logically* impossible; that so-and-so is a contradiction in terms. Or perhaps we mean that so-and-so is *empirically* impossible, that is, contrary to known or supposed empirical laws. Now both kinds of impossibility are quasi-syntactic properties. Let us consider the first kind of impossibility, logical impossibility. This property has as its syntactic correlate the syntactic property, defined last Thursday, of *contradictoriness:* that is to say, any sentence of the form "Log impos (----)" is equivalent to the sentence "Contrad ("----")"; the two sentences are consequences each of the other. For example, let "----" be the sentence "It is both raining and not raining". The sentence "It is logically impossible that it is both raining and not raining" is equivalent to the sentence " 'It is both raining and not raining' is contradictory."

Whereas "log impos (----)" *contains* within itself the sentence "----", on the other hand "Contrad ("----")" contains rather ""----"", and *mentions* the sentence "----", attributing to it the syntactic property of contradictoriness. The sentence "It is impossible that it is both raining and not raining" purports to tell us something about rain; on the other hand the syntactic translation: " 'It is both raining and not raining' is contradictory" does not mention rain, but only mentions a sentence, or expression, which in its turn mentions rain. The syntactic property, which this sentence attributes to the sentence "It is both raining and not raining", namely the property of contradictoriness, was so defined last Thursday as to depend only upon the formative and transformative rules of the language in question. A sentence is contradictory which embraces all sentences among its consequences.

What has been said of logical impossibility applies equally to logical possibility, logical necessity, contingency, and logical implication. The sentence "It is logically possible that ----" becomes in the syntactic idiom "The sentence '----' is not contradictory". The sentence "It is logically necessary that ----" becomes in the syntactic idiom "The sentence '----' is analytic". The sentence "It is contingent (that is, neither necessary nor impossible) that ----" becomes "The sentence '----' is synthetic". The sentence "That ----, logically implies that ····", becomes in the syntactic idiom "The sentence '····' is a consequence of the sentence '----'."

Possibility, impossibility, necessity and contingency are often expressed by the modal auxiliaries *can, cannot, must* and *may or may not*. My present remarks concerning the modalities apply of course also to those words.

Thus the so-called logical modalities, namely logical possibility, impossibility and necessity, contingency and logical implication, all arise merely through the quasi-syntactic idiom. When we translate into the syntactic idiom, all these notions drop out and we are left only with sentences and syntactic properties of sentences, such syntactic properties namely as contradictory, non-contradictory, analytic, synthetic and consequence. These syntactic properties were all defined last Thursday in terms merely of the formative and transformative rules of whatever language happens to be in use.

It has been customary in philosophy to talk of a realm of possibility as distinct from the realm of actuality. This has been referred to differently in different philosophies. Plato has his realm of ideas. The new realists, following Russell, speak of *subsistent entities* as against *existent entities*. Even those who do not deliberately engage in philosophy presumably entertain, for the most part, some vague notion of a realm of the possible which is set over against the actual.

Then philosophy proceeds to encounter philosophic problems due to the notion of the realm of the possible: problems as to how fragments of the possible are actualized, and what it *means* for a possibility to be actualized, and why certain possibilities are actualized rather than others. These are metaphysical questions, and are dealt with differently by different metaphysics; for Leibniz, for example, the actualization of a possibility takes place through a divine act of creation, and the choice of one possibility rather than another depends upon the goodness of the Creator, who so chooses as to effect the best of all possible worlds—best according to a certain irreducible aesthetic standard.

The modality of logical *impossibility* also creates metaphysical problems. The realm of non-actualized possibility is a tenuous realm, but the realm of impossibility is still more tenuous. Among the obvious difficulties of such a realm there is one theological difficulty which has led to metaphysical activity: the difficulty, namely, that an omnipotent creator cannot create what is impossible.

Now this whole appalling development depends, Carnap claims, upon use of the quasi-syntactic rather than the syntactic idiom. When we forsake the quasi-syntactic idiom in favor of the syntactic, the modalities give way to syntactic descriptions of sentences. There is no longer any talk of possible, impossible, necessary and contingent states of affairs; there is talk only of non-contradictory, contradictory, analytic and synthetic *sentences, expressions*. A given state of affairs either is or is not; the world is either thus and so, in the indicative mode, or it is otherwise. Beyond this we have no commerce with further modes of being such as impossibility, necessity, contingency and so on, once we eliminate the quasi-syntactic idiom; instead we have only syntactic properties of certain expressions, and these syntactic properties depend on the purely syntactic rules, formative and transformative, of the language used. The philosphy of modalities gives way to the syntactic rules of our language.

Thus far I have spoken only of the *logical* modalities; but the modalities are also extended, in common speech, to what we might call *empirical* modalities: empirical impossibility, empirical necessity, empirical contingency and so on. Here, as in the strictly logical modalities, we also use the modal auxiliaries "can", "cannot", "must" and "may or may not" as shorthand for "it is possible that", "it is impossible that", "it is necessary that" and "it is contingent that". Discussion of a couple of these will serve. Empirical impossibility is impossibility in view of accepted empirical laws. Now ⟨this⟩ is a quasi-syntactic property, having as its syntactic correlate what we may call *empirical contradictoriness*. Namely, a sentence S may be said to be empirically contradictory if that set of sentences is *contradictory* which contains S along with the accepted empirical laws of the given stage of science, say in 1934. Empirical contradictoriness as thus defined is a syntactic property, but belongs to empirical syntax rather than formal syntax. As just now defined, empirical contradictoriness depends upon the notion "contradictory" of formal syntax together with the empirical, anthropological notion "laws accepted in 1934". But the property of empirical contradictoriness is none the less a syntactic property.

An example involving the quasi-syntactic property of empirical impossibility is the sentence "It is impossible that a mechanism be frictionless". The syntactic translation would read "The sentence 'A mechanism is frictionless' is empirically contradictory." Both sentences are synthetic; but the first one quasi-syntactic, while the other belongs to empirical syntax.

Again, the property of *empirical contingency* is a quasi-syntactic property, having as its syntactic correlate what we may call empirical syntheticness. Namely, a sentence S might be said to be *empirically synthetic* if neither it nor its denial is *empirically contradictory*. Thus the quasi-syntactic sentence "It may or may not rain tomorrow" would have as its syntactic translation the sentence "The sentence 'It will rain tomorrow' is empirically synthetic"; that is, "The sentence 'It will rain tomorrow' and 'It will not rain tomorrow' are neither of them empirically contradictory."

Thus the empirical modalities are, like the logical modalities, quasi-syntactic; sentences involving them can be translated into the syntactic idiom so as to eliminate mention of those modalities. Sentences involving *logical* modalities have as their syntactic translations sentences of formal syntax—in every case analytic or contradictory sentences, never synthetic sentences. Sentences involving *empirical* modalities have as their syntactic translations sentences which, though syntactic, are synthetic: synthetic in referring, empirically, to a given state in the history of scientific pronouncements.

Both the logical modalities and the empirical modalities thus appear as needless complications. When we pass over to the syntactic idiom, we are concerned only with actual fact plus syntax; the modes disappear. Of course, we are left with other notions which have to be handled instead of the modalities; such syntactical notions as consequence, contradictory, analytic, synthetic and so on. But these are properties of signs, and are defined in terms of the formative and transformative rules of our language; their manipulation is not a question of metaphysics, but a precise matter of conventions as to the use and the interrelationships of expressions.

The danger of the material idiom which I have considered so far is the danger of losing sight of what we are talking about; in the quasi-syntactic idiom we appear to be talking about certain non-linguistic objects, when all we *need* be talking about is the sign or signs themselves which are used for denoting those objects. Thus the quasi-syntactic idiom gives us, among other things, the expressions of modality, which are for all the world properties not of names, or sentences, but of things or situations. These modality-properties or pseudo-properties then involve us in difficulties from which we turn to metaphysics for extrication. When the syntactic formulation is used, so that whatever in effect concerns language is made explicitly to concern language, these difficulties vanish in favor of syntax.

Preparatory to such further cases of the quasi-syntactic idiom as I am going to consider, it will be necessary to explain a few further syntactic properties. Formal syntactic properties depend, like all syntax, upon the language in which we choose to work. But relatively to any language which is not completely revolutionary we will be able, for example, to frame a syntactic definition of *predicate*. Suppose our language is a semi-symbolic language in which we write "Red (x)", "Brother (x, y)" and "Between (x, y, z)" to mean "x is red", "x is a brother of y" and "x is between y and z". The sign "Red" here is a one-place predicate, the sign "Brother" is a two-place predicate, and the sign "Between" is a three-place predicate. Now relatively to this hypothetical language we can define the syntactic property of being a *predicate*: namely, a sign φ is a predicate if and only if there is an expression E such that the expression "φ (E)" is a sentence. This definition of *predicate* depends only upon the formative rules of the hypothetical language in question: these rules tell us what expressions are sentences, and this definition explains the predicate in terms of the sentence.

Again, we can define in analogous fashion the more special syntactic notion *one-place predicate*. Relatively to our hypothetical language we may say that φ is a one-place predicate if there is an expression E *containing no commas*, such that "φ (E)" is a sentence. Similarly a predicate φ may be defined to be a two-place predicate if it is not a one-place predicate and if there is an expression E, containing only one comma, such that "φ (E)" is a sentence. In the same way three-place and n-place predicates can be characterized in turn. More generally, a *many-place predicate* can be defined as a predicate which is not a one-place predicate.

Again, the syntactic notion of *substantive* could be defined in terms of this hypothetical language by saying that an expression E is a substantive if there is a one-place predicate φ such that "φ (E)" is a sentence. That is, a substantive is a sign to which a one-place predicate can be applied.

What has thus been done for this hypothetical language could be done in corresponding but more complex fashion for English, or any language which is built along at all familiar lines.

Now it is to be noted that the property of being a property, and the property of being a relation, are themselves quasi-syntactic properties! The syntactic correlate of the property of being a *property* is the syntactic property of being a one-place predicate. For example, the sentence "Populousness is a property" has as its syntactic translation the sentence "The word 'Populous' is a one-place predicate." Again, the syntactic correlate of the property of being a *relation* is the property of being a many-place predicate. For example, the sentence "Seeing is a relation" has as its syntactic translation the sentence "The word 'sees' is a many-place predicate."

Just as we saw earlier that philosophical problems involving the modalities can be thrown over in favor of syntax by translating the quasi-syntactic idiom into syntactic form, so now we see that the philosophical difficulties of the *universals*—properties and relations—can be reduced similarly to syntax.

I have of course been using the quasi-syntactic idiom throughout this lecture, in speaking of quasi-syntactic *properties* and *relations*. All that I have said *could* be put over into syntactic form, in terms of one- and many-place predicates; but I shall continue, for the sake of intuitiveness, to use the quasi-syntactic idiom.

In addition to "predicate", "one-place predicate", "substantive", etc., there are many further important expression-classes which we can define syntactically in terms of our language, whatever it may be. One such class is the class of *numerical expressions;* how this definition will run will of course depend upon the details of the language in question, but it can obviously be done for any language whose syntax is such as to provide analytically for arithmetic.

This being done, the property of being a *number* becomes a quasi-syntactic property, having as its syntactic correlate the syntactically defined property of being a *numerical expression.* The sentence "5 is a number" thus becomes quasi-syntactic, and has as its syntactic translation the sentence " '5' is a numerical expression." The philosophical question "What is a number" thus gives way, under syntactic translation, to a question merely as to the syntactical rules governing the use of numerical expressions within the language in question.

Without carrying out such details any further, we may merely look at some selected philosophical sentences of the quasi-syntactic idiom and compare them with their syntactic translations according to Carnap. One such sentence is this: "Within the ultimate *given* there are relations." As a syntactic translation Carnap gives this, in effect: "Among the signs which are defined neither explicitly nor implicitly (that is, through the transformative rules), there are many-place relations." Assuming for the sake of argument the technical defensibility of this syntactic translation, there are two important results to be noted. First, the terms of the sentence become quite clear: they are ordinary syntactic concepts. But second, the proposition in question completely loses its absolutistic character, and becomes avowedly relative to the language in question. Metaphysically there may be endless dispute as to whether or not the ultimate given includes relations. The opposition may claim that relations are never ultimately given, but depend only upon the properties of the terms related. Carnap would translate this assertion of the opposition, in turn, as the following syntactic sentence: "All many-place predicates are defined on the basis of one-place predicates." The opposition disappears when the sentences are thus translated into syntax. If one man claims that many-place predicates occur undefined, while another claims that they are all defined in terms of one-place predicates, the solution of the difficulty is immediate: the languages to which the two men tacitly refer differ in point of syntax.

One example of a different kind may be in order. To the sentence "Time has no beginning and no end", Carnap gives the syntactic translation "There is no smallest and no largest time-coördinate"— where "time-coördinate", presumably, has been given a definition in terms of the syntax of the language in question.

The *relativity* observed in these cases runs throughout. In its quasi-syntactic form a sentence of philosophy is, ostensibly at least, a sentence about things, reality, etc.; thus conceived, the truth or falsity of what is expressed must be regarded as absolute, rather than as depending merely upon the syntax of one or another language. When on the other hand such a sentence is given its syntactic translation, its relativity to specific language becomes clear. All syntactic sentences are relative to a language; they are ambiguous until the intended language is specified, and may differ as to truth or falsity according to what language is selected.

Carnap's process of syntacticizing philosophy is thus seen to depend entirely upon translating the quasi-syntactic into syntactic form. Of course philosophy does not have a monopoly of the quasi-syntactic; everyday language is full of it, this lecture has been full of it, and Carnap's writings are avowedly full of it. But in each case, in order to detect precisely what is necessary to the truth of the sentence, and also in order not to lose sight of the relevance of syntactic relativity, we must be ready to translate into the syntactic idiom.

We must not be carried away with the idea that everything thus becomes syntax. There are abundant sentences, sentences about the world, sentences such as "Boston is populous", which are neither syntactic nor quasi-syntactic. No criticism whatever is levelled against such sentences. It is in sentences dealing with reference, mention, meaning, denotation that we must be on our guard; also in modal sentences, both logical and empirical; and also, finally, in sentences involving categoric words such as "property", "relation", "number", "the ultimate given" and so on.

When these quasi-syntactic sentences are all translated into syntactic sentences, the resulting syntactic sentences are *not* all of them sentences whose truth or falsity we can decide purely by a syntactic analysis of our language. Many of these syntactic translations turn out rather to belong to empirical syntax, and to involve history of science or anthropology. Such was seen to be the case, for example, with the empirical sentences about mentioning; such was also seen to be the case with the empirical modalities. In general, of course, the empirical quasi-syntactic sentences are bound to turn out, upon translation, as sentences of empirical syntax and not formal syntax.

On the other hand the quasi-syntactic sentences of philosophy itself, when translated into the syntactic form, appear rather as sentences of *formal* syntax. These sentences are not synthetic, but are analytic or contradictory. Such a sentence may be analytic when construed as having to do with the syntax of one language, and contradictory when construed as having to do with the syntax of another language; and until the language is specified, the sentence is simply ambiguous, or, at least, a statement as to how the speaker proposes to frame the syntax of *his* language.

All this, assuming it to be valid, points to the dissolution of much philosophic controversy. Controversies about modalities, controversies about universals, controversies about the nature of number, controversies about the ultimate given, all become merely descriptions of dissimilar syntaxes, once the quasi-syntactic is abandoned in favor of the syntactic rendering.

This syntactic view of philosophy is commonly referred to, along with *physicalism* and related theories, as *logical positivism;* but the designation is unfortunate, and Carnap himself avoids it. For this syntactic viewpoint leads no more toward Mach's positivism than toward realism or any other metaphysical doctrine. A main thesis of the positivist, in the traditional sense of the word at least, is that a thing is a complex of sense-perceptions; a main thesis of realism, put of course in a ridiculously oversimplified form, is that a thing is a complex of atoms. Carnap's answer here as in similar philosophic controversies is that *both* sentences are quasi-syntactic, and, put into syntactic form, come merely to characterize the syntaxes of dissimilar languages. The term nominalism, if applied to Carnap without great caution, presents an analogous danger.

This is not the end of Carnap's contribution; rather it is only the starting point. For his purpose is not merely to advance a negative doctrine, nor to construe philosophy as trivial. His concern is rather to clear away confusion and lay the foundations of a rigorous and fruitful study of the logic of science: for it is the logic of science, in the broadest sense of the phrase, the analysis, criticism and refinement of the *methods* and the *concepts* of science, that Carnap regards as the defensible province of philosophy. And the medium for all such studies is, according to Carnap, syntax.

Views will differ as to the success of Carnap's total thesis that all philosophy is syntax. Carnap has made a very strong case for this thesis; but it must be admitted that there are difficulties to be ironed out. We cannot be sure that we have found the key to the universe. Still Carnap *has* provided us, at worst, with a key to an enormous part of the universe. He has in any case shown conclusively that the bulk of what we relegate to philosophy can be handled rigorously and clearly within syntax. Carnap himself recognizes that this accomplishment stands *independently* of the thesis that *no* meaningful metaphysics remains beyond syntax. Whether or not he has really slain the metaphysical wolf, at least he has shown us how to keep him from our door.

[THE QUINE-CARNAP CORRESPONDENCE]

[1.   CARNAP TO QUINE   1932-12-5]

Prof. Dr. Rudolf Carnap
   Prag XVII.   , den 5. Dezember 1932.
N. Motol, Pod Homolkou

Mr. W. V. Quine, Ph.D.   *Wien.*

   Ich erhielt Ihren Brief vom November d.J. durch die
Vermittlung des Dekanates der Philosophisch en Fakultät der
Deutschen Universität in Prag. Da ich vom 12.–15.Dezember
nach Wien komme, könnten wir Ihre Fragen mündlich
besprechen. Ich bitte Sie, mir noch hierher Ihre Adresse zu
schreiben, damit ich mich in Wien mit Ihnen in Verbindung
setzen kann.

                 Hochachtungsvoll
                 R. Carnap

[1.E   CARNAP TO QUINE   1932-12-5]

Prof. Rudolf Carnap
Prague XVII
N. Motol, Pod Homolkou   December 5, 1932

Mr. W. V. Quine, Ph.D.   *Vienna.*

   I received your letter of this November by way of the Dean of
the Philosophical Faculty at the German University in Prague.
Since I am coming to Vienna from the 12th through 15th of December, we can discuss your questions orally. Please send your
address to me here, so that I can contact you in Vienna.

                 Yours Respectfully
                 R. Carnap

[2. CARNAP TO QUINE 1933-2-6]

Prof. Dr. Rudolf Carnap
    Prag XVII.   Prag, den 6.Febr.1933.
N. Motol, Pod Homolkou

Sehr geehrter Herr Q u i n e !

Falls Ihre Absicht noch besteht, zum Anfang des hiesigen
Sommersemesters herzukommen, möchte ich Ihnen einige Infor-
mationen geben.

Ich lege den Ankündigungszettel meiner Vorlesungen bei. Die
Vorlesung über Geschichte bringt nichts Neues; es wird sich für
Sie nicht lohnen, sie zu besuchen. Dagegen werden Sie
vielleicht in der Vorlesung Logik II (und in dem dazu gehörigen
Seminar) einiges finden, das Sie interessiert; ich will in dieser
Vorlessung meine neueren Untersuchungen zur logischen Syntax (Metalogik, Semantik) vortragen.   Am 23.Febr. ist noch
kein Seminar, sondern nur 1 Stunde Vorlesung. Am 27. Febr.
fallen die Vorlesungen wegen Fastnacht aus. Sie würden daher
nur 1 Stunde der Vorlesung versäumen, falls es Ihnen besser
passt, erst am Donnerstag, den 2.März, zur Vorlesung zu
kommen.

Das Mathem.Institut, in dem meine Vorlesungen stattfinden,
und das Physikal. Institut (Prof.Frank, den Sie auch aufsuchen
sollten; er hat ein ausgezeichnetes neues Buch über das
Kausalgesetz geschrieben) befinden sich im Naturwiss. Institut,
Vinivna 3 (Tel. 37628) (auf dem Plan mit "2" bezeichnet).

Hotel Splendid, das ich Ihnen fürs Erste empfehle: Plan 10.

Ich habe hier draussen leider kein Telephon. Bitte schreiben
Sie mir, wenn Sie nach Prag kommen, und teilen Sie mir mit,
wo Sie wohnen.

Ich freue mich, Sie bald hier begrüssen zu können.

                    Mit besten Grüssen
                    Ihr
                    R. Carnap

[ATTACHED AS A PARTIAL PAGE TO PRECEDING LETTER]

Prof.R. C a r n a p

S.-S.1933

1) *Kritische Geschichte der Philosophie der Neuzeit.* 2-st.
Sa. 11–13. Hörs.f.Math.

2) *Logik II.* (Für Fortgeschrittene). 3-st. No.17$\frac{1}{2}$-19$\frac{1}{2}$, Do.17–18
Hörs.f.Math.

3) *Seminar:* Logik (im Anschluss an die Vorlesung). 2-st.
Do.18–20. Math.Institut.

Beginn der Vorlesungen: Do 23. Febr.

[2.E   CARNAP TO QUINE   1933-2-6]

Prof. Rudolf Carnap
Prague XVII
N. Motol, Pod Homolkou   Prague, Feb. 6, 1933

Dear Mr. Quine:

In case you are still planning to come here at the beginning of
our summer semester, I would like to give you some
information.

I have attached a slip announcing my lectures. The lecture on
history contains nothing new; it would not be worth it for you
to attend. On the other hand, you might find something in the
lecture Logic II (and in the seminars connected with it) which
interests you; in this lecture I will discuss my new research on
logical syntax (metalogic, semantics). On Feb. 23rd there is no
seminar, but only a one-hour lecture. On Feb. 27th classes are
canceled because of Shrove Tuesday. Hence, if it would be better
for you to start attending the lectures on Tuesday the 2nd of
March, you would miss one hour of lecture.

The Mathematical Institute, where my lectures are given, and
the Physical Institute (Prof. Frank, whom you should look up;

he has written an excellent new book on causal laws) are located in the Natural Sci. Institute, Vienna 3 (Tel. 37628) (marked "2" on the map). Hotel Splendid, which I recommend to you most highly: Map 10.

Unfortunately, we have no telephone out here. Please write to me, when you arrive in Prague, and tell me where you are staying.

I am happy to be able to welcome you here soon.

With best wishes,

Yours,

R. Carnap

[ATTACHED AS A PARTIAL PAGE TO PRECEDING LETTER]

Prof. R. Carnap
S.-S. 1933
1) *Critical History of Contemporary Philosophy.* 2 hr. Sat. 11–1. Math. Lecture Hall.
2) Logic II (for advanced students). 3 hr. Mon. 5:30–7:30, Thurs. 5–6. Math. Lecture Hall.
3) *Seminar:* Logic (in conjunction with the lecture). 2 hr. Thur. 6–8. Math. Inst.

Beginning of lectures: Thur., Feb. 23.

[3.   QUINE TO CARNAP   1933-3-8]

Prag, 8. März. 1933

Sehr geehrter Herr Professor!

Letzten Montag erwähnte ich Ihnen eine Idee für eine mögliche Umformung von deskriptiven Sätzen, wodurch solche Sätze keine Funktoren und keine Gleichungszeichen sondern nur Zahlzeichen (und Klammern und Beistriche) enthalten würden. Seitdem habe ich einerseits eine Antwort zu Ihrem Einwand gefunden, aber andererseits bin ich überzeugt worden, dass solche Umformung weniger wichtig sein würde, als ich zuerst gemeint hatte.

Zuerst werde ich die Idee selbst kurz abreissen. Denken wir uns die Qualitätsarten (z.B. "Temperatur", "Farbe") untereinander irgendwie geordnet und durch Zahlzeichen dargestellt, genau so wie Sie die Qualitäten selbst unter einer bestimmten Art (z.B. die verschiedenen Temperaturen) schon betrachtet haben. Vorausgesetzt Einfachheit halber, dass jede Qualität von gegebener Art durch eine natürliche Zahl ausdrückbar ist, dann können wir jetzt jede Qualität von *beliebiger* Art durch ein Zahlpaar ausdrücken, wo die erste Zahl die Qualitätsartzahl ist und die zweite die Qualitätszahl unter dieser Art ist. Sei z.B. "Farbe" durch "9" gezeichnet, und habe Blau (einer gewählten Helle usw.) die Farbezahl 5, dann wird Blau durch das Paar "9,5" ausgedrückt; die Temperatur 5° andererseits wird "6,5", wo 6 die Qualitätsartzahl für Temperatur ist. Non können wir für die Aussage, "Blau tretet am Punkt auf, dessen Koordinaten 6,9,3 sind," die Schreibweise "Blau(6,9,3)" gebrauchen; da Blau durch "9,5" ausgedrückt wird, diese Aussage wird "(9,5)(6,9,3)". Entsprechend wird die Form "t(x,y,z)=n", wo "t" "Temperatur" heisst, durch "(m,n)(x,y,z)" ersetzt, wo m die Qualitätsartzahl für Temperatur ist. Hier kommen Funktoren und das Gleichungszeichen gar nicht vor.

In Antwort zu Ihrer Frage, wie man denn Sätze von der Form "t(a,b,c) = t(x,y,z)" ausdrücken könnte, bringe ich die Form

$$(\exists n)[(m,n)(a,b,c) \cdot (m,n)(x,y,z)]$$

vor, wo m so wie oben die Qualitätsartzahl für Temperatur ist. Wenn es gewünscht wird, den Operator $(\exists n)$ nur in der beschränkten Form anzuwenden, dann liegt es uns nur, eine hinreichend grosse Beschränkungszahl zu wählen.

Diese Umformung scheint mir aber weniger Wichtigkeit zu besitzen, als ich zuerst glaubte. Es scheint jetzt keine Ausdehnung Ihrer Methode sondern nur ein Anschlag zu sein, wodurch Funktoren durch Prädikate etsetzt werden können; und dies hat keinen offenbaren Vorteil über Ihrem Verfahren, welches Prädikate durch Funktoren ersetzt. Die Einführung von Zahlen für die Qualitätsarten ist nur ein Detail der obigen

Entwickelung, und führt natürlich nur eine flache Notationsänderung ein.

Ihr ergebener
Willard V. Quine

Herrn Prof. Dr. C a r n a p

[3.E   QUINE TO CARNAP   1933-3-8]

Prague, March 8, 1933

Dear Professor:

Last Monday I mentioned to you an idea for a possible revision of descriptive sentences in which such sentences would contain no functors and no identity signs but only numerals (and parentheses and accents). Since then on the one hand I have found an answer to your objection, but on the other hand I have been convinced that such a revision would be of less importance than I had thought at first.

First, I shall briefly set out the idea itself. Imagine qualitykinds (e.g., "temperature", "color") as somehow ordered among themselves and represented by numerals, precisely as you have already regarded the qualities within a certain kind themselves (e.g., the various temperatures). For simplicity's sake assume that each quality belonging to a given kind is expressible by a natural number; we can now express any quality of whatever kind by a number pair, where the first numeral is the qualitykind numeral and the second numeral is the quality numeral of this kind. If for example "color" is indicated by "9" and if blue (of a certain brilliance, etc.) has the color numeral "5", then blue is expressed by the pair "9,5"; the temperature 5° on the other hand would be "6,5" where 6 is the quality-kind number for temperature. Now for the statement "Blue appears at the point whose coordinates are 6,9,3" we can write "Blue (6,9,3)"; since blue is expressed by "9,5" this statement becomes "(9,5)(6,9,3)". Correspondingly, the form "t(x,y,z) = n", where "t" signifying "temperature" is replaced by "(m,n)(x,y,z)", where m is the quality-kind number for temperature. Here functors and the like do not occur at all.

In answer to your question about how one could express sentences of the form "t(a,b,c) = t(x,y,z)", I propose the form

$(\exists n)[(m,n)(a,b,c) \cdot (m,n)(x,y,z)]$

where m as above is the quality-kind number for temperature. If one desires to use the operator $(\exists n)$ only in the restricted form, then we need only choose a sufficiently large restriction number.

This revision seems to me, however, to possess less importance than I believed at first. It seems now no extension of your methods but only a device whereby functors can be replaced by predicates; and thus has no obvious advantage over your procedure which replaces predicates with functors. The introduction of numbers for the quality-kinds is only a detail of the foregoing development and introduces only a superficial change of notation.

Yours truly
Willard V. Quine

Prof. *Carnap*

[4. QUINE TO CARNAP   1933-3-14]

Prag, 14. März. 1933

Geehrten Herr Professor C a r n a p !

Gestern erwähnte ich Ihnen eine Idee, wodurch arithmetische Identität mit Hilfe vom Prädikat Gr("grösser als") sich definieren lässt, nämlich

$x = y .=.$ non $Gr(x,y)$. non $Gr(y,x)$ Df

Dagegen wendeten Sie ein, dass Ihre Definition von "Gr" von den Begriffen "arithmetisch identisch" und "grösser oder gleich" [Grgl] abhängt, obwohl dieser letzte Begriff, Grgl, unabhängig von Identität definiert ist.

Aber die arithmetische Identität lässt sich leicht durch Grgl definieren, nämlich

$x = y .=. Grgl(x,y) . Grgl(y,x)$ Df

Sehr wahrscheinlich haben Sie schon hieran gedacht.

Mit besten Grüssen,

Ihr ergebener
Willard V. Quine

[4.E   QUINE TO CARNAP   1933-3-14]

Prague, March 14, 1933

Dear Professor *Carnap:*

Yesterday I mentioned to you an idea whereby arithmetic identity may be defined with the help of the predicate Gr ("Greater than"), namely

$$x=y = \text{not } Gr(x,y) \qquad \text{not } Gr(y,x) \qquad Df$$

Against my idea you objected that your definition of "Gr" depends on the concepts "arithmetically identical" and "greater or equal" [Grgl], although this latter concept, Grgl, is defined independently of identity.

But arithmetic identity may easily be defined through Grgl, namely

$$x=y = Grgl(x,y) \qquad Grgl(y,x) \qquad Df$$

Very likely you have already thought of this.

With best wishes,

Yours truly
Willard V. Quine

[5.   CARNAP TO QUINE   1933-4-30]

Prof. Dr. Rudolf Carnap
    Prag XVII.   Prag, den 30.April 1933.
N. Motol, Pod Homolkou

Lieber Herr Dr. Quine !

Besten Dank für Ihren freundlichen Brief zum Abschied von Prag. Wir hoffen, Sie haben inzwischen eine angenehme und interessante Reise durch Italien und bis Afrika gehabt.

Für Warschau schicke ich Ihnen hier einen Stadtplan.
Lukasiewicz, Lesniewski und Kotarbinski wohnen in 1 Haus:
Brzozowa 12 (Plan G6, Kreuz). Tarskis neue Wohnung weiss ich
nicht (Sulkowskiego 2 m.5). Hotel Saski, wo ich wohnte: G7,
Kreuz. Ich rate Ihnen doch dringend, nicht allein zu suchen.
Besuchen Sie zuerst Tarski und lassen Sie sich Ratschläge geben,
in welcher Gegend Sie suchen sollen, wie die Preise sind usw.
Vielleicht weiss er auch zufällig ein Zimmer. Das vornehm
eingerichtete Zimmer, das ich anfangs hatte, war immer noch
billiger als das ganz primitive Hotelzimmer.

An Tarski werde ich noch schreiben; wie Sie gewünscht
haben, nicht über Zimmerbestellung.

Feigl schreibt, dass das erste Heft der auf beiliegendem Zettel
angekündigten Zeitschrift in November erscheinen soll.

Von Rockefeller und Lewis hab ich noch nichts gehört.
Vielleicht werde ich selbst mal an R.F. schreiben; aber ich will
zunächst mal die Antwort von Lewis abwarten.

Im Ferienmonat April war ich fleissig an meinem Manuskript.
Aber es bleibt noch viel daran zu tun.

Seit gestern ist mein Schüler und Freund Hempel aus Berlin
hier; er bleibt 6 Wochen. Es wird erfreuliche Diskussionen
geben.

Ihnen und Ihrer Frau herzliche Grüsse, auch von Ina,

Ihr
R. Carnap

[5.E   CARNAP TO QUINE   1933-4-30]

Prof. Rudolf Carnap
Prague XVII
N. Motol, Pod Homolkou   Prague, April 30, 1933

Dear. Dr. Quine:

Thanks very much for your friendly letter on departure from
Prague. Meanwhile we hope you are having a pleasant and interesting trip through Italy and to Africa.

I am enclosing a city map of Warsaw for you. Lukasiewicz,

Lesniewski, and Kotarbinski live in 1 house: Brozozowa 12 (Map G6, cross). I am not acquainted with Tarski's new apartment (Sulkowskiego 2, n. 5). Hotel Saski, where I lived: G7, cross. However, I urge you strongly not to search alone. First visit Tarski and let him advise you about what neighborhood you should search, about prices, etc. Perhaps he also knows by chance of a room. The elegantly furnished room that I had at first was still cheaper than a completely primitive hotel room.

I will still write to Tarski; as you asked, however, not about arranging a room.

Feigl writes that the first volume of the journal announced in the enclosed note should appear in November.

I have heard nothing from Rockefeller or Lewis. Perhaps I will write once to the R.F. ⟨Rockefeller Foundation⟩ myself; but first I want to wait for the answer from Lewis.

In the vacation month of April I worked hard on my manuscript. But there remains much to do on it.

My student and friend Hempel has been here from Berlin since yesterday; he is staying 6 weeks. That will allow delightful discussions.

Best wishes to you and your wife, also from Ina.

Yours
R. Carnap

[6. CARNAP TO QUINE   1933-6-4]

Prof. Dr. Rudolf Carnap
  Prag XVII.   Prag, den 4.Juni 1933.
N. Motol, Pod Homolkou

Lieber Herr Dr. Q u i n e !

Besten Dank für Ihren ausführlichen Brief aus Warschau. Wir haben uns gefreut, zü hören, dass Sie beide eine so schöne und interessante Reise gehabt haben. Das unglück Ihrer Frau hat uns sehr leid getan. Ich weiss aus meiner Erfahrung in Wien im Dezember, wie unangenehm es ist, in einer fremden Stadt ins Hospital zu müssen. Wir hoffen aber, dass der Fuss inzwischen wieder vollständig heil ist, sodass Sie beide auf Ihrer weiteren Reise unbehindert sind.

Ich freute mich auch sehr, zu hören, dass der Warschauer Aufenthalt für Sie so fruchtbar gewesen ist. Die Menschen dort sind ja ausserordentlich freundlich und hilfreich, mehr als in einem andern Land Europas. Und sie machen ausgezeichnete Arbeiten. Hat Tarski Ihnen gesagt, ob seine grosse Arbeit polnisch oder deutsch erscheinen wird? Ich hoffe sehr, das letztere.

Im Mai bekam ich Nachricht von Lewis, dass er an die Rockefeller-Stiftung geschrieben hat. Ich habe dann auch noch selbst dorthin geschrieben. Man hat mir geantwortet, dass die Reisepläne so besetzt sind, dass der Vertreter vor dem späten Sommer oder frühen Herbst nicht herkommen kann, dass man aber diesen notwendigen Besuch so bald als möglich machen will. Ich schliesse hieraus, dass man der Ansicht ist, dass das Stipendium für mich wenigstens nicht ganz unmöglich ist; ferner, dass ich es zwar nicht mehr für diesen Herbst bekommen kann, aber vielleicht dann doch nicht bis zum Herbst 1934 warten muss. Jedenfalls sehe ich nun der weiteren Entwicklung dieser Angelegenheit mit Ruhe entgegen. Für das freundliche Anerbieten Ihrer Hilfe herzlichen Dank! Sollte es später einmal erforderlich sein, so werde ich es gern annehmen. Solange aber die Aussicht auf das Rockef.—Stipendium noch nicht ganz verschwunden ist, will ich keine direkten Schritte wegen einer Stellung in Amerika unternehmen. Denn ich denke mir: wenn ich zunächst ein Jahr mit R.-Stipendium drüben sein kann, die Sprache gut lernen kann, Vorträge halte, and vielleicht auch eine engl. Uebersetzung meines Buches inzwischen erscheinen würde, so würde mir das alles die Erlangung einer Professur wesentlich erleichtern.

Malisoff schreibt mir soeben, dass das erste Heft der neuen Zeitschrift Okt.–Nov. erscheinen soll. Unter den Herausgebern sind Lewis, Bridgman, Whitehead, Cohen. Ich soll Herausgeber für Europa sein. Es liegen schon Manuskripte vor von Feigl, Blumberg, Haldane, Reiser, Watson, Bell, Struik. Ich hoffe, Sie werden auch bald unter den Mitarbeitern auftreten!

Vorgestern ist Hempel abgereist. Wir haben viel über Wahrscheinlichkeit, Induktion, Protokollsätze diskutiert.

Ihnen und Ihrer Frau herzliche Grüsse von uns beiden, und beste Wünsche für ein gute Ueberfahrt!

Ihr

R. Carnap

[6.E CARNAP TO QUINE   1933-6-4]

Prof. Rudolf Carnap
Prague XVII
N. Motol, Pod Homolkou   Prague, June 4, 1933

Dear Dr. Quine:

Thanks very much for your detailed letter from Warsaw. We were happy to hear that you both had such a lovely and interesting trip. Your wife's misfortune made us very sad. I know from experience in Vienna in December how unpleasant it is to have to go to the hospital in a foreign city. We hope, however, that the foot in the meantime is completely healed again so that you both are unimpeded for the rest of your trip.

I was also very happy to hear that your Warsaw stay was so fruitful for you. The people there are certainly extraordinarily friendly and helpful, more than in any other European country. And they do excellent work. Has Tarski told you whether his important work will appear in Polish or in German? I very much hope the latter.

In May I received a report from Lewis that he had written to the Rockefeller Foundation. Consequently I wrote them myself. They responded that their travel plans are too full for their representatives to come here before late summer or early fall, but that they intend to make this necessary visit as soon as possible. I conclude from this that they think the fellowship is at least not completely impossible for me, but rather that I indeed cannot get it this fall, but perhaps need not wait until fall 1934. In any case I look forward to the further development of this business with equanimity. Many thanks for the friendly offer of your help. Should it be necessary later on I will gladly accept. As long, however, as the prospect of the Rockef. fellowship is not yet completely gone, I will undertake no direct steps for a position in America. For I imagine if, first, I can get a one-year fellowship, learn the language well, deliver lectures, and perhaps an Engl. translation of my book will appear in the meantime as well, then all of this will naturally facilitate obtaining a professorship.

Malisoff just wrote me that the first volume of the new periodical should appear in Oct.–Nov. Among the editors are Lewis, Bridgman, Whitehead, Cohen. I am supposed to be the editor for Europe. There are already manuscripts by Feigl, Blumberg, Haldane, Reiser, Watson, Bell, Struik. I hope that you will soon appear among the contributors.

The day before yesterday Hempel left. We discussed a lot about probability, induction, and protocol sentences.

To you and your wife kind regards from us both and best wishes for a good crossing!

> Yours,
> R. Carnap

[7. CARNAP TO QUINE   1933-10-9]

Prof. Dr. Rudolf Carnap
   Prag XVII   Prag, den 9.Oktober 1933.
N. Motol, Pod Homolkou

Lieber Herr Dr. Quine!

Meinen Brief vom 4.Juni haben Sie hoffentlich noch in Hamburg bekommen. Inzwischen werden Sie sich wieder ganz in Amerika eingelebt haben. Hoffentlich sind die in Europa bekommenen Anregungen fruchtbar für Ihre weitere Arbeit.

Meine Angelegenheit mit der Rockefeller Foundation ist noch nicht weiter gekommen. Doch habe ich jetzt direkte Nachrichten durch Dr. Felix Kaufmann aus Wien (vielleicht erinnern Sie sich an inh aus dem Zirkel), der in Paris gewesen ist und mit

Dr. Miller gesprochen hat. Dieser wird wahrscheinlich noch im Lauf des Jahres 1933 nach Prag kommen. Inzwischen soll ich erwirken, dass Urteile namhafter Gelehrter über mich an die R.F. geschrieben werden. Ich habe soeben deswegen auch an Lewis geschrieben, und ihn gebeten, zu veranlassen, das auch Sheffer, Huntington und vielleicht auch Whitehead Urteile über mich schreiben. Es ist schade, dass mein Buch noch nicht fertig ist, um diese Urteile darauf stützen zu können. Vielleicht können aber Sie Lewis Einiges über meine "Syntax" berichten.

Ich habe mein Buch in diesem Jahr vollständig umgearbeitet. Jetzt bin ich beinahe fertig damit. Ich denke, dass es in einigen Wochen in Druck gehen wird.

Wie steht es mit Ihrem Buch? Was für Probleme wollen Sie jetzt weiter bearbeiten? Besten Dank für die beiden Sonderdrucke, die ich im Juni bekommen habe!

Für die neue Zeitschrift "Philosophy of Science" habe ich einen kurzen Aufsatz geschrieben, den Blumberg übersetzt.

Es ist nicht ausgeschlossen, dass ich das Stipendium (falls ich es bekomme) in Februar 1934 antreten kann; andernfalls hoffe ich auf Herbst 1934. Der Beginn im Februar wäre aber nur dann möglich, wenn ich angeben kann, ob und wie ich die Sommermonate drüben nutzbringend verbringen könnte. Was macht man in Harvard im Sommer? Ist da niemand dort? Und ist es dann sehr heiss dort?

Wir waren im Juli für einige Tage in Wien. Da habe ich einige Male im Zirkel referiert und auch etwas diskutiert. Aber leider war die Zeit nur sehr knapp. Aber mit Gödel, der jetzt eben (durch v.Neumann) an das Institute for Advanceed Study in Princeton zur Grundlagenforschung der Mathematik gerufen wurde (für 10 Monate), habe ich mehrmals ausführlich gesprochen. Wenn ich das Stipendium bekomme, will ich auch einige Zeit nach Pr. gehen, um dort mit Gödel und v.Neumann zusammenzuarbeiten.

Anschliessend an die Wiener Tage waren wir noch 2 Wochen in Steiermark. Und nun sind wir seit Anfang August wieder hier, ich arbeite mein MS nochmals durch, meine Frau tippt es für den Druck ins Reine. In einigen Tagen beginnt das Semester wieder. Es tut mir leid, Sie nicht mehr unter meinen Hörern zu haben.

Bitte grüssen Sie auch Ihre Frau herzlich von uns bieden. Haben Sie den Sommer gut verbracht?

Mit besten Grüssen Ihr
R. Carnap

[7.E CARNAP TO QUINE 1933-10-9]

Prof. Rudolf Carnap
Prague XVII
N. Motol, Pod Homolkou   Prague, October 9, 1933

Dear Dr. Quine:

I hope my letter of June 4 reached you in Hamburg. In the meantime you will have gotten completely settled again in America. Hopefully, the ideas you got in Europe are fruitful for your further work.

My business with the Rockefeller Foundation has not progressed at all. However, I now have direct reports through Dr. Felix Kaufmann of Vienna (perhaps you remember him from the Circle), who was in Paris and spoke with Dr. Miller. The latter will probably still come to Prague in the course of 1933. In the meantime I should make sure that well-known scholars write their assessments of me to the R.F. I have therefore just written to Lewis as well and asked him to arrange that Sheffer, Huntington, and perhaps also Whitehead write assessments of me. It is too bad that my book is not ready yet so that these assessments could be based on it. Perhaps, however, you could report to Lewis something about my *Syntax*.

This year I have completely revised my book. Now I am about ready with it. I think that it will go to press in a few weeks.

How is your book? What sort of problems will you work on now? Many thanks for the two offprints which I received in June.

For the new periodical *Philosophy of Science* I wrote a short paper which Blumberg translated.

It is not impossible that I could begin the fellowship (if I get it) in February 1934; otherwise I hope for the fall 1934. Beginning in February would be possible, however, only if I can say whether and how I can usefully spend the summer months over there. What does one do at Harvard in the summer? Is anyone there? And is it very hot there then?

In July we were in Vienna for a few days. There I lectured a few times in the Circle and also discussed some things. Unfortunately, however, time was very short. But I spoke at length with Gödel, who has just now (with v. Neumann's help) been invited to the Institute for Advanced Study in Princeton for foundational research in mathematics (for 10 months). If I get the fellowship I will also go to Pr. ⟨Princeton⟩ for some time in order to collaborate there with Gödel and v. Neumann.

Following the days in Vienna we spent 2 weeks in Steiermark. And now since our return here at the beginning of August, I am working through my MS once again, and my wife is typing a clean copy of it for publication. In a few days the semester will begin again. I am sorry not to have you among my students any more.

Our kind regards to you and your wife. Have you spent the summer well?

> With best wishes
> Yours
> R. Carnap

[8. QUINE TO CARNAP 1933-12-7]

> 65 Mount Auburn Street
> Cambridge, Mass., U.S.A.
> den 7. Dezember 1933

Lieber Herr Professor Carnap!

Besten Dank für Ihre zwei Briefe. Ich bin sehr gefreut über die Nachricht der weiteren Entwickelungen in Bezug auf das Rockefeller—Stipendium. Es ist unsere ernsteste Hoffnung, Sie und Ihre Frau schon diesen Februar hier in Cambridge wiedersehen zu können!

Whitehead und Sheffer habe ich gebeten, für Sie an die Rockefeller Foundation zu schreiben. Ich weiss bestimmt, dass Sheffer und auch Lewis und Huntington schon geschrieben haben. Whitehead hat mir und auch dem Scheffer ernst versprochen, auch hinzuschreiben; ich weiss aber nicht, ob er es getan hat oder nein, denn er ist sehr alt und ich weiss aus eigenen früheren Erlebnissen, dass er in solchen Bezügen nicht besonders zuverlässig ist. Jedenfalls aber haben die drei geschrieben, und vielleicht auch der vierte.

Damit ich von Ihrer Wahl früher erkündigt werden könnte, als es durch Sie über das Meer möglich wäre, habe ich gestern ein Gesuch an die Rockefeller Foundation geschrieben, mir die Liste aller neuen Gewählten zu schicken, so bald wie es fertig wird. Ich hoffe sehr, bald un günstig erkündigt zu werden.

Es würde eine Freude sein, zu wissen, dass wir diesen Februar die Gelegenheit haben würden, Ihrer Frau und Ihnen im Aufsuchen einer Wohnung zu helfen Jedenfalls aber werden Sie in kurzem kommen können: wenn auch das Stipendium nicht vorkommt, werden Sie ohne Schwierigkeit eine Professur erhalten können.

Ich freute mich, in Ihrem letzten Brief zu lesen, dass Ihr Buch fast fertig war. Hoffentlich ist es jetzt schon zum Druck gegangen, und bald zu erscheinen. Seit meiner Rückkehr habe ich viele Gelegenheiten gehabt, bei Interessierten meinen Enthusiasmus für das Buch zu betonen. Daher hat z.B. mein Freund B. F. Skinner, der sich in den Beziehungen zwischen experimentaler Psychologie und der Logik interessiert, eine entworfene Arbeit aufgeschoben, um sich zu ermöglichen, erst einmal Ihr kommendes Buch zu lesen. Ich bemerke dass sehr viele Menschen hier an Harvard Ihr *Logischer Aufbau* kennen und hoch preisen. Mein Freund Cooley schreibt seine Doktorthese über Ihre publizierte Ideen.

Besprechungen mit Tarski hatten mich überzeugt, aus meinem Buche eine keine Basische Rolle spielende Idee über die gebundene Variable wegzulassen; wann ich so einmal zum Entwurf einer Aenderung des Buches guzwungen wurde, entschied ich auch eine basische Idee einzukörpern, die mir vor einem Jahre gekommen war. Dies hat mir eine baträchtliche Umarbeitung des Buches gefordert Ich arbeitete also wieder auf dem Buche und entdeckte plötzlich dazu, dass wenn ich bei der Abstraktion "$\hat{x}$ (----)" auch den Fall einschlösse, wo "x" in "----" *nicht* vorkommt, würde eine erfreuende Verminderung meiner Grundbegriffe dadurch ermöglicht werden. Zusammen haben diese Erwägungen eine durchgehende Umarbeitung des Systemes und des Buches bedeutet. Das fing ich während zufällinger Stunden im Laufe unserer Reise nach Litanen, Lattland, Danzig, Deutschland, Dänemark, Schweden, Niederland und Irland an. Auf dem Schiffe nach Amerika hatte ich viele Zeit zu arbeiten. So kam ich an Harvard am Ende Juni und lernte, das mein Buch vor einigen Tagen endlich zum Druck gegangen war! Der Drücker hatte aber nur angefangen und ich nahm mein Manuskriptum weg. Seitdem habe ich fleißig auf dem Buche gearbeitet. Früh in Jänner wird es hoffentlich nochmals fertig für den Drück sein.

Ihnen und Ihre Frau herzliche Grüße von uns beiden, und beste Wünsche in Bezug auf das Stipendium.

Ihr

[8.E   QUINE TO CARNAP   1933-12-7]

65 Mount Auburn Street
Cambridge, Mass., U.S.A.
December 7, 1933

Dear Prof. Carnap:

Many thanks for your two letters. I am delighted about the report of further developments regarding the Rockefeller fellowship. It is our most earnest hope to be able to see you and your wife again here in Cambridge.

I have asked Whitehead and Scheffer to write to the Rockefeller Foundation. I know definitely that Scheffer and also Lewis and Huntington have already written. Whitehead solemnly promised me and even Scheffer to write; I do not know, however, whether or not he has done it, because he is very old and

I know from my own earlier experience that in such respects he is not especially reliable. In any case, however, the three have written and perhaps also the fourth.

So that I could inquire about your election earlier than would be possible for you across the ocean, I wrote a request to the Rockefeller Foundation to send me a list of all new appointments as soon as it is ready. I very much hope soon to inquire favorably.

It would be a delight to know that we have the chance this February to help you and your wife to find an apartment. In any case, however, you will be able to come in the near future: if the fellowship is not forthcoming, you can find a professorship without difficulty.

I was happy to read in your last letter that your book was almost ready. I hope it has already gone to press and is soon to appear. Since my return I have had many opportunities to emphasize to those interested my enthusiasm for the book. Thus, for example, my friend B. F. Skinner, who is interested in the relations between experimental psychology and logic, postponed a planned work in order to make it possible for him to read your forthcoming book right away. I notice that very many people here at Harvard know of your *Logischer Aufbau* and praise it highly. My friend Cooley is writing his doctoral dissertation on your published ideas.

Conversations with Tarski have persuaded me to omit from my book an idea about bound variables which plays no basic role; since I had to make one change in the draft of the book I also decided to incorporate a basic idea that occurred to me a year ago. This required me to substantially rework the book. Thus I worked on the book again and suddenly discovered in addition that if with abstraction "$\hat{x}$ (----)" I included also the case where "x" does *not* occur in "----", then this enables a gratifying reduction of my fundamental concepts. Together these considerations mean a thoroughgoing reworking of the system and of the book. I began it during chance hours on our trip racing through Lithuania, Latvia, Danzig, Germany, Denmark, Sweden, the Netherlands, and Ireland. On the ship to America I had a lot of time to work. Thus I came to Harvard at the end of June and learned that my book had finally gone to press a few days before! The printer, however, had only begun, and I took my manuscript away. Since then I have worked industriously on the book. Early in January it will, I hope, once more be ready for press.

To you and your wife kind regards from us both, and best wishes in regard to the fellowship.

Yours

[9. CARNAP TO QUINE   1934-1-6]

Prof. Dr. Rudolf Carnap
    Prag XVII   Prague, January 6, 1934
N. Motol, Pod Homolkou

Dear Mrs. and Mr. Q u i n e ,

We try to write to you in English, preparing for our journey to America. But this does not mean, that we shall come soon. We have not yet any answer from the Rockefeller Foundation, nor has been anybody from the F. in Prague. Many thanks for your intervention in this case at Whitehead and Sheffer! We heard also from Bertrand Russell, J. von Neumann-Princeton, Marcel Boll-Paris, Louis Rougier-Paris, Eino Kaila-Helsingfors, that they wrote in my favour to the Foundation. Since we have heard not yet anything, it seems quite impossible to get the Fellowship for this February. Now we hope for the fall. Yesterday we wrote to the F. asking, what their opinion is about my chance. When we have answer, we shall write.

The "Logische Syntax der Sprache" has gone to the publisher in the middle of December. There has been added a "General Syntax" and many new details; therefore it lasted so long time. I hope, you will like it in this new form.

I am pleased, that your friend Cooley is working about my ideas. But it is a pity, that Cooley has not seen the "Syntax". I think my earlier publications surpassed by this new book. But perhaps you have told to your friend about the new ideas too.

The treatise about "Die physikalische Sprache als Univer-

salsprache der Wissenschaft" will come out in English as volume of the "Psyche Miniatures", translated by M.Black. You
know, the "Psyche" is edited by C.K.Ogden, who also edits the
"International Library". By the occasion of this translation I got
nearer contact with Ogden, and Ogden sent me a lot of his publications; the most are about Basic English (volumes of the "Psyche Miniatures"), one about Bentham, and one is called "The
Meaning of Meaning". Ogden and his staff (it seems that he has
a sort of institute, called "Orthological Institute") have interesting ideas about language; but they are more based on common-
sense than on subtle knowledge of logic. Do you know anything
about Basic English? I was occupied all the holydays by this
books, and I dream even in English.

Have you seen the new periodical "Philosophy of Science"? I
am glad, that really this baby has been born and I hope for
good growth. And what do you think about? (Perhaps you
found already some mistakes in the translation of my treatise;
the passage quoted from Hume was not the right one.)

How did you spend your summer-holydays? And how du ⟨*sic*⟩
you live now? In which form has realised your stipendium?

Considering our hope to come in the fall to USA, we would
be very interested to hear which effect on the prices the Dollar-
Baisse has had. We heard, that the Rockefeller F. askes for a
proposal of the Fellow, how much he believes to need; therefore
it would be good to know, how much we will spent with moderate pretensions. Perhaps Mrs. Quine will be so kind to write
about this subject.

Many thanks for your nice Xmas card! We send you in return
our best wishes for the New Year!

I am eager to read your book. When will it appear?

Would you be so kind as to send back one copy of this letter
with your corrections, when you write the next time (it is not
urgent)? We will do the same, if you send a second copy of
your german letters. But I see from your very well expressed
german letter, that your letters will not be such a red ocean as
ours will be.

Your idea of admitting the case, that ‚x' does not occur in the
operand of ‚x̂', is certainly a good one. I also did so with the
(propositional) operands in my system. I think quite generally,

that a system will become simplier ⟨*sic*⟩, if such so to speak
empty cases are not excluded.

Hearty greetings to you both from my wife and

yours truly
R. Carnap

[10. CARNAP TO QUINE 1934-2-25]

Prof. Dr. Rudolf Carnap
Prag XVII   Prague, February 25, 1934.
N. Motol, Pod Homolkou

Dear Mrs. and Mr. Q u i n e ,

I am very sorry I must say you today, that the Rockefeller
Foundation has sent me now a negative answer. In January one
of the representatives has been there, who told me, that my
chances to get a fellowship are very small. His reasons were: 1)
special fellowships were given very seldom, and now, as the
foundation has little money, more seldom than ever; 2) the field
of my works seems not to agree with the program of the foundation (for they give not fellowships for philosophy and they
didn't look at my works as pure mathematics; I had asked for a
fellowship of foundations of mathematics); 3) for the reason the
foundation has little money, they got order to prefer physics to
all other sciences and not to spend so much money for the others. Meantimes those reasons have caused the negative decision
of the Foundation.

Nevertheless I hope to come to America. If not with a fellowship, then perhaps by an invitation for lectures for one or half a
year. By my studies in the last time I have improved my English. I realise this in my speech with the Rockefeller man in
January; the speaking went on much smoother than in the last
year with you. So I think I would be able to give lectures in
English next fall. Today I asked Lewis for a suggestion how to
get an invitation. Do you know any way for this?

In the case that at present it will not be possible to get an
invitation, I hope for the effect of my book, especially because

there is a chance to get out an English translation of it. Mr. Ogden wrote me about an opportunity for this. The question is not yet decided; it depends upon if the English and the German publishers will come to an egreement. I hope, they will do. The book is now in print; I got already half of the proof-prints.

We are very well. Now we have been one week in the Giant mountains for skiing. I like this sport more than any other. It gives such a good combination of pleasing movement and of enjoying the beautiful winter woods and mountains.

Are you both well, healthy and happy? When will appear your book?

Do you know Prof. Charles W. Morris (University of Chicago)? Feigl has discussed with him, and he seems much interested in our Vienna Circle. He wrote me that in Spring or Summer 1934 he intends to come to Europe and spend some months at Prague and Vienna. (In his first letter he wrote also about Berlin; but he seems to have dropped this intention, perhaps because Reichenbach is no more in Berlin, he is now professor in Istanbul). On account of the judgement of Feigl about Morris, I am very pleased to get the opportunity of seeing him and speaking with him.

Sincerely yours
R. Carnap

[11. (FIRST PART) QUINE TO CARNAP 1934-3-12]

Kopie   65 Mt. Auburn Street
Cambridge, Mass. USA
d. 12. März. 1934

Lieber Herr C a r n a p!

Die ungünstige Nachricht betreffs des Stipendiums hat uns sehr leid getan. Hoffentlich werden Sie aber statt dessen etwas noch besseres erhalten. Es ist sehr gut, daß Sie an Lewis geschrieben haben.

Wann ich Ihren letzteren Brief bekam, ging ich gerade an | a. Whitehead, um ihm vertraulich mitzuteilen, daß Sie eine zeitliche oder beständige Professur in Amerika gern annehmen würden. (Er hatte mir seine hohe Achtung für Ihre Arbeit schon früher erwähnt.) Er war sehr interessiert und schlug vor, daß ich sofort einen Brief an Langford (University of Michigan) schreibe und seinen (Whitehead's) Name anwende. Gestern schrieb ich also an Langford einen höchst behutsamen Brief, der hoffentlich irgendeinen Erfolg gewähren wird.

    John Cooley kennt Northrop (Yale) and wird ihm auch die
b. | Sache diplomatisch erheben.

    Heute habe ich mit Lewis gesprochen. Der ökonomischen Lage wegen gibt es natürlich fast keine freie Stellen im ganzen Lande; nichtsdestoweniger schien Lewis hoffnungsvoll zu sein, denn es muß Ihres Ruhmes und der Wichtigkeit Ihrer Arbeit
c. | wegen jedenfalls in irgendeiner guten Amerikanischen
d. | Universität eine Stelle geben. Er fragtete mir nach Ihrem Englisch, worüber ich ihn ruhig machte. Er hat versprochen, einige Briefe dahinzuschicken, wo sie die besten Erfolge liefern sollen. Von Whitehead und auch Lewis wurde die Idee einer Stellung an Harvard überhaupt nicht erwähnt; daraus dürfen Sie
e. | aber nichts ableiten, da so ein Begriff scheinlich etwas nicht vorauszuerwähnendes ist.

    Naomi hat mich plötzlich unterbrochen, um vorzuschlagen, daß ich englisch schreibe, damit Sie Übung bekommen. Ihr Englisch wird zu einem näheren praktischen Zweck gefordert, als mein Deutsch.

    I am glad your book is with the printer, and am very eager to see it.

[ENDE DER KOPIE]

[CARNAP'S CORRECTIONS OF QUINE'S GERMAN:]

a. 'Wann' changed to 'Als' and 'an' changed to 'Zu' ⟨Als ich Ihren letzteren Brief bekam, ging ich gerade zu Whitehead, . . .⟩.
b. 'erheben' is underlined, over it is written 'nahelegen, fragen (ihm nahelegen oder: ihm in dieser Sache fragen)'.
c. 'Amerikanischen' is decapitalized.
d. 'fragtete' changed to 'fragte', 'mir' changed to 'mich', and

'ruhig machte' changed to 'beruhigte' ⟨Er fragte mich nach Ihrem English, worüber ich ihn beruhigte.⟩.

e. 'Begriff' is parenthesized with 'Idee, Plan' written above. Carnap also adds 'wahr' to 'scheinlich' ⟨wahrscheinlich⟩ and also suggests: 'oder: scheinbar'.

[11.E   QUINE TO CARNAP   1934-3-12]

Copy   65 Mt. Auburn Street
Cambridge, Mass., USA
March 12, 1934

Dear Mr. Carnap:

The adverse report concerning the fellowship has made us very unhappy. I hope, however, that instead of this you will get something even better. It is very good that you have written to Lewis.

When I got your last letter I went straight to Whitehead in order to inform him confidentially that you would gladly accept a temporary or permanent professorship in America. (He had already mentioned to me earlier his high opinion of your work.) He was very interested and suggested that I immediately write a letter to Langford (University of Michigan) and to use his (Whitehead's) name. Therefore, yesterday I wrote Langford an extremely careful letter which I hope will produce some results.

John Cooley knows Northrop (Yale) and also will raise the matter with him diplomatically.

Today I spoke with Lewis. Owing to the economic situation, there are almost no available places in the whole country; nevertheless Lewis seems hopeful that because of your reputation and the importance of your work a position in some good American university must still turn up. He asked me about your English, about which I reassured him. He promised to send out a few letters where they should produce the best results. The possibility of a position at Harvard was not raised at all by Whitehead nor by Lewis either; do not draw any conclusions from this, however, because such an idea is apparently something never raised before.

Naomi suddenly interrupted me to suggest that I write in English so that you can get practice. Your English will be put to practical application sooner than my German. ⟨*Translation ends here.*⟩

I am glad your book is with the printer, and am very eager to see it

[end of the copy]

a. | in its final form—as also are many of my asssociates, to whom I have expressed my enthusiasm for the book.

Thank you for the offprint from *Philosophy of Science*. I had read your article earlier in the library, but was very glad to have a copy of my own. I thought the article an effective and elegant summary of your doctrine of philosophy as grammar. I did not think Malisoff's translation altogether unexceptionable, however—for example, wouldn't your use of "inhaltlich" be best translated as "material", the usual English correlative of "formal"? I suggest that as relevant to the projected translation of your book.

I am greatly impressed by the new quarterly—both by the imposing array of editors and contributors and by the quality of its make-up and typography. The journal fulfills an urgent need. It is the first good philosophy periodical published in this country. (The *Monist* and the *Journal of Philosophy* are miserable rags, as you know.)

Last week, finally, I finished the thoroughgoing rewriting of my book and put it into the hands of the printer (Harvard University Press). Beyond the gain in generality afforded by the suppression of individuals in favor of sequences, the system has almost nothing in common with the form in which I sketched it to you in Prague. The system is now much simpler, and at the same time a much more radical departure from tradition, than it was in the earlier form. The book will have about 225 pages. Whitehead is writing a short preface for it. Since the book could not appear before June in any case, the publishers will probably hold it until September, since they deem that the best season for the marketing of an academic work.

I am glad to hear of the steps toward an English translation of your *Logische Syntax,* and of the projected translation of the *Die physikalische Sprache usw.* I am slightly acquainted with the Psyche Miniatures, and in fact have just now read Richards' *Basic Rules of Reason,* in Basic English. I am very much pleased with Basic English; it is an ingenious practical simplification, and not without a certain logical interest as well. For the most part Richards' little book resounds very naturally upon the orthodox English ear. The simplicity of vocabulary is aesthetically good, and conducive moreover to greater clarity by virtue of its greater Eindeutigkeit (we have no usual English word for this; the nearest is "univocal"). In using Basic English as an approach to standard English it must nevertheless be kept in mind that some of the Basic locutions are inadmissible in the regular language— *e.g.* "take a look at", excessive use of "get", et al. But Basic English is always thoroughly intelligible, and the bulk of it is idiomatically orthodox as well.

I am acquainted with *The Meaning of Meaning.* It is an entertaining book, and says much that is sound and important, but, as you have remarked, it makes no pretense of subtle analysis.

I have recently discovered John Horne Tooke: *EΠEA ΠTEROENTA* ⟨i.e. *EΠEA ΠTEPOENTA*⟩, *Or The Diversions of Purley* (late 18th century). It is both a highly amusing and an enlightening work, and one which I recommend to you if you have not seen it. Tooke writes that Locke's *Essay* is properly construed if for every occurrence of the word "idea" therein we substitute the word "word". Tooke is a philologist and a philosopher; as a philosopher he practically, but not quite explicitly, subscribes to your doctrine that philosophy is grammar. On the other hand he naïvely seeks to establish his doctrines by philological data; insofar as he does this he is of course a natural scientist, specifically an anthropologist, rather than a logician or grammarian. The book is a delight to read, especially the leisurely 18th-century vein of ridicule with which he fills his copious footnote-references to his contemporaries.

The three-year appointment which I am now enjoying is an ideal arrangement. My annual salary is $ 2250, I am given full library and lecture-attendance privileges, and I have no duties whatever; full time for research in any form I may choose. We must provide our own lodgings, but I am allowed all the meals I please in the university dining halls without cost. This is a convenience for me most noons and such other times as Naomi may have other plans. Unmarried appointees are provided with lodgings, but their stipend is reduced correspondingly.

The Society of Fellows (the group under consideration) has a suite of rooms, where we have one luncheon and one dinner together a week. The weekly dinner is followed by conversation which lasts till about midnight. It is always interesting and stimulating, for besides us six appointees (upper age limit of appointment 28) there are the so-called Senior Fellows, or sponsors, comprising seven more or less distinguished scholars, among them Whitehead. The six junior appointees will be added to each year until there is a total of 24, which will then be kept about constant; the Senior Fellows on the other hand will remain seven. This is the first year of the project; six to ten more young men are now being selected, from applicants all over the country, to join us next year. The object of the foundation is opportunity for three years of unhindered productive research or preparation. It is part of the policy that no credit toward degrees is allowed for work produced or courses attended during incumbency; this is of course irrelevant to the two of us who already have our doctorates.

The fall of the dollar has resulted in only a slight rise in prices. Rents in Cambridge, however, have always been high. A suite of several furnished rooms would cost you about $ 45 a month as a minimum, with gas, electricity, water and heat included. An unfurnished apartment (= "flat", in Engld.) of an acceptable kind might be had for $ 30, and gas and electricity would cost about $ 3 a month additional. If you furnished such a place very simply and cautiously from second-hand stores, with our help—the procedure which we adopted two years ago—you could probably pass a year more cheaply than in furnished rooms, and you would have the added privacy of a separate entrance, whereof one usually cannot be assured in furnished lodgings. $ 25 a month would be ample for meals, prepared at home.

But such information is hardly relevant now that you are planning for a teaching position rather than a Rockefeller Fellowship. Your income will be far greater with the former than with the latter, and you will have less reason to worry over expenses than we now have. Note incidentally that if you should be at some university other than Harvard your rent will be much less—at some places little more than half as much.

In any case of course we are looking forward to the pleasure of accompanying you in the search for lodgings and furniture—unless you should happen to be called to some such distant point as Iowa, Texas or California. Our hope is of course that you will be with us here at Harvard.

Many thanks for the two photographs. We were very happy to get them, and they are excellent pictures.

To return to the question of living expenses, I might mention that on my salary—which is certainly less than you will receive—we have been living in an attractive, light and centrally situated apartment with two large rooms plus bedroom, bathroom, hall and tiny kitchen. We have furnished the apartment completely with new and attractive furniture, which we shall have finished paying for in two more months. The furniture is all of first quality, but slowly and cautiously purchased—so slowly in fact that we were sleeping on the floor and I was using a board for a desk for a few weeks last September! But don't let me alarm you; the caution was necessary merely in order to acquire our permanent furniture all at one time and at lowest prices.

With heartiest greetings to you both, also from Naomi,

Sincerely yours,

[MARGINALIA ON QUINE'S COPY (TOP OF SECOND PAGE):]

a. 3-12-34 page 1 to be returned by Carnap

[12.   CARNAP TO QUINE   1934-4-8]

Prof. Dr. Rudolf Carnap
    Prag XVII   Prague, April 8, 1934.
N. Motol, Pod Homolkou

Dear Mr. Quine,

many thanks for your letter of March 12th. I return you the copy of the German part of your letter; you write such a good

German that I had only to change some expressions. I am very obliged to you for the trouble you took in order to advance my America-aims. We were very pleased to see that Ina was right: she said to me from the first moment of her acquaintance with Naomi and you: "you will see, Quine will become good friends to us". — Meantimes I got a letter from Lewis; he wrote that he will write in my favor to two places, he had heard of the possibility of an invitation for one semester. He did not mention the possibility of an invitation from Harvard. It is a pity, Ina and I would have been very happy to be in the same town where Naomi and you are. I heard from different parts that it would not be difficult for a University which has the wish to invite a professor but has not money enough to get a share from the Rockefeller Foundation; perhaps this is still a possibility for me to come over.

Now I got an invitation of the University of London for a course of three lectures. I expect to go to England in the middle of September—after the Internat. Congress for Philosophy in Prague—and to spend there some weeks for learning good English pronunciation. The lectures will be in the first half of October.

The translation of the "Die physikalische Sprache usw." is now finished; the little book will appear soonly. The agreement with Ogden about the translation of the Logische Syntax is also ready; but now I have to negociate with my German publisher about his consent; this will be a hard work. But I hope to come to a good end.

I am glad to hear that you finished the rewriting of your book. I am very interested to learn about your simplifications and your departure from tradition. What a pity that it will appear so late!

You are right: "inhaltlich" would be best translated as "material"; so I suggested to Mr. Black for his translation of the Physikalische Sprache. I heard from Schlick, that Malisoff's translation of my article is not a good English. What do you think about? I ask this for the future; because it is the simpliest way for me that Malisoff himself translates the articles.

I don't know the book of Tooke and am very pleased to hear your report. Sorry I shall not get it here in the library.

We were glad to hear that you are quite content with the circumstances in which you live now. It is surely of great value for you that you have now three years only for your work without considerable sorrows about the subsistence. What makes Naomi all the time? Ina is very interested to hear about.

Would you perhaps be willing to write a review of my "Syntax" in an American journal? In this case the best way is that the administration of the journal requests a review-copy from the publisher (J. Springer, Wien I, Schottengasse 4) mentioning your name as writer of the review. If you do not like to review please write me; in this case it will be a pleasure for me to send you a complimentary copy.

With heartiest greetings to you both, also from Ina,

Sincerely yours,
R. Carnap

[13. CARNAP TO QUINE   1934-6-8]

Prof. Dr. Rudolf Carnap
    Prag XVII   Prague, June 8, 1934
N. Motol, Pod Homolkou

Dear Dr. Q u i n e ,

My book "Logische Syntax" is not quite ready. I think it will appear in 2 weeks. Concerning the English translation I have come to an agreement with the German publisher; I am sorry I must make the concession that the English edition is not to appear before April 1, 1935. May I ask you for your advice in some *terminological questions* regarding the English translation?

1. *Satz*: sentence (I think this is better than ‚proposition', because the series of signs is meant, not its meaning; and a second | a. advantage: as a syntactical gothic letter I could keep , $\mathfrak{S}$ (gothic S)).

~~2. (Ein Satz ist) *Folge* (anderer Sätze): conclusion (consequence?)~~ | b.

3. *Gehalt*: content. | c.
4. *gehaltgleich*: equal in content (is there no simple word?) | d.

e. | 5. *Alloperator:* universal (or: general) operator.
f. | 6. *Ausdruck* (any series of signs): expression.
      7. Strich (e.g. in ‚o$^|$'): stroke (or would this produce a confu-
g. | sion with Sheffers Stroke ‚|', which does not occur in my "Syn-
tax"?), dash.
      8. *Strichausdruck* (e.g. ‚o$^{|||}$'): stroke expression (if no danger
of confusion with e.g. ‚p|q' which however does not occur; the
advantage would be that I could keep the gothic sign , **𝕿** '
(=St) as in German), dash expression.
h. | 9. *Spielraum* (as in Wittgenstein, p.98): domain, range.

a-Begriffe:	*f-Begriffe:*
10. *Ableitung:* derivation.	17. *Folgereihe:* conclusion-series (?)
	18. *Folgeklasse:* conclusion-class, class of conclusions.
11. *Beweis:* proof (demonstration?)	
12. *ableitbar:* derivable	19. *Folge:* conclusion (consequence).
13. *beweisbar:* provable (demonstrable?)	20. *gültig:* valid.
i. 14. *widerlegbar:* disprovable	21. *widergültig:* contra-valid (I think, ‚invalid' would not do)
j. 15. *entscheidbar:* decidable	22. *determiniert:* determinate.
16. *unentscheidbar:* indecidable	23. *indeterminiert:* indeterminate.

Explanations: Ableitung and Beweis are certain finite series of sentences. Folgereihe is a series of classes of sentences. The concepts in left column (a-Begriffe) have the meaning of something which can really be done; therefore I think that for (12)–(16) words with the ending ‚-able' are preferable. The concepts in the right column (f-Begriffe) have a meaning which is in a certain sense absolutistic. For (19): a sentence can be a Folge of an other sentence or of a class of sentences.

      24. *Zahl-* (-Ausdruck, -Zeichen, -Variable): numerical (expres-
k. | sion, sign, variable) or numeral?

25. *freie und gebundene* Variable: (I would prefer not to take, as Russell, ,real' and ,apparent variable') free, bound variable.

In your answer you may simply refer to the numbers of the concepts.

With best greetings 2:2 ⟨presumably: from the two of us to the two of you⟩

> very truly yours
> R. Carnap

[MARGINAL NOTES ON QUINE'S COPY OF 13:]

a. sentence
b. consequence
c. OK
d. equipollent
e. universal quantifier
f. OK
g. accent
h. range
i. refutable
j. resoluble
k. ⟨Quine underlines 'sign' and 'numbered' and connects them with an identity sign ('=')⟩

[14. QUINE TO CARNAP   1934-6-29]

Cambridge, Mass, U.S.A.
June 29, 1934   a.

Dear Professor Carnap,

We are leaving Cambridge tomorrow night, for the summer. During these last days in Cambridge I have been kept extremely busy with proofs of my book; it was desirable that I accomplish as much as possible of that work before my departure. Now, finally, I have an hour's respite.

We shall spend the summer with my parents, at the following address:

16 Orchard Road, Akron, Ohio, U.S.A.

While there I shall finish all proof-reading and indexing of my book, which will appear about Sept. 1 under the title *A System of Logistic*. Also I hope to have time for a little other writing. On Sept. 13 we shall leave on a three-weeks' cruise to Haiti. By Oct. 5 we shall be back here in Cambridge again, at a not yet determinate address. (But I can always be reached care of Department of Philosophy, Harvard University.)

I have arranged with the *Philosophical Review* to review your *Logische Syntax*, and the editor has arranged with the Springer Verlag to send me a copy. I shall set to work at it immediately when my copy arrives. I am very eager to see the book.

Regarding your terminological questions, I agree with your suggestions to the following extent:

1) *Satz* = Sentence,
3) *Gehalt* = Content,
6) *Ausdruck* = Expression,
10) *Ableitung* = derivation,
11) *Beweis* = proof,
12) *ableitbar* = derivable,
13) *beweisbar* = demonstrable,
20) *gültig* = valid,
22) *determiniert* = determinate,
23) *indeterminiert* = indeterminate,
25) *freie, gebundene Variable* = free, bound variable.

In my book also I have used "free, bound" in preference over "real, apparent."

Perhaps (11) and (13) seem inconsistent choices. They represent, however, commonest usage: for (a) "proof" is the more natural noun in English, and "demonstration" a laborious *mot savant*, whereas (b) "provable" is a *tour de force*, like "doable," "eatable," etc., and is hence usually avoided in favor of the purer Latin adjective "demonstrable" (just as "doable" and "eatable" are avoided in favor of "feasible" and "edible").

Regarding (2), I should prefer

2) *Folge* = consequence.

"Conclusion" does not quite serve, but answers rather to "*Schluss*."

c. b.
d.

As to (4), *"Gehaltgleich"*, I agree that a single word is desirable. This requires the introduction of a special technical word for the purpose. I suggest "equipollent," which according to my dictionary, had much the desired meaning in traditional logic years ago. Etymologically also "equipollent" seems appropriate for the purpose. I heartily recommend its use.

If however you should decline this word in favor of a phrase such as "equal in content," I suggest that you adopt rather the phrase *"alike* in content." (Even if you use "equipollent," this point is relevant when you come to define that word.) "Alike" is of course etymologically cognate with *"gleich."* The word *"equal"* suggests rather likeness of quantity; ! "equal in content" would thus mean "having the same *amount* of content⟨"⟩. ("Equal" and *"gleich"* thus coincide only in the comparison of numbers, *e.g.*, 5=3+2.)

As to (5), your suggestion of "universal operator" for *"Alloperator"* is admissible. But in my own work I have preferred to adopt "universal *quantifier,"* on the basis of fairly prevalent English usage. But this is an unimportant matter; meaning is clear in either case.

As to (7), I suggest

7) *Strich* = accent.

It is usual in English to read x' as "x prime", but to refer to the mark ' itself as an *accent* (*not* a "prime"). As you say, "stroke" would create confusion with Scheffer's sign; furthermore it would not suggest the mark ' to an English reader even unacquainted with Sheffer's notion. "Dash" is impossible, for a dash is always horizontal.

Perhaps (8), then, should be construed thus:

8) *Strichausdruck* = accented expression.

Under (9) I advise

9) *Spielraum* = range,

when the word is used in Wittgenstein's sense. One speaks also of the *range* of a variable. The word "domain" is better confined to the technical sense of *Principia Mathematica* (=*Bereich*, or *Vorbereich*). Finally in the case of the *Spielraum* or *Bereich* of an operator, meaning thereby the segment of a given expression which the operator governs, the proper translation is "scope." | e.

For (14) I suggest

14) *widerlegbar* = refutable.

"Disprovable" has the shortcoming attributed earlier to "provable."

(15) and (16) are difficult, as shown by the fact that even in English the German words "*Entscheidungsproblem*" and "*Entscheidungsverfahren*" are frequently used. Of course that procedure is undesirable. But *against* "decidable" and "indecidable" there are two objections:

a) "Decide" does not, like "entscheiden," suggest the determination of the truth or falsity of a proposition; in any case, therefore, use of the word would amount to the introduction of a special technical usage.

f. | b) "Decidable" is an uncommon word, and grates upon the English ear because it has no French or Latin precedents "décidable," "decidabilis".

As one alternative I suggest

15) *entscheidbar* = determinable,

16) *unentscheidbar* = indeterminable,

if you do not object to thus emphasizing the parallelism with (22) and (23). Otherwise I suggest

15) *entscheidbar* = resoluble,

16) *unentscheidbar* = irresoluble.

Very likely this last choice is best. The verb corresponding to "*entscheiden*" would then become "resolve."

June 30

Our furniture, books etc. are now all packed and moved into storage. In two hours we shall be off for Ohio. I have made the sad discovery that I have packed your last letter, leaving out the next to the last by mistake. So I shall have to attempt to finish answering your terminological questions from memory.

According to my suggestion under (2), your tentative terminology "conclusion-series," for "*folgereihe*," would have to become "consequence-series" instead. But doesn't the mediaeval

g. | terminology "sorites" fit the meaning?

Similarly your "conclusion-class" or "class of conclusions," under "*Folgeklasse*," would become "consequence-class" or "class of consequences," But I thought you identified this with *content-Gehalt*. If that is the case, and the word "*Folgeklasse*" is used only temporarily for expository purposes leading up to that identification, then use "class of consequences" for that temporary purpose rather than "consequence-class"; the latter is more a technical word than a description, and its introduction would be justified only by permanent use.

I believe that disposes of (17) and (18). I have forgotten what (19) was, but will send a postscript next week covering it. Your letter is somewhere in our Ohio-bound baggage, rather than in storage.

As to (21), I think you will have to coin a word, as you suggest. But you had best make a finished job of the coinage by omitting the hyphen, thus:

    21) *widergültig* = contravalid

I have just now remembered (19). It duplicates (2), which you had crossed out.

    19) *Folge* = consequence.

As to (24), I suggest the following:

    24) *Zahlausdruck* = numerical expression
        Zahlzeichen = numeral !
        Zahlvariable = numerical variable

Please pardon the hasty and unfinished character of this letter; it is unavoidable unless the letter be delayed until we get to Ohio. Despite the haste of writing, the above conclusions have all been carefully considered; I had made all the decisions with full deliberation a day earlier than the beginning of this letter. I hope the suggestions will be of help, and am very glad that the English translation of your book is coming.

I am very grateful to you for my copy of *The Unity of Science or Physics as a Universal Language*. It makes a splendid little volume, and I greatly enjoyed reading it through again in translation. On the whole I thought the translation fairly successful.

Thanks also for the reprint of your two book-reviews. I have not yet had a chance to read it thoroughly, so I am taking it along with me.

I am told that members of the *psychology department here* are becoming much interested in your writings regarding that subject.

Naomi and I are very unhappy not to be able to look forward to seeing you in America this autumn. Surely however you will have news of something in America before very long.

You ask my opinion of Malisoff's translation. I thought it rather ordinary, but not definitely bad. Meaning was clear throughout, but idiom might have been improved somewhat. I think however that there would be no harm in having him translate further articles; I noticed no serious faults in his work.

We were glad to hear of your invitation to the University of London. You will enjoy it, and it will be good training in the language. I hope your stay in London will be followed shortly by a one-way trip to America!

Naomi joins me in greetings and best wishes to you both.

Sincerely yours,
W.V. Quine

⟨It is difficult to determine on this letter which of the underlining is Quine's and which Carnap's. That which seems to be Quine's is reproduced here (by italicizing the underlined material, in conformity with the practice adopted throughout this edition of representing underlining by italics).⟩

[MARGINAL NOTES ON CARNAP'S COPY (IN GERMAN SHORTHAND):]

a. Terminol for "Syntax"
b. ⟨above 'provable'⟩ (But in the dictionary also OD)
c ⟨above 'doable'⟩ (*not* in the dictionary)
d ⟨above 'eatable'⟩ (in the dictionary)
e. operand
f. ⟨above 'decidable'⟩ (but in the OD)
g. no

[15. QUINE TO CARNAP   1934-11-24]

Kopie   52 Garden Street
Cambridge, Mass., USA
d.24.Nov.1934

Lieber Herr Carnap!

a. | Ich habe sehr viel Ihnen mitzuteilen; daß werde ich der zeitlichen Reihenfolge nach.

In Antwort Ihres Schreibens des 3. Juni schrieb ich Ihnen | b.
einen ausführlichen Brief. Hoffentlich erhalten Sie ihn und
fanden etwas nützliches unter meinen terminologischen
Vorschlägen.

Ihr Buch hat mir natürlich sehr gefallen. Ich habe es für die
Philosophical Review rezensiert. Das passiert aber spät. Durch
irgendeinen Unfall bei dem Herausgeber mußt ich für meinen | c.
Exemplar des Buches vier Monate warten; inzwischen mußte ich
fünf mal schreiben: zweimal an die Zeitschrift, zweimal an
Springer, und einmal an den Postamt. In September kam | d.
endlich das Buch und ein Paar Wochen später sandte ich meine
Rezension ab.

In der Universität habe ich während dieses Monates drei
öffentliche Vorträge über Ihre letzteren Arbeiten gehalten. Eine | e.
sehr befriedigendes Interesse wurde gezeigt. In dieser Gegend
werden Sie sehr viel besprochen. Eine Gruppe der jungen
Doktoren plant nun, für die Besprechung Ihrer Ideen periodisch
zusammenzutreten.

Gerade nach meinem vorgestrigen Schlußvortrag über Ihre
Arbeit hat Prof. David Wight Prall mir gesagt, daß er sehr gern
die *Logische Syntax* ins englisch übersetzen möge. Dies war mir | f.
eine außerordentlich erfreuende Nachricht. Ein gewißer Tom
Chambers (Chemie) und Dr. Fred Skinner (Psychologie) und Naomi und ich schickten Ihnen dann gemeinsam die
Kabeldepesche, die Sie vermutlich am 23. d.M. erhalten haben,
um Sie zu überzeugen, den Uebersetzungsvorgang aufzuhalten,
falls er nicht schon etwa halbeswegs durchgeführt worden sei.

Ich hoffe sehr, daß es noch nicht zu spät ist, die
Uebersetzungsarbeit dem Prall zuzuerkennen. Das letztere wäre
aus folgenden Gründen sehr vorteilhaft:

1) Prall ist nicht etwa unbekannter Dozent in Tennessee,
sondern Professor an Harvard. In dem Kreis amerikanischer
Gelehrter ist er schon gut errichtet und hoch geachtet. | g.

2) Einerseits ist Prall über Ihre Arbeit sehr begeistert;
andererseits aber wird Prall sozusagen von Seiten der
Feindeslager, d.h. der ausgesprochenen Philosophen, als
ordentlicher Kollege angesehen. Politisch ist ein solche Lage
offenbar vorteilhaft.

3) Prall ist ein geschickter Schriftsteller.

h. | 4) Er ist ein sehr energischer und mit dabei ein sehr
sorgfältiger Arbeiter. Jede Einzelheit der Terminologie usw.
würde von ihm behutsam und geschickt behandelt werden. Es
würde sein aufrichteges Ziel sein, eine stolzwürdige
i. | Uebersetzung zu erzuegen. Daß er auf dieses Ziel gelangen
würde, ist ausgerechnet.

Daher springt es ins Auge, daß es Ihnen geziemt, jeden
schon enstandenen Uebersetzungsvertrag gerade wegzutun,
und die Arbeit dem Prall zuzuerkennen, wenn das noch heute
überhaupt möglich ist.

Es ist mein aufrichtigster Wunsch, Sie nicht nur in Amerika
sondern an Harvard möglichst bald errichtet zu sehen; das ist
auch der Wunsch einer Menge meiner Kollegen. Was ärgerlich
j. | ist, ist die Langsamkeit unserer Universitätsmächte in allen
solchen Vorgängen. Täglich wird es aber diesen Mächten stärker
k. | bestätigt, wie wichtig es sei, Sie hereinzuladen.

Ueber Ihre Definition von "quasi-syntaktisch", Seiten 178–
179, möchte ich eine Frage stellen. Innerhalb dieser Definition
scheint es nicht festgesetzt zu sein, daß Sg_2 ein syntaktisches
Prädikat sei. (Freilich muß Sg_2 der Sprache S_2 zugehören, welche
l. | Sprache aber *enthält* eine Syntax für S_1 und sonst im allgemeinen
übriges.) Wenn nun Sg_2 ein nicht syntaktisches Prädikat sein
darf (obwohl freilich es lauter Zeichen als Argumente annimmt),
warum denn könnte Sg_2 nicht irgendein ungünstiges dem
Begriff "wahr" betreffendes Prädikat sein, Ihren Bemerkungen
am Ende der S. 179 zuwider?

m. | Andrerseits nehme man an, Sg_2 müße syntaktisches Prädikat
sein. Nach Ihrer Definition von "syntaktischs" heißt dies, daß
Sg_2 innerhalb einer logischen Sprache liegt, und daher (nicht
wahr?) daß jeder Vollsatz von Sg_2 entweder analytisch oder
kontradiktorisch ist. Wenn aber jeder solchen Vollsatz dem
entsprechenden Vollsatz von Sg_1 gehaltgleich ist, so muß jeder
Vollsatz von Sg_1 ebenfalls entweder analytisch oder
kontradiktorisch sein. Unter diesen Voraussetzungen erhalten
wir aber das unwillkommene Resultat, daß ein Prädikat nur
dann quasi-syntaktisch sein kann, wenn jeder seiner Vollsätze
entweder analytisch oder kontradiktorisch ist.

Bitte zeigen Sie mir doch, worin mein Mißverständnis liegt.

[Ich bemerke nun, daß ich oben stets "Prädikat" anstatt "Satzgerüst" geschrieben habe. Dasgleiche soll aber beiderseits gelten, wenn es überhaupt gilt.]

Betreffs S. 116 habe ich eine geringere Frage zu stellen. Sie schreiben, "Zur Feststellung des Wahrheitswertes einer Implikation muß man die Wahrheitswerte der beiden Glieder feststellen." Dagegen möchte ich auszeichnen, daß wir günstigenfalls mit nur einer Gliedfestellung abhören dürfen, | n. nämlich wenn das zunächst festzustellende Glied das erste bzw. das zweite Glied ist und wird als falsch bzw. wahr festgestellt.

Ferner scheint es mir, daß wir günstigenfalls auf das Feststellen | o. des Wahrheitswertes überhaupt eines Gliedes verzichtern können und den Wahrheitswert des Ganzen einfach durch eine allgemeine logisch abgeleitete Beziehung feststellen.

Mit den Ideen Ihres Buches bin ich natürlich ganz einverstanden; es sei nur das obige Paar technischer Beipünkte | p. hervorgehoben.

Das Drücken meines Buches hat eine ungeheure Zeitlänge | q. gedauert. Letzte Woche ist es endlich erschienen. Ein komplimentäres Exemplar wird Ihnen direkt von dem | r. Herausgeber geschickt.

Separat sende ich Ihnen einige Sonderabdrücke. | s.

Ich hoffe, daß Ihr Aufenthalt in England angenehm war. Herzlichste Grüße Ihnen beiden, auch von Naomi.

Ihr

W. V. Quine

[CARNAP'S CORRECTIONS OF QUINE'S GERMAN:]

a. 'daß' changed to 'das', and 'tun.' added ⟨. . . das werde ich der zeitlichen Reihenfolge nach tun.⟩.
b. 'des' changed to 'vom' ⟨. . . Schreibens vom 3. Juni . . .⟩.
c. 'für' changed to 'auf', and 'meinen' changed to 'mein' ⟨. . . mußte ich auf mein Exemplar . . .⟩.
d. 'den' changed to 'das' ⟨. . . an das Postamt.⟩, and 'In' changed to 'Im' ⟨Im September . . .⟩.

e. 'letzteren' changed to 'letzten' ⟨. . . über Ihre letzten Arbeiten . . .⟩.

f. 'englisch' changed to 'Englische', and 'möge' changed to 'möchte' ⟨. . . ins Englische übersetzen möchte.⟩.

g. 'errichtet' is underlined and under it is written: '(augesehen)'.

h. 'mit' is crossed out ⟨. . . und dabei ein . . .⟩.

i. 'auf dieses' is changed to 'zu diesem' ⟨Das er zu diesem Ziel . . .⟩, and 'ausgerechnet' is underlined and next to it is written: $\left(\genfrac{}{}{0pt}{}{\text{ausgemacht.}}{\text{sicher}} \right)$.

j. 'Universitätsmächte' changed to 'Universitätsbehörden'.

k. 'hereinzuladen' changed to 'einzuladen' ⟨. . . Sie einzuladen.⟩.

l. Carnap circles *'enthält'* and moves it to the end of the sentence ⟨. . . welche Sprache aber eine Syntax für S_1 und sonst in allgemeinen übriges *enthält.*⟩.

m. "müße' changed to 'müsse' ⟨. . . Sg_2 müsse syntaktisches . . .⟩.

n. 'abhören' changed to 'aufhören' ⟨. . . Gliedfestellung aufhören dürfen, . . .⟩.

o. 'wird' moved to the end of the sentence ⟨. . . und als falsch bzw. wahr festgestellt wird.⟩.

p. 'Beipünkte' changed to 'Nebenpunkte' ⟨. . . technischer Nebenpunkte hervorgehoben.⟩.

q. 'Drücken' is changed to 'Drucken' ⟨Das Drucken meines Buches . . .⟩, above this is written: 'drücken = to press; drucken = to print'.

r. 'komplimentäres' is changed to 'Geschenk-', and 'Herausgeber' is changed to 'Verlag' ⟨Ein Geschenkexemplar wird Ihnen direkt von dem Verlag geschickt.⟩. An arrow from 'Verlag' points down to

      Herausgeber: editor (a scientist)
      Verleger: publisher (a businessman)

s. 'Sonderabdrücke' is changed to 'Sonderabdrucke'.

[15.E   QUINE TO CARNAP   1934-11-24]

52 Garden Street
Cambridge, Mass., USA
Nov. 24, 1934

Dear Mr. Carnap:

I have very much to tell you; I shall do so in chronological order.

In answer to your letters of June 3 I wrote you a detailed letter. I hope you got it and found something useful among my terminological suggestions.

Your book of course, pleases me very much. I have reviewed it for the *Philosophical Review*. That, however, occurred recently. Through some mischance with the editor I had to wait four months for my copy of the book; in the meantime I had to write five times: twice to the journal, twice to Springer, and once to the post office. In September, the book finally came and a couple of weeks later I mailed my review.

This month at the university I delivered three public lectures on your recent work. A very satisfying interest was manifest. In this area you are very much discussed. A group of young Ph.D.s now plans to meet periodically to discuss your ideas.

Right after my last lecture on your work the day before yesterday Prof. David Wight Prall said to me that he would be very happy to translate the *Logische Syntax* into English. This was extraordinarily gratifying news to me. One Tom Chambers (chemistry) and Dr. Fred Skinner (psychology) and Naomi and I jointly dispatched the cablegram to you which presumably you received on the 23rd of this month in order to persuade you to halt the current translation if it is not already about halfway complete.

I hope very much that it is not yet too late to award the translation work to Prall. The latter would be very advantageous on the following grounds:

1) Prall is not some unknown assistant professor in Tennessee, but a professor at Harvard. In American scholarly circles he is already well established and highly regarded.

2) On one hand Prall is very enthusiastic about your work; on

the other hand, however, Prall will be viewed by the enemy camp so to speak, i.e., by the outspoken philosophers as a sound colleague. Obviously, such a situation is politically advantageous.

3) Prall is a skilled writer.

4) He is a very energetic and thereby a very meticulous worker. Every particular of terminology etc. would be treated by him carefully and skillfully. It would be his sincere aim to produce a translation to be proud of. That he would achieve this aim is certain.

Hence, it seems obvious that it would be proper for you to cancel any translation contract already existing, and award the work to Prall, if that is currently possible at all.

It is my sincerest wish to see you established as soon as possible not only in America but at Harvard; that is also the wish of a group of my colleagues. What is vexing is the slowness of our university authorities in all such matters. How important it is to invite you, however, is reaffirmed to these authorities more powerfully every day.

I should like to pose a question about your definition of "quasi-syntactical", pages 178–179. Within this definition it does not seem to be settled that Sg_2 is a syntactical predicate. (Of course Sg_2 must belong to language S_2 which, however, *contains* a syntax for S_1 and, as a rule, for others.) Now if Sg_2 cannot be a syntactical predicate (although of course it takes only expressions as arguments), then why cannot Sg_2 be some predicate referring to the untoward concept "true", contrary to your remarks at the end of p. 179?

On the other hand, it is assumed, Sg_2 must be a syntactical predicate. According to your definition of "syntactal" this means that Sg_2 is located within a logical language, and, hence (right?), that every full sentence of Sg_2 is either analytic or contradictory. However, if every such full sentence is equipollent to the corresponding full sentence of Sg_1, then each full sentence of Sg_1 must likewise be either analytic or contradictory. On these assumptions, however, we obtain an unwelcome result, that a predicate can be thus quasi-syntactical only if each of its full sentences is either analytic or contradictory.

Please show me where my misunderstanding lies.

[I notice now, that above I have written "predicate" instead of "sentential framework". The same should hold both ways, if it holds at all.]

Concerning p. 116, I have a smaller question to pose. You write "In order to determine the truth value of an implication, the truth values of both components must be determined." Against this I should like to point out that at best we may stop with determining only one component, namely when the first component to be determined is the first (or second) component and is determined as false (or as true respectively). Moreover it seems to me that at best we can dispense with the determination of the truth value of any component at all, and determine the truth value of the whole simply through a general logically derived relation.

Naturally, I am in complete agreement with the ideas of your book; it should be emphasized that the above are only a pair of technical side issues.

The printing of my book has taken an enormous length of time. Last week it finally appeared. A complimentary copy will be sent to you by the press.

Separately I am sending you several offprints.

I hope that your sojourn in England was agreeable. Best wishes to you both, also from Naomi.

Yours
W. V. Quine

[16. CARNAP TO QUINE   NO DATE (COVER LETTER
TO 17)]

Prof. Dr. Rudolf Carnap
    Prag XVII
N. Motol, Pod Homolkou

Dear Dr. Quine,

I wish to say you my best thanks for your letter of Nov. 24 and the cable, and also for your letter of June 29, to which I did not answer. I am very grateful for your kind and good help, as well in the terminological questions as now in the problem of the translator of my book. And I thank you most cordially for your book. First I made a run through it and found many interesting features, and now in the last days I studied it in detail (as a Christmas pleasure) and enjoyed much the good structure of your system with very fine new devices and simultaneously the clarity of your explanations. My remarks to the book I am writing separately.

I am very glad that you gave three lectures about my "Syntax" and other things, and that you had an interested audience.

I was very surprised by your cable (please give my thanks also to Mrs. Quine, Mr. Chambers and Dr. Skinner) and by your letter about the proposal of professor Prall. I should be very glad if that proposal would be realised. Unfortunately the decision is not mine but Ogden's; because he made the agreement with the translator and I do not even know on what lines. I wrote him twice, with long quotations from your letter, and I strongly recommended the proposal. Ogden answered but postponed the decision till after Christmas. He wrote that Countess Zeppelin had sent to me some time ago the first part of the translation. I must confess, I am in doubt whether that is true; at least I did not get anything so far. Ogden writes Dec. 20: "I was hoping to see the Countess Zeppelin today, but am giving her till after Christmas before making a decision. Her last letter said that the "Logical Syntax" would be complete in less than a month. Even if she is unable to do it by then, there is much to be said against an American if the book is to have an English public—in addition to the loss of time at so great a distance." That is of course nonsense, because even for the English public an Harvard professor will be more attractive than C. Z. So it seems to me that Ogden gives pretexts instead of his real reasons which I don't know and which seem to be against the project. On Dec. 22 Ogden writes that he did not yet succeed to meet C. Z., but he had a telegramm from her saying that the translation will be complete by January 31. Now I wrote him again, but I am afraid that nevertheless his decision will be in the negative. I should regret that very much especially in consideration of my future projects. In any case say please already now to prof. Prall my most cordial thanks; there is still a chance however little. As soon as I shall know Ogden's decision I shall write you.

I am very grateful to you that you wrote a review of my book. I suppose it was the first written, because the book appeared not before July and most of reviewers take several months (sometimes even years) for writing the review.

To *your questions* about "Syntax":

1. *Definition of 'quasi-syntactical"*, p. 178–179. You are right, an addition is here necessary. But it is sufficient to replace "$\grave{S}\grave{g}_2{}^n$" (the accent ` marks Gothic letters) on p. 178, last line, by "ein $\grave{S}\grave{g}_1{}^n \grave{S}\grave{g}_2$". Then $\grave{S}\grave{g}_2$ belongs to the logical sub-language S_2' of S_2 and is a syntactical $\grave{S}\grave{g}$, because S_2' is a syntactical language for S_1 and $\dot{Q}_1[\dot{A}_1]$ etc. are suitable arguments for $\grave{S}\grave{g}_2$. — It is not possible to define a *logical* $\grave{S}\grave{g}_2$ in such a way that for every $\grave{S}_1$ of S_1 $\grave{S}\grave{g}_2(\dot{Q}_1[\grave{S}_1])$ has the sense of "$\grave{S}_1$ is true"; because in this case, if we take a synthetic $\grave{S}_1$, $\grave{S}_1$ must be equipollent with $\grave{S}\grave{g}_2(\dot{Q}_1[\grave{S}_1])$ which is a logical and hence a not-synthetic sentence, and that is impossible. — Not every full sentence of $\grave{S}\grave{g}_2$ is L-determinate, but only every f. s. having logical arguments. If we add a *descriptive* description of an expression (e.g. "the expression written at that and that place") as an argument to $\grave{S}\grave{g}_2$, then the full sentence will in general be synthetic. Thus e.g. the quasi-syntactical sentences 1a (p. 215) and 12a (p. 217) are synthetic. But the qu.-synt. predicate "treats of" ("handelt von"), used in these sentences, is a logical one, because a full sent. of this predicate with logical arguments (logical descriptions of expressions) is L-determinate.

2. (p. 116). You are right, the *truth value of an implication sentence* can often be found in other way. But in the special case concerned here we cannot (according to the meaning of the objection which I reject however) use a general sentence, because the objection is based on the (erroneous) opinion that a general sentence has to be tested by testing the single instances. — Sometimes it is indeed sufficient to find the truth-value of one of the two parts, but not in this case, provided we do not make use of the definition of ‚P_3''.

Many thanks also for your *offprints*, which you kindly sent me. I had some doubt in respect to some points in your "Ontological Remarks", but perhaps you yourself would formulate it today in a somewhat different way. Especially interesting is your report about Whiteheads new approach (but hard to understand because of its shortness); is the propositional calculus of his new system intensional like that of Lewis?

The four weeks which we spent together in *London* were a very interesting and stimulating time. I was very glad to make the acquaintaince of Stebbing, Ogden, Richards, Woodger and others. The three lectures which I delivered at the University are now in print; you will soon have the little book. Professor Stebbing seemed very satisfied with the lectures and their effect upon the audience, and so I think that it may be a help for America also.

The terminological remarks in your former letter have been very valuable for me. I accepted your suggestions in the terminological list for the translator (if it will be Prof. Prall I will send it to him), and I used them already, as you will see, for the London lectures.

I sent you recently an offprint "Antinomien" and some time ago a little pamphlet "Wissenschaftslogik" which is merely a popular explanation of some ideas of the last chapter in "Syntax". I shall send you some older offprints about physicalism for you or others interested in these problems.

Prof. Charles W. *Morris* of the University of Chicago was here in August for some weeks. We spoke often together; he is very interested in constructing bridges between Pragmatism and the view of the Vienna Circle which he considers complementary doctrines. He seems to have the serious intention to help me to come to America.

Through the help of the American Institute at Prague I am in connection with the Institute of International Education, New York, asking them to organize a lecture tour through the U. S. beginning in October 1935. Perhaps that will be a suitable way for coming in personal connection with some universities. But it would be a stretching enterprise, I suppose. And I hope to get in some way or other an invitation for some months at one place; of course I should prefer that to a tour of permanent travelling.

If it will not be too much loss of time, could you perhaps send back the enclosed copy with corrections? It suffices of course to correct the serious grammatical mistakes (not expressions which are merely unsuitable). Please send me copies of your German letters (also of the last), if you think corrections useful.

Thanks for your kind Christmas greeting. My wife and I, we send you and Naomi our best greetings and wishes for the New Year. May your work go on successfully as it started so promising; and let us hope to meet again, perhaps in the now beginning year.

Sincerely yours,
R. Carnap

[17. CARNAP TO QUINE   VARIOUSLY DATED, PROBABLY 1934-12-28]

(enclosure in 16)

Prof. Dr. Rudolf Carnap
    Prag XVII
N. Motol, Pod Homolkou

Remarks about Quine's Logistic.

I find your book in the whole excellent. Your system is an essential improvement of the usual system-form, and your explanations are clear and exact. I have the intention to write a re- | a.
view of the book for "Erkenntnis". It was for me a great plea- | b.
sure to read it.

I regret that we cannot discuss some points verbally. So I shall write some remarks.

1. I should find it suitable if you had given explicitly *formation rules*, i.e. definitions of "sentence", "n-ad expression" (esp. "class expr." and "sequence expr.") and others (see 2, 3c), including the expressions containing defined symbols.

2. You have a much higher degree of exactness than P. M. ⟨*Principia Mathematica*, by Whitehead and Russell⟩, and there remain now only very few demands for accomplishing exactness. So e.g. it was a lack of exactness in P. M., that no *formation rules for definitions* are given but only a practice. It will be good if you will supply that for your system. Because a reader, seeing your

c. | practice, could perhaps think that it were allowed to introduce the abbreviation "A" for an expression like "V,x" (or "O,α" or others), which of course would lead to contradictions.

3. *Substitution*, p.42. a) It seems to me very good, that you demand in your explanation of substitution the rewriting of certain variables. That is better than my procedure (prohibiting subst. in such cases and thereby compelling indirectly the rewrit-

d. | ing before subst.)

b) I should prefer to say instead of "written in lieu of" (p.42): "written in lieu of every free". Then you may leave out "free" in the rule; and the convention at the end of p.44 (containing the not quite exact expression "construed as cases") will be unnecessary.

c) It seems to me necessary to restrict in your rule of substitution the range of expressions allowed for substitution. You restrict it only by the condition that the result must be significant (i.e. must be a sentence). But that condition is not sufficient. E.g. your rule allows to infer (p. 86) $4 \cdot 1 \ (x / y \ . \supset . \sim (z = z))$ which gives the obviously false result "V,y.$\supset$.$\sim$(z = z)".

4. p. 51. I think we cannot treat parentheses by extra-formal

e. | conventions, but we must give explicit rules for them (as you do in fact). There is a fundamental difference between the use of

f. | parentheses and the use of the different sortes of variables in

g. | your system. The latter is in fact unessential (as you say), but not the former, because you cannot leave out the par. Therefore I should prefer to call the parentheses primitive symbols and to take notice of them in the formation rules (demanded above), as you did already in your informal explanations.

5. Your device of discarding *descriptions* and keeping only "α ⟨x" defined as a sum of classes is very fine.

6. Likewise admirable is your treatment of *operators*, using "x̂" as sole operator, replacing all other sortes by combinations of "x̂" with class expressions. I think this is an essential improve-

h. | ment. Just now I got a paper from Ajdukiewicz containing the question whether such a replacement will be possible. Now I

i. ' have written him that you solved this problem already. I recom-

j. mended your book and suggested him to send you an offprint of his paper.

7. It is a great advantage of your *hierarchy of types* that it in-

cludes also sentences. Hereby the desire may arise to find a way
of including also some other symbols which now have no type | k.
(see 8.).

8. You discarded operator symbols and *replaced them by class
symbols*. That is a very good simplification of the system. Perhaps we may go one step or some steps further in this direction
and replace some further symbols, now being without type, by | l.
class symbols.

a) There are some symbols which are now already predicates
(in the wide sense of this word in "General Syntax") but are not | m.
class symbols in your system and have no type; these are the
symbols of implication, identity, equivalence, denial and conjunction. We can easily take them as class symbols, writing e.g.
"⊃,p,q", "~,p" and so on. Then the dots are discarded which
in your system are primitive symbols (and ought to be enumerated among those).

b) All defined symbols, with exception of class symbols and
those just mentioned, are functors. If we keep "⁽" (being the | n.
fundamental and indispensable functor) we can replace all others by class symbols. This is possible because all definienda of
those symbols are now already class expressions. | o.

Instead of: we may write:

$\exists x$ $\exists^{(}x$

$\alpha \supset \beta$ $\supset^{(}(\alpha,\beta)$ or: imp $^{(}(\alpha,\beta)$

$\bar{\alpha}$ $-^{(}\alpha$ "   neg $^{(}\alpha$

$\alpha \cap \beta$ $\cap^{(}(\alpha,\beta)$ "   pr $^{(}(\alpha,\beta)$

$\alpha^{(}{}^{(}\beta$ distr $^{(}(\alpha,\beta)$

α_β relpr $^{(}(\alpha,\beta)$

$\alpha \uparrow \beta$ per $^{(}(\alpha,\beta)$

α conv $^{(}\alpha$

$\vec{\alpha}$ coll $^{(}\alpha$

[or:$\vec{\alpha}^{(}x$ coll $^{(}(\alpha,x)$?]

Then all defined symbols with sole exception of "⁽" will be class
symbols. In my view this will be an advantage, because they belong then to the system of types, and we have variables for them.

c) I should prefer to replace the primitive symbols "[]" also
by a class symbol. (The symbolised notion has in my feeling too | p.
much weight for being symbolised by punctuation symbols like

brackets; but that is of course only a subjective feeling.) There

q. | are some possible ways:

A) We may write "cong $^\iota\alpha$" instead of "$[\alpha]$". And then:

A$_1$) either we take "$^\iota$(" as a new primitive symbol;

A$_2$) or we take first "cong (" as *one* symbol (without type);

r. | we define later on "(" and show that "cong (" can now be taken as a combination of that "(" and a class symbol "cong".

B) (Perhaps preferable to A). We take "$\subset$" as prim. class symbol (writing "$\subset,\alpha,\beta$" instead of Russell's "$\alpha\subset\beta$"). Then we may

s. | define, if desired, "cong $^\iota\alpha$" by "$\hat\beta(\subset,\alpha,\beta)$", or use only the latter (in order to avoid "(" at this stage).

d) I should prefer to take "(" as primitive symbol. [Do you

t. | believe that it will be possible to define then "cong" (or "$\subset$")? If not, I should take both "(" and "$\subset$" as pr.s.] If we take "(" as pr.s., the system will contain only these 3 kinds of symbols:

1) punctuation signs: comma, inverted comma, parentheses

y. | "()",

2) variables,

3) class constants.

u. | *All defined symbols are class constants;* hence will come a great simplification for the formation rules for definitions (see above 2).

And the discarding of all functors, excepted "(", will simplify the syntactical definition for "class expression" (and thereby that for

v. | "sentence"), because every class expression has the form "α" or "$\hat{x}(\ldots)$" or "$\alpha^\iota\ldots$". The system of types includes every symbol

w. | with exception of the punctuation signs.

x. | 9. p. 5. We due the remark about the assertion sign to Witt-

z. | genstein, I believe.

10. p. 144, line 25. "$\hat{y}(\alpha,y,x)$".

R. C.

⟨Concerning the date of this item, there are several copies even among Carnap's papers. One is dated "28.12.34" (Dec. 28, 1934) apparently in Carnap's hand. Internal evidence of the letter somewhat confirms this. There are, however, other copies dated "18 Dec. 1934" among which is one bearing Quine's grammatical and stylistic corrections on Carnap's text. This date may be in error.⟩

[QUINE'S GRAMMATICAL AND STYLISTIC CORRECTIONS:]

a. 'have the' crossed out, and 'intention' changed to 'intend' ⟨I intend to write . . .⟩.

b. 'for me' moved after 'pleasure' ⟨It was a great pleasure for me to read it.⟩. Also marked: 'better, omit 'for me' entirely'.

c. 'were allowed' changed to 'would be allowable'.

d. 'indirectly' moved back before 'compelling' ⟨That is better than my procedure (prohibiting subst. in such cases and thereby indirectly compelling the rewriting before subst.)⟩. Carnap had started to type 'indirectly' in that place but had crossed it out. Quine writes in the margin: 'better the first time!'.

e. Quine changes this sentence to read: 'I do not think we can treat parentheses by extra-formal conventions; I think rather that we must give explicit rules for them (as you do in fact).' Quine also writes in the margin: 'My correction here looks illogical, but it is the English idiom.'

f. 'sortes' changed to 'sorts'.

g. 'unessential' changed to 'inessential'.

h. 'got' changed to 'received' and 'will' changed to 'would' ⟨Just now I received a paper from Ajdukiewicz containing the question whether such a replacement would be possible.⟩.

i. 'have' inserted before 'solved' ⟨Now I have written him that you have solved this problem already.⟩.

j. 'to' inserted after suggested, and 'to' changed to 'that he' ⟨I recommended your book and suggested to him that he send you an offprint of his paper.⟩.

k. 's' in 'inclusing' is changed to 'd' ⟨Hereby the desire may arise to find a way of including also some other symbols which now have no type (see 8.).⟩.

l. 'being' crossed out ⟨. . . , now without type, . . .⟩.

m. 'wide' changed to 'broad' ⟨. . . in the broad sense . . .⟩.

n. 'being' changed to 'which is' ⟨If we keep "(" (which is the fundamental and indispensable functor) . . .⟩.

o. 'are now already' changed to 'have become' ⟨This is possible because all definienda of those symbols have become class expressions.⟩.

p. 'in my feeling' changed to 'to my way of feeling' ⟨The symbolized notion has, to my way of feeling, too much weight . . .⟩.

q. 'There' changed to 'Here'.

r. 'first' inverted with ' "cong (" ' and 'we define' inverted with 'later on' ⟨or we take "cong (" first as *one* symbol (without type); later on we define "(" and show . . .⟩.

s. 'a' inserted before 'prim.', and ', if desired,' inverted with ' "cong (" ', and 'by' changed to 'as' ⟨Then we may define "cong (", if desired, as "β̂(⊂,α,β)", . . . ⟩.

t. 'a' inserted before 'primitive' and 'be possible to define' inverted with 'then' ⟨ . . . take "(" as a primitive symbol. Do you believe that it will then be possible to define "cong" (or "⊂")?⟩.

u. 'there' inserted after 'hence', 'come' changed to 'result', and 'for' changed to 'of' ⟨. . . hence there will result a great simplification of the formation rules for definitions (see above 2).⟩.

v. 'for' changed to 'of' twice ⟨. . . will simplify the syntactical definition of "class expression" (and thereby that of "sentence"), because . . .⟩.

w. 'the' inserted before 'exception' ⟨. . . every symbol with the exception of . . .⟩.

x. 'due' changed to 'owe' ⟨We owe the remark . . .⟩.

y. On Carnap's copies of this item (17) he added 'circumflex,' at the end of d)1). On one of his copies he wrote (in shorthand) in the margin here: 'Added in the next letter! Written 14.2.35' (i.e., Feb. 14, 1935). That next letter is in fact dated March 14, 1935. Quine also corrected his copy of item 17 both here and at the point marked by marginal note z.

z. Carnap and Quine corrected their copies at this point either by inserting 'p. 94' after 'Wittgenstein' or (on one of Carnap's copies) by writing in German shorthand 'Wittgenstein p. 94'.

[18.   CARNAP TO QUINE   1935-3-14]

Prof. Dr. Rudolf Carnap
   Prag XVII   March 14, 1935.
Pod Homolkou 146

Dear Quine,

Ogden delayed—as he always does—the decision concerning the translator of "Syntax", and writes now that the translation is almost completely ready. So it seems that he had never the intention to change the translator. I regret that very much, but it is a matter of his decision only and I can do nothing but agree.

In the meantime I wrote a review of your fine book. But the 2 next issues of "Erkenntnis" will only contain a report of the Prague-Conference and no reviews. Thus the review will appear in Nr. 3. I got a review-copy from the publisher. As I have already your complimentary copy, I put the second copy to your disposal (I know from my own experience that one has never too much free copies). Please write me whether I am to send it to you or to any other address. I think that among European logicians the following would be most interested: Gödel, Tarski, Hempel, Jörgensen, Lukasiewicz, Lesniewski, Scholz.

To my *"Remarks"* (of Dec. 1934) I have to add
p. 4, d. 1: "circumflex";
p. 4, No. 9: "Wittg. p. 94".

Short time ago I had a letter from President of the Harvard University, inviting me to take part in the Symposia of the Tercentenary in September 1936 and to deliver then a short lecture. You can imagine how glad I am about this first American invitation. They pay so well, that it will cover the travel-expenses for Ina and me. Now the bridge over the big water is once constructed, I have good hope that further steps may follow. I suppose that the papers which you read did a good deal in leading the attention of the professors and boards to my work. I am very grateful for your good help!

I should be very glad if perhaps there might be an opportunity of explaining my thoughts in some circles of Harvard more in details than it is possible in a single lecture of about half an hour's length; but that is no urgent question, perhaps later on it will clear itself.

Just one day before the Harvard letter I had a letter from the Institute of International Education, New York, which I had asked for organizing a lecture-tour. They write that under the present economical conditions a tour of lectures specially in Philosophy has not sufficient chances. Later on I shall write to the Institute about the Harvard invitation, and I suppose that the announcement of this invitation will have good effect upon other institutions and universities.

How did you spend all the time? We have been in the mountains for skiing at Christmas and now in February between the terms. And all the other time I am busy with lectures and small papers and all the little things which cost so much time but are unavoidable. And we both are well and happy.

With warmest regards to Mrs. Quine and to you from us both,

> very sincerely yours,
> R. Carnap

[19.   QUINE TO CARNAP   1935-3-31]

> 62 Garden Street
> Cambridge, Mass.
> March 31, 1935

Dear Mr. Carnap,

What a delight to plan definitely on seeing you both in America next year! This has been our fondest wish for two years, and we are extremely happy and excited about finally seeing it realized. I wish it were happening this September, but that it is definitely fixed in the not distant future is splendid news.

It is, I should think, certain that in thus coming to America you will come to stay. There will unquestionably be offers. My chief hope, of course, is that you will stay at Harvard, so that the four of us can be neighbors: for it seems likely that I shall be continuing here.

My three-year research fellowship expires in June 1936, but I am assured (unofficially, at this early date) of a teaching position at Harvard afterward. Hence, barring an offer of *far* better pay elsewhere, we shall be living in Cambridge when you come. We are looking forward keenly to meeting your boat and taking you home with us. You must be our guests!

Professor L. J. Henderson, distinguished as a biochemist but now interested chiefly in Pareto, was the direct force behind your invitation to the tercentenary. He is one of the most influential figures behind the Harvard administration. I see him regularly at the weekly dinners of the Society of Fellows, and on those occasions I interested him in your work. He readily became interested, because his own attitude is extremely antimetaphysical and skeptical. (You, however, would find his state of mind unsatisfactorily confused and naïve.) As a result he bought and read (in part) your *Logische Syntax* when it appeared; and it was he (and, independently, or Rafael Demos) who suggested to the philosophy department last fall that I be asked to give some lectures on your doctrines. The particular set of tercentenary lectures in which yours will occur was a subsequent idea of his own, and a couple of months ago he consulted me on the notion of including you.

Another ally, valuable but somewhat less powerful than Henderson, is Charles P. Curtis, dilettante and prominent Boston lawyer, who is a trustee of Harvard. He is a follower of Henderson's in the study of Pareto, and co-author with Homans in a recent popular book *Introduction to Pareto*. Like Henderson he is a sponsor of the Society of Fellows, so that I see him each week. Like Henderson he became interested in your work and read the not too technical portions of the *Logische Syntax*. He attended my lectures and is at present studying over the manuscript of them, together with your new *Philosophy and Logical Syntax*. He is very enthusiastic; and he has a vote and a persuasive voice in university policy. He, like Henderson, will be a strong factor in brightening the future.

Many thanks for the copy of your *Philosophy and Logical Syntax*, a very fine little book, very well written, and constituting an excellent simplified synopsis of your doctrine. The need of such a book has been made known to me again and again since my lectures on your work: for laymen and semi-laymen have been asking to reread the manuscript of my lectures, and urging me to bring out a little non-technical book in English, some sort of "Introduction to Carnap," serving the same purpose. Your *Philosophy and Logical Syntax* is therefore good news to many.

Thanks also for the offprint of your valuable article "Die Antinomien etc." I am also very glad to have the duplicate stock of *Erkenntnis* papers; I am reserving them for as judicious distribution as possible, hoping to place them only where they will be studied and used most seriously. Incidentally I was happy to be able to appropriate a copy of the "Protokollsätze" paper for myself for I had lacked that paper, and am anxious to keep my Carnap library as complete as possible.

Thanks, fourthly, for your painstaking and valuable commentary on my book. I shall follow your numbering in commenting on the comments.

1)2) It would surely have been well to present a rigorous development of the formative rules. But the policy which, motivated by considerations of expository simplicity, I deliberately adopted in the book, was to present as little in the way of rigorous (and laborious) *metamathematical* analysis as was compatible with moderately unconfused expression of the *logical* system. Such *e.g.* was my reason for using the intuitive blanks "———", "---", ". . ." etc. instead of introducing expression-variables. I even went so far as to suppress syntactic expressions in favor of quoted logical expressions in many cases where I knew it to be strictly (if trivially) *incorrect* from a subtly syntactical point of view. On the same score, like Lewis and *Principia*, I left the notion of *significance* at an unanalyzed level of this sort; "expressions constructible in terms of the primitive signs, by the tacit but obvious rules of combination, restricted however by the conditions imposed by the theory of types"; and I did not deliver myself explicitly even to the above extent. My attitude was that any reader *already* syntactically oriented could supply the wanted rigor by a routine application of the general methods published by you, and, in a less thoroughgoing way, by Gödel, Tarski, etc.; and as for the not yet syntactically oriented reader, I was not concerned in this book with orienting him, nor did I want to exclude him by *presupposing* his orientation. But whether or not this elliptical procedure was ill-advised, my *chief* mistake was in not including the above remarks in the introduction!

3b) I do not see how this will make the convention on p. 44 unnecessary, for that convention is required by the rule of *subsumption* rather than substitution.

3c) Quite right! This of course is tied up with my above remarks on 1)2).

4) Since in my book I talk in a deliberatively quasi-syntactic idiom [because of what I have said concerning 1)2)], and thus discuss for the most part *elements* and *operations* rather than primitive *symbols*, I should prefer this third method of dealing with parentheses: Let the parentheses be *part*-of the symbolism of the primitive and defined operations—*e.g.* let the symbolism of ordination and abstraction be respectively "(. . . , . . .)" and ".ˆ.(. . .)" rather than ". . . , . . ." and ".ˆ. . . .", and then let certain parentheses be dropped by explicit convention. [I used this *kind* of procedure, different in detail, in my paper in last October's *Bull. Amer. Math. Soc.*] But it is true in any case that the point of view on p. 51 is bad; an unnecessarily evil result of the attitude explained above *in re* 1)2).

8) I am very much pleased by your suggestion to eliminate operation signs as far as possible in favor of class-signs; this would be a great advance in elegance, and would greatly simplify the syntax of the system and shorten the (mainly tacit) syntactical rules. I am not sure that this would be worth the price of an extra primitive operation (classial correlation), but I should certainly favor carrying your process as far as it can be carried *without* paying that price. In any case the method could be applied to all operations defined *after* classial correlation, and definitions or primitives could be so shifted about and revised as to bring in classial correlation very early. Still, this compromise procedure would fall short of the highly desirable principle that *all* defined symbols be class constants. But in whatever way these considerations may balance, the direction (Richtung) suggested is an attractive one.

10) Thanks; I hadn't yet found that misprint. Here are some more: p.115, end of line 19, add "the"; p. 163, third from last

line, omit first "of"; p. 187, fourth from last line, for " " put " ";
p. 200, column 2, line 8, for "negates" put "negate"; ninth line
from end, for "151" put "149". Two of these mistakes I had corrected on the proofs, and the printer overlooked the corrections;
these of course are especially annoying.

A fifth object of thanks is your kindness in writing a review
of my book for *Erkenntnis,* of which I am very glad.

Three days ago I mailed you offprints of my reviews of Peirce
III and IV.

You are kind to suggest sending me your extra copy of my
book. I should like very much to have it for my own shelf, for,
strangely, I do not at present own a copy; I gave my last away
and have not yet bought another.

I suppose there is even at this late date a slight possibility of
your being given an American offer for the coming year. I like
to hope so. But otherwise, since you must be here in any case
in September 1936, can't you come in June 1936 and spend the
summer in America instead of in the Tatra or the Tyrol?
Whether or not we shall be at Harvard after September 1936
(which, however, we almost certainly shall), in any case we
shall be here that summer. We are impatient to see you.

As soon as our present lease expires (end of this August) we
plan to move out of the city, much as you have done in Prague.
We hope to move into an even less populous quarter, however,
than Novi Motol; a definitely rural region. We must of course be
within about thirty minutes' transportation of the university,
and I think that will be possible. Our reason for moving is that
we (especially I) can no longer endure the noise of radios, bark-
ing dogs and swarms of children. Hence when you come you
will find us much more pleasantly and comfortably situated
than in our present crowded city flat. There will be room, isolation and fresh air, and we will be able to take walks over the
New England countryside at a moment's notice without any preliminary transportation. For convenience in getting to the university an automobile will be desirable; we shall probably have one
by the time you come, and it will enable us all to make pleasant
little trips together.

You will find a third Quine when you come. Naomi expects a
baby five months from now.

With heartiest regards to both, also from Naomi, and with an 'auf Widersehen' this time in a *definiten Sprache*,

Cordially yours,

P.S.—In speaking of your work, in English, I always say "formative rule" and "transformative rule", which strikes the English ear as more elegant than "formation rule" and "transformation rule". Also I have tended of late to say "formal (or material) *idiom*"; the latter word emphasizes that it is a linguistic concept. However, "mode" is not unsatisfactory—indeed, I approved "mode" in an earlier letter.

I see there are further points I have failed to touch, so I shall continue this postscript.

It is clear that the very slight change which you suggest for the last line of p. 178 of your *Syntax* completely surmounts the difficulty I had raised.

Whitehead's new scheme, though still fragmentary, has now been published in a fuller form than I had been able to give it in my short synopsis; namely, see Whitehead's article in *Mind* XLIII (NS) pp. 281–297. It is full of misprints, for Whitehead was too ill to read proofs when they reached them; but you will be able to decipher the errors—*e.g.* "Ǝ" should be inverted iota at top of p. 287; the sign of logical addition should be replaced by the sign of inclusion at various points on p. 286.

Although Whitehead's scheme depends (as does my *Logistic*) upon construing propositional *identity* in a much stronger way than as mere sameness of truth-value, still (as in my system) there is no trace of anything approaching Lewis' modality functions. Perhaps his notion of propositional identity would (unlike mine) turn out to approach Lewis' "strict equivalence" if Whitehead were to enlarge upon the topic; but this is purely speculative, since neither postulates nor discussion are as yet forthcoming to determine this aspect. Such verbal questions as I have put to Whitehead on the subject have led only into metaphysical mazes; yet he will no doubt purge the finished product of any considerable metaphysical ingredients, as he has hitherto done in his technical logical writings.

I am glad of your connection with Morris of Chicago—his efforts will add to the chances of your being brought to America a year early. As to the year *after* next, of course, I am thoroughly confident that you will be here to stay.

Prall and I were of course both disappointed that he could not translate the *Syntax,* but I gave him to understand fully that the decision was Ogden's and counter to your wishes and protests.

I enclose corrected copies of your recent letters. Your English is becoming very good. Practically all the corrections are of idiom rather than grammar, and the idiom itself is vastly improved.

Following your kind suggestion I also enclose a copy of my last letter for correction of the German.

With further greetings,

[20. CARNAP TO QUINE   1935-4-25]

Brussels, April 25, 1935.

Dear Quine,

my best thanks for your very kind letter with its interesting and satisfying contents. As soon as I shall be back in Prague, I will answer you (I suppose, in the first days of May). Your optimistic views filled our hearts with optimism too. We are here for some days, visiting Hempel and discussing logistic and probability.

With best regards from 2:2

Cordially yours
R. Carnap

[21. CARNAP TO QUINE   1935-5-5]

Prof. Dr. Rudolf Carnap
     Prag XVII   May, 5, 1935.
Pod Homolkou 146

Dear Q u i n e ,

Your letter of March 31 was very satisfying for me, as well by your optimism concerning my further chances in USA as by your great personal kindness.

We too had already considered the plan of coming some time

before August 1936 to the US in order to spend the summer there, to see friends and to learn English. Your very kind proposal gives us a strong stimulus in this direction.

I hope with you that the Harvard invitation will have a strong effect on other American universities, and I suppose, that this effect will be strengthened by the fact that, according to the President's letter, the Honorary Doctorate of Science will be conferred upon me. Do I owe this also to Prof. Henderson?

You have rendered an extremely effective help by interesting Prof.Henderson and Mr.Curtis on my work. Would you, please, give me their addresses and those of other people which you would consider to be worth for sending separata? It would be very useful for me, if you gave me kind suggestions as to which separata would be of interest for each of them. You may simply note the numbers, according to the following list:

*(5.   Physikalische Begriffsbildung.)

*(7.   Der Logische Aufbau der Welt.)

*(8.   Scheinprobleme.)

*(9.   Abriss der Logistik.)

*13   F. L'Ancienne et la Nouvelle Logique. (Translation of Erkenntnis I, p.12.

*19   F. La Science et la Metaphysique. (Translation of Erkenntnis II, p.219). (I have no more offprints of the German originals 13 and 19.)

*20   E. *Unity of Science.*

21.   Psychologie in physikalischer Sprache. (Erkenntnis)

22.   Erwiderung auf Zilsel und Dunker.   ("   )

23.   Protokollsätze.   ("   )

26.   *On the Character of Philos.Problems.* (In: Phil.of Science)

*28.   Logische Syntax der Sprache

*31.   *Philosophy and Logical Syntax.*

34.   Formalwissenschaft und Realwissenschaft. (Just appeared in "Erkenntnis"; offprint has been sent to you.)

35.   Les Concepts Psychologiques et les Concepts Physiques. (Is to appear soon in the French Periodical "Synthèse").

*Appeared not in periodicals, but as independent issues. Please note also, if somebody has already something of the list (bought, or as subscriber of the journal, or offprint given by you.) I would like to keep my card-index complete; everybody who has offprints of mine, is contained in it.

Please write me whether you yourself have all of the list. Perhaps not (5) and (8) (if my card-index is right); if so, I shall send them. And would you like to have (13 F) and (19F) in French?

In the next time you will receive an offprint of a paper (33) "Ueber ein Gültigkeitskriterium. . . .". The contents of this paper and the previous one (32) "Antinomien" will be contained in the English translation of "Syntax". Therefore in general I do not send offprints of these papers to American readers, with few exceptions.

May I perhaps read a copy of the manuscript of your lectures?

The English translation of "Syntax" is said to be nearly complete. Ogden sent me Ch.I and II of it. I had to spend much work in revising and correcting them; I found a lot of mistakes, misunderstandings and unsuitable expressions. Therefore I suggested Ogden once more most urgently to take another translator. But he answered that this were impossible; he went through all my corrections and asserts that there were only 5 (!) real mistakes. He promises that the rest will be examined very carefully before it comes to me. Thus I hope that the translation after all will not be too bad. You may imagine that after these experiences I am still more angry about that Ogden did not accept the proposal of Prall in January.

Concerning my remarks on your book. 1)2). You may be right in making the syntactic explanations of your system as simple as possible, considering the class of supposed readers. Your use of the intuitive blanks "---", ". . ." etc. instead of special syntactical symbols seems to me very suitable for the purpose. Nevertheless I think it would be desirable or even necessary to state formation rules; that may be done in a simple form, using your blanks, e.g.: "Every class expression has one of the following forms: 1.) variable in class-position, 2.) "x̂(. . .)" where ". . ." has sentencial form, 3.) ". . .". And analogously for "sentence". Then it will be easy to formulate the rule of substitution so as to avoid the contradiction 3c.

3b). I am not quite sure whether or not my considerations are right, but still the following seems to me to be the case:

A) The addition of "every free" in the definition of "substitution" p.142 is necessary; for we do not wish to call the transformation of

$$(1) \qquad \ldots \alpha \ldots \hat{\alpha}(\text{-- } \alpha \text{ --})$$

into
$$(2a) \qquad \ldots V \ldots \hat{\alpha}(\text{--V--})$$

or into
$$(2b) \qquad \ldots V \ldots \hat{V}(\text{--V--})$$

a substitution.

B) When the mentioned addition is made, the word "free" may be left out in the rule of substitution.

C) If that addition is made and the convention at the end of p.44 is left out, a theorem of the form

$$(3) \; [\alpha], \; \hat{x}(\text{--}\hat{x}(. \; . \; .)\text{--})$$

does not seem to me to be dangerously ambiguous. Or do you think, it is so? Could you perhaps give me an example of a contradiction resulting from it? or a proof of a theorem which we should not wish to be demonstrable?

My best thanks for your reviews of Pierce III and IV.

Simultaneously I send you your book.

I proposed the terms "formative rules" and "transformative r." to the translator already in a letter of June 1934; but she did not accept them. As you find them preferable, I too shall use them in the future.

I enclose your German letter with my corrections. If you wish to exercise your German I am of course always ready for correcting German letters; it does not take more than a minute.

We are glad that in the next year we shall find you as a triad. We send Naomi our most hearty wishes for her hard examination in August; that is more than writing logic. And we are glad too that you will soon be living on the countryside and have it more quiet. That will be good for health and work.

With cordial greetings 2→2,

Yours

R. Carnap

Prof. Dr. Rudolf Carnap
  Prag XVII   May 31, 1935.
Pod Homolkou 146

Dear Quine,

Now I have a new invitation from Harvard for the Summer
School 1936. I need not tell you that I am very happy about it.
Many thanks for this fine effect of your activity. I am enclosing a
copy of the inviting letter. May I ask you some questions about
it?

1. I understand that each of the two courses goes through
the whole time of 6 weeks and thus contains 30 meetings. Am I
right in this?

2. The letter says *"meetings"*, not "lectures". Is there a difference? Does the word "meeting" imply the inclusion of discussions? or something else?

3a. As to the *topics,* do you suppose that the demand for the
second course to be about "history of philosophy, ethics, aesthetics, etc." (what may be indicated by this "etc."?) is meant
strictly? As I am not inclined to lecture about ethics or aesthetics, I should in this case deliver a historical course, perhaps
about the development of modern scientific philosophy in Europe, or such like. But of course I shall prefer systematic topics
to historical ones. In my answer I have said that I shall later on
make proposals concerning the topics. Do you think I could propose something like "Introduction to Philosophy" (or ". . . Exact
Philosophy" or ". . . Scientific Phil.")? I should be ready to deliver such a course in a rather general, not too technical way,
not supposing any preliminary knowledge of logic; thus such a
course would fulfil the demand of being "relatively elementary".
But might it be accepted as belonging to "history etc."?

3b. Concerning the *first course,* belonging to my own field, as
the letter says, there are of course no difficulties. But at any rate
your suggestions will be very valuable for me. I suppose that
this course may have a somewhat more technical character. Can
I presuppose here some knowledge of elementary logistic or
would that restrict too much the number of possible hearers? If I

can do so, I could perhaps choose "Logical Syntax of Language". I should of course give a short survey of the elements
of logistic in the first lectures; but for people who never before
had heard of logistic, that would not suffice. If necessary, I
could announce "Logic and Logical Syntax"; in this case I
should explain a logistical language in detail and simultaneously
construct and explain its syntax. — Or would you think that a
subject like "The Logical Foundations of Mathematics" would
find more interest? But such lectures would of course not contain much of my own.

Usually the summer term here ends about (or a little before)
the middle of June. Thus in 1936 we should have to go then
immediately to America. I shall consider the possibility of taking
my leave here somewhat earlier in order to have in the U.S.
some time for learning English, becoming acquainted with people, for leisure etc., before the courses go on.

In the meantime my letter of May 5 will have reached you.

> Very cordially yours,
> R. Carnap

Warm regards from Ina to Naomi.

[23.   RALPH BARTON PERRY TO CARNAP   1935-5-13
         (ENCLOSURE IN 22)]

HARVARD UNIVERSITY
DIVISION OF PHILOSOPHY AND PSYCHOLOGY

Department of Philosophy   Emerson Hall
                                                 Cambridge, Mass.
                                                 May 13, 1935.

My dear Professor Carnap:

My colleagues and I are delighted to learn of your acceptance
of the invitation to attend the Tercentenary Celebration here in
the autumn of 1936. I am now writing to ask whether you would
be willing to offer two courses in the Harvard Summer School of
1936. The stipend would be $1400, which would be designed to
cover both instruction and a part of your travelling expenses. If

this proposal is, as I hope, agreeable to you I should like to discuss with you the matter of the two courses which you would be expected to offer. There would be five meetings per week in each course, each meeting lasting for about fifty minutes. One course would, I hope, be in the philosophy of science, or whatever you would consider the proper designation of the field in which you are most interested. A second course could be offered in ethics, history of philosophy, aesthetics, etc. It would be well to consider at the same time whether one of your two courses could be of a relatively elementary nature.

The period of the Summer School is from July 6 to August 15.

We all hope very much that you will accept this invitation and in this way extend the period of your visit to Harvard.

With sincere regards,

Very truly yours,

Ralph Barton Perry
Chairman

Professor Rudolf Carnap.

[24. QUINE TO CARNAP   1935-6-19]

Kopie   52 Garden Street
Cambridge, Mass.
d. 19. Juni 1935

Lieber Herr Carnap!

Wir sind höchst erfreut, daß Sie eingeladen worden sind, Vorträge hier im Sommersemester zu halten. Betreffs Ihrer ersten Frage hebe ich ausfindig gemacht, daß die Anzahl der Klassenversammlungen im Laufe des Sommers 30 ist. Ob diese Versammlungen aus lauter Vorträgen oder aus Vorträgen und Besprechungen bestehen, scheint von dem Vorzug des Lehrers a. | abzuhangen. Ich würde erwarten, daß Ihre Kürse Besprechung b. | umfaßen würden.

Was Perry mit "etc." bedeutet, weiß ich auch nicht;

mindestens aber schafft diese Abkürzung eine bequeme | c.
Spielraum. Es wäre Ihnen und gleichfalls dem Publikum
vorzüglichst, wenn nicht nur der erste sondern auch dieser
zweite Kurs hauptsächlich aus Ihren Ideen gebildet würde. Ich
empfehle also etwas u.d.T. "wißenschaftliche Philosophie", | d.
worin Sie in elementarer und untechnischer Weise derartigen | e.
Ideen darstellen könnten, wie Sie in *Erkenntnis* u.a.O. entwickelt
haben. Das sollen Sie mindestens dem Perry vorschlagen, bevor
Sie sich mit einem rein geschichtlichen Kurs aussöhnen.

Betreffs des ersten Kurses, der gewiß Ihrem eigenen Bereich
angehören wird, glaube ich, daß Sie kaum Kenntnis der Logistik
voraussetzen dürfen, denn es wird hier fast nichts darüber
gelehrt. Also meine ich, daß ein Kurs u.d.T. "Logik und
logische Syntax" meist zu empfehlen ist. | f.

Vielen Dank für das Exemplar meines Buches, auch für die
Sonderabdrücke Ihrer Schriften 33–35, die ich mit vielem In- | g.
teresse gelesen habe. Für Henderson [Prof. Lawrence J. Henderson, Fatigue Laboratory, Soldiers Field, Boston, Mass.] und Curtis [Mr. Charles P. Curtis, Jr., 30 State Street, Boston, Mass.]
wird 35 außerordentlich wertvoll sein; 34 empfehle ich auch fur
beide. Für Henderson empfehle ich noch 13F und 19F. Ich
glaube, daß Curtis schon 19F besitzt, aber 13F gern bekommen
würde. Ich schlage auch vor, daß Sie jedem jede zukünftige
leicht verständliche Schrift senden. Wann ich Henderson und | h.
Curtis im September wiedersehen werde, werde ich ausfindig
machen, welche übrigen Schriften Sie besitzen. Inzwischen weiß | i.
ich aber, daß Curtis 28 hat, und daß weder Curtis noch Hender-
son die oben empfohlenen Schriften haben. | j.

Weiter weiß ich, daß Skinner [Dr. B. Frederic Skinner, John
Winthrop House F35, Cambridge, Mass.] mindestens 8 und 28
hat, daß Cooley [Dr. John C. Cooley, 6 Story Street, Cambridge,
Mass.] 28 hat, und mit dabei das alles als Abonnent hat, das in | k.
Erkenntnis erschienen ist, und daß Haskell [Mr. Edward F. Haskell, 5207 15th Avenue, Brooklyn, N. Y.] den Sie in Prag
kennengelernt haben, 21 von mir bekommen hat. Ich empfehle,
daß Sie an Cooley jede zukünftige und an Dennes [Prof. Will R.
Dennes, Department of Philosophy, University of Carlifornia,
Berkeley, California] jede nicht sehr technische zukünftige

Schrift senden. Bei Cooley verzichten Sie aber auf *Erkenntnis*, die er schon bekommt, und bei jedem dieser Menschen verzichten Sie natürlich auf Bücher, die eine Menge kosten. Für Cooley und Dennes empfehle ich auch 35, und für Dennes und Haskell 34. Dennes braucht 34 sehr.

Meinerseits möchte ich sehr gern die von Ihnen gütigst gebotenen Schriften 5, 8, 13F und 19F bekommen.

Mit Ihren letzten Bemerkungen über mein Buch bin ich endlich ganz einverstanden. Ursprünglich verstand ich nicht recht, was für Fehler Sie durch Ihr 3b) [Dez.1934] ausschließen wollten, und meinte, der einzige Zweck wäre, die Festzetzung auf S. 44 zu vermeiden; durch A) [Mai 1935] aber wird alles klar,

l. | und die Verbesserung 3b) wird gezeigt, bewünschenswert zu sein. Betreffs C) [Mai] haben Sie wieder recht, so scheint es mir: es erscheint nämlich, daß C3) nur indirekt mittels der *Rule of Concretion* zum Widerspruch führen könnte, und dieser Weg

m. | zum Widerspruch wird dadurch abgeschloßen, daß die Definition des Wortes '*substitution*', das in dieser *Rule of Concretion* vorkommt, der Verbesserung 3b) unterworfen wird.

o. | n. | Ich gratuliere Sie auf dem honorären Doktorat der Wißenschaft. Ich weiß, daß Curtis sich darin interessiert hat.

Meine Vorlesungen über Sie werden diesen Sommer von Dennes und einem Parr seiner Schüler in Kalifornien

p. | angewendet. Wann ich sie wiederbekommen werde, werde, ich sie sofort Ihnen schicken.

Mein guter Freund Tom Chambers, junger Chemiker und Mitglied, wie ich, der *Society of Fellows*, wird umgefähr am 17.

q. | Juli an Prag kommen. Er möchte gern Sie kennenlernen und wird Ihnen schreiben oder Sie telefonisch anrufen. Er versteht aber, daß Sie sehr wahrscheinlich weg sein werden.

r. | Morgen werde ich mit zwei Freunden auf einer zweiwochigen Reise nach Neufundland und St.-Pierre abfahren.

Naomi was sehr erfreut, den freundlichen Brief von Frau Carnap zu bekommen und wird bald antworten.

Wir sehen Ihrer Ankunft nächsten Juni mit größter Freude entgegen. Mit besten Grüßen Ihnen beiden,

Ihr

s. | W. V. Quine

[CARNAP'S CORRECTIONS OF QUINE'S GERMAN:]

a. Umlaut added to 'abzuhangen' (. . . des Lehrers
   abzuhängen.).
b. 'Kürse' is changed to 'Kurse' with footnote '2)' added,
   'Besprechung' is changed to 'Besprechungen', and 'umfaßen'
   is changed to 'umfassen' with a footnote '1)' added (. . . daß
   Ihre Kurse Besprechungen umfassen würden.). Footnotes 1)
   and 2) (and 3)) are at the end of the letter.
c. 'eine bequeme' is changed to 'einen bequemen' (. . . diese
   Abkürzung einen bequemen Spielraum.).
d. 'wißenschaftliche' is changed to 'wissenschaftliche'
   (. . . "wissenschaftliche Philosophie", . . .).
e. 'derartigen' is changed to 'derartige' (. . . Weise derartige
   Ideen . . .).
f. 'meist' is changed to 'am meisten' (. . . Syntax" am meisten
   zu empfehlen ist.).
g. 'Sonderabdrücke' is changed to 'Sonderabdrucke' (. . . für
   die Sonderabdrucke Ihrer Schriften . . .).
h. 'Wann' changed to 'Wenn' with a footnote '3' added (Wenn
   ich Henderson . . .). Footnote 3) is at the end of the letter.
i. 'Sie' changed to 'sie' (. . . Schriften sie besitzen.).
j. 'empfehlten' is changed to 'empfohlenen' (. . . die oben
   empfohlenen Schriften haben.).
k. 'das' is changed to 'was' (. . . hat, was in *Erkenntnis* . . .).
l. 'und die Verbesserung 3b) wird gezeigt, bewünschenswert
   zu sein." is changed to 'und es wird gezeigt dass die
   Verbesserung 3b), wünschenswert ist.'
m. 'abgeschloßen' is changed to 'abgeschlossen' with a footnote
   '1)' added (. . . wird dadurch abgeschlossen, daß . . .).
n. The whole sentence is changed to read: "Ich gratuliere Ihnen
   zu dem Ehrendoktorat der (Natur-(?)) Wissenschaft." A footnote '1)', is added.
o. 'darin' is changed to 'dafür' (. . . sich dafür interessiert hat.).
p. 'Wann' is changed to 'Wenn' and a footnote, '3)', is added
   (Wenn ich sie . . .).
q. 'an' is changed to 'in' and 'kommen' is changed to
   'ankommen' (. . . am 17. Juli in Prag ankommen.). Also, 'Sie

gern' is changed to 'gern Sie' (Ere möchte gern Sie
kennenlernen . . .).

r. 'einer zweiwochigen' is changed to 'eine zweiwöchige'
(. . . auf eine zweiwöchige Reise . . .).

s. At this point are Carnap's footnotes:

1) im *Druck:* (a) zwischen Vokalen: nach langem Vokal
„ß", z.B. Füße, saßen, Maße (=measures).
nach kurzem Vokal „ss" z.B. Flüsse,
hassen, Masse (=mass).

(b) am Ende der Silbe: numer „ß" (auch bei
kurzem Vokal), z.B. Haß.

beim *Schreiben* wird oft anstatt „ß" „ss" geschrieben (so tu
ich es meist)

2) in Fremdwörtern meist kein Umlaut.

3) wenn = $\begin{cases} \text{if} \\ \text{when} \end{cases}$

wann = when, nur in direkter oder indirekter *Frage.*

Translated into English these footnotes read:

1) in print: a) between vowels: after long vowels 'ß'
e.g. Füße, saßen, Maße (= measures)
after short vowels 'ss' e.g. Flüsse, hassen,
Masse (= mass).

b) at the end of the syllable: [use] „ß"
(also with the short vowels), e.g. Haß.

in writing, often instead of 'ß', 'ss' will be written (I do
this usually)

2) in foreign words usually no umlaut

3) wenn = $\begin{cases} \text{if} \\ \text{when} \end{cases}$

wann = when, only in direct or indirect questions.

[24E. QUINE TO CARNAP   1935-6-19]

52 Garden Street
Cambridge, Mass.
June 19, 1935.

Dear Mr. Carnap:

We are extremely happy that you have been invited to lecture
here during the summer semester. Regarding your first question

I have discovered that the number of class meetings over the course of the summer is 30. Whether these meetings consist of only lectures or of lecture and discussion seems to depend on the preference of the instructors. I would expect that your courses would include discussions.

What Perry means by "etc." I also do not know; at least, however, the abbreviation provides some convenient maneuvering room. It would be most convenient for you and likewise for the public if not only the first but also the second course consisted chiefly of your ideas. I recommend, therefore, something under the title "Scientific Philosophy", in which you can present in an elementary and non-technical way the sort of ideas that you have developed in *Erkenntnis* and other works. You should at least suggest that to Perry before you reconcile yourself to a purely historical course.

Regarding the first course which certainly belongs to your own area, I believe that you can hardly presuppose a knowledge of logistic because it is almost never taught here. Thus, I think, a course under the title "Logic and Logical Syntax" is to be recommended most.

Many thanks for the copy of my book, also for the offprints of your publications 33–35, which I have read with much interest. 35 will be extraordinarily valuable for Henderson [Prof. Lawrence J. Henderson, Fatigue Laboratory, Soldiers Field, Boston, Mass.] and Curtis [Mr. Charles P. Curtis, Jr., 30 State Street, Boston, Mass.]; I recommend 34 also for both. For Henderson I recommend 13F and 19F besides. I believe that Curtis already possesses 19F, but would be glad to get 13F. I suggest also that you send to each all future easily understood publications. If I see Henderson and Curtis again in September, I shall find out which of the remaining publications they possess. In the meantime, however, I know that Curtis has 28, and that neither Curtis nor Henderson has the publications recommended above.

Further I know that Skinner [Dr. B. Frederic Skinner, John Winthrop House F35, Cambridge, Mass.] has at least 8 and 28, that Cooley [Dr. John C. Cooley, 6 Story Street, Cambridge, Mass.] has 28 and with that, as a subscriber, everything that has appeared in *Erkenntnis*, and that Haskell [Mr. Edward F. Haskell, 6207 15th Avenue, Brooklyn, N.Y.], whom you met in Prague, has received 21 from me. I recommend that you send to Cooley all future publications and to Dennes [Prof. Will R. Dennes, Department of Philosophy, University of California, Berkeley, California] all not very technical future publications. For Cooley dispense with *Erkenntnis* which he already receives, and with each of these men dispense with books, of course, which cost a lot. For Cooley and Dennes I also recommend 35, and for Dennes and Haskell 34. Dennes needs 34 very much.

As for me I would very much like to receive publications 5, 8, 13F and 19F which you kindly offered.

I am finally in complete agreement with your last remarks about my book. Originally I misunderstood what sort of mistake you wanted to preclude by your 3b) [Dec. 1934] and thought the sole purpose would be to avoid the postulate on p. 44; however, A) [May 1935] makes everything clear and shows that the improvement 3b) is desirable. Concerning C) [May] it seems to me you are right again: namely it seems that C) can lead to contradiction only indirectly by means of the *Rule of Concretion,* and this route to contradiction is closed by the fact that the definition of the word *'substitution'* which occurs in this *Rule of Concretion,* is subject to the improvement 3b).

I congratulate you on the honorary Doctor of Science degree. I know that Curtis took an interest in that.

My lectures on you will be used this summer by Dennes and a pair of his students in California. When I get them back, I shall forward them immediately to you.

My good friend Tom Chambers, a young chemist and member, as am I, of the *Society of Fellows,* will be driving around, arriving in Prague on July 17. He would like very much to meet you and will write to you or call you on the telephone. However, he understands that you will very probably be away.

Tomorrow I shall depart with two friends on a two-week trip to Newfoundland and St. Pierre.

Naomi was very happy to receive the friendly letter from Mrs. Carnap and will answer soon.

We are looking forward to your arrival next June with greatest joy. Best wishes to you both,

Yours
W. V. Quine

[25. CARNAP TO QUINE   1935-7-28]

Pod Homolkou   Prague July 28, 1935

Dear Quine,

My best thanks for your kind letter of June 19th. I enclose the copy with my corrections, and you see that your German is becoming very good; the letter contains only very few mistakes.

Thanks for your suggestions concerning the titles of my courses. As to the elementary one, Nagel wrote me that there are difficulties in translating "wissenschaftliche Philosophie"; therefore he proposes "analytic philosophy". But I should not like this title very much. Would you think that "Introduction into Scientific Philosophy" would not be quite suitable? Does it sound for American ears as meaning "Philosophy of Natural Sciences", which of course would be—though not quite false—nevertheless too narrow. Or how would you translate "wissenschaftliche Philosophie"?

I got your letter during a travel. Therefore I have sent the offprints to the addresses suggested by you only now. I am obliged for your suggestions.

On August 1rst we shall start once more, this time for a longer travel. During August we shall be in Tyrol, together with Woodger and his wife and 4 children, and Feigl. W. is trying with good success to apply logistics to biology, as you know perhaps. Feigl is coming from Iowa to Europe for two months only. At the beginning of September I shall visit friends in Munich, and then I shall go to Paris for our Congress, while Ina will visit friends in North Italy and in Dresden.

Tom Chambers, your friend, has been here. He visited us twice and Ina spent one afternoon with him for sight-seeing.

With best wishes to Naomi for the third Quine from both of us—Ina thanks for Naomi's letter and intends to reply from Tyrol—and cordially regards to you,

                              Yours
                              R. Carnap

[26.   CARNAP TO QUINE   NO DATE [1935] (PROBABLY
WITH 24)]

Prof. Dr. Rudolf Carnap
  Prag XVII
N. Motol, Pod Homolkou

My address:

> until August 31: Landhaus Schultze, *Hintertux*
> (Zillertal, Tirol)   Austria.
> until September 8: *München*, bahnpostlagernd.
> until September 22: c/o American Express Co, *Paris*, rue
> Scribe 11. then *Prague.*
> Letters addressed to Prague will always be forwarded to
> me.
>   We were pleased to speak with your friend about you
> and to hear from you by him.

⟨Marked 1935, apparently in Quine's hand.⟩

[27.   QUINE TO CARNAP   1935-9-23]

91 Washington Avenue
Cambridge, Mass., U.S.A.
d. 23. Sept. 1935

Lieber Herr Carnap!

a. | Es freut uns sehr, zu lernen, daß Sie früh nach Amerika
b. | kommen werden! Wir sehen das Ende Dezembers mit größtem
   | Vergnügen entgegen. Es ist der Hauptzweck dieses Briefes, Sie
c. | überzuzeugen, daß es am besten ist, hinreichend früh
abzureisen, mindestens eine Woche bei uns verbringen zu
können, bevor Sie nach Baltimore fahren werden.
   Ich habe schon festgestellt, daß Sie als Gast bei der
"Kerlgesellschaft" [eine bei mir übliche Bezeichnung, die von
einer Zweideutigkeit des englischen Wortes "fellow" abhängt]
am Abend des 23. Dezember höchst willkommen sind, wenn
d. | auch es sonst keinen der üblichen wöchentlichen Schmäuse so

nah an den Weihnachten geben würde; es wird nämlich
letztenfalls einen besonderen um Ihren willen gahalten, worin | e.
alle diejenigen der Gesellschaft teilnehmen werden, die noch so
nah an den Weihnachten vorhanden sind. [Auch habe ich
gelernt, daß einige vorhanden sein werden, wenn Sie da sein | f.
werden, die sonst weg sein würden.] Da würden Sie einige der
wichtigsten der Behörden kennen lernen, u.a. den Dekan der
Universität, möglicherweise den President der U., bestimmt den
vormaligen President, auch Henderson und Curtis. Auch | g.
würden Sie während Ihrer Aufenthalt die verschiedenen | h.
Philosophen kennenlernen. Ich meine sehr (so meint auch mein
Freund Dr. Skinner), daß es Ihnen vom Standpunkt einer
zukünftigen hierigen Professur sehr vorteilhaft wäre, | i.
betreffende Gelehrte möglichst früh kennenzulernen. Die Räder
mahlen langsam.

Sofern handelt es sich nur um akademische Vorteile. Nun
möchte ich hinzufügen, daß es unser ernster Wunsch ist, Sie
beide möglichst bald zu sehen, und Sie bei uns für die
Weihnachten zu haben. Ich möchte Sie also pressen, ein Schiff | j.
direkt für Boston zu nehmen [dadurch würden Sie die umgefähr
15 Dollars sparen, die es zwei Personen kostet, von Neu-York
nach Boston mit Zug zu fahren], derart, daß Sie vor dem 23.
Dez. ankommen werden. In unserer neuen Wohnung haben wir
Platz genug; und Sie werden bei uns so viel Arbeiten dürfen,
wie Sie wollen. Nah am Ende des Jahres werden Sie und ich
zusammen nach Baltimore fahren können, mit irgendeinem
anderen, z.B. Cooley, der eine Auto besitzt. In Vergleich mit | k.
dem Zugfahrgeld würde das Verteilen der Autodepense uns viel
Geld sparen; auch würde es angenehmer sein. Inzwischen wird
Ina mit Naomi bleiben können, und um solche Zeit nach Chi- | l.
cago abreisen, mit Ihnen während der Reise zusammen-
zukommen. (Sie würden vermutlich von Baltimore nach Chicago
direkt mit Zug fahren.) | m.

Ich hoffe sehr, daß dieser Vorschlag annehmlich sein wird. | n.

Besten Dank für die Schriften 5, 8, 13F und 19F, die es mich | o.
sehr freut, zu besitzen. Außerdem hatte ich 5 und 13F sogar nie
gelesen; ihr Lesen hat mir vieles Vergnügen und (insbes. 5) | p.
vielen Nutzen geleistet.

Besten Danke für die schöne Rezension, die Sie meinem

Buche gewährt haben, und für die Exemplare davon, die Sie mir geschickt haben.

Curtis war sehr erfreut, Ihre drei Sendungen zu bekommen,
q. | und hat mich unterrichtet, Ihnen seinen herzlichen Dank mitzuteilen. Eine Antwort von Haskell wird hier beigeschloßn.

Die Gastfreundlichkeit, womit Sie meinen Freund Tom Chambers bewillkommen haben, wird von ihm und auch von mir
r. | sehr verdankt. Der Besuch bei Ihnen, und der Ausflug an den Hradschin bilden für ihn angenehme Erinnerungen.

Der Exemplar meiner voriges Jahr behaltenen Vorträge über
t. | s. | Ihrer Arbeiten ist mir noch nicht zurückgeschickt worden. Wann ich es bald bekommen werden, werde ich es Ihnen gleich schicken; sonst werden Sie es in Amerika lesen können.

u. | Wir haben jetzt ein gesundes 26 Tage altes "Elisabeth" gennantes Kind. Naomi hat Schwieriget gahabt, ist jetzt aber genesend.

Ihr Brief an Langford hat mich sehr interessiert. Damit bin ich na-
v. | türlich ganz einverstanden, meines Studiums Ihrer Arbeit wegen.

Die Bezeichnung "Scientific Philosophy" bringt die Philosophie der Naturwissenschaften (die vielmehr "Philosophy of Science" zu bezeichnen wäre) gar nicht bei, sondern die in wissenschaftlicher Weise getriebene Philosophie. Insofern scheint die Bezeichnung zu passen. Nichtsdestoweniger klingt sie mir gar nicht gut—ich weiß nicht genau warum. Vielleicht hängt dies irgendwie von dem Mißbrauch ab, den das Wort "sci-
w. | entific" in Amerika geleidet hat (z.B. in den unredlichen Geschäftsreklamen—für Zahnpaste usw.—, auch beim religiösen
x. | Fadismus). Das Wort bleibt gebrauchlich, aber man muß auf den Klang der Zusammenhang sehr aufpassen. Ich kann keine
z. | y. | allgemeine-Regel aufstellen, nur mein Gefühl in einzelfällen mitteilen. Z.B. klingt mir "Philosophy as a Science" ganz gut— auch "Scientific Method in Philosophy", wenn dies nicht schon
a.a. | von Russell vorgekauft wäre. Oder warum nicht Ihr früher angewandter Titel "Philosophy and Logical Syntax"?

Mit besten Grüßen Ihnen beiden, auch von Naomi,

Ihr
W. V. Quine

P.S. Ich sende gleichzeitig noch einige Exemplare meiner Rezension Ihres Buches.

[CARNAP'S GRAMMATICAL CORRECTIONS ON QUINE'S COPY:]

a. 'lernen' changed to 'erfahren' ⟨. . . , zu erfahren, daß Sie . . .⟩.
b. 'das' changed to 'dem' ⟨Wir sehen dem Ende . . .⟩.
c. 'zu' inserted after 'Sie' ⟨. . . Briefes, Sie zu überzuzergen, . . .⟩.
d. 'auch' inverted with 'es' ⟨. . . , wenn es auch sonst . . .⟩.
e. 'besonderen' changed to 'besonderer' ⟨. . . ein besonderer um Ihren . . .⟩.
f. 'gelernt' changed to 'gehort' ⟨Auch habe ich gehort, daß . . .⟩.
g. 'President' changed twice to 'Präsident' ⟨. . . den Präsident der U., bestimmt den vormaligen Präsident, . . .⟩.
h. 'Ihrer Aufenthalt' changed to 'Ihres Aufenthalts' ⟨. . . während Ihres Aufenthalts . . .⟩.
i. 'hierigen' changed to 'hiesigen' ⟨. . . einer zukünftigen hiesigen Professur . . .⟩.
j. 'pressen' changed to 'drängen' ⟨Ich möchte Sie also drängen, ein Schiff . . .⟩.
k. 'eine' changed to 'ein' and 'In' changed to 'Im' ⟨. . . der ein Auto besitzt. Im Vergleich . . .⟩.
l. 'um solche' changed to zu solcher' ⟨. . . , und zu solcher Zeit . . .⟩.
m. 'einem' inserted after 'mit' ⟨. . . direkt mit einem Zug fahren.⟩.
n. 'annehmlich' changed to 'annehmbar' ⟨. . . Vorschlag annehmbar sein wird.⟩.
o. 'es' omitted and 'zu besitzen' moved to its place ⟨. . . , die zu besitzen mich sehr freut.⟩.
p. 'vieles' changed to 'viel' and 'geleistet' changed to 'gebracht' ⟨. . . mir viel Vergnügen und (insbes. 5) vielen Nutzen gebracht.⟩.
q. 'unterrichtet' changed to 'gebeten' ⟨. . . hat mich gebeten, Ihnen . . .⟩.
r. 'bewillkommnem haben, wird von ihm und auch von mir sehr verdankt.' changed to 'bewillkommnet haben, danken er und auch ich Ihnen sehr.'

s. 'Der' changed to 'Das' ⟨Das Exemplar . . .⟩, and 'behaltenen' changed to 'gehaltenen', and 'Ihrer' changed to 'Ihre' ⟨. . . Jahr gehaltenen Vorträge über Ihre Arbeiten . . .⟩.

t. 'Wann' changed to 'Wenn' and 'werden' changed to 'werde' ⟨Wenn ich es bald bekommen werde, werde . . .⟩.

u. Commas inserted around '26 Tage altes' ⟨. . . gesundes, 26 Tage altes, "Elisabeth" . . .⟩.

v. 'ganz einverstanden' moved to the end of the sentence ⟨. . . natürlich meines Studiums Ihrer Arbeit wegen ganz einverstanden.⟩.

w. 'geleidet' changed to 'gelitten' ⟨. . . in Amerika gelitten hat . . .⟩.

x. 'gebrauchlich' changed to 'gebräuchlich' ⟨Das Wort bleibt gebräuchlich, . . .⟩, and 'der Zusammenhang' changed to 'des Zusammenhangs' ⟨. . . den Klang des Zusammenhangs sehr . . .⟩.

y. 'allgemeine-Regel' changed to 'allgemeine Regel' ⟨. . . keine allgemeine Regel aufstellen, . . .⟩.

z. 'einzelfällen' capitalized ⟨. . . in Einzelfällen mitteilen.⟩.

aa. 'vorgekauft' changed to 'vorweggenommen' ⟨. . . von Russell vorgenommen wäre.⟩.

[27.E   QUINE TO CARNAP   1935-9-23]

> 91 Washington Avenue
> Cambridge, Mass., U.S.A.
> Sept. 23, 1935

Dear Mr. Carnap:

We are very glad to learn that you will soon come to America! We look forward to the end of December with the greatest pleasure. It is the chief purpose of this letter to persuade you that it is best to leave sufficiently early to allow yourself at least a week with us before you travel to Baltimore.

I have already arranged for you to be most welcome as a guest of the "Kerlgesellschaft" [my usual designation; it depends on the ambiguity of the English word "fellow"] on the evening of December 23rd, even if none of the usual weekly banquet is given so close to Christmas. In the latter case we want to hold a special banquet for you, in which all the members of the Society who are around so close to Christmas shall take part. [Also I have heard that a few, who otherwise would not be there, will be around if you are there.] There you will meet a few of the most important officials, among others, the dean of the university, possibly the president of the u., definitely the former president and also Henderson and Curtis. You will also meet various philosophers during your stay. I very much believe (as does my friend Dr. Skinner) that it would be very advantageous for you from the standpoint of a prospective professor here to meet relevant scholars as soon as possible. The wheels grind slowly.

Thus far it is a question only of academic advantage. Now I would like to add that it is our most earnest wish to see you both as soon as possible and to have you with us for Christmas. I want, therefore, to urge you to take a ship directly for Boston [you would save about 15 dollars thereby, which is what it costs for two persons to travel by train from New York to Boston]. In this way you can arrive before Dec. 23. We have room enough in our new apartment; and you may work as much as you like at our place. Near the end of the year, you and I shall be able to travel together to Baltimore, with someone else, e.g., Cooley, who owns an automobile. Compared to the cost of train travel sharing the automobile expenses will save us a lot of money; it will be more pleasant as well. In the meantime Ina can stay with Naomi and depart for Chicago in time to meet you during the trip. (You would presumably travel by train directly from Baltimore to Chicago.)

I very much hope that this proposal will be acceptable.

Many thanks for publications 5, 8, 13F and 19F, which I am very happy to own. Otherwise I had never even read 5 and 13F; reading them brought me much pleasure and (esp. 5) profit.

Many thanks also for the nice review you gave my book, and for the copy thereof which you sent me.

Curtis was very glad to receive your three parcels and has asked me to communicate to you his sincere thanks. An answer from Haskell will be enclosed herein.

My friend Tom Chambers and I thank you very much for the hospitality with which you welcomed him. The visit with you and the excursion on the Hradschin was a memorable experience for him.

The copy of the lectures on your work I delivered last year has still not been returned to me. If I receive it soon I shall send it to you at once; otherwise you will be able to read it in America.

We now have a healthy 26-day-old child named "Elisabeth". Naomi had difficulty but is now recovered.

Your letter to Langford interested me very much. Naturally, I am in complete agreement, because of my study of your work.

The designation "Scientific Philosophy" does not convey at all the philosophy of the natural sciences (which, on the contrary, would be designated "Philosophy of Science") but rather philosophy done in a scientific way. In this respect the designation seems to suit. Nonetheless it does not sound good to me at all—I do not know exactly why. Perhaps it somehow depends on the misuse which the word "scientific" has suffered in America (e.g., in dishonest commercial advertising—for toothpaste etc.—, also with religious fadism). The word remains useful, but one must watch out for the sound of the combination. I can state no general rule, only express my feeling in individual cases. E.g., "Philosophy as a Science" sounds good—also "Scientific Method in Philosophy", if this were not already preempted by Russell. Or why not the title you used earlier, "Philosophy and Logical Syntax"?

Best wishes to you both, also from Naomi,

Yours
W. V. Quine

P.S. I am simultaneously sending a few more copies of my review of your book.

[28.   CARNAP TO QUINE   1935-10-28]

Prof. Dr. Rudolf Carnap
    Prag XVII   October 28, 1935.
N. Motol, Pod Homolkou

Dear Quine,

Many thanks for your kind letter of Sept. 23.
Above all our most cordial congratulations to your daughter

Elizabeth. We wish that she might grow and develop in the best way, and we hope that Naomi has overcome all difficulties and is recovered entirely.

Your invitation to come to Cambridge and stay in your home is extremely kind. We are happy to come, but we decided to live in a hotel at Cambridge. I think it is for both parts more convenient. We shall then of course be very glad when we may come sometimes to your home and be together with both of you.

We shall arrive at New York on Dec. 21st. (For financial reasons we took a German boat and they don't go to Boston.) Could you perhaps inform me of the trains from N.Y. to Boston (time of departure and arrival)? We should like to be in N.Y. during Dec. 22 and meet Dr. and Mrs. Nagel and other friends whom we know from Vienna. I should like to call at the International Institute of Education too, but I suppose it will be impossible because the 22nd is a sunday. I have asked them to organize a lecture tour for April and perhaps May 1936 (I am enclosing a list of the lecture titles.) I hope there is a train arriving at Boston in the afternoon (23.) early enough for me to participate in the dinner of your fellow society on Dec. 23rd. You are right, this opportunity of meeting several university people would be very valuable for me.

Your plan of riding together to Baltimore in the car of a friend of yours is very fine. It will take 2 days, I suppose?

Many thanks for the copies of your review.

Neurath gave me some copies of various papers of his for my friends. I am sending them to you simultaneously.

A pamphlet containing the french translations of 29 and 34 appeared (called "29–34F"). If it seems desirable for you or somebody else, please let me know.

Tarski (Warsaw) will send you the amount of 35 $. Please keep it for me.

The last summer I finished a paper "Testability and Meaning", a reply to Lewis' paper. It has become rather long. Therefore and for the reason that I wish to have it read not only by philosophers but also by philosophically interested scientists I will publish it not in the "Philosophical Review", but in "Philosophy of Science". I gave a copy to Feigl for the editor. Another copy I sent to Lewis for his information.

I intend to deliver at the Baltimore meeting a paper which is to explain in short the chief ideas of that longer paper. Prof. Murphy, the secretary of the Phil. Ass. to whom Lewis sent a letter about my paper wrote me that it would be more advisable for me to deliver a paper on probability because the session dealing with probability will have a more prominent place in the program. Nevertheless I prefer to deliver a paper on testability because at present I have no time for preparing an entirely new paper on probability; perhaps I might make a short informal remark in the discussion on probability. To-day I have sent a letter to Murphy in this sense.

I have sent to Prof. Perry a statement of my courses to be given at the Harvard Summer School. A copy is enclosed here.

We are now terribly busy in collecting our papers necessary for the visa. It takes ages at the Czechoslovakian authorities! Further we are dividing our things into groups for a short, a longer and a lasting stay in America. The next five weeks are not expected to be a mere pleasure.

Post will reach me here till Dec. 10, between 10th and 15th on board S.S. "Bremen", Cabine 482, Bremen.

With warmest regards and wishes from both of us to you three,

Very sincerely yours,
R. Carnap

[29. QUINE TO CARNAP   1935-11-26]

91 Washington Avenue
Cambridge, Mass.
d. 26. Nov. 1935

Lieber Herr Carnap!

Es freut uns sehr, dass Sie in Dezember nach Cambridge kommen können. Um 10 Uhr vormittags gibt es einen Zug ab N.Y., der um 3 Uhr nachmittags an Boston kommt. Sie werden also bequem den 22. Dez. in N.Y. verbringen können, wie Sie wollten, und diesen Zug um 10 Uhr den 23. Dez. nehmen. Auch gibt es einen Zug ab N.Y. um Mittag, an Boston um 5 Uhr

5. Dieser würde auch ausreichende Zeit lassen, um an die Society of Fellows um 6:30 zu gelangen. Dort trägt man einfach Geschäftskleider. Der Zug um 10 Uhr bietet den Vorteil, mindere Eile zu fordern; der Zug um Mittag bietet aber den Vorteil, den Vormittag des 23. für einen Besuch beim International Institute of Education in N.Y. offen zu halten.

Bitte schreiben Sie mir mit Eilpost (Special Delivery), welchen dieser Züge Sie nehmen werden. Das können Sie während der Seereise; Postschachtel gibt es an Bord. Der Brief wird mich den 22. oder den Vormittag des 23. erreichen. Dann werde ich Ihnen am Bahnhof in Boston treffen. Steigen Sie an South Station aus, welche der letzte und wichtigste der Bostoner Bahnhöfe ist. Ich werde auf dem Bahnsteig sein, um Sie eben beim Aussteigen zu finden.

Der Zug fahrt von dem Grand Central Terminal in N.Y. ab. Sie werden erfahren, dass die amerikanischen Züge die besten der Welt sind; wohl aber die teuersten, im Sinne, dass es keine dritte Klasse gibt. (Deswegen habe ich die europäischen Züge lieber.) In amerikanischen Zügen hat man zwei Klassen worunter zu wählen; sie heissen aber nicht erste und zweite Klasse, sondern "Pullman" and "Day Coach". ("Pullman" heisst nicht nur Schlafwagen; tags auch bleibt die dadurch bezeichnete Klasseneinteilung vorhanden.) Nehmen Sie jedenfalls die billigere dieser zwei, d.h. Day Coach. Die neuen Day Coaches auf dieser Strecke sind prachtvoll: behagliche Sessel und gewaschene Luft. Passen Sie auf, dass Sie in einem diesen neuen Day Coaches sitzen, denn es bleiben auch einige der älteren Art innerhalb derselben Züge ohne Kostenunterschied.

Für unsere Reise nach Baltimore ist alles in Ordnung. Ein gewisser Goodman, der sich mit Ihrer Schrift 7 beschäftigt hat, wird uns in seinem grossen Auto nehmen. Prall wird mitgehen, auch ein gewisser Leonard, Dozent in Philosophie mit logischen Interessen. Diese drei bilden ein Teil einer Gruppe, die seit einen Monat zur Besprechung Ihrer 28 bei mir wochentlich zusammengekommen ist. Wir werden den 28. Dez. abfahren, um an Baltimore den 29. um Mittag zu kommen. Der Kngress wird von Mittag den 29. bis Mittag den 31. dauern. Dann werden Sie direkt von Baltimore nach Chicago reisen können. Naomi hofft, Ina bei Ihr in Cambridge während unserer Reise nach Baltimore zu haben. Ina wird dann mit Ihnen in Chicago zusammenkommen können.

Ich möchte betonen, dass es uns eine Enttäuschung sein wird, wenn Sie für die fünf Tage in Cambridge ein Hotelzimmer nehmen. Wir haben wirklich ausreichenden Raum, Ihnen zwei Bette und Platz zur ungestörten Arbeit bieten zu können, ohne uns zu belästigen. Auch wäre es für Naomi keine Bürde, weil Sie seit dem Geburt des Kindes täglichen Hausdienst mietet.

Ausser dem Abendessen bei der Society of Fellows hat es für Sie vorteilhaft geschienen, die zwei folgenden Ereignisse zu planen:

(1) 26. Dez., 4:00–6:00, Tee. Vermutlich anzusein: Sheffer, Perry, Huntington und Frau, Hocking (Vorsitzender der philosophischen Fakultät) und Frau, Birkhoff (Mathematiker und Dekan) und Frau, Prall und Schwester, und Frau Langer.

(2) 26. Dez., 8:00, Besuch bei den Whitehead.

Andere Sachen, die für Sie minder wichtig sind, und die sich kürzer vorausplanen lassen, haben wir Ihrer Neigung gelassen. Wir haben folgende betrachtet:

(3) ein Abend zur Besprechung mit jüngeren Interessierten;

(4) mit Sheffer zu Mittagessen;

(5) Umschau der Bostoner Sehenswürdigkeiten.

Ich habe das Gelt von Tarski bekommen und behalte es für Sie.

Vielen Dank für die Sonderdrücke von Neurath, die mir sehr gefallen haben. "Physicalisme" hatten Sie mir schon früher gegeben; diesen zweiten Exemplar werde ich also entweder Ihnen zurückgeben oder jemandem anderen geben können.

Betreffs Ihr 29–34F weiss ich nicht, was '29', welches in dem in Ihrem Briefe des 5. Mai enthaltenen Register nicht vorkommt, bezeichnet. Falls ich 29 nicht besitze, möchte ich 29–34F sehr gern haben; diesenfalls könnte ich Ihnen 34 zurückgeben.

Dem Wiedersehen am 23. Dez. sehen wir mit grosser Freude entgegen. Gute Reise!

Ihr

W. V. Quine

Ihre vorgeschlagene Vorträge klingen sehr gut; auch ihre Titel.

91 Washington Avenue
Cambridge, Mass.
Nov. 26, 1935

Dear Mr. Carnap:

We are very happy that you can come to Cambridge in December. At 10 o'clock in the morning there is a train from N.Y.
which arrives in Boston at 3 o'clock in the afternoon. You will be
able to spend Dec. 22 comfortably in N.Y., however you want,
and take this train at 10 o'clock Dec. 23. Also there is a train
from N.Y. at noon arriving Boston at 5:05. This would permit
sufficient time in order to reach the Society of Fellows at 6:30.
The members simply wear business clothes. The train at 10
o'clock has the advantage of requiring less haste; the train at
noon has, however, the advantage of leaving open a visit on the
morning of the 23rd to the International Institute of Education
in N.Y.

Please write to me express (Special Delivery) which of these
trains you will take. You can do that during the ocean voyage;
there are mail bags on board. The letter will reach me the 22nd
or the morning of the 23rd. Then I shall meet you at the train
station. Get off at South Station, which is the last and most important of the Boston train stations. I will be on the platform in
order to find you just as you get off.

The train departs from Grand Central Terminal in N.Y. You
will learn that the American trains are the best in the world;
true, but the most expensive in the sense that there is no third
class. (On that account I prefer the European trains.) In American trains one has two classes to choose between; they are not
called first and second classes, however, but "Pullman" and
"Day Coach". ("Pullman" means not only sleeping car; during
the day the class distinction remains in effect.) In any case, take
the cheaper of these two, called Day Coach. The new Day
Coaches are splendid on this stretch: comfortable seats and
fresh air. Make sure that you sit in one of these new Day
Coaches, for a few of the older kind also remain within the
same trains without any cost change.

Everything is in order for our trip to Baltimore. A man by the name of Goodman, who is busy with your publication 7, will take us in his large car. Prall will go with us, also someone by the name of Leonard, assistant professor of philosophy with an interest in logic. These three form part of a group which for a month has met weekly at my house for a discussion of your 28. We shall depart Dec. 28 in order to arrive at Baltimore at noon on the 29th. The convention lasts from noon on the 29th till noon on the 31st. Then you can travel directly from Baltimore to Chicago. Naomi hopes to have Ina with her in Cambridge during our trip to Baltimore. Ina can then meet you in Chicago.

I would like to stress that it will be a disappointment for us if you take a hotel room for the five days in Cambridge. We really have sufficient room to be able to offer you two beds and a place for undisturbed work. Also it would be no burden for Naomi because since the birth of our child she has hired daily maid service.

Other than the dinner at the Society of Fellows it seems advantageous for you to make plans for the two following events:

(1) Dec. 26, 4:00–6:00, Tea. Presumably to be there: Scheffer, Perry, Huntington and wife, Hocking (chairman of the philosophical faculty) and wife, Birkhoff (mathematician and dean) and wife, Prall and sister, and Mrs. Langer.

(2) Dec. 26, 8:00 Visit with Whitehead.

Other matters which are of minor importance to you, and which allow of briefer preplanning we left to your preference. We have considered the following:

(3) an evening for discussion with interested students

(4) lunch with Scheffer

(5) seeing the Boston sights

I have received the money from Tarski and am keeping it for you.

Many thanks for the offprint by Neurath, which I like very much. You have already given me "Physicalism"; I shall, therefore, either return this second copy to you or I can give it to someone else.

Concerning your 29–34F I do not know what '29', which does not occur in the index contained in your letter of May 5, denotes. In case I do not possess 29, I would like very much to have 29–34F; in this case I can return 34 to you.

We look forward to seeing you again on Dec. 23rd with great joy. Have a good trip!

Yours,
W. V. Quine

Your suggested lectures sound very good, as do their titles.

[30.   CARNAP TO QUINE   1935-11-?
(POSTED 1935-11-18)]

RUDOLF CARNAP   PRAG, November 1935
                       XVII, Pod Homolkou 146

Für die Zeit bis September 1936 gelten die untenstehenden Adressen. Die Daten bezeichnen den Ankunftstag der letzten Post; ein Brief braucht von Mittel-europa nach Amerika etwa 10 bis 14 Tage.

Rudolf Carnap

1935:	bis. 10. Dez.:	Prag (wie oben)
	bis 14. Dez.:	Hotel Nordischer Hof, Banhofstr., Bremen
	bis 21. Dez.:	c. o. S. Broadwin, 433 Beechmont Drive, New Rochelle N. Y. (USA)
	bis 27. Dez.:	c. o. Dr. W. V. Quine, 91 Washington Ave., Cambridge Mass. (USA)
	bis 31. Dez.:	c. o. American Express Co., 213 North Charles Street, Baltimore Md. (USA)
1936:	bis 15. März:	University of Chicago, Dept. of Philosophy, Chicago Ill. (USA)
	bis 30. Juni:	(Aufenthalt wechselnd: adressieren:) c.o. American Express Co., 65 Broadway, New York City (USA)
	bis. 20. Sept.:	Harvard University, Dept. of Philos., Cambridge Mass. (USA)

[30.E CARNAP TO QUINE 1935-11-? (POSTED
1935-11-18)]

RUDOLF CARNAP   PRAGUE, November 1935
                                       XVII, Pod Homolkou 146

The addresses below are valid for the period until September
1936. The dates indicate the arrival date of the last post; a letter
takes about 10 to 14 days from central Europe to America.

                                                    Rudolf Carnap

1935: till Dec. 10: Prague (as above)
       till Dec. 14: Hotel Nordischer Hof, Banhofstr., Bremen
       till Dec. 21: c.o. S. Broadwin, 433 Beechmont Drive,
                      New Rochelle N. Y. (USA)
       till Dec. 27: c.o. Dr. W. V. Quine, 91 Washington Ave.,
                      Cambridge Mass. (USA)
       till Dec. 31: c.o. American Express Co., 213 North
                      Charles Street, Baltimore Md. (USA)
1936: till Mar. 15: University of Chicago, Dept. of Philoso-
                      phy, Chicago Ill. (USA)
       till June 30: (In Transit; address mail:) c.o. American Ex-
                      press Co., 65 Broadway, New York City
                      (USA)
       till Sept. 20: Harvard University, Dept. of Philos., Cam-
                      bridge Mass. (USA)

[31. CARNAP TO QUINE 1935-12-9]

Prof. Dr. Rudolf Carnap
    Prag XVII
N. Motol, Pod Homolkou 146   Prague, Dec. 9, 1935.

Dear Quine,

Thanks for your letter. Your invitation is extremely kind. Perhaps Ina will not come to Cambridge this time, but stay in N.Y.;
Mrs. Broadwin wishes to have her there (we know them from
Vienna). In this case I shall dare to come to you without being
afraid to cause you to much trouble.

I do not know whether this letter will reach you before I shall come myself. I shall write once more from the steamer. I expect to take the earlier train, arriving at 3 p.m. at Boston (South Station). If it will be necessary because of the Institute in N.Y. to take the second train, I shall inform you, if necessary by telegramme.

Thanks for the fine programme projected. I agree perfectly. I shall like very much to have a discussion with young people. If possible, I prefer afternoons to evenings for discussion. But sightseeing is perhaps better delayed to the next time, because now time is so short.

Simultaneously I send you a MS "Testability and Reduction". I intend to read it at Baltimore in the Meeting. I should be very obliged to you if you kindly correct it. And then please let it be retyped at my expense, or at least those pages on which there are many corrections. Of course it is not necessary to bring it in a fine style; it need only to be correct and clearly comprehensible. I should not even wish an elegant style, because in German also I prefer a simple style to an elegant and rhetoric one. It would not even matter if it sounded a little awkward. The MS need not be ready at my arrival, of course. I suppose that it will arrive not much time before myself.

We are in a chaos here, all things come in a store. 41 boxes with books are already away.

I am in a hurry, excuse the mistakes!

I am very happy to see you soon.

With best regards to you and Naomi, also from Ina,

yours
R. Carnap

[32.   ĊOURSE DESCRIPTION   NO DATE (1935?)]

Prof. Dr. Rudolf Carnap
    Prag XVII
N. Motol. Pod Homolkou 146

Harvard Summer School 1936.
1. *Elementary Course. Introduction to Philosophy*
   The psycho-physical problem and other metaphysical prob-

lems. Critical analysis of these problems. The functions of language. Distinction between cognitive meanings and emotive appeals. Formal and factual (empirical) science. Formal logic. Logical foundations of mathematics. Epistemological problems of factual sciences. Verification. Induction. Causality. Physicalism. The unity of science. Logical syntax. Scientific method of philosophizing.

2. *Advanced Course. Logic and Logical Syntax.*

Symbolic logic. Logical foundations of mathematics. Logical syntax. Application of the method of logical syntax to philosophical problems.

[33.   LECTURE DESCRIPTION   NO DATE (1935?)]

Prof. Dr. Rudolf Carnap
  Prag XVII
N. Motol, Pod Homolkou 146

International Institute of Education,

New York

Single Lectures:

1. *Scientific Philosophy in Contemporary Europe.*
   (Origines. Present tendencies. Chief problems. The 1st International Congress on Scientific Philosophy, Paris 1935.)
2. *Philosophy and Logical Analysis.*
   (The stages in the development of scient. philosophy: rejection of speculative metaphysics; rejection of the apriori.
   The present task: transformation of the epistemology into logical syntax.)
3. *The Unity of Science.*
   (The method of reduction of concepts. Positivism and Physicalism. The unity of science on a physical basis.)

Lecture (1) is rather elementary. For lecture (2) some elementary knowledge of philosophical problems is desirable. For lecture (3) some knowledge of the simplest elements of logic is desirable but not necessary.

Lecture Course (of 3 to 8 lectures, with discussions):
  Logical syntax—the basis for a scientific philosophy.
  (The method of logical syntax. Language-systems. Formative
  and transformative rules. The pseudo-object-sentences of philosophy. Translation of philosophical problems into the syntactical language.)

[34. INA CARNAP TO NAOMI QUINE, WITH NOTE 1936-1-7]

Chicago, Jan. 7, 1936

Dear Mrs. Quine,

Thank you so very much for your Xmas parcel. Did Mr.
Quine report to you, that this was the only Xmas present,
which I got this year. But what a shame that I had simply nothing for you. How did you know, that I really needed the little
sewing bag and that I had only European-thick stockings. Your
present met first two real needs of mine!
So far we are not finally settled. It is rather difficult to find a
furnished apartment not too far from our taste and habit of living. Most of the apartments, which I have seen, are either dark
or noisy or horrid petit-bourgeois furnished or all these three
together. We stay now in an apartment-hotel, where it is at least
light and agreeably furnished, but so near to the railway that it
is not at all an ideal solution. Prof. Morris and his wife are very
helpful and friendly, but it is a hard job to find the right thing.
Thank you also very much for all your kindness concerning
Carnap and his stay in your home. I am really sorry that I
haven't seen you that time. But I was very miserable just those
days and I had to leave for my friends in Canada also on Dec.
28th. But I expect to see you probably in April. and I am very
keen of seeing your offspring Elizabeth. Carnap praised her in
high words.
I haven't got land-legs for Chicago till now. It is all a little

strange and very tiring for me. Carnap stands it much better in spite of train noise during the nights.

    With very warm regards 2:3

Yours

Ina C

a. |

Thanks for forwarding mail.

Hearty thanks and regards! I enjoy still in memory the fine Xmas-days in your home and all your and Quine's immense kindness. I am looking forward to seeing you again in Spring.

Yours

R. Carnap

a. ⟨This afterthought (in Ina's hand) is upside down over the salutation.⟩

[35.   QUINE TO CARNAP   1936-1-28]

91 Washington Avenue,

Cambridge, Mass.,

January 28, 1936.

Dear Mr. Carnap,

    I enclose a copy of my letter to Langford, and with it I return Langford's letter for your files.

    It was a great pleasure having you with us in Cambridge, and I was very glad to be able to prolong the pleasure by the trip to Baltimore. The one disappointment was that Mrs. Carnap could not be with us too; we are looking forward keenly to April and the summer, when you will both be here. And above all, it is to be hoped that there will be no returning to Bohemia in the fall! Surely the Chicago plan will be realized for the coming year. I am very anxious to have news as soon as it exists. Given provision for the coming year at Chicago, subsequent years will take care of themselves: you will have Chicago always in reserve, while awaiting preferable alternatives farther east.

    When you come in April, Mrs. Whitehead is going to bring

you and Dean Birkhoff together; you had little contact with him on the two previous occasions. She is aware of the desirability of your being brought to Harvard. That cannot be effected for the coming year, of course, but is to be hoped for soon after.

Paul Weiss says that Bryn Mawr College wants to be included in your lecture tour; also Hocking, the chairman of the Harvard philosophy department, told me he hoped we could have a lecture while you are here in April.

There is a young mathematician of my acquaintance named Korgan, who is interested in foundations and will attend your lectures this summer. He was planning to order a copy of the *Syntax*, and, acting on your kind suggestion, I told him that you would be willing to order it for him and give him the advantage of your discount. He also wants a copy of the *Abriss*, and I thought you could order it for him at the same time, if the edition is not exhausted. I told him that you would communicate direct with him regarding cost, etc.; the address is: Mr. R. L. Korgan, 38 College Street, Brunswick, Maine.

A year ago I met a precocious boy of 16 named Carey Gulick, who has budding interest in logic and philosophy. I discussed with him at some length, introducing him to your point of view, and lent him "The Unity of Science" and "The Character of Philosophic Problems". Recently I had him in for another evening of discussion; he returned "The Unity of Science", but remembered nothing of the *Philosophy of Science* reprint, which, unfortunately, is therefore lost. Though reprints are generally irreplaceable, I lend them because it is in such ways that science is propagated; and actually this is the first loss that has resulted. If you are not running short of reprints of that paper, I would be very grateful for another.

This letter is proving to consist mainly of asking favors; there is one more. Cooley and Goodman have urged me to ask you if you have a temporarily dispensable copy of your paper "Testability and Meaning"—not the short Baltimore paper, but the whole as designed for publication. We are anxious to see the detailed theory, and would be very glad not to have to wait for its appearance in print. Or is it already about to appear?

On the way home from Baltimore I heard, for the first time, an account of the work which Leonard and Goodman have been carrying on. Like the *Aufbau* it is a constitution-system, but its basis is fundamentally different from that of the *Aufbau*, and Goodman expects it to behave differently at the *mittlere Stufe*; indeed, he doubts the necessity of forsaking definability in favor of your more liberal notion of reducibility, and this is a reason why we are especially anxious to see your paper. I have not yet been through all the details of the Leonard-Goodman structure, but I have begun meeting with them periodically for that purpose. From what I have heard of it thus far, their scheme interests me very much; and I am anxious to hear your criticism of it when Goodman sends you some of it to read, as he hopes to do before long.

I hope that by now you have found satisfactory quarters. The lodging problem is a difficult one; and in our experience the most difficult condition to fulfill is quiet. We are moving again in August, as we have every year, because of noise. (Our place seemed quiet to you, but only because the noisy family downstairs was away for the holidays.)

Naomi joins me in kindest regards to both.

Yours,

Encs.

[36. CARNAP TO QUINE   1936-2-25]

Prof. Dr. Rudolf Carnap
     Prag XVII   Chicago, February 25, 1936.
N. Motol, Pod Homolkou 146

Dear Quine,

Thank you very much for your letter of January 28th and for the copy of your letter to Langford. I think you explained it to him excellently!

So far nothing has been decided concerning the Chicago plan. But Morris thinks, the decision has to be pretty soon. But I would not estimate my chances more than 40%.

I had a letter from Hocking, asking for a lecture in April. Do you think "Verification and the Unity of Science"[1] or "Mathematics and Empirical Science"[2] would be the better theme? The Institute in New York is arranging the date; it has proposed either April 8–10 or April 27–29 to Harvard. I think, we could perhaps spend about 5 days in Cambridge. We also are looking forward keenly to meeting both of you.

Neither I nor the Institute has received a word from Bryn Mawr that they wish me for a lecture.

I have ordered a copy of the "Syntax" from Springer for *Korgan* and I have sent him a copy of the "Logistik" from my stock. I have written him that you had asked me in his name to do so.

I have sent you to-day another copy of the *Philosophy of Science* paper. It was a pleasure for me.

I hope the "Testability and Meaning" paper has arrived in the meantime. I had given it to Murphy, he had given it to Lovejoy, and so I had to ask the latter for sending it to Cambridge. I am very interested to hear more about the Leonard-Goodman structure in April.

In the daytime we like our apartment very much; in the night it is so noisy from the railway and the streetcar that I have to sleep with closed windows. And that is a shame. The lodging problem is really rather difficult. Though I think, one could find the right place for a longer time and unfurnished. Well, nearly two thirds of our stay in Chicago have already passed.

Do you know a man called Lewis Feuer in Cambridge? Malisoff sent me a paper of Feuer, asking whether he should take it for the *Philosophy of Science*. It seems that Feuer has delivered this paper before the Philosophical Club in Harvard last December? I do not think that he has a clear idea about my views.

Ina was ill about three weeks, but now she is again well.

With our warmest regards to both of you,

Yours,
R. Carnap

[1] The method of reduction of concepts. Positivism and Physicalism. The unity of science on a physical basis.
[2] The instrumental function of mathematics in the operations of empirical science.

[37.   QUINE TO MORRIS   1936-3-6]

91 Washington Avenue
Cambridge, Mass.
March 6, 1936

Dear Professor Morris,

Your own high opinion of Carnap has my enthusiastic support. It is no wonder that he is becoming one of the most discussed of current philosophers, when we survey what he has produced in the past decade. His *Logischer Aufbau der Welt* marks the advent of logistic method in epistemology. It is a bold attempt to carry out, explicitly and rigorously, the reduction of the physical world to immediate experience; a reduction of which generations of philosophers had talked, but which none had seriously undertaken. The program of the *Aufbau* bears the same relation to science in general that the program of *Principia Mathematica* bears to mathematics; and the former program is more ambitious even than the latter, just as the philosophy of science in general is a vaster subject than the philosophy of mathematics. A pioneer work which aims so high would be expected to be tentative and provisional in proportion; but the *Aufbau* is a monumental beginning, a work of amazing technical subtlety, and an indispensable base of reference for all further researches in this important direction. Too difficult technically to draw many readers, the book is only now coming into its own. Its growing influence is witnessed e.g. by the requests for a French translation, by the important supplementary researches in which Leonard and Goodman are now engaged, and by the fact that Leonard is to teach the subject at Harvard beginning next fall.

Following upon the *Aufbau* were Carnap's *Erkenntnis* papers and numerous other brief publications, dealing with problems of scientific and philosophical method; and these developments have now culminated in his *Logische Syntax der Sprache*, wherein the same technical subtlety characteristic of the *Aufbau* is now brought to bear upon the most general problems of philosophy. The *Logische Syntax* and associated publications occupy so central a position in current thought that representatives even of the unsympathetic philosophical schools now see in Carnap a major force with which they must reckon.

And the evolution does not end here. Carnap would regard the contribution of the *Syntax* as methodological rather than systematic; and its methodological power has worked not only to cope satisfactorily with some philosophical problems, but also to clear the way to further ones, which remain to be attacked by the same methods. It is with these further problems that Carnap is now engaged; and results of major significance may be expected all along the line, for he has introduced scientific method into philosophy.

Now a word, more particularly, concerning Carnap's status in mathematical logic. All who are actively engaged in this field would agree, I should think, in rating Carnap as of first rank. His *Abriss der Logistik*, to begin with, strikes me as the best practical manual of mathematical logic; I wish it existed in English for textbook purposes. But Carnap's importance in relation to logic runs far beyond such pedagogical concerns, and may be summed up rather under the following four heads:

(1) Carnap, far more than anyone else, has pointed the way to scientific application of logistical technique. There is some interest in this direction in the *Abriss*, but chiefly in the *Aufbau*; the latter is not only the first considerable instance of applying logistical technique to empirical subject matter, but an extremely impressive instance in point of results achieved.

(2) Carnap has seen, more fully than any other writer, the philosophical implications of the logistical point of view. It is basically an analysis of the nature of logistical systems that leads Carnap to the whole notion of logical syntax, the keynote of the new positivism.

(3) In the course of his practical use of logistic as of (1), Carnap has elaborated special logistical techniques, for purposes at hand, which are considerable technical contributions in their own right.

(4) His philosophical consideration of logistic has issued not only as of (2), but also in several contributions of first rank regarding central problems in the foundations of logistic and mathematics. The chief of these contributions is his distinction between the demonstrable and the analytic, and between the

refutable and the contradictory. This work has the importance, for current foundational developments, of ameliorating the difficult situation which results from Gödel's proof of the incompletability of arithmetic. It discloses a new sort of completeness which may still be sought, and reëstablishes the distinction, blurred by Gödel's theorem, between mathematics and physics. Through this contribution alone Carnap takes his place as one of the chief figures in the new foundational crisis.

Very sincerely yours,
Willard V. Quine

⟨While obviously not a letter to Carnap, this letter has been included here because of what it reveals of Quine's opinion of Carnap. Other letters such as letters of recommendation and referee reports will also be included for the same reason.⟩

[38. CARNAP TO QUINE   1936-3-15]

Prof. Dr. Rudolf Carnap
    Prag XVII   March 15, 1936.
N. Motol, Pod Homolkou 146

Dear Dr. Quine,

I told Dr. Weinberg, that he might ask you for sending him my manuscript "Testability", when you will have finished it. I have now changed my mind: if you have not yet sent it, I shall send him another copy; if you have already sent it, please let me know.

I bought the book "Essays for Whitehead" and I studied your paper with very much interest. I am very keen of discussing it when we meet in April.

Prof. Hocking wrote me that I should "make use of the facilities of the Faculty Club" in April. Does he mean that I should stay there or does it mean the permission of taking meals there?

Please, could you kindly recommend us a quiet Hotel in Cambridge? I remember your kind invitation to stay with you very well. But since Ina is coming with me and since we intend to stay from April 8–13, we would prefer to stay at a Hotel.

So far, my affair here is still undecided.

With warmest greetings from Ina and me to both of you,

> Very sincerely yours,
> R. Carnap

[39.   INA CARNAP TO QUINE   1936-3-17]

The Midway Apartment Hotel,
1535 East, 60th Street,
    Chicago, Illinois.   March 17, 1936.

Dear Dr. Quine,

A good thing has happened: Carnap has got an offer from Princeton University. The inofficial question whether he would be interested in such a position came 2 weeks ago, and yesterday the official offer came: 5000$ a year, 10 hours teaching a week. These 10 hours comprehend only 2 or 3 hours graduate lectures and all the other time is undergraduate work, not all lecturing, but partly discussions. The offer is understood as being next (to) for one year and becoming prolongated or even permanent if there is mutual satisfaction.

You can imagine how glad we were, especially because the affair here does not look so very splendid. Carnap will delay the final answer to Princeton as long as possible for seeing how it will turn out in Chicago. But it was a great relief for him to see that the problem of the next year seems to be solved either so or so.

I thought you might be interested to know it as soon as possible. That is the reason why I am writing while Carnap is not here. He has left for Urbana yesterday.

The sky is blue and the sun is shining and perhaps we shall buy a car before we leave Chicago and shall make the lecture

tour in our own car. It would be fun. Only so far we are beginners in driving. But we both like it very much.

Please give my love to Naomi. I am very glad to see you both
in a short time!

Very sincerely yours,
Ina Carnap

[40.   CARNAP TO QUINE   1936-3-29]

Chicago, March 29, 1936.

Dear Dr. Quine,

Thank you very much for your wire! We shall leave Chicago
on March 31st in the morning and go in our new car to the
East. Since we are both beginners in driving, we wish to take it
easy and therefore we will need a lot of time. I shall be in Buffalo on April 6th. Would you please be so kind as to write me
just a line to this place—c.o. Prof. M. Farber, Department of
Philosophy—giving the name of the hotel in Cambridge, which
you can recommend us. You probably know that I put much
weight on quietness. May I ask you a second favour? If you
have concluded from my last letter that I was meant to stay in
the Faculty Club by Prof. Hocking, would you please phone
him, that I shall come with Mrs. Carnap and therefore I shall go
in a hotel?

It is hard for me to figure out what day we shall arrive in
Cambridge, either in the afternoon of April 8th or more probably some time on April 9th. And my plans are now so, that I
would have to leave Cambridge on the 12th. But in this case I
should try to come again for a few days more at the end of the
month.

With our best regards and warmest greetings to both of you
from Ina and me,

Very sincerely yours,
R. Carnap

[41. QUINE TO CARNAP   1936-4-2]

91 Washington Avenue
Cambridge, Mass.
April 2, 1936.

Dear Mr. Carnap,

I am sorry to be so late in replying. Three weeks ago I found
what looks to be a solution to the problem in which I have been
mainly interested for several years; and I have been hurrying to
work out the details and write up a brief account for quick publication in the *Proc. Nat. Acad. Sci.* I postponed my reply to you
until accomplishing this, because I thought always that I could
finish my paper earlier than has actually proved to be the case.
Now, having finally mailed the paper last evening, I am shocked
to see that it is April 2, I just now set about to write you this
letter in duplicate, and send one copy to Chicago and the other
to your American Express address in New York; but this course
was made unnecessary by the arrival, a few minutes ago, of
your letter containing the Buffalo address.

The point of the paper in question is indicated by the title: "A
Theory of Classes Presupposing No Canons of Type". You shall
see a copy of the manuscript when you come.

We are very happy about all the good news. The Princeton
opening is very fine; and Princeton is a good place to be. You
are now in a position to choose between Princeton and Chicago
at least, on the basis of the relative merits of the two offers; and
the important thing is, you are certain to stay permanently in
America! The wish of three years has finally been realized. We
are disappointed that you will not be here in Cambridge with us
next year, but this is relatively a detail; and one which I hope
will be rectified before long.

How fine to have your own car, and to drive about the
country!

Naomi has investigated hotels and other lodgings, and has
found something that looks good. Brattle Inn is an establishment near the university comprising a dining room, some rooms
for transients, and other rooms occupied through the year. The

latter are occupied chiefly by young Harvard instructors, among them John Cooley. The place consists of a group of three houses, very clean and comfortable, and run by high-grade people; less pretentious than a hotel, but quieter. Naomi has inspected a suite of two rooms and bath there, simple but comfortable, with a big desk in one of the rooms; this can be had for a total of $3 a day. This is just half what two rooms and bath would cost in a hotel, for hotels are very expensive here.

Remember that you are more than welcome to stay with us; but if you feel the other plan would be more practical, Brattle Inn is to be recommended. Naomi has tentatively reserved the described suite, so there is nothing that you need to do.

Come first to us in any case when you reach Cambridge, for we are very anxious to see you both; then we can lead you to your destination at your leisure. For finding us it will be simplest, no matter which route you take from Buffalo to Boston, to adopt Arlington, Mass. (next town to Cambridge) as your destination. Certain routes from Buffalo would take you to Arlington automatically on the way to Boston. If on the other hand you come via Route 20, which is most likely, Arlington is slightly out of the way; but very slightly, and still simplest. If you come via Route 20, you must leave Route 20 in the city of Waltham (near Boston); immediately past the central point of Waltham you will see a sign directing you leftward for Arlington. If you have to inquire for Arlington and are asked what part you want, ask for Arlington Center; but the described route takes you right to it.

For what follows, Arlington Center is the starting point. As mentioned, you may have reached this point from either of several directions, depending upon the route chosen from Buffalo. From Arlington Center, now, follow Massachusetts Avenue, the chief highway of Arlington, toward Cambridge and Boston. Be careful at the start to select Massachusetts Avenue; here is a map of Arlington Center:

⟨Presumably there was a map here, but none survives on Quine's carbon copy of this letter.⟩

Follow Massachusetts Avenue 2.4 miles. (After about the first mile you will have entered the city of Cambridge.) You then find yourselves at Porter Square, which is very close to our home. Here is a map showing how to get to us:

⟨Presumably there was a map also here but again none survives on the carbon.⟩

We will be at home constantly on the 8th and 9th, expecting you. If you have the slightest difficulty in finding the way, telephone me (ELIot 0488) and I will bicycle to you.

Many thanks for the second reprint of "On the Character etc.", which I am very glad to have. Thanks also for having your very interesting manuscript sent to us; several of us have read it together with great interest and profit. I am keeping it here, to deliver it to you when you arrive.

When Mr. Hocking offered the Faculty Club he intended lodging, not knowing that Mrs. Carnap was coming. It seems however that there are no lodging facilities for women. But you are both to have meals there. (I have not talked with Mr. Hocking, but with the department secretary, who knows all these things best.) I shall be glad to phone Mr. Hocking today, as you requested in this latest letter.

With kindest regards to both,

Sincerely yours,
W. V. Quine

[42. CARNAP TO QUINE   1936-4-6]

April 6, 1936.

Dear Quine,

Once more good news: I have received an offer from the University of Chicago, permanent professorship, $5500, about 6 hours teaching a week, mostly for graduates. I think, this conditions are very fine, especially the amount of teaching hours is less than I dared to hope to find in this country. Very probably I shall accept this offer, but in any case I shall delay the decision till I have spoken with the Princeton people. I am very happy.

The travel in our car is great fun; we enjoy it very much. But of course it is stretching and tiring for beginners. And likewise the late parties and discussions in Ann Arbor. For the next two days we shall have rather great distances to drive. Therefore I should like to find some rest during the days in Cambridge. For the first day (April 9) the programme contains lecture, dinner and discussion. During the other two days we should like to see you and Naomi, perhaps have a conversation with you, Lenard and Goodman and to see Mr. and Mrs. Whitehead, if they like. Perhaps we ought to delay other appointments until our return at the end of April. As to appointments for April 10 and 11 I would prefer afternoon to evening.

Perhaps this evening I shall find news from you at Professor Farbers home. But I want to send this without delay.

With kindest regards from both of us,

> yours,
> R. Carnap

[43. CARNAP TO QUINE   1936-6-2]

6-2-36.

Dear Quine, we are living in such a bungalow, but in a more isolated one, and enjoy sunshine, fresh air and fine landscape. Fortunately we decided to go southwards (not before the morning when we left Ithaca). At this height here it is not at all too hot; in the evenings sometimes even rather chilly. On the whole, the climate is very agreeable. I am rewriting the Testability paper. It becomes still longer therefore I consider the question of publishing it as a little book. Do you think it would be possible at Harvard Press?

Best greetings $2 \rightarrow 3$, your R. Carnap

⟨This and the following item (44) are postcards. This one is a picture postcard showing on the reverse "A few of the Rustic Bungalows at Skyland, Virginia, Shenandoah National Park."⟩

[44. CARNAP TO QUINE   1936-6-5]

R. Carnap. (At least until June 10:) Skyland Va.

June 5, 1936.

Dear Quine, The Ass. f. Symb. Logic asks for the title of my
lecture in September. The other day we talked about the possibility of lecturing about "demonstrable" and "analytic"; what do
you thing of the title: "(The Concept of) Truth in Mathematics
(and Logic)"? (with or without the words in brackets?) or have
you a better suggestion?

Just I received the programm of the Summer School (via
Prague). I am sorry, my lectures are not, as Hocking wrote me,
according to my wishes, at 11 and 12, but at 9 and 10; and at 11
and 12 are the lectures of Prall. But I guess, now it is to late for
any change. And perhaps Prall wanted these hours; then it is of
course alright.

We have a very fine time here. Best regards.

R. Carnap

[45. QUINE TO CARNAP   1936-6-8]

91 Washington Avenue
Cambridge, Mass.
June 8, 1936

Dear Carnap,

I should favor the title "Truth in Mathematics and Logic".

MacLane tells me that Curry has written you and not had a
reply; perhaps another case of mismanagement of mail at the
Am. Express. What Curry wants to know (among other things
perhaps) is the title of the paper, for the list of papers is to go to
press on June 15. I told MacLane that, if a reply should not be
received from you in time for the printing, the title suggested
above should be printed; for this was one of the four possibilities suggested on your recent card.

The Am. Math. Soc. has requested me to summarize your

coming lecture of Sept. 1; the summary is to be printed
promptly after the lecture, and I was told that they would like
to have the summary even before the lecture if possible. I
thought it would be both easier and more satisfactory for you to
write the summary yourself, and have consequently replied with
the suggestion that they make that request directly of you.

We are glad to hear you are enjoying your trip, and are looking forward to seeing you again in a few weeks.

Excuse the hurriedness; I am late (as usual) to an
engagement.

Best regards to both.

> Yours,
> Quine

[46. CARNAP TO QUINE   1936-6-17]

June 17, 1936.

Dear Quine,

We are still in Skyland; it is very quiet and beautiful here but
we would have gone a little farther if my work on the Testability
paper were finished. But rewriting it I have completely changed
the first parts and it seems to get the length of a little book now.
I hope to be through with it in a few days and perhaps then we
shall change the place.

Thank you very much for your letter of June 8. I did not
answer Curry before your letter came, because in his letter to
me he asked for the title and an abstract of 200 words until July
10th. So I thought, I had plenty of time to wait for your answer
concerning the title. Now I have given him the title "Truth in
Mathematics and Logic" and promised to send an abstract until
July 10. Do you not think, I could use the same abstract also for
the Am. Math. Soc. or had it to be longer? Of course, I prefer to
write it myself.

Sometimes I find myself dreaming that Smith have rented
their house to somebody else and that we shall find us, coming

back, not only without a shelter but also that all our mail from
Europe and America which we have ordered to be sent there
will never get in our hands. Can you comfort my soul and as-
sure me that we are to stay in Smith's house? Do you have the
keys for us or the Cohins? We intend to come back on July 3rd.

Feigl has written that he intends to come to Cambridge about
the middle of July; he will attend my classes.

I hope, you all are well and not too hot. Please give our best
regards to Naomi!

Yours,
R. Carnap

[47.   CARNAP TO QUINE   1936-6-18]

June 18, 1936

Dear Quine,

Yesterday I received a letter from Hocking telling, that Dr.
Leonard and Dr. Arnold Isenberg have applied for being assistant to me during the summer school. It seems that I have a
choice in this case. Whom would you recommend? There is no
hurry to decide because whether there will be appointed an assistant at all depends upon the number of students enrolling for
my courses; if over 20 are enrolling, they will appoint an assistant. What has such an assistant to do??

Further I got a letter from Mrs. Robert W. Sayles inviting us
to stay in their home during the Tercentenary days. Since we
hope to stay in the Smith's house I intend to refuse.

Did you happen to hear any thing about the hours of my
lectures?

I hope, I shall have finished "Testability" in another two days
and shall be able to enjoy holidays after that.

With best regards 2:2,

Yours,
R. Carnap

[48.   QUINE TO CARNAP   1936-7-18]

CORRECTIONS OF *LOGISCHE SYNTAX* DUE TO McKINSEY OR QUINE
(UNLESS ANTICIPATED BY OTHERS)

McKINSEY:

a. |
(1) P. 29, RI 2. (McKinsey showed the rules to be inadequate. Quine showed how to make the correction.)

(2) P. 55, D 29 and next few lines. (McKinsey showed the original form to be wrong. Carnap showed how to make

b.
the correction.)

(3) P. 60, D 64. (McKinsey showed both the error and the correction.)

(4) P. 62, D 83. McKinsey showed the inadequacy of the *Schranke*.

QUINE:

c. | (1) P. 29, RI 2. (See (1) above.)

d. | (2) P. 175, line 14: insert negation sign.

(3) P. 178, foot. (Quine showed the error [letter of Dec. 1934]; Carnap showed how to correct it.)

W. V. Q.
18, VII, 36

[MARGINALIA ON CARNAP'S COPY AND IN CARNAP'S GERMAN SHORTHAND:]

a. Tarski
b. §21, 22 McKinsey/3 Improvements in Chapter II
c. Tarski
d. §62, 63 Quine Quine

[49.   CARNAP TO QUINE   1936-8-21]

Bethlehem, Aug. 21., 1936.

Dear Quine,

today we decided to leave this cottage near Bethl., perhaps you got in the mean time my card sent to Franklin describing its

situation. We intend to go to Maine, to the Northern lake region. Address: Rangeley (Maine), general delivery. If you come
there you can learn our address and place at the post office in
R. Probably we shall be there until Aug. 30. It would be very
fine to see you there. If you decide to come, send a wire so that
we could inform you in case of change of place.

With best regards to you and Na from the three of us, yours

R. Carnap

⟨Postcard⟩

[50.   QUINE TO CARNAP   1936-8-24]

61 Frost St.
Cambridge, Aug. 24, 1936

Dear Carnap,

I just returned from a good 6-day trip with Loesch, the friend
whom we have been expecting. We were sorry not to be able to
look you up, but we decided not to visit the White Mts.; instead
we went into the woods of northern Maine and climbed
Katahdin. This is the most impressive mtn. in New Eng.,
though not the highest. Then we passed Moosehead Lake and
proceeded to Quebec.

You remember Curtis—you haven't met him, but have sent
him reprints. His, I think, is the chief responsibility for your
tercentenary nomination. He is the one who was recently fired
from the corporation of Harvard because of his divorce and re-
marriage. He is very intelligent; a lawyer, but with a broad
range of academic interests: very enthusiastic, and good company. He has been wanting to meet you, and would like to arrange to take you and Ina and Naomi and me to supper when
you come in September. Are you willing to have your solitude
broken by another Cambridge social engagement? Any evening
but Friday, Sat., and Sun. seems to be possible for Curtis. As

soon as I hear from you as to the possible dates (if any!) I will pass the word on to Curtis.

With best regards to you both and to Feigl,

> Yours,
> Van

[51. QUINE TO CARNAP 1936-11-15]

> 61 Frost St., Cambridge
> Nov. 15, 1936

Dear Carnap,

I enclose a copy of a paper which I am ready to send off for publication, and which I plan also to use (minus footnotes) for my invited address before the Math. Assn. at Durham, N. C. on Dec. 31.

I am anxious to have you look this over as soon as possible, to see whether you have reason to suppose the system contradictory: for it looks dangerous, and on the other hand if consistent it looks important. Read the last three pages first, to see both the significance and the dangers of the system. The whole paper will not take long to read, for it is not in the condensed style of most of my papers. There are some matters on pp. 6–8 which I think will interest you incidentally (though they do not contribute to the doubtful aspect).

Ina would dislike the first five pages.

I am glad of the invitation to speak before the Association because it may help bring offers of jobs. I hope for such offers, either for acceptance as improvements over the present job, or as bases for asking advancement here.

Many thanks for the recent reprint answering Schrödinger. It is valuable in revealing an aspect of your position which people tend to miss.

I will be very grateful for your views on the enclosed.

Naomi joins me in best regards to Ina and yourself. I hope the work at Chicago is proving pleasant. I am enjoying my two graduate courses very much; the tutoring less. We are all well, and Elizabeth almost talks.

Yours,

⟨Quine symbol⟩

⟨This letter is signed with a symbol in Carnap's shorthand for 'Quine'. Curiously the symbol is explained only at the bottom of Carnap's next letter. Conceivably, after receiving 52, Quine could have gone back to his own previous letter and marked the carbon with the symbol. Since the symbol is difficult to reproduce, it will be indicated as above (except in 52).⟩

[52.   CARNAP TO QUINE   1936-11-19]

RUDOLF CARNAP
Department of Philosophy
  University of Chicago   Chicago, Illinois   Nov. 19, 1936.

Dear Quine,

   I read your paper very carefully and with the highest interest. If it will be found to avoid the known antinomies it will indeed be extremely interesting and valuable. So far, I do not see any contradiction in the system itself, i.e., without the definitions. But I share your feeling that the whole looks rather dangerous. The *contradictions* which I shall explain (connected with the definitions) can themselves be avoided, I suppose, by modifying the definitions. But I am not quite sure, whether they are not perhaps symptomatic for a more general character of the system itself which then would lead to other contr. if these ones are excluded.

   Thus I shall in the following raise my objections against the definitions as if they belonged to the system. You will then have to find out whether the defects are only superficial and do not affect the system itself.

1. The definitions, as written, seem to me to be such that a different temporal order of their application leads to essentially

different results, espec. with respect to D 9. Therefore we can construct a contradiction (provided I did obey all your rules; I am not quite shure). Let "a" be defined as a class symbol; we define: $\qquad$ b $\qquad$ for $\qquad$ $-a$ $\hfill$ (1)

The following is demonstrable:

$$(\imath x)\ (x \in y)\ \in b\ \equiv\ (\imath x)\ (x \in y)\ \in b \tag{2}$$

Now we transform first only the left side; first we eliminate the description by D9

$$(\exists z)\ ((z \in b)\ \cdot\ (x)\ ((x{=}z)\ \equiv\ x \in y))\ \equiv\ \text{- - - (as above)} \tag{3}$$

Now we elim. "b" and "-":

$$(\exists z)(\sim(z \in a)\ .\ (x)(.\ .\ .))\qquad\qquad \equiv \qquad\qquad \text{- - -} \tag{4}$$

Now we transform the right side, but here we elim. first "b" and "-":

$$\text{-- -- --}\qquad\qquad \equiv \sim((\imath x)(x \in y)\ \in a) \tag{5}$$

and then the description:

$$(\exists z)\ (\sim(z \in a)\ .\ (x)\ (.\ .\ .))\ \equiv\ \sim(\exists z)\ ((z \in a)\quad.\ (x)\ (.\ .\ .)) \tag{6}$$

This is contradictory. (If we put e.g. "Λ" for "y" the right side becomes analytic, the left side contradictory, therefore the whole contradictory).

Way out: a rule concerning the order of applying the definitions.

2. I have some serious doubts as to *D 10*. If I am not mistaken it leads to the following result. If the describing function in the description ". . ." is contradictory then every sentence of the form "$y \in$ . . ." is, according to D 10, contradictory; hence, acc. to P1, ". . ." is synonymous to "Λ". If I am right in this, a contradiction arises. Let "e" be a defined constant.

Def.: $\qquad$ c for $(\imath x)\ ((x \in e)\ .\ \sim(x \in e))$ $\hfill$ (7)

It follows, with the help of D $10\frac{1}{2}$

$$(y)\ (\sim(y \in c)) \tag{8}$$

hence $(y)\ (y \in c\ \equiv\ y \in \Lambda)$ $\hfill$ (9)

hence, acc. to P1: $\qquad\qquad$ c $= \Lambda$ $\hfill$ (10)

Let d be a class to which Λ belongs (e.g. $\{\ \Lambda\}$):

$$\Lambda \in d \tag{11}$$

(10), (11): $\qquad$ c $\in$ d $\hfill$ (12)

(12) (7):　　　　　$(\imath x) ((x\in e) . \sim(x\in e)) \in d$　　　　　(13)

(13), D 10:　　　$(\exists z) (z\in d . (x)$

　　　　　　　　$((x=z) \equiv (x\in e \quad . \quad \sim(x\in e)))$　　　　(14)

hence:　　　　　$(\exists z) (z\in e . \sim(z\in e))$　　　　　(15)

This is contradictory.

3. There are two possible ways (chiefly) for defining
"$x \ni (. . .)$":

　　a) $y \in x \ni (. . .)$ for $(. . .) \binom{y}{x}$ (substitution)

　　b) by a description, as in D11.

I have some doubts as to *D 11*, in connection with D 10. Let us take as "$. . .$" a function which is not stratified, e.g. "$\sim(x \in x)$". (This function is not contradictory; I suppose e.g. that "$\sim(\Lambda \in \Lambda)$" is demonstrable; therefore this point is different from 2). As you say correctly on p. 16, it can be shown that there is no class corresponding to this "$. . .$":

　　　　$\sim(\exists u) (x) ((x\in u) \equiv \sim(x\in x))$　　　　　(16)

On the other hand, let us put

　　c' for $x \ni(\sim x\in x)$　　　　　(17)

(17), D 11: $(y\in c') \equiv y\in (\imath z) (x) ((x\in z) \equiv \sim(x\in x))$　　(18)

(18), D10: $(y\in c') \equiv (\exists u) ((y\in u) . (z) ((z=u) \equiv (x) ((x\in z \equiv$
$\sim(x\in x)))))$　　　　　(19)

　　　$(y\in c') \supset (\exists u) (y\in u . (x) (x\in u \equiv \sim(x\in x)))$　　(20)

(20) (16): $(y) (\sim(y\in c'))$　　　　　(21)

hence, analogous to (8), (9), (10): $c' = \Lambda$　　　　　(22)

Hence there is still a class corresponding to the function
"$\sim(x\in x)$", in contradiction to (16); this leads probably to Russell's antinomy.

Way out: perhaps restrict D 11 to stratified functions !

Some minor remarks:

4. p.2, last line is not quite clear.

5. p.11, note 13. R5 and R2 have also been used by Hilbert a. Ackerman 1928.

6. p.13, line 10. "$n \geqq 1$".

7. p.16, line 9 from below. Instead of "derivability": "demonstrability".

8. p.7, D9 and 10. Interesting method, avoiding Russell's awkward operator "[(ıx) (- - -)]". The price, paid for this, is—as you certainly have seen—that certain sentences cannot be formulated by the help of a description, e.g. "the only member of y is not a member of z". The formula "~((ıx)(x∈y)∈z)" does not mean this, because if y has several members this formula is true while the sentence mentioned before is false. I should not regard this to be a serious disadvantage, but for D 11 which makes all class expressions descriptions.

Best thanks for your recent offprint!

Can you give me the address of Leonard?

I hope very much that you will be able to overcome all difficulties.

We are quite well. I have good audiences.

With best regards to Naomi and yourself, from both of us,

yours,
Carnap

I keep your MS so you may refer to it in your answer if you wish to. Please write whether you want it back!

⟨There then appears the following illustration indicating how to write 'Quine' in Carnap's German shorthand:⟩

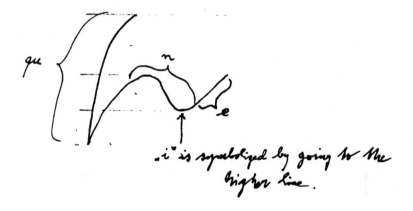

[53.   QUINE TO CARNAP   1936-11-21]

Cambridge, Nov. 21, 1936

Dear Carnap,

Many thanks for reading and criticizing my paper so promptly and carefully.

While I also am doubtful of the consistency of the system, and three contradictions derived in your letter seem to depend on applying the rules illegitimately to defined expressions. We are to think of R1, R2, R3', R4, R5 as applied ultimately to formulae in primitive notation (see p. 3 of paper), and therefore any contradiction derivable by help of the def'ns should be derivable without that help—unless the def'ns fail of unique eliminability.

Consider 1 of your letter. Here "b" is short for "−a", hence for "z∃ ~ (z∈a)" hence for "(ıw) (z) ((z∈w) ≡ ~ (z∈a))". (But see also note 5 of paper; choice of letters depends on the definition of "a".) Hence each side of your (2) is short for "((ıx) (x∈y)∈ (ıw) (z) ((z∈w) ≡ ~ (z∈a)))". And there is only one way of expanding this, in view of p. 7 (foot); viz., the first stage in the expansion* is "(∃t) ((t∈(ıw) (z) ((z∈w) ≡ ~ (z∈a))) · (x) ((x=t) ≡ (x∈y)))".

The fallacy in 1 is your equivalence (5), which depends on the invalid assumption that ((ıx) (x∈y) ∈−a) ≡ ~ ((ıx) (x∈y) ∈a). True, we have the theorem "((u ∈−v) ≡ ~ (u∈v))"; but substitution here of a description "(ıx) (x∈y)" for the variable "u", or an abbreviated description "a" for the variable "v", is not in general valid—not in general capable of being accomplished by R1, R2, R3', R4, R5. Substitution of a description for a variable must be justified by a syntactical theorem, showing how the corresponding operation could be performed in primitive notation by R1, R2, R3', R4, R5. *Any* step of inference involving definitional abbreviations needs the same sort of justification.

This perhaps makes the system appear technically awkward: a description or an abstractive class expression (which is also a description) cannot in general be substituted for a variable. How-

*I here ignore proper choice of letters

ever I can prove the syntactical theorem that, *given* a theorem E! $(\imath\alpha)\ \phi$ [i.e., $(\exists\beta)(\alpha)((\alpha = \beta) \equiv \phi)$], we can substitute $(\imath\alpha)\ \phi$ for any variable. Also, the stronger theorem syntactical that $((\beta)\ \omega \supset (E!\ (\imath\alpha)\ \psi \supset {}^{(\imath\alpha)\psi}_{\omega\ \beta)}$ is always demonstrable (granted obvious stipulations regarding scopes of bound variables). Since R3′ and P1 provide in general that E!y $\ni$ --- [i.e., E!($\imath$z) (y) ((y$\in$z) $\equiv$ ---)] for any stratified formula "---", it becomes possible to substitute "y$\ni$ ---" for variables whenever "---" is stratified. The substitution is also possible, of course, whenever we manage (as on p. 16) to prove "E!y$\ni$ ---" for unstratified "---".

Perhaps this clears up your 2 and 3 also, and the last sentence of 8.

Thus, in 2, (8) and (9) are valid but (10) is not. (10) depends on substituting "c" for "x" and "Λ" for "y" in P1. Granted, "Λ" *can* be substituted for "y" in P1—more accurately, the formula (primitive notation) whereof the result of this substitution is an abbreviation can be derived by the rules from P1. This can be shown, as mentioned earlier, because we can prove that E!Λ. But "c" *cannot* be substituted for "x", because, by (7), ~E!c.

Again, in 3, (16)–(21) are correct but (22) not. The derivation of (22) is blocked by the circumstance observed above in connection with (10).

But your argument in 1 reveals this inaccuracy in the paper: p. 7, end of last paragraph, add "except in degenerate cases"— meaning, cases where ~E!($\imath$x)---.

My objection to your definition a, under 3, is that it does not explain "(x$\ni$ --- $\in$y)" ("y" being a variable).

I agree with your point in 8 (except for last sentence, concerning which see above). Of course the same objection applies to Russell's method insofar as the operator "[($\imath$x)---]" is suppressed: for this is suppressed where the scope is minimal. But it may be said in Russell's defense that he can always accommodate sentences such as your example by restoring the operator; whereas in my method the only recourse would be to primitive notation.

But I am now tending to favor the following course: define descriptions so as to provide the intended meanings in all cases where E!($\imath$x)---, but without caring what the contexts come to mean in the trivial cases where ~E!($\imath$x)---. Indeed, this attitude motivated my treatment of descriptions in *System of Logistic,* and perhaps also your theory of the K-operator. Hence I incline, in my lectures, to still simpler definitions than D9-10; viz.,

viz., $((\imath\alpha)\ \phi \in \beta)$ for $(\alpha)(\phi \subset (\alpha \in \beta))$

and $(\beta \in (\imath\alpha)\ \phi)$ for $(\alpha)(\phi \subset (\beta \in \alpha))$.

Obviously these are equivalent to D9-10 and also to Russell's definition whenever E!$(\imath x)$---. On second thought I believe I will use these simpler definitions even in the paper.

As to 4 of your letter: I am glad to have the obscurity pointed out, and will change the phrasing. The intention is to interpret "∈" as follows: if y is an individual, $(x \in y)$ if and only if $x = y$; if y is a class, $(x \in y)$ if and only if x is a member of y. An obvious alternative course would be to decide that $\sim(x \in y)$ wherever y is an individual; but this would require providing P1 with the hypothesis that y is not an individual, and this hypothesis is inexpressible in my primitives. For a peculiarity of the present course, however, see p. 3, note 3.

I am very glad to learn of the misprint 6; also of the bibliography 5. I am changing note 13 accordingly. But it seems that Hilbert-Ackermann cannot be said to use R2; they have a certain formal axiom, using predicate variables, and a rule of substitution in addition. My new note 13 will thus refer to Hilbert-Ack. in a form roughly parallel to the original reference to Tarski. But I am also going to make sure tomorrow that there is no anticipation in your *Logische Syntax;* that book is in my office in Eliot House, and I am now home.

I will not need your copy of the MS.

Leonard's address is: 21 Waverley Avenue, Newton, Mass. a good street for a logistician.

Now a word of admonition to Ina: "sure", not "shure"!

Again, many thanks for your help. With best regards,

Yours,
⟨Quine symbol⟩

⟨The footnote in the third paragraph is Quine's own.⟩

[54. QUINE TO CARNAP   1936-11-27]

61 Frost St., Cambridge
Nov. 27, 1936

Dear Carnap,

Lines 2 to 7 of page 3 of my last letter (Nov. 21) are to be disregarded. The two definitions stated there give undesirable results when the variables α and β are the same letter. Thus we get:

$$((\imath x)\ (x{=}y)\ (\in x) \quad \equiv \quad (y{\in}y))$$
$$\text{instead of:} \quad ''\quad''\quad''\quad'' \quad \equiv \quad (y{\in}x));$$
$$\text{likewise:} \quad (x{\in}\ (\imath x)\ (x{=}y)) \quad \equiv \quad (y{\in}y))$$
$$\text{instead of:} \quad ''\quad''\quad''\quad'' \quad \equiv \quad (x{\in}y)).$$

Thanks for the interesting reprint on Extremalaxiome. I have only skimmed it so far, but will soon read it carefully.

Yours,
⟨Quine symbol⟩

⟨The first sentence refers to letter 53, paragraph 12, sentences 3 through end: "Hence I incline, in my lectures, . . . even in the paper."⟩

[55. CARNAP TO QUINE   1937-1-26]

RUDOLF CARNAP
Department of Philosophy
University of Chicago   Chicago, Illinois, January 26, 1937

Dear Quine,

Thank you very much for your two letters. While I would like very much to discuss the questions and problems of your letters further, I think, it takes to much time to do it by writing; but I hope to see you in not too far a time.

A few weeks ago a part of my books from Europe arrived and I found several copies of "Der Raum" in them; thus I shall send you one copy in the next days.

I cannot see from my notes whether you already have these two reprints of mine:

(30) "Methode der logischen Analyse" (Philosophenkongress Prag)

~~(31) "Philosophy and Logical Syntax" (3 lectures delivered in London)~~

(I see, you have it)

If you do not have them and would care to have them, please let me know.

I also found several reprints of other authors among my books which I have twice. I enclose a list of those and you may choose all you like.

The translation of the "Syntax" is to appear very soon. And the second part of "Testability" will be out in a few days. I ordered the reprints of "Testability" both parts in one cover, and as soon as the second part appears, you will get an offprint. Likewise I have ordered to send you a copy of the "Syntax" as soon as it will be out.

Prof. Frank has sent money to several addresses in order to accumulate money here for his planned trip (he is only permitted to send money to different addresses, not a greater amount to one person). If you have received money for him, the simplest thing to do would be to send it to me.

A book of Waismann has been published: "Einführung in das mathematische Denken" (Verlag Gerold & Co., Wien I., Stefansplatz 8). It is not the book about Wittgenstein for which we have been waiting so long. It does not contain new things, but is a very good introduction in my eyes. Since Waismann too would like to come to America, he is very interested to see his book reviewed in an American Journal by a good man. Do you know somebody who could do it for the "Journal of Symbolic Logic", if you do not care to do it yourself?

Many thanks to Naomi and you for the nice Xmas card. I hope, you had nice holidays. We were not quite lucky this time. Just the day before our planned skiing trip I became sick. Something was wrong with my spine. The doctor thinks it was a combination of strain by doing exercises as a preparation for the skiing trip and a rheumatic attack. It was stupidly painful the first days, I had to lie on a hard surface—I did it on the floor—

and to wait for the healing. I was better after a week but had to lie in bed for another 10 days. Now I can be up, being supported by a brace, but I still do not feel quite allright, and I get tired quickly. But I hope that this symptoms will disappear in another few weeks. If you happen to see Mr. Curtis, give him our best regards. We regretted very much not to have been able to see him when he was in Chicago.

With love from us to both of you,

Yours,
R. Carnap

[56. QUINE TO CARNAP   1937-1-27]

61 Frost St.
Cambridge, Mass.
Jan. 27, 1937

Dear Carnap,

Naomi and I were very sorry to hear of your spinal difficulty, and hope the last signs of it will now soon be gone. Too bad you had to miss the skiing in Wisconsin. Hard floors are ill adapted to vacations.

I am glad I am going to have a copy of "Der Raum". Also I do not yet have "Methode der logischen Analyse", and would like to have it. And I have taken great pleasure in checking over your generous list of duplicate works of other authors and determining my wants, which are as follows: (3), (4), (5), (6), (13), (18), (19), (20). There are seven others which I neither selected nor already had, viz. (7), (12), (14), (15), (16), (17), (21); if you feel that certain of these (whereof I know nothing) would interest me as much as the next prospective recipient, I would of course be glad to have those also. E.g., I hesitated over (15). The remainder, viz. (1), (2), (8), [=1 (9)?], (10), (11),a and (22), I already have. Mention of this last and subtlest document reminds me:

(a) Jones or not Jones.
(b) x or not x.

If these are mere tautologies, why are they false? How can logical syntax hope to deal with basic problems such as this???

I am looking forward also to the English *Syntax* and the combined "Testability" reprint. I will be going through these with one at least of my tutees next half year, with omissions no doubt in the case of the *Syntax*.

Tom Chambers, by the way, would like a reprint of "Testability". During the past year or more his main interest has been moving toward method 'primarily of chemistry', and months ago in reply to his inquiry after general literature I suggested this as most relevant. His present address is:

The Athenaeum (τὸ ᾽Αθηναῖον)
California Institute of Technology
Pasadena, California

A money order for $8.32 in Kc came from Mrs. Frank some months ago; at first I thought of writing her in inquiry, but decided against this for fear of causing trouble with Bohemian authorities. Enclosed is a check for the amount; if you just deposit it to your account there, rather than trying to cash it, there will be no red tape.

I am writing Church about Waismann's book: He will select a reviewer if he finds that the book overlaps enough on symbolic logic (as he presumably will; I haven't seen it).

With best regards to both, also from Naomi,

Yours,

P.S.—We are invited to the Curtises' Sunday; I will give your message.

[57.   QUINE TO CARNAP   1937-2-17]

Cambridge, Feb. 17, 1937

Dear Carnap,

In my last letter I forgot to mention a request from Louis Harab, librarian of Robbins Library of Philosophy (Emerson Hall, Cambridge, Mass.), for a "Testability and Meaning" reprint. Though they have Philosophy of Science, he would like to bind this separately as a book for the library.

This term is much harder than last. Instead of my two graduate courses (phil. math. and math. logic) I have one graduate course (math. logic) and one elementary (logic): also 5 tutees as usual. The elementary course is rather depressing; the math. logic lectures come almost as a relaxation.

I hope all traces of that spinal disorder are now gone.

Naomi joins me in best wishes to you both.

> Yours,
> ⟨Quine symbol⟩

P.S.—Many thanks for the "Testability" reprint which you sent me. It makes a good book. I wish it were accessible to the general public thus in book form.

[58. QUINE TO CARNAP   1937-2-28]

> 61 Frost Street
> Cambridge, Mass.
> Feb. 28, 1937

Dear Carnap,

Many thanks for the many recent presents—"Der Raum" and the many accompanying reprints, and subsequently the English edition of the "Syntax". The latter is a very attractive job. I have a graduate student whom I am about to drive through the book—he will study it and then consult with me bi-weekly.

Thanks also for the references to me in the English edition; I am very grateful for the bibliography.

With best regards,

> Yours,
> ⟨Quine symbol⟩

[59. CARNAP TO QUINE 1937-3-5]

RUDOLF CARNAP
Department of Philosophy
  University of Chicago   Chicago, Illinois, March 5, 1937.

Dear Quine,

Thanks for your letters of February 17 and 28. I sent a copy of
"Testability" to Robbins Library.

Main purpose of this letter: The Department of Philosophy
here is working out a plan which sounds very attractive to me—
if it should succeed: a Research Seminar, meeting three quarters
each year (my idea: 1. Qu.: Formal Logic, Syntax, Semantic, 2.
Qu.: Foundations of Mathematics, 3. Qu.: Logic of the Empirical
Sciences). The plan is that there should be created a few assistantships with salaries between $1000–1500 a year; the research
assistants would have to participate in and to stimulate the seminar discussions, do a little teaching besides that and work on
their own problems. You know, how delighted I would be of
having you work with me. But unfortunately so far the budget
cannot be expanded for higher positions. Since this seminar is
to be made under my supervision (a similar one is planned under T. V. Smith for ethics etc.), I am to prepare a list of names of
possible assistants. Do you know of people in Harvard who
would be willing and able to do this job? I had Leonard and
Cooley in mind. But I suppose, they have both positions at Harvard; and since the Chicago plan is to change the participants in
the seminar every year, I do not know, whether they would like
to leave Harvard for such an uncertain job. In addition to this
doubt I would very much like to hear *your* opinion about their
scientific qualities. Is there somebody else you would recommend? I would be very obliged to you if you could send me
your answer so that I have it until next Thursday, because I
have to turn in the list on Friday. Please list the names in the   a.
order of your appreciation and answer the following questions
as well as you can do without much trouble and looking up
people: age; studies, where and when; degrees; married or not;
publications; teaching experience; present position and salary if
any. It is not quite certain that the president will back the plan

[231]

and it is not yet definite how many positions he will grant, I expect between 1 and 3. You can imagine how pleased I would be to do this work, especially in later years when the foundations will be built. Is it not a nice dream?

My spinal difficulties have not completely gone, but I feel much better.

With love to both of you,

> Yours,
> R. Carnap
> and ina. (how is Naomi and Elizabeth?)

P.S. If you should hear about somebody's intention of buying the English "Syntax": I can get it at the author's price of $4.70, whereas the retail price is $7.50!

⟨The small parenthetical question after Ina's name is in her hand. Marginalia on Quine's copy (in Carnap's hand):⟩

a. (please airmail!)

[60. QUINE TO CARNAP   1937-3-8]

> 61 Frost St.
> Cambridge, Mass.
> March 8, 1937

Dear Carnap,

Apart from (or perhaps even including) Olaf Helmer, whom you know more about than I do, my first recommendation for the proposed assistantships would be:

Dr. J.C.C. McKinsey. Ph.D. in math. received I think at Berkeley, Cal. Age unknown; looks 24 or less. Good mathematical insight, and very industrious. Probably one of the two or three most careful readers of the *Logische Syntax*. Publications:
"On the independence of Hilbert and Ack.'s postulates for the calculus of prop'l func'ns", *Am. Jour. of Math.* 57 (1936), pp. 336–344.

"On Boolean functions of many variables", *Trans. Amer. Math.
 Soc.* 40 (1936), p. 343–362.
"Reducible Boolean functions", *Bull. Amer. Math. Soc.* (1936), pp.
 263–267.
"On the generation of the functions Cpq and Np of Lukasiewicz
 and Tarski by means of a single binary operator", ebenda, pp.
 849–851.
"Boolean functions and points", *Duke Math. Journal* 2 (1936), pp.
 465–471.
There may be even more. He is a candidate at present for a
National Research Fellowship; but he might prefer your assis-
tantship. His present address is:

New York University, Washington Square, New York, N.Y.

I would recommend Henry Leonard just as highly; McKinsey
excels him in tangible logical accomplishments, but Leonard
makes it up in philosophical background and proved teaching
ability. (I know nothing of McK's teaching.)
Leonard's publications:
Essay in *Philosophical Essays for A. N. Whitehead*.
"The pragmatism and scientific metaphysics of C. S. Peirce",
 Phil. Review 4 (1937), pp. 110–121.
Review of my book, *Isis* 24 (1935), pp. 168–172.
Review of your "Testability and meaning" forthcoming in *Jour.
 Symb. Logic*.
Leonard is an excellent teacher, with about 7 years experience.
Ph.D. at Harvard in philosophy, about 1930. (Thesis in logic.)
Age about 31. Wife and child. Probably getting between $2000
and 2500 here. Plans for next year uncertain. I suppose he
couldn't accept $1500, with his family.

My next recommendation would be H. Nelson Goodman, 607
Boylston St., Boston. Candidate for Ph.D. Age about 30. Very
competent and industrious. An authority on the *Logischer
Aufbau*, and conversant with your later work. Well grounded in
philosophy and logic. As you know, he is in business—which
accounts for the lateness of his Ph.D. I am not sure that he
would not be interested in the assistantship. Teaching experience and publ'ns, none.

Next comes John C. Cooley, Leverett House, Cambridge,
Mass. Ph.D. at Harvard (phil.) in 1934. Thesis on you (mainly

Aufbau). Has developed a good background in logic, and some in fdtns. of math. Primary interest is scientific philosophy. Two or three years teaching experience (asst). Next to no salary. No publications. Unmarried; age perhaps 29.

a. | Another possibility is C. L. Stevenson, 39 Walker St., Cambridge, Mass. Ph.D. at Harvard (phil.) 3 or 4 years ago. 2 or 3 yrs. teaching expce. (asst. and tutor). Inclines to scientific philosophy—somewhere between you and the Cambridge (Eng.) people. Knows some logic, but less than Cooley. Publication: a paper on **values**, in current number of *Mind.*

Regarding **industry** and dependability, I know nothing of Cooley and Stevenson, but can rate Leonard and Goodman high; regarding teaching ability I know nothing of Goodman and Cooley, but can rate Leonard and Stevenson high.

Another possibility is Wm. T. Parry, 96 Prescott St., Cambridge, Mass. Ph.D. about 1932. 5 or 6 years teaching experience (asst). Knows elementary logic thoroughly. Seems to be slipping away from modal functions, which were the theme of his two short publications (*Mind* 43, pp. 78–80, and *Erg. math.Koll.*). But I am not sure about his interests in scientific philosophy; his spare time goes to *Science and Society,* of which he is business mgr. He is about 29, unmarried, and receiving negligible pay as assistant here.

I wish that new plan involved also a $3500 job—how I would like to take part in such a program!

Elizabeth now walks; also speaks a few meaningful words, but mostly meaningless chatter. She is in best of health. Naomi is fairly well—blood still not quite normal. She joins me in love to both.

Yours,
Quine

[MARGINALIA:]

a. Wife & 2 children   about 1500 supplemented privately
   Age 28.

[61. QUINE TO CARNAP   1937-3-16]

Cambridge, March 16, 1937

Dear Carnap,

Acting on the offer made in your last letter, I am enclosing a check from
Mr. Thomas G. Henderson
Eliot House D22
Cambridge, Mass.
for $4.70, for which he would like a copy of the English SYN-
TAX. He was greatly pleased to hear he could get it thus at
author's price.

I can now say pretty confidently that Goodman would be interested in the research assistantship there—though I cannot be
sure he would finally accept.

With best regards,

⟨Quine symbol⟩

[62. CARNAP TO QUINE   1937-4-5]

RUDOLF CARNAP
Department of Philosophy
University of Chicago   Chicago, Illinois, April 5, 1937.

Dear Quine,

Thanks for the check of Mr. Henderson for one copy of my
"Syntax". I ordered it right away and trust that he will have
received it.

Unfortunately the big plan concerning the Research Seminar
seems to have collapsed for financial reasons. There was a Meeting of the Board of Trustees where they decided a cut in expenses and this means practically no creation of new jobs.
McKeon thinks now, if there is any chance at all for the realiza-
tion of the plan, then in the best case 1 or two assistants could
be granted with a salary of at most $1000 a year. I had placed
Hempel and Helmer on top of my list of candidates. Thus—at

least for the coming year—Goodman would not be taken into consideration. Thank you very much for your notes and comments on the other candidates. I still hope to get McKinsey another year. Helmer also told me that he had met McKinsey in New York and that he had a very good impression of his personality. Helmer himself needs a job badly. So far nothing has turned out for him. And if he reaches the bottom of his resources he will just have to go back. I think he is very able and I want very much to help him. But how?

Ina is very keen to hear whether the Smith have blamed poor Naomi very much for having brought us to their house. It is unavoidable that one spoils one thing or another. Can you quiet Ina's conscience? We have enjoyed the summer and staying in this house very much and it was *very* good of Naomi that she has arranged it in this way. Tell this to Na and that Ina is sending her her love. Ina is very busy with her new study and all my correspondence and all my manuscripts are suffering under the negligence of my secretary.

With best regards to both of you

Yours,
R. Carnap

P.S. Do you think, the Harvard professors have the publications of the Tercentenary? or is it still worthwhile to send them offprints of my paper on logic?

[MARGINALIA ON BOTTOM OF LETTER:]

Answered in negative, Apr. 27

[63. QUINE TO CARNAP   1937-5-23]

61 Frost St.
Cambridge, Mass.
May 23, 1937

Dear Carnap,

Sheffer says he never received a reprint of "Testability and Meaning", and would like very much to have one. Address: Prof. H. M. Sheffer, Emerson Hall, Cambridge.

Perhaps you will soon hear from your Schwiegerlandsmann, Prof. Haberler, with a check for a copy of the English syntax at author's price.

I hope you are both now free from backaches. Naomi feels remarkable well these days, considering the extremity of her condition. The latest estimate places the birth just two days hence. Naomi's sister, who came by bus from California to be on hand during Naomi's confinement, is now here lifting all work and worry.

When will we see you? Will you come to Cambridge before sailing? If not, it would be fine if I could see you in New York; the probability is very small, but I would like, to know your schedule in case opportunity arises.

With best regards 3 ½ : 2,

Yours
⟨Quine symbol⟩

[64. QUINE TO CARNAP   1937-5-28]

61 Frost St.
Cambridge, Mass.
May 28, 1937

Dear Carnap,

Another friend of mine is taking advantage of your willingness to supply the English *Syntax* at author's price:
Dr. William Frankena
45 Trowbridge St.
Cambridge, Mass.
I enclose my check for $4.70, for which he has reimbursed me.

He would like very much to have a reprint of "Testability and Meaning", if you can spare it. He is regarded as our best Ph.D. in several years. He is not a logical positivist, but leans in that direction; influenced mainly by the analytic philosophy of G. E. Moore and his followers.

Yours,
⟨Quine symbol⟩

[65. CARNAP TO QUINE   DATE UNKNOWN, POSSIBLY
1937-6-5]

RUDOLF CARNAP
Department of Philosophy
University of Chicago   Chicago, Illinois   May 5 1937.

Dear Quine,

to-morrow we shall leave. We are packing in a hurry and, in addition, Ina had to-day her examination.

I ordered 5 copies of the Syntax for you from Harcourt. Please give one to Frankena, another to Haberler (if he wants one; he did not write to me), and the rest keep for later similar occasions. When somebody gets a copy, he may send me a cheque. (I got yours for Frankena). I sent a copy of "Testability" to Frankena.

I sent you some programms of the Research Seminar, perhaps you meet people who might be interested. More programs may be ordered from the Dept. of Philos.

It would be excellent to see you at New York. But I scarcely can hope that you will find it worth while to come since we could not have very much time together, I am afraid, because we have to do a lot of things. Maybe, I even have to fly to Washington because we do not have our Reentry Permit so far. Without it we cannot leave. Because of a misunderstanding we applied too late for it. But we hope that some phoning or wiring between the Immigration Offices in N.Y. and in W. will do.

With cordial regards to all four Quines (what is the structure-characteristic of the parent-relation in your family, represented by the maximal dual number, according to Logistik § . . . ? I believe: (0) 110000000000110.), from Ina too (with us:0000),

yours
R. Carnap

⟨The date of May 5, 1937, is clearly in error since the letter replies to letters 63 and 64.⟩

[66. QUINE TO CARNAP   1938-2-4]

[Note new address]

21 Waverley Av.
Newton, Mass.
Feb. 4, 1938. | a.

Dear Carnap,

I have been hoping to write for a long time, and have been accumulating many things to communicate; but I have been very busy. We have thought of you often, and gathered all possible news from the Goheens. Also I talked at length with Hempel, learning your new views. He has told you I am alarmed by them; v. infra. I was glad to meet Hempel, and liked him very much.

Last term I gave a course on "Logical Positivism", which is to say "Carnap". I enclose a copy of the exam; also a copy of the exam in my graduate course in Mathematic Logic.

I also enclose a copy of my Princeton talk. Nothing of importance, but I thought you might like to see what was in it, since the abstract gives little indication. Actually I made some last-minute changes not shown in this copy, but they were merely improvements in clarity and organization.

I have found three misprints in the English *Syntax*, as follows:
P. 21, line 11: initial inverted comma lacking.
P. 26, 11th line from foot: "Z" should be "Z_1".
P. 170, last line: initial inverted comma lacking.

Also I have found various non-typographical errors (unless I am mistaken), as follows:
P. 21, line 20: After "partial sentence" you should insert "or nu- | b.
merical expression", in order to provide for the case where A_2 is a K-operator.
P. 22, just above the example: "$A_1(\frac{z}{z}1)$" should be enclosed in | c.
inverted commas.   d.
P. 170, line 11: "some" should be "any". (German idiom has survived here, reversing the intended meaning.)
P. 290, second full-length line: drop all inverted commas. | e.

Simplification: On p. 30, last line of PSI 11, both denial signs
f. | could be avoided by contraposition.
Circularity: On p. 21, "bound" is defined in terms of "sentence"
(and "numerical expression"); on p. 26, vice versa. Could be
remedied by a more complex recursive definition using an auxil-
g. | iary notion of "rank". Note similar circularity *within* p. 26, be-
| tween "numerical expression" and "sentence". (I recognize that
these circularities do not survive in the arithmetized syntax.)

Also I found more far-reaching difficulties in the notion of
"quasi-syntactic". Insofar at least as these difficulties concern the
application to "denotation" etc., I gather that you are now
aware of them yourself. Another difficulty is that your formal
definition of "quasi-syntactic" seems to provide only for those
cases where the syntactic translation is logical, and thus does
h. | not support your descriptive examples.

It occurred to me that it might be amusing to add to your
syntactical concepts the concept of *the subject matter of* S: it could
i. | be defined as the content of S plus the content of ~S.

You may be interested in the following simplification of the
definition of similarity circle in the *Abriß* (p. 49):

$$\text{Sim'R} = {}_{df} \hat{\alpha}[\alpha = \hat{x}(\alpha \subset \vec{R} \, 'x)]$$

The definiens here is equivalent to yours, and uses no notations
which yours does not use; but it is only half as long. Alternative
j. | definientia, perhaps preferable psychologically:

$$\hat{\alpha}(x)(x \in \alpha \, . \, \equiv \, . \, \alpha \subset \vec{R} \, 'x)$$

$$\hat{\alpha} \, (x) \, [x \in \alpha \, . \, \equiv (y) \, (y \in \alpha \, . \supset . \, yRx)]$$

Your definition of quality class (*Aufbau*, p. 153) can also be
k. | shortened by half, as follows:

l. | $\text{qual} = {}_{df} \hat{\alpha}(\alpha = p \, '\hat{\beta} \, [\beta \in \text{ähnl} \, . \, \text{Nc'} \, (\alpha \cap \beta) > \text{Nc '} (\alpha - \beta)])$

Next I proceed to inveigh against your recent intensional pro-
pensities, as reported by Hempel. First I schematize your motivation, as I understand it:

(1) Intensional languages are legitimate, by the principle of
tolerance.

(2) Therefore our syntax language must be adequate also to
treating intensional languages.

(3) But now we find that the syntactical treatment of languages must in general be supplemented by semantic treatment.

(4)   To treat a language semantically we must be able to translate the language into ours.

(5) Hence, to treat intensional languages adequately we must be able to translate them into ours.

(6) It results that our language also must be intensional.

The course I should prefer is to repudiate (2). As I told Hempel, I fear your principle of tolerance may finally lead you even to tolerate Hitler. If we decide we are interested only in extensional languages, I take it that we can still get along with an extensional metalanguage, even in the face of the need of semantics; and if this is the case, I think it is unfortunate to be led into the complexities and the philosophical dangers of using intensional language, merely in order to provide for the analysis of a type of language which we regard initially as unimportant. | n.

I also dislike the notion of sentences as names—even as names of truth values—so long as we can get along without it. The fact that the notion simplifies other semantic constructions is not important, for once we have made the more complex constructions we can still proceed by simple methods, just as in arithmetic after finishing the construction of number from logic.

I like the following rule of thumb: *hypostasis* of a realm of entities, said to be *denoted* by the signs of a given syntactical category, corresponds (on the formal side) to the adoption of *bound variables* in that category. In *this* sense hypostasis of *classes,* to be denoted by *predicates,* is presumably essential to classical mathematics; and subsequent semantic treatment must proceed as if predicates were names of classes. (I am assuming extensionality here.) But use of bound sentential variables is unnecessary, and accordingly I regard the hypostasis of designata here as gratuitous. | o.

Psychologically also there is this argument: The notion of sentence designatum is not even entrenched in uncritical common-sense*, as is the designatum of predicate, numeral, etc.; sentence-designatum is historically a by-product rather of a confused analogy between sentential variables and arithmetical variables, all of which is late. Recognition of sentence-designata, if

---

*Common sense says rather: sentences are not names. Grammar forbids their use in noun position.

unnecessary as argued above, thus appears to give gratuitous help to the forces of philosophical confusion.

I should add, however, that I am not really so emotional or dogmatic about these matters but what I can be affected by arguments to the contrary.

I have been wanting to urge upon you the following terminology—although it is perhaps less appropriate in the light of your new views as regards sentence-designata. Namely, in my own work I have been suppressing the terminology "implication" and "equivalence", as applied to the truth-functions, in q. | favor of "conditional" and "biconditional". The latter are most naturally construed as modes of statement-composition ("if-then", "if and only if") coördinate with alternation and conjunction, whereas "implication" and "equivalence" are more naturally construed as denoting metalogical relations between statements, expressed by inserting verbs ("implies", "is equivalent to") between names of statements. Implication might indeed by identified with the converse of consequence, and r. | equivalence with equipollence; or, implication and equivalence might be construed semantically, in a way independent of transformative rules; or, for a while at least, the words "implication" and "equivalence" might simply be avoided.

Even if we accept the notion of sentence-designatum (horrid thought), the course recommended above retains the advantage of endowing "⊃" and "≡" with a terminology parallel to "alternation" and "conjunction".

s. | I have been finding out some rather interesting things about the theory of types; also an alternative way of avoiding the contradictions which is perhaps more striking than the method in terms of stratification ("New Fdtns") and which is adapted to my reduced primitives of inclusion and abstraction (see Jour.Symb.Logic, Dec. 1937). I am presenting these things in a lecture at New York on Feb. 24, and hope to send you a mimeo-t. | graphed abstract of it soon. I will publish it somewhat later.

I haven't sent you reprints of my last three articles, because you receive the Jour.Symb.Logic. But I will be glad to send them if you prefer having them in reprint form.

Let me know whenever you want some or all of those four

copies of the English *Syntax* returned. I have had no further requests for them so far, but there is one request pending.

Love to both, also from Naomi.

Yours,

Quine

u.

[MARGINALIA (ALL EXCEPT L. BY CARNAP) (MOST ARE IN GERMAN SHORTHAND):]

a. noted
b. simpler: "partial expression"
c. right in the original
d. errors of the translator
e. just as with the remarks on Ex. 8b, 9b
f. simple correction: I delete "is a free variable" twice on p. 26.
g. No, see explanation p. 26 above!
h. He apparently means only in §75 (Example 1b, 12b, 15c, 16c). To this: today I would translate the examples into semantics instead of syntax, the mentioned examples not into "pure" semantics, but into pragmatics (concerning, besides linguistic expressions and their designata, also persons, ⟨illegible⟩, etc.)
i. noted
j. noted
k. Right; is equivalent with my def. and much simpler
l. Has advantage of avoiding fractions. ⟨This note is by Quine.⟩
m. !
n. I have used intens. —Method.—language only for very special purposes: interesting results for translation relations between ext. and int. languages; for this int. semantical languages are necessary
o. Are classes of classes less objectionable? Or more customary in colloquial language? In my opinion the pred. variables are already very dangerous, and the higher levels perhaps more dangerous than bound sentence variables.
p. (That is questionable) I doubt it.
q. That's good.

r. No, that is L-implied; implication is a semantical relation between propositions.

s. very interesting

t. ⟨I⟩ am looking forward ⟨to it⟩

u. Grammar also forbids "red" in noun position; ⟨it⟩ replaces it,
however, with "Redness"; just as ⟨it⟩ replaces the sentences
with "my arrival"

[67. CARNAP TO QUINE   1938-2-11]

February 11, 1938

a. | Dr. W. V. Quine,
21 Waverley Av.,
Newton, Mass.

Dear Quine,

I thank you very much for your letter and the manuscript. I
enjoyed very much reading both of them. Let me first make
some remarks to your letter. I am very grateful for your corrections in the English Syntax. On page 21 I shall simply put "partial expression". The errors on Page 22 and 170 have been made
by the translator. The correction on page 290 is right; It applies
also to the explanations for examples 8 b, 9 b. About circularity:
The first one can be avoided, I think, by crossing out "as a free
variable" twice on page 26. That will cause a certain restriction
as to possible limit expressions, but without doing much harm.
The second circularity on page 26 does, however, not exist, I
b. | believe. See my explanation on top of page 26.

Concerning "quasi-syntactic". I suppose, you think chiefly of
examples in §75. Today I would translate these examples not
into a syntactical language but into a semantical one. The examples 1 b, 12 b, 15 c, and 16 c do not belong to "pure" semantics
but to pragmatics, i.e. the part of meta-theory concerning, besides expressions and their designata, also other things e.g. persons, letters etc.

Your simplifications of three definitions have really great
advantages.

Your sermon against my sin of intensionality has made a great impression upon me. But I may say as an apology, I do not indulge in this vice generally and thoroughly. I used an intensional meta-language only for certain special purposes and I found it useful and even necessary for these purposes, namely for the investigation of the relation of translation between an extensional and an intensional language. It seems to me that certain interesting results are found in this way. Although we usually do not like to apply intensional languages, nevertheless I think we cannot help analyzing them. What would you think of an entomologist who refuses to investigate fleas and lice because he dislikes them? Now, for a syntactical analysis of an intensional language an extensional meta-language will do; but not for a semantical analysis.

c.

Concerning designata of sentences. This is indeed a very interesting and serious problem. I see the danger involved in speaking about such designata. On the other hand it seems to me very convenient to speak about them *if* we decide to make semantics. I think that variables of predicates of a higher than the first level are at least as dangerous as bound sentential variables, perhaps even more so. And I doubt whether sentence designata are not referred to in every-day language. The customary grammar forbids also predicates in noun position, but it replaces them by corresponding nouns e.g. "red" by "redness"; in the same way it replaces sentences in noun position by corresponding expressions as e.g. "my arrival" or "his being opposed to this". In any case I think the question should be discussed much more and my view about it is not at all definitive.

The term "conditional" seems good to me. "Implication" can then be used for a certain semantic relation (the first being false or the second true), while the converse of consequence would be called S-implication.

d.

I am looking forward to reading the abstract of your results about types. I shall be very much interested in it. Your paper "New foundations . . ." was discussed in the discussion group, led by Hempel and Helmer, in the last quarter; and in this quarter we discuss it in detail in my seminar. I hope to have an opportunity some day to talk with you about it. It is especially for the purpose of semantics that a language without type restrictions would have considerable advantage because the relation of designation has to refer to entities of different types.

We thought of arranging a small private conference for the discussion of a few present problems. In the first place we would like to discuss semantics and especially your and Nagel's objections and suspicions against it. Would you have inclination, time and money to come at some date before the beginning of June? The second point we would like to discuss is the question of a language without type restrictions. And further the problem in which sense truth in logic and mathematics is based on conventions. This question is closely related to that of your Princeton paper. And therefore we hope to get a most valuable contribution to our discussion through your conception. Especially the short indications which you make at the end (from page 10 on) are extremely interesting for me, although I could not see quite clearly how they are meant. I would like very much to get more detailed explanations, if possible, by conversation.

I just received Mrs. Langer's book on Symbolic Logic. Some of the introductory parts of it may be helpful to students but in the whole I was a little bit disappointed. Nearly the whole of the book is devoted to the old Boolean Algebra, so that the interesting but still elementary parts of symbolic logic are exhibited only at the end in a very short way or not at all, as e.g. the theory of relations. What do you think about this book?

Please let me know soon whether and what time you could come here. Unfortunately, Helmer and Hempel intend to sail about June 11; otherwise we could have made our discussions about the middle of June somewhere in the East. Now I hope you and Nagel will find it possible to come here for a couple of days.

Very probably we shall not go to Europe this summer. We plan to go to the mountains and perhaps even to California. If you cannot come here during spring, when & where could we see you during the summer?

I was very much interested to see your examination questions for the two courses. In both cases I am full of astonishment and admiration with respect to the level, provided that really these questions have been answered in a satisfactory way.

With best regards, also from Ina, to you and Naomi,

yours,
Carnap

[MARGINALIA ON QUINE'S COPY:]

a. encl. check for $4.7 (Ravven)
b. My error. Indeed, Carnap's full expl'n is virtually the method of "rank" I suggest.
c. This is a useful sense in which an intensional language might (intolerantly) be called semantically meaningless!
d. Better, give "implication" a less trivial semantic sense: S implies T if there is a term which, replaced by a vbl. turns S & T into statement forms S' & T' such that S' is not false for all values of "x", nor T' true for all values S'^"⊃"^T' is true for all values.

[68.   QUINE TO CARNAP   1938-2-15]

21 Waverley Av.
Newton, Mass.
Feb. 15, 1938.

Dear Carnap,

I see now that the last of my list of corrections (circularity, within p. 26) was indeed amply covered on that very page. I had found the supposed circle while looking something up, rather than while reading consecutively. Mistake of not checking.

I am glad we agree in wanting to be extensional where extensionality suffices. Your analogy of fleas and lice is forceful; we | a. must study intensional languages as a human phenomenon. But will a syntactical treatment not satisfy us here?—as in the case of *metaphysical* expressions, which are devoid of denotation,

[247]

truth, falsehood? Indeed, the impossibility of extensional semantic treatment of intensional languages might serve as a conve-
b. | nient (though intolerant) Kennzeichnung of meaninglessness. I
c. | am thinking on paper; undecided.

I agree that bound predicate variables of non-minimal level
are more dangerous than bound sentential variables. But my
point was rather that the former are *needed* for classical mathematics, while the latter are not. Indeed, the latter could even be
introduced by contextual definition, if they would be convenient, so they would still have no status at the primitive level.
In my suggested sense of "hypostasis of designata", then, it
would remain true that designata only of predicates and not of
sentences would be hypostatized. Your argument that everyday
language does after all support sentence-designata must, I
guess, be admitted (contrary to my previous argument); but I
suppose I am affected mainly by Occam's razor.

I think also that a semantic definition of "implication" is a
good plan. But I think your suggested "material" sense (first
false or second true) is gratuitous—for though I favor the material *conditional* whole-heartedly, I think such a notion of "implica-
d. | tion" *would* indeed have all the faults which loose-thinking crit-
ics have in the past confusedly attributed to the "⊃" which I
approve. Instead I would favor some semantic notion of implication such as this: S_1 implies S_2 if there is some term whose replacement by a variable turns S_1 and S_2 into statement forms
(open sentences) S'_1 and S'_2 such that S'_1 is not false for all values of the variable, S'_2 is not true for all values of the variable,
and $S'_1 \supset S'_2$ is true for all values of the variable. (I.e., $(\exists v)\, S'_1$,
$(\exists v) \sim S'_2$, and $(v)\, (S'_1 \supset S'_2)$ are true, where 'v' is the variable
chosen.) (You remember Tarski's suggestion; different, but in
same general direction.)

I still have not looked at Mrs. Langer's book; had not been
anxious to, for Cooley had been impatient with it. Said there
was too much metaphorical talk *about* logic; too little logic.

The private conference you suggest would be extremely pleasant and valuable. I would come if at all possible. But I am very
unhopeful, because of the expense. I find that a family of four,
with an instructor's salary, presents problems. It is for this rea-

son, in fact, that I am very anxious to be offered a more remu-
nerative job somewhere.   e.

I enclose my check for one of the copies of the *Syntax*; sold to
one of my students, Robert Ravven.   f.

About the examination questions, I should say that in the advanced course (Math 19) the showing was quite good; nearly
half the students scored 85 per cent perfect or better. But I had
an unusually good class. In the intermediate philosophy course
(Phil 16, Logical Positivism) the students were not outstanding,
but the average student answered the exam questions fairly intel-
ligently. But the generousness of choice (6 out of 12) should be
kept in mind as a mitigating factor of that exam. I made the
questions rather technical to exclude empty essay answers; then
conceded compensatory latitude of choice.

Nancy Goheen told us about your apartment, which sounds
fine—convenient, rational, pleasant.

With best regards to Ina and yourself,

> Yours,
> Quine

[MARGINALIA (IN SHORTHAND) ON CARNAP'S COPY:]

a. But intensional languages are *not* meaningless
b. That would really be too narrow!
c. yes
d. That is a danger only with the term "implication", which I
   still retain, however, for certain analogous reasons.
e. !
f. received, noted.

[69. QUINE TO CARNAP   1938-5-22]

May 22, 1938

Dear Carnap,

The Association is holding a joint meeting with the Philosophical Association on December 28, at Wesleyan University

(Connecticut). Are you willing to serve on the program committee? and to act as its chairman? I don't want to urge this if it would be a burden, but I know that by putting the arrangements in your hands we would get the best selection of papers.

Since we are meeting with the philosophers, it is perhaps best to draw two members of the committee from philosophy departments and one from a mathematics department. I will delay the selection of the rest of the committee until hearing from you; and I would appreciate any suggestions.

I cannot serve on the committee myself, because we will be abroad next term. I have a half year off for writing.

Here is a question to try on your students. I used it in the Ph.D. preliminary exam, and nobody got it right.

Do the following conditions determine the class A uniquely? Defend your answer.
1) Every member of A is a nephew of a local person.
2) Every member of A is a nephew of a lawyer.
3) All local people are Cantabrigians.
4) Every nephew of a Cantabrigian lawyer is a member of A.

Naomi joins me in love to Ina and yourself. Are we going to see you soon? We will be here till late in August, for I am giving an introductory course in mathematical logic in summer school.

Yours,

[70. CARNAP TO QUINE   1938-5-26]

RUDOLF CARNAP
Department of Philosophy
University of Chicago   Chicago, Illinois   May 26, 1938

Dr. W. V. Quine,
21 Waverley Ave.,
Newton, Mass.

Dear Quine:

I thank you very much for several letters and two checks. Thanks for your proposal to join the program committee for the December meeting. But it seems to me, I cannot do it because probably I shall not be in Chicago during the autumn quarter. I have no teaching duties during that quarter in order to give me time to write something presumably about semantics.

Do I understand correctly that you will spend the next fall and winter in Europe? Do you intend to visit the Polish logicians or where do you intend to go? At present Europe does not seem very attractive. Let us hope that the situation will change until you will come there. Do you take all your family with you? We intend to go to the Rocky Mountains and to look around to find a nice and quiet place where I can work. We did not have a car during the winter but we intend soon to buy one. I should like to come to the East at the beginning of the summer vacation in order to see you and a few other people, but I do not know whether I can really do it because it is just the opposite direction from our aim.

Your examination question seems to me, although elementary, rather hard for the average student. I would put the answer in this way: "no; although $R^{((}(\alpha^\cap\beta) \subset R^{((}\alpha^\cap R^{((}\beta$, the inverse does not necessarily hold".

In the meantime I read your abstract about the problem of types. It is indeed very interesting, but just in the essential point it does not give enough information how you intend to construct this system. Therefore, I am looking forward to reading the whole paper as soon as it will appear.

Can you give me the address of Maisel, the author of "An Anatomy of Literature" who apparently knows you. A letter sent to him care of his publisher came back. Hempel sends you the enclosed photo with best regards. You look here like a Tibetan monk, very wise, and indulgently smiling about the poor human creatures.

Recently we had during the weekend some discussions about semantics and connected problems. Langford and Kleene came here. I regretted very much that we could not have you here.

With best regards, 2 to 4:

Yours,
Carnap

[71. QUINE TO CARNAP   1938-5-28]

May 28, 1938

Dear Carnap,

I feel pretty sure that this letter will come as a relief to you—otherwise I would not take this step. But the following two considerations have arisen since my last letter:

(1) I find that the name and address of the chairman of the program committee must be sent in at once for publication in the Journal, in order that we may call for volunteer papers. I was not aware of the ruch when I wrote you.

(2) I have heard from Curry, urging selection of committee members located fairly close to one another and to the Phil. Assn. secretary at Middletown.

Curry did not know of my intention to ask you to serve. But I can see the value of having the committee close enough together to allow a conference or two—particularly since Curry says he was criticized last year for not consulting the rest of the committee sufficiently.

A likely committee would appear to be: Lewis, Nagel, Bennett. This has the advantage also of allowing immediate action as regards chairman; for I have been able to arrange with Lewis by phone as to his acceptance and other details, and thus to notify Church today for publication.

I would not have resorted to these high-handed methods if I knew you less well, or if I were not so confident that you dislike committee activities as thoroughly as I do. And in Nagel I am getting a good representative of our point of view.

It is politically good to have Nagel countered on the committee by Lewis, I think, for there have been indications of restiveness among the anti-positivists in the Association. Bennett is there to represent the members of math. departments.

Two of my graduate students (Callis, Rosenbaum) would like to avail themselves of your author's discount on the *Aufbau*, if you are willing and if the book is still to be had. If so, please let me know the cost and I will have them send checks to you direct.

And can you give me the addresses of Bachmann and Gödel?

Yours,
⟨Quine symbol⟩

P.S. Somebody showed me an error in the bibliography to the English *Syntax:* Weiß mixed with Whitehead. I can't be more explicit, for my copy is at my office.

[72. CARNAP TO QUINE   1938-6-7]

RUDOLF CARNAP
Department of Philosophy
University of Chicago   Chicago, Illinois   June 7, 1938

Dr. W. V. Quine,
Emerson Hall,
Harvard University,
Cambridge, Massachusetts

Dear Quine:

Your arrangement concerning the program committee is, of course, quite satisfactory for me, as you will have seen in the meantime from my letter of May 26th.

Author's price for the "Aufbau": bound $3.00, in paper cover $2.50. If I have no word from you at the beginning of the next week, I shall send two paper cover copies to your address; because we intend to leave about the middle of next week. The addresses you wish:

Dr. Kurt Gödel, Wien VIII, Josefstädterstr. 43/II

Dr. Friedrich Bachmann, Münster i.W., Melchersstr. 52 pt. Yes the title of Weiss was put under Whitehead.

We plan to go to some place in the Rocky Mountains, we do not know where. Letters will be forwarded.

I am very sorry not to see you in the near future.

Yours,
R. Carnap

[73. QUINE TO CARNAP   1938-6-10]

76 Grozier Rd.
Cambridge, Mass.
June 10, 1938

Dear Carnap,

Thanks for the addresses, and also for your willingness to
provide copies of the *Aufbau* at author's price. Better not send
these to me; I have just now notified the two students that they
should send checks direct to you, to reach you by Monday, if
they want to get the books now. So if you do not hear from
them (one or both) by Monday you may as well drop the matter
till next year.
Address of Maisel Disclaimer.
Not to Europe, but phps. to Azores.
Back for logic mtg.
Thanks to Hempel.

⟨This letter is marked 'copy' at the top, and judging by the last
lines it is not complete.⟩

[74. CARNAP TO QUINE   1938-10-25]

RUDOLF CARNAP
DEPARTMENT OF PHILOSOPHY
UNIVERSITY OF CHICAGO   CHICAGO, ILLINOIS

Carmel, Cal., Oct. 25, 1938

Dear Quine,

Enclosed find a copy of my letter to Cooley concerning his
notes on logic. Since you helped him—supposedly a good
deal—perhaps you may be interested in my remarks.

Where are you? And how do all of you spend your time? Is
dear Naomi well? And how about Elizabeth and Norma? We

should be very pleased to get an account of the happenings in your family!

We have already spent three months in Carmel and intend to stay at least one more. I have not been too well this summer. My back trouble (strained ligaments) has happened six times and I had to stay in bed for about ten weeks. I have been up these last ten days and hope that this is the final turn for the better. While I had to lye quietly I have written my contribution to the "Encyclopedia". I expect it will be printed in January. I have finished about two thirds of the manuscript for a new German edition of my "Abriss der Logistik"; Rosinger intends to translate it into English for an English edition to be published by the Chicago U. Press. For the last two weeks I have been working on considerations about semantics. As you perhaps know, the University gave me this quarter off in order to give me time to work on semantics. — Please answer this detailed account with a similar one of what you have done.

The Franks are in America, as you probably have heard. He is on a lecture tour, is right now in Chicago and will come to see us in between lectures on the West Coast about the middle of next month. He also has an invitation from Harvard but I don't know for what date. The German University in Prague most likely will have ceased to exist in the mean time. Don't you think the European situation terrible?

Our love to both of you. Ina has had an attack of shingles, and she thinks "perfectly lousy" is the only fitting description of the status.

Very cordially yours,
Carnap

⟨Concerning the translation of the *Abriss* . . . , Kurt Edward Rossinger had been asked in 1934 by T. N. Whitehead (son of A. N.) to translate the book for his own (Whitehead's) use. Quine had in fact been the conduit for this request. Apparently the translation provided to Whitehead was quite literal, but the project expanded, as is seen here, toward a translation aimed at publication.⟩

[75.   CARNAP TO JOHN COOLEY   1938-9-22]

CARNAP
Carmel, Cal.   Carmel, Sept. 22, 1938.
(until the end of October)

Dear Mr. Cooley,

I read your 'Outline of Symbolic Logic' with great interest, and I think it is a very good introduction to the field. It would be very useful for my students. I am glad to learn that you intend to enlarge and improve it. Will it then be printed as a book? or mimeographed like this one? I shall certainly recommend it to my students as the best introduction available in English.

I should like to buy a copy. Please let me know whether I can keep this one or where I can order one, and what its price is. Perhaps you will be interested to see my 'Notes for Symbolic Logic'; I have no copies left but shall write to Chicago and order one. Its purpose is of course entirely different from that of your book, because it does not give explanations. I am writing a new and entirely changed edition of my 'Abriss der symbolischen Logik'; and the Chicago University Press plans to publish an English translation to be made by Rosinger, but that will not be before 1940. I believe your and my books will not compete but complement each other; because mine will be on a more technical level and especially stress the application in non-logical axiomatic systems.

Your explanations are nearly all perfectly correct and clear so that I have to make only few remarks.

The one point where I have the impression that a revision would be necessary and essential, is the treatment of *variables*. Your deviation from the customary notation is of course all right; but you have to take care to bring your explanations in agreement with the modified system. In the present formulation the fundamental distinction between blanks and variables does not become clear. A blank (e.g. '. . .' or '--' as used by Quine and sometimes by myself, or 'p' and 'p_x' in your text) belongs to the meta-language, not to the object-language, i.e. the symbolic system dealt with. A variable, on the other hand, (e.g. 'X', 'x',

'F', in Hilbert's notation, 'p', 'x', 'F' in my notation (language II in "Syntax", and "Notes"), 'x' in your notation) belongs to the object-language. It is important that the reader understand the difference; many logicians are not clear about this point, chiefly because Princ. Math. was not clear. You explain 'x' p. 62 as part of a blank 'p_x', but on page 63 'x' is suddenly used as a variable in the object-language. And on p. 118 f. it does not become quite clear what 'y' is. — I do not know whether to suggest that you take 'p' in the new text as a variable, or keep it as a blank. Perhaps the first is simpler, but certainly both procedures are correct and feasible. But in either case it should be made quite clear what 'p' is.

Terminology. When students will read your and my publications, I do not think that it will cause any serious difficulty for them to find some terms of yours (e.g. 'conditional', 'alternation', 'scope', 'quantified' etc.) which differ from my corresponding terms. Perhaps I shall even accept some of your terms for my own use. On the other hand, I am afraid that the readers will get into difficulties and confusion, when you use a term in a meaning different from mine. I will mention some examples. You use 'variable' not in the sense in which it is used by myself (and the logicians on the Continent: Hilbert, the Poles, etc.) but for what I would call a blank. Further 'implication' for the converse of consequence; I am now (in the Encyclopedia) using ('logical implication' or) 'L-implication'; if you do not like this, I hope you will find another word. My advise is in any case decidedly against 'implication'; the reader would be terribly confused, e.g., by p. 115 footnote when he simultaneously reads in 'Syntax' my emphasis upon the distinction between the consequence relation (or its converse) and implication. — 'derivation' of a statement form; perhaps 'construction'. — It seems to me not to be advisable to use the same term 'proof' both for proofs and derivations (e.g. p. 12); the difference is important, but neglected by many logicians.

I am occupied since some time with an attempt of what I call a standardized word language. Therefore I am much interested in your "standard expressions". Did you independently come to this idea? I developed many forms but am in many cases not sure which choice is the best. I took 'for every x' (would you think 'any' is better?) and 'for some x' (because it is in better analogy and shorter than 'there is. .').

Some minor remarks. p. 6 ff. 'substitution'; here better 'replacement', and 'subst.' reserved for the special case (for a variable). — p. 13 footnote. Better a new valid form of inference:

$$\frac{\begin{array}{l} p \\ q \end{array}}{p \text{ and } q}$$

— p. 25, l.2. f.b. instead of 'positive sense': 'denial'. — p. 27. I believe, it is customary to take TF as second case. — p. 31 Would it not be advisable to give a truth table for 'not'? — p. 36. I should prefer to make a distinction between a set of sentences and their conjunction (see remark to p. 13). — p. 156 bottom. This restriction is *not* necessary, since you admit vacuous quantification. But the inverse restriction is necessary. (You give it p. 160). The example p. 158 bottom is excluded by the latter. — p. 161 middle. (7) is true and (8) is false. — p. 164 bottom. This restriction is not sufficient; in '(x) [. . .(y)(. .x. .y. .)]' 'y' must not be rewritten as 'x'.

With many congratulation for what you did so far and best wishes for the further work on this book,

Sincerely yours,
R. C.

⟨This is the enclosure with item 74. Hence, it is printed here out of chronological order.⟩

[76. QUINE TO CARNAP   1938-11-17]

Posta restante
Ponta Delgada
a. | Azores, Nov. 17, 1938

Dear Carnap,

I was glad to hear from you, and to have the copy of your letter to Cooley. His use of the terminology "conditional", "biconditional", "alternation" etc. is a result of my insistence. But I agree that his use of the word "implication", without adjective, is dangerous. In the book on which I am working I use
b. | "logical implication" for substantially this sense. I agree also that

his treatment of variables wants ironing out. In my own work I prefer to avoid "p", "p_x", etc. entirely, as in your Language I; and to use "x" etc. only as bound variables, supplementing individual-names and class-names (or predicates, used with " " indiscriminately). The usage last mentioned is tied up with my scheme for avoiding the theory of types—on which see the next Jour. Symb. Logic.

I am responsible for Cooley's use of truth tables in the form:

T	T
F	T
T	F
F	F

which you criticize on the ground that the form:

T	T
T	F
F	T
F	F

is more usual. I am inclined to defend the upper arrangement, for I find it more convenient. The essential advantage lies in the fact that it is the 2-case of the following general scheme:

T	T	T	T	T	. . .
F	T	T	T	T	. . .
T	F	T	T	T	. . .
F	F	T	T	T	. . .
T	T	F	T	T	. . .
F	T	F	T	T	. . .
.	.	.	.	.	
.	.	.	.	.	
.	.	.	.	.	

The arrangement which you prefer does not lend itself to generalization in a table building outward thus from the upper left corner. The above general array can be characterized thus: in the ith column the "T"s and "F"s are alternated in groups of 2^{i-1}.

We are spending my whole free semester stationary here in Ponta Delgada. Continued travel is impossible with the children, and anyway I need the whole time for my work. I am working on a general book of mathematical logic, which will start at the elementary level but include higher developments such as

Gödel's proofs of the completeness of quantification theory and incompleteness of arithmetic.

The place is, strictly speaking uncomfortable—straight armless chairs corn-husk mattresses, swarms of flies, and hordes of microbes which make themselves known with warning touches of fever when the annoying little precautions are relaxed. But such things are, for five months anyway, a moderate price for the picturesque background. A complete change is provided by the topography, the architecture, and the life, human and otherwise. The first of these three categories consists of an odd heap of old volcanoes, now well eroded and covered with green; never very high (limit about 1000 meters), but spectacular in spots. The second category is characterized by red tile roofs and plaster walls, white or delicately tinted; narrow cobblestone streets, mosaic sidewalks with balconies overhead. The third category includes hooded barefoot peasants with urns and baskets on head; oxen, donkeys, goats, and sheep pulling carts through the city; dogs carrying baskets; weird varieties of fish; an occasional lizard on the bedroom wall; palms, dragon trees, tea plants, banana trees, pineapples. The food is good, and living is cheap. We live in a boarding house, where we have two big rooms and abundant good board for the whole family at a million reis ($43.86) a month.

We are very sorry to hear about the continued trouble with your back, and Ina's affliction of shingles. I hope these things are over now.

Our best regards to the Franks. Their trip to the U.S. proved to be opportune; I hope they can stay there. The mess in Europe is incredible. In the last days of September it looked as though Hitler was due for a showdown and the forces of democracy still had a good chance; but now the hope of frustrating Hitler's world domination begins to look like wishful thinking.

With love to both, also from Naomi,

Yours,
Quine

[MARGINAL NOTE IN QUINE'S HAND ON HIS COPY:]

a. Postcard next day:
> This card has two purposes: (1) to show you the town;
> (2) to make the following corrections to my letter of yes-
> terday: (a) line 8, for "supplementing" read "supplant-
> ing"; (b) line 9, fill blank with "ϵ"; (c) fifth line from end
> of 1st page, insert comma after "speaking".

⟨In the text, corrections (a) and (b) occur in the sixth sentence
and correction (c) occurs in the first sentence of the fourth
paragraph.⟩
b. accords well with my 'L-implication'

[77. CARNAP TO QUINE   1939-3-11]

RUDOLF CARNAP
Department of Philosophy
University of Chicago   Chicago, Illinois   March 11, 1939

Dr. W. V. Quine,
Emerson Hall,
Harvard University
Cambridge, Mass.

Dear Quine:-

Thanks for your letter and check. In the meantime I read with
very great interest your new paper about avoiding the Theory of
Types in the J. S. L. I should like to talk with you especially
about semantics. In the spring quarter, beginning at the end of
March, I shall again give a seminar about semantics, and there
develop some new views. I hope very much that when we shall
come to the East in September, we shall find time to talk about
these things.

Prof. Findlay from New Zealand will come to Harvard for
some time in the next future. I suggested him to get in contact
especially with you. He was here for about two months and
came regularly to all of my courses. He is very much interested

in logic and logical syntax, but his training is, of course, far from perfect due to the isolation in which he works at home. I am not sure whether he is entirely free from metaphysics, but he tries to become so, and he is really anxious to learn. Therefore, I believe he deserves any help which we can give him by suggestions for reading and conversations.

I am glad that my friend Hempel is now with you. I am sure he will enjoy it very much. I suppose that your Department think that they have enough logicians. But if you occasionally learn of some other University or College looking for an instructor in philosophy, I would be grateful for either informing them about Hempel or informing Hempel or myself about them. I think that Hempel is an excellent man, and his outstanding abilities for teaching and discussing will make him a very good teacher.

With our love to you and Naomi,

Yours,
Carnap

[78.   QUINE TO CARNAP   1939-4-23]

76 Grozier Road
Cambridge, Mass.
April 23, 1939

Dear Carnap,

We much enjoyed having Hempel with us. I hope he gets a good job soon. I was surprised to find he is not on the list of refugee scholars circulated by the American Philosophical Association. I am writing them, on the assumption that Hempel does fall within the refugee category.

Also I hope Prof. Frank gets something. It has been suggested to me that you write to Prof. Harlow Shapley, Harvard Observatory, Concord Avenue, Cambridge, Mass., urging Frank's virtues. Shapley is a distinguished astronomer here, who is doing more than anyone else hereabouts in trying to find places for exiled scholars.

I have talked with Prof. Findlay (New Zealand) several times, and he has been attending my seminar in the Philosophy of Mathematics regularly. I am scheduled to have another talk with him tomorrow.

I suppose you have seen my friend Ed Haskell recently, whom you first met with us in Prague. He is at the University of Chicago, working on anthropology; he seems to be interested largely in general methodological questions at present, and was planning to seek an interview with you.

I am working hard—wishing always to push on with my book, but finding little or no time for it on account of pressure of other duties (including onerous matters in behalf of Association for Symbolic Logic). We are all well, and hope the same applies to you.

Yours,
Quine

P.S.—We are looking forward with great pleasure to seeing you and Ina this September.

[79.   QUINE TO CARNAP   1939-5-16]

May 16, 1939

Dear Carnap,

Sad news: whereas the department recommended me for promotion, I have learned just today that the administration rejected the recommendation—on some impersonal grounds of policy.

The prospect of further years as instructor is so distasteful that I would accept a fair offer from elsewhere with unbounded delight. The fact that the department did recommend me for promotion is a strong point in my favor. The important thing for me is that the right people learn the facts fast, for the season is late. I would be deeply grateful to you for dropping a word wherever you think it might do some good.

With best regards to Ina and yourself.

Yours desolately,
⟨Quine symbol⟩

[80.   CARNAP TO QUINE   1939-6-3]

RUDOLF CARNAP
Department of Philosophy
University of Chicago   Chicago, Illinois   June 3, 1939

Dr. W. V. Quine,
76 Grozier Rd.,
Cambridge, Mass.

Dear Quine:-

I am very sorry and surprised to learn that your promotion
has not been granted. But is your pessimism really justified?
Since the department recommended your promotion is there not
a very good chance for you to get it next year or in any case at
sometime in the near future? Is the rejection not merely based
on economic reasons? In our department every year several people are recommended either for an increase in their salary or for
promotion. We are surprised when such a recommendation is
accepted, not when it is declined. Last year three assistant professors were recommended for increase in salary; this year one
professor was recommended for the same, and I was recommended for permanent tenure without increase in salary. None
of these five recommendations of these two years have been accepted, and none of us was surprised. I talked your situation
over with Morris because he has a better knowledge of practical
questions, and I asked him what I could do for you. He doubts
whether you are wise in spreading around the information that
you are willing to leave Harvard. He is afraid that this might
have an unfavorable re-effect upon the attitude of your University towards you, and he wonders whether you should not wait
a little bit more before you even take into consideration going
away. Therefore, I did not write to other Universities; but I shall
be very glad to do so if you want me to do it. I could, e.g.,
write to Gomperz and to Reichenbach, if you think you would
take the two Universities at Los Angeles into consideration. I
heard from Nagel that he got direct information from you. I had
transmitted your information to McKeon and Cohen before Morris cautioned me.; they have many connections.

Thank you also for your letter of April 23rd. Frank was already in contact with Prof. Shapley, and it seems now that the negotiations are close to a successful end. Haskell wrote to me too that he would come to Chicago, but he has not yet showed up.

If you have a spare copy of "Philosophy 20 m, Topics for papers" which I saw with Hempel, I should be very grateful for one.

May I ask you to reserve a room for me in a Dormitory for the time of the Congress? I should like it as quiet as possible; I suppose that in other respects there will not be a great difference between the rooms. Ina is not much interested in Congress meetings, and will perhaps stay at Marblehead.

Reach, who took his Dr.'s degree with me in Prague, sent me some reprints and summaries for distribution in order to get people interested in his work because he wants to immigrate, if possible, to the United States. He will perhaps read a paper at our Congress. I am sending you a reprint and a summary, | a.

Minor remarks to your paper: "Completeness". (J S L 3, p.37) The introduction of "F" violates the rule that a definiens must not contain a free variable not contained in the definiendum. If I remember correctly, you yourself objected to this procedure when Jörgensen applied it. Of course, in your paper, in contradistinction to Jörgensen's, this procedure does not do any harm.

As you probably know, an exchange of Sheffer and myself is planned for the whole year of 1940/41. One of the chief attractions of this plan for me is your presence there. I hope very urgently that you will not run away before that time.

I shall teach here during this Summer Quarter, and then shall be free in the fall. Thus we shall stay in Chicago until August 25th, and then start our trip to the East.

With best regards to you and Naomi from both of us,

Yours,
Carnap

[MARGINALIA ON ORIGINAL:]

a. ⟨unclear but probably partially missing:⟩
Praha XIX
ad Král. Oborou 17
BOHEMIA

[81. QUINE TO CARNAP 1939-6-8]

Eliot House E14
Cambridge, Mass.

June 8, 1939

Dear Carnap,

Many thanks for your commiseration, for your kindness in talking of my situation to McKeon, Cohen, and Morris, and for you willingness to go farther.

I think I am not more pessimistic than justified. I recognize that my chances of ultimate advancement do not look bad; but the administrative board has made it clear that advancement is impossible both now and next year. If it were a question of promotion from assistant professorship to associate professorship, I would be content to bide my time. What I find unsatisfactory is the idea of remaining *instructor* for at least two more years, despite my scientific productivity over the past seven years.

For some time past, many have regarded my status as anomalous. Now the department is indignant over the administration's refusal of my promotion. The fact that I have told friends of my willingness to improve my situation by leaving Harvard would not, therefore, surprise the department. They would be sympathetic, I believe; for they are aware that contemporaries of mine, whom they have let go while retaining me as first choice, have already fared far better elsewhere than I here. Nor do I see harm in the discovery by our administrative officers that I am becoming restive as instructor.

I would not, indeed, burn my bridges yet by filing formal applications at other institutions: but I hope there may be places where news of my present essentially unattached state might precipitate an offer. I am thus inclined to waive Morris's warning, though genuinely grateful to him for it. I am sustained in this by a couple of friends who are top-flight professors here (outside philosophy).

Yes, I would take the two universities at Los Angeles into consideration—with especial enthusiasm, in fact. So I urge you to write to Gomperz and Reichenbach, as you so kindly proposed.

As to my definition of "F" in "Completeness", I suggest the following as summing up my attitude on definitions:

(1) Definitions are foreign to the object language. I do not even write:

$$p \vee q \, . \;\; = \;\; _{df.} \; {\sim}p \supset q,$$
$$F \;\; = \;\; _{df.} \; p \supset p,$$

or

$$p \vee q \, . {\equiv} . \; {\sim}p \supset q \quad \text{(Def.)}$$
$$F \;\; {\equiv} . \; p \supset p, \quad \text{(Def.)}$$

but rather: $\ulcorner \phi \vee \psi \urcorner$ for $\ulcorner {\sim}\phi{\supset}\psi \urcorner$

"F" for "p ⊃ p"

(or more accurately: "F" for "(p ⊃ p)").

(2) All proofs are supposedly carried out in primitive notation. When I use defined abbreviations in a theorem and its proof, I imagine the abbreviations expanded throughout. The abbreviations are only an unofficial agreement with the reader, for saving space-time.

(3) In view of (2), it is essential to frame the definitions with a view to notationally unique eliminability: and this is for me the only requirement. In definitions I specify even the choice of bound variables, arbitrarily; e.g.:

$\ulcorner \zeta \subset \eta \urcorner$ for $\ulcorner (\alpha)(\alpha{\in}\zeta . \supset . \alpha{\in}\eta) \urcorner$ where α is the alphabetically earliest variable foreign to ζ and η.

On the other hand definition of "T" as "p ⊃ p", or *even of* "G" *as* "p ⊃ q", is legitimate—uniquely eliminable. But note that "T" does *not* abbreviate "q ⊃ q", nor does "G" abbreviate "p ⊃ r". Substitution of "s" for "p" in a context containing "T" (or "G") involves dropping "T" (or "G") in favor of "s ⊃ s" (or "s ⊃ q"); this is clear from (2).

(4) It is *convenient* to frame our definitions in such a way that in practice we can apply our rules of inference directly to the

abbreviated forms without reaching any theorems which could not be reached through primitive notation. By this canon, the abbreviation of "p ⊃ p" as "T" is convenient (when accompanied by postulational provision for the theorem "T ≡. q ⊃ q", i.e. "p ⊃ p .≡. q ⊃ q"), whereas abbreviation of "p ⊃ q" as "G" is inconvenient. But even the latter abbreviation is not *dangerous*, unless coupled with the mistaken belief that we have adhered to the convenient canon (4). Definition of "T" as "p ⊃ p" is likewise dangerous *if* (a) we have not provided postulationally for "p ⊃ p .≡. q ⊃ q" and (b) we proceed under the mistaken belief that we have adhered to the convenient canon (4). For, we might then conclude from the theorem "T ≡. p ⊃ p" (i.e., "p ⊃ p .≡. p ⊃ p") that "T ≡. q ⊃ q" is a theorem, which (by (a)) it is *not* (though true).

I think highly of Reach, for whose paper in J. S. L. I was the referee. His summaries of contents of unpublished papers indicate that he has a lot of interesting and important material coming along. I hope very much he can be rescued from Bohemia. Would he be eligible for attention of the committee on refugee scholars, which is connected with the Am. Phil. Assn.? (Did I mention, by the way, that I wrote them on Hempel? He is a fine person and an extraordinarily able thinker; I hope he soon gets his deserts.)

Another man much in need of attention is Tarski. He is invited to both the Unity of Science congress and the 1940 mathematical congress; and he will come to both if anything at all in the way of a job can be found to tide him over the intervening year. I have talked with people here, with Curry, and with Weyl, and have written Morris. A 1940 summer-school job has been fixed up for him at Harvard, but more is needed.

I wonder if there could have been an ambiguity in Haskell's letter to you; for he has been in Chicago right along, for several years, except for short trips outside.

I was much excited when I heard of the plan to exchange you and Sheffer. It would be hard for us to leave on the eve of that prospect. Time will tell.

Yours,
Quine

[82. CARNAP TO QUINE 1939-8-7]

RUDOLF CARNAP
Department of Philosophy
University of Chicago   Chicago, Illinois   August 7, 1939

Dr. W. V. Quine,
Eliot House East 14
Cambridge, Mass.

Dear Quine:-

Thank you very much for your letter of June 8th. I have immediately written to Gomperz and Reichenbach about you (on June
11th), so let us hope that in some future something will come
out of it.

Your explanation of your conception of definitions is very
clear, and solves the problem which I had in connection with
that special instance completely.

I am not certain whether you noted my request for a room in
a former letter of mine. Therefore, I am enclosing a blanc for
this purpose.

We shall be in Chicago until August 26th, then we shall drive
leisurely towards the east. (Address until August 31st, General
Delivery, Albany, N.Y.).

We are looking forward very much to seeing you and Naomi
soon.

Yours,
Carnap

[83. CARNAP TO QUINE ET AL. 1939-8-7]

Rudolf Carnap
Faculty Exchange
University of Chicago
Chicago, Ill.   Aug. 7, 1939

To *Church*,   please forward to *Quine*
To Nagel,   "   "   " Helmer
To Hempel,   "   "   " Tarski

Questions on Terminology of Semantics

I should like to get your answers to the following questions; they are connected with one another and partly overlapping. It is sufficient to mention the number of the question (e-g. '/b') and the letter of the answer (e-g. 'B'). Indication of reasons is desirable but not necessary. If necessary, add further proposals.

Quest. 1:

How to use the word *'function'*? (A) for certain symbols (functors), (B) for certain (open) expressions, (C) for certain designata (of functors). I took (B) previously, but am now inclined to (C) because customary in mathematical terminology. (Church thinks (A) is customary in mathematics; but I believe this appears to be so only because some mathematicians often neglect the difference between a symbol and its designation.)

Quest. 2:

Terms for designata

	expression		designatum
2a	predicate or functor	(A)	function (wider sense);
		(B)	concept;
2b	predicate	(A)	attribute; (B) propositional function; (C) relation
2c	one-place predicate	(A)	property; (B) quality
2d	more-place predicate	(A)	relation
2e	functor	(A)	function (narrower sense); (b) correlation
2f	sentence	(A)	proposition; (B) state of affairs.

My preference is for (A) throughout.

Quest. 3:

In case of answer 1C, my former use of 1B (in "Syntax") must be abandoned; how to replace it?

Instead of: (as used in "Syntax")		Now proposed:
3a. function	(A)	open expression;
	(B)	schema
3b. sentential function	(A)	open sentence (or, with respect to systems containing only closed sentences: open sentential expression)
3c. numerical function	(A)	open numerical expression

3a (B) is used in "Syntax" with a different meaning (for a syntactical description of a form of sentences, e.g. 'primitive sentence schema'). My preference is for (A).

Quest.4:

Which method shall we apply for forming *names for particular calculi?*
(A) names referring to a kind of expressions
(B) names referring to a kind of designata (of those expressions)
Previously, I used (A), but not consistently (e.g. 'sentential calculus', 'calculus of predicates'; but also 'functional calculus' and 'calculus of relations'). I am now considering to adopt (B), because it seems more frequently used among logicians and mathematicians (see examples to question 5).

Quest.5:

If 4B is chosen, which (probably several ones) of the following methods shall we admit?
(A) noun before 'calculus' (e.g. 'class calculus');
(B) adjective before 'calculus' (e.g. 'functional calculus', 'propositional calculus')
(C) 'calculus of . . .' (e.g. 'calculus of classes', c.o. 'relations' 'c.o. functions' 'c.o. propositions', 'c. of real numbers')
(D) 'calculus for . . .'
It seems to me that the examples mentioned here are customary. (D) is not customary but perhaps more clear than (C)

(thus (1) a calculus with sentential variables will be called 'calculus for propositions', (2) a calculus with (variables for) names of sentences 'calculus for sentences'; if we took instead 'calculus of sentences' for (2) then it might easily be mistaken as meaning (1)). Leaving aside the objection just mentioned against (C), I think we could admit all four forms.

Quest.6:

How to name *kinds of variables?* (and analogously kinds of constants).
(A) with reference to the kind of expressions (symbols) substitutable for them (e.g. 'predicate variable', 'functor variable', 'sentential variable').
(B) with reference to the designata of those expressions (e.g. 'individual variable', 'class variable', 'propositional variable', 'functional variable').
It seems to me that the examples given are customary; hence the customary usage is not consistent. (B) seems more customary, but awkward if used in connection with the name for the corresponding kind of symbols (i.e. variables and constants) (e.g. "a propositional variable is a sentence"; "the predicates are divided into property variables and property constants"; "function variables and other functors. . . ."). Therefore, my preference is for (A).

[84. CARNAP TO QUINE   1939-8-8]

Rudolf Carnap
Faculty Exchange
University of Chicago
Chicago, Ill.   Aug. 8, 1939

Terminology for English Translation of my
"Abriss der Logistik" (new edition)

Several terms are marked for easier reference by 'A', 'B' etc.
Please, state your preference simply in this way: "§2, 1B" (this would mean that you prefer 'quality'). State your agreement also where only one term A is given. If you prefer a term not listed, add it

with a new capital. My preference is for that term or one of
those terms which are not included in parentheses. Inclusion in
double parentheses means that I am strongly against that term,
e.g. § 1, 6B.
Abbreviations following a term and indicating an author who
used that term:
    PM   Principia Mathematica
    Q   Quine
    Sy   Carnap, Syntax (English)
§ 1:   1. Logistik: A symbolic logic (B logistic) | a.
         2. Zeichen: A sign, B symbol
         3. Grundbegriff A primitive concept.
         4. Formregel   ) siehe
) § 17
         5. Umformungsregel   )
         6. Satz: A sentence ((B proposition))
         7. Relationskalkül: A calculus of relations (B relational
            calculus)
         8. Axiomatische Methode: A axiomatic method (method
            of postulate)
         9. Antinomie: A antinomy (B paradox on)
§ 2.   1. Eigenschaft: A property (B quality)
         2. Einstelliges (Prädikat): A one-place (Sy), B one-term
         3. Vollsatz: A full sentence (Sy) | b.
         4. Vollausdruck: A full expression (Sy) | c.
         5. Attribut: A attribute
         6. Satzkonstante: A sentential constant. | d.
         7. Funktor: A functor (Sy)
§ 3.   1. Satzverknüpfung: A sentential connection (B sentential | e.
            junction (Sy))
         2. Deskriptiv: A descriptive
         3. Verknüpfungszeichen: A connective (Q)(B junction
            symb. (Sy))
         4. Disjunktion: A disjunction (B alternative C logical |
            sum) | f.
         5. Konjunktion: A conjunction (B logical product)
         6. Implikation: A implication (Sy) (B conditional (Q))
         7. Aequivalenz: A equivalence (Sy) (B bi-conditional (Q))

8. Folge: A consequence
9. Klammern: (both for '()' and '[]'): A brackets (B parantheses)

§ 4.   1. Wahrheitswerttafel: A truth value table, B truth table
2. Teilsatz: A component

§ 5.   1. Spielraum: A range (Sy, Wittg..)
2. Analytisch: A analytic (Sy), (B analytical)
3. Synthetisch: A synthetic (Sy)
4. Lehrsatz: A theorem
5. Gemeinsamer Spielraum: A common range

§ 6.   1. Gehalt: A content (Sy)
g. | 2. Satzvariable: A sentential variable
3. Einsetzen: A substitute
4. Wendung: A transposition
5. Ableitung: A derivation (Sy)

§ 7.   1. Allsatz: A universal sentence (Sy)
2. Existenzsatz: A existential sentence (Sy)
g. | 3. Individualvariable: A individual variable
4. Operator: A operator (Sy), B quantifier
5. Operand: A operand (Sy), B scope
6. Gebundene (Variable): A bound (sy), (B apparent (PM))
7. Freie (Variable): A free (Sy), (B real (PM))
h. | 8. Offener (Satz): A open (Sy)
i. | 9. Geschlossener (Satz): A closed (Sy)
10. Satzfunktion: A sentential function (Sy)
j. | (B oder sollen wir anstatt 'Satzfunktion' Lieber
'offener Satz' sagen, weil das Wort 'Funktion'
vielleicht besser für gewisse Designata genommen
wird., nämlich solche von Funktoren oder Prädikaten,
k. | anstatt für Ausdrücke bestimmter Art?)
11. Implikation (= Implikationssatz): A implication, B im-
l. | plication sentence

§ 8.   1. Prädikatvariable: A predicate variable
2. Beweis: A proof (Sy), (B demonstration (PM))
3. Ersetzen: A replace (Sy), ((B substitute))

§ 9.   1. Definition: A definition
      2. Definiendum: A definiendum
      3. Definiens: A definiens

§10.   1. Stufe: A level (Sy), (B order)
      2. nullte Stufe: A zero level

§11.   1. Identität: A identity
      2. Kardinalzahl: A cardinal number

§12.   1. Funktor: A functor (Sy)
      2. Prädikatausdruck A predicate expression
      3. Erstglied: A first member
      4. Glied: A member

§13.   1. Isomorphie: A isomorphism
      2. Isomorph: A isomorphic, B isomorphous
      3. einmehrdeutig: A one-many
      4. mehreindeutig: A many-one
      5. eineindeutig A one-one
      6. Korrelator: A correlator
      7. Struktur: A structure

§14.   1. Objektsprache: A object language
      2. Metasprache: A metalanguage
      3. Semiotik: A semiotic (B -ics)
      4. Pragmatik: A pragmatics
      5. Pragmatisch: A pragmatical (B -ic)
      6. Semantik: A semantics
      7. semantisch: A semantical, (B semantic)
      8. Sprachsystem: A language system
      9. Bezeichnungsregel: A rule of designation
      10. Wahrheitsregel: A rule of truth
      11. Syntax: A syntax
      12. Syntaktisch: A syntactical (B -ic)
      13. Kalkül: A calculus
      14. Kalküle: A calculi (B calculusses)
      15. Deduktionsregel: A rule of deduction (B deductive rule)
      16. Deutung: A interpretation

§15.   1. Fraktur(zeichen) A Gothic (Sy) | m.
§16.

§17. 1. Formregel, Formbestimmung: A rule of formation, (B formative rule)

2. Umformungsregel, -bestimmung: A rule of transformation, (B transformative rule), (C rule of deduction, (D deductive rule)

3. Grund(zeichen): A primitive

4. Definitionsregel: (=Definition in Form einer Regel; nicht: Regel für eine Definition): A definition rule

n. | §18. 1. Grundsatz: A primitive sentence

2. spitze (Klammern) A pointed, B angular

3. Auswahlprinzip: A principle of selection (Sy), B principle of choice, (C multiplicative principle (PM)

4. Kennzeichnung: A description (PM)

5. Satzkalkül: A sentential calculus (Sy) (B propositional calculus)

6. (Grundsatz) Schema: A schema, B scheme

7. Schlussregel: rule of inference (Sy)

8. Einsetzungsregel: A rule of substitution

o. | 9a Implikationsregel: A rule of implication

b Abtrennungsregel: A rule of abruption (Woodger), B rule of separation

p. | §19ä 1. beweisbar: A provable (B demonstrable (Sy))

§20. 1. ableitbar: A derivable

§23. 1. Grund(typus): A basic, B primary

2. umfangsgleich: A coextensive

§24. 1. Relationsprodukt: A relational product, (B relative product (PM))

2. Potenz (einer Relation): A power

3. Konverse: A converse (PM, Sy)

§25. 1. Bestandliste (einer Relation): ?

2. Pfeilfigur (einer Relation): A arrow diagram

q. | 3. Matrix (einer Relation): A matrix

4. symmetrisch: A symmetric, (B symmetrical)

5. total-reflexiv: A totally reflexive
6. zusammenhängend: A connected (PM)
7. Reihe: A series (PM)

§26. 1. Leere Klasse: A null class
2. Allklasse: A universal class
3. Vereinigungsklasse: A sum
4. Durchschnittsklasse: A product
5. Teilklasse: A subclass
6. Anfangs(glied): A initial
7. End(glied): A final, (B ending)

§27. 1. Einerklasse: A unit class
2. erbliche (Eigenschaft): A hereditary
3. structurelle (Eigenschaft): A structural

§33. 1. abzählbar: A denumerable

§ 32. 1. wohlgeordnet: A well ordered
2. dicht: A dense
3. Dedekindsche (Reihe): A Dedekindian
4. stetig: A continuous

§34. 1. Beschränkter (Operator): A limited
2. Rekursive (Definition): A recursive, (B regressive)

§ 35 1. (Quantitative) Bestimmung: (A determination, B term, C concept)

§ 36 1. Axiomatische Methode: A axiomatic m.
2. Axiom: A axiom (B postulate)
3. Axiomensystem: A axiom system
4. Modell: A model
5. Explizitbegriff: A explicit concept

§38 Umgebung: (A neighborhood) (so Russell, An. of Matter, p.296 ff) B environment

innerer Punkt: A inner point
Randpunkt: A border point
Gegiet: A region
Randmenge: A border set
Grenzpunkt: A boundary point
Berührungspunkt: ? | r.
Häufungspunkt: A cluster point (Russell behält das Wort 'Häufungspunkt')

s. | Verdichtungspunkt: ?
isolierter Punkt: A isolated point

⟨Besides marginalia there is also significant underlining. It is clumsy to reproduce it, and that information is duplicated in the next letter. The following are Quine's marginalia (with the exception of k., which is first a translation of the German, in square brackets, and then the marginal remark):⟩

a. or: mathematical logic
b. sentence, or statement If there *are* free variables, *statement matrix,* Inclusive of both: *formula*
c. name [vs: name matrix; inclusive of both: term]
d. [sentence sign]
e. ⟨Quine crosses out 'connections' and writes 'composition'.⟩
f. ⟨Quine crosses out 've' in 'alternative' and writes 'on', i.e., 'alternation'.⟩
g. ⟨Quine circles both 6.2A and 7.3A, connects them and writes 'spurious parallelism?'.⟩
h. matrix
i. (see p. 1)
j. sentence matrix
k. [(B or should we rather say 'offener Satz' instead of 'Satzfunktion', because the word 'Funktion' is perhaps better used for certain designata., namely such as functors or predicates, instead of for expressions of a specific kind?] Yes!
l. conditional
m. *German* ("gothic" is something else; see any printer's catalogue!)
n. axiom
o. conditional
p. c modus ponens
q. table (as in "truth table")
r. point of contact?
s. point of condensation?

[85. QUINE TO CARNAP 1939-8-18]

Emerson Hall
Harvard University
Cambridge, Mass.
August 18, 1939

Dear Carnap,

I am coming to Chicago a week from today, to stay six days. Unfortunately your departure so nearly coincides with my arrival that I probably won't see you till Cambridge. But I will telephone on the 25th.

Meanwhile here are answers to your two interesting terminological questionnaires:

SEMANTICS (Aug. 7):

1:	C	
2a:	class	[My recommendation of "class" in these 3 cases involves no ambiguity from my
2b:	class	point of view, since I regard a function
2c:	class	as a one-many relation and a relation in analysis of couples (whose copulands may in turn be couples, etc.).]
2d:	axiom	
2e:	function	
2f:	A	
3a:	matrix	
3b:	statement matrix	[I think of formulae as falling into statements and statement matrices: and of
3c:	numeral matrix (special kind of name matrix	terms as falling into names and name matrices. I don't regard statements as names; i.e., I repudiate propositions.]
4:	B	[Apparently I am now inconsistently voting for "propositional calculus". Actually I regard this appropriate so long as variables "p", "q", etc. are
5:	ABC	used: I don't use them, and hence have no such
6:	B	calculus, but would regard use of the variables as committing one to propositions (designata). N.B.: one can countenance propositions as *fictions*, by introducing quantified "p", "q", etc. through con-

textual definition.)] [Note that I prefer to use only general variables "x", "y", etc. (repudiating type), and to use these only in name-positions (rather than statement positions, e.g.).]

ABRISS (Aug. 8):

§1.	1:	B or: mathematical logic
	2:	A
	3:	A
	6:	statement
	7:	A
	8:	A
	9:	A
§2.	1:	A
	2:	A
	3:	statement
	4:	name or statement
	6:	statement sign
	7:	A
§3.	1:	statement composition
	2:	A
	3:	A
	4:	alternation
	5:	A
	6:	B
	7:	B (without hyphen)
	8:	A
	9:	A
§4.	1:	B
	2:	A
§5.	1:	A
	2:	A
	3:	A
	4:	A
	5:	A
§6.	1:	A
	2:	propositional variable
	3:	A

	4:	A
	5:	A
§7.	1:	universal quantification
	2:	existential "
	3:	A
	4:	B
	5:	B
	6:	A
	7:	A
	8:	matrix (statement matrix) [8 plus 9: formulae]
	9:	statement
	10:	statement matrix
	11:	conditional
§8.	1:	(see preceding page) ⟨nos. 4, 5, and 6 under SEMANTICS above⟩
	2:	A
	3:	A

§9.–§13.: A throughout

§14.   A throughout *except:*

	2:	[it hurts me to fuse Greek and Latin in a single word. But I have no good substitute—unless possibly "metasystem" or "semiotic language".]
	12:	B

§15.   German. (Gothic is something else; see printer's catalog.)

§17.	1:	B
	2:	B
	3:	A
	4:	A
§18.	1:	axiom
	2:	B
	3:	B
	4:	A
	5:	B
	6:	A
	7:	A (stet)
	8:	A
	9a:	rule of conditional
	9b:	A, or: modus ponens

§19.   1:   B
§20, §23: A throughout
§24:   1:   B
        2:    A
        3:    A
§25.   1:   catalogue
        2:    A
        3:    table [as in "truth table"]
     rest: A
§26-§36: A throughout
§38.   Berührungspunkt: point of contact
        Verdichtungspunkt: point of condensation
        rest: A

Yours,
Quine

P.S. I am very grateful for the letters you wrote to California. I have turned in your room reservation.

[86.   QUINE TO CARNAP   1939-11-12]

Elliot House E14
Cambridge, Mass.
Nov. 12, 1939

Dear Carnap,

   I am applying to the American Philosophical Society for a grant to pay for clerical help in finishing my book. The blank calls for the names of several experts who are acquainted with my work, and with your permission I should like to include yours.
   Tarski has job.
   I envy you the tropics, and hope you are enjoying them.
   We are looking forward to having you here next year. From Sheffer's remarks I gather that it is pretty definite.
   Meanwhile look out for fever, alligators, etc. Love to Ina.

Yours,
Quine

[87.   CARNAP TO QUINE   1939-11-19]

R.Carnap   Windermere, Florida, Nov. 19, 1939.
                                               (until Dec. 26)

Dear Quine,

You have general permission always to give my name as reference. I shall always be very glad if I can express the very good
opinion I have of you and your work. By the way, does the
A.P.S. sometimes give money for clerical help? Is that meant
e.g. for typing MS's? I think I might use that also occasionally,
or will they think that a professor gets salary enough to pay
such things himself? Ina is now too busy with her own work to
type for me.

Nagel wrote me that CCNY was considering Tarski. Therefore
I wrote there to the Committee of Appointments recommending
T. very highly. I am glad to learn from your letter that he will
have a job there. Is it only for one term, or is there good hope
for prolongation? I heard (I believe from Nagel) that there was
also a chance for T. at Harvard. Was that in Phil. or in Math.?
And did anything come out of it?

We have a nice little house near a lake. I swam often, am
mostly sitting on the porch, writing something about Semantics.
Would you or Tarski or both have time to look at it? I should
like you to see some parts of it before it will go to print. It will
probably be typed about Christmas or in January.

Korzybski wrote whether I would become Honorary Trustee
of his Institute. I declined of course. What is your final judgment about him? Do you think it worth while to read his "Science and Sanity"? The letter states that the invitation went
simultaneously to many people, among them Lesniewski and
Lukasiewicz. If I remember correctly, the opinion of Warsaw logicians on Korzybski was not very favorable. Does Tarski know it?

Has Tarski any news of his family? And does he know anything about the university people we knew in Warsaw?

Best regards, also from Ina, to you and Naomi, and to Tarski
if he is still with you,

                              yours,
                              R. C.

[*283*]

[88.   CARNAP TO QUINE   1939-12-10]

R. Carnap   Windermere, Florida, Dec.10, 1939.
                                   (until Dec.23)

Dear Quine,

I wrote to APS in support of your application and I hope for best success.

The secretary of the Guggenheim Foundation wrote me that the first meeting of the Committee will not be before February. Therefore I could not wait for his inofficial information about my chance which he had promised to give me after that meeting. Therefore I decided to come to Harvard next year as was planned. If, against probability, the G.F. will grant me a fellowship, I may postpone its consumption for one year, I was told.

Here copy of my letter to Hocking for your information and perhaps for suggestions as to formulation for the titles of my courses. I shall be very glad to get students who will have had training by you. And above all, I shall be very happy to see you then often. I have wished so often to talk to you during these years, and I was disappointed that in Chicago and in Cambridge in Sept., the time was too short for any serious talk.

Here a photo by Hempel which I got twice by chance.

                                   Yours,
                                   Carnap

[89.   CARNAP TO ERNEST HOCKING   1939-12-5]

                          Windermere, Fla., December 5, 1939.
                                   (Until Dec. 26th)

Professor Ernest Hocking,
Chairman, Department of Philosophy,
Harvard University,
Cambridge, Mass.

Dear Professor Hocking:

Your kind letter of November 24th was forwarded to me from Chicago. I am very grateful to you for your suggestions, and, as you will see, I am following them in the choice of my topics. My own plans are in agreement with your indications as to the interests in the department.

I should like to give two consecutive half-courses as my lecture course. In the first semester I propose to give an introductory course, a survey of the problems in the different fields of philosophy from my point of view, perhaps under a title like "Introduction to Analytic Philosophy". In the second semester I propose to lecture about theory of knowledge, perhaps under the title "Principles of Empiricism". This second course would presuppose either the first one or some equivalent reading. (In Chicago I should indicate this in the Announcements by the remark: "Prereq.: Course No. . . . or Consent of Instructor".) For the seminar I should prefer to take a full-course, running through the whole year. I should like to deal with problems in modern logic, especially in semantics and logical syntax, perhaps under the title: "Logic, Semantics, and Syntax". This seminar would be on an advanced level, presupposing familiarity with symbolic logic.

I do not know the customary arrangement of hours for courses in your department, and whether there is any possibility of choice left. For the case that there is, I am indicating some preferences. If it should fit easily into the schedule my first choice for the hour of the lecture course would be 11 A.M., the second 10 A.M. I suppose that seminars are in the afternoon as in Chicago. Any time between three and six P.M. on one of the two days between my lectures would suit me, preferably the earlier of the two days. I do, of course, not expect that it will be possible to satisfy all these preferences. Above all, I do not want to inconvenience somebody else.

I am looking forward very much to joining your department for the next year.

Sincerely yours,

⟨This letter is the enclosure mentioned in the previous letter.⟩

[90. QUINE TO CARNAP   NO DATE]

Dear Carnap,

I spoke to Lewis about the plan of issuing your semantics books unbound. He strongly opposes this on the ground that it would greatly reduce the sales, in view of U.S. habits. Libraries also would in large part be deterred, because of having to bind the books. Whether or not he is right, there would be no chance of departmental action counter to his strong advice in this matter. So I suppose you better continue to be interested in the Chicago alternative. It remains that our department *would* in my opinion be likely to favor substantial subsidy toward (a) the finished two volumes in one, which you find unsatisfactory, or (b) eventual publication of all three or four volumes in one, or (c) publication of *just* the first volume. Maybe the first volume would sell well enough so the Press would afterwards take the second *without* subsidy, or with such little subsidy as the A.C.L.S. alone might provide?

In any case it is of course just as well to hear what the Harvard Press has to say in the way of an estimate.

Yours, Van

⟨This is a postcard. Because it lacks a date, it is hard to order with respect to the other letters. This is where it appeared in Quine's files, but perhaps it should have appeared slightly later.⟩

[91. INA CARNAP TO NAOMI QUINE   1940-1-11]

1-11-40

Dear Naomi,

Since I don't have Mary Ann's address, will you do me the favor & ask her to come with you & Van next Saturday & to stay also for an early supper? Perhaps 5 o'clock would be a good time? I am going to ask Farrell too, he seems a nice boy.

Love, ina

⟨This is a postcard.⟩

[92. CARNAP TO QUINE ET AL. 1940-2-12]

R. Carnap

February 12, 1940

Prof. Dr. Egon Brunswik, Prof. Herbert Feigl, Dr. C. G. Hempel,
Prof. Charles W. Morris, Prof. Ernest Nagel, Dr. W. V. *Quine*

Dear Friends:

I would like to inform you of the present situation of Prof.
Heinrich Gomperz, (3919 ½ Dalton Ave., Los Angeles, Cal.), of
which I just learned by a letter from him. His teaching in the
Dept. of Philosophy at the University of Southern California will
be reduced to one semester from next year on, and accordingly
his salary will be cut into half. The University suggests that he
looks for teaching possibilities at other places for the second half
of each year.

I talked the situation over with our Department and Dean
McKeon. But, unfortunately, nothing can be done here, even
not with respect to a temporary invitation because of financial
reasons. McKeon, however, who is himself an expert in Greek
and Greek philosophy, told me that Gomperz, although he is
somewhat overshadowed by the high reputation of his father, is
regarded with high esteem in the field of Greek philosophy. His
English is very good. In case that you learn of a place where
they need somebody for the history of philosophy and especially for Greek philosophy, even if only temporarily, I should be
very grateful to you for either informing those people of Prof.
Gomperz' availability if you know them well enough, or, otherwise, inform Gomperz.

> With best regards,
> Yours,
> R. Carnap

[93. QUINE TO G. J. LAING   NO DATE]

65 Sparks St.

Mr. G. J. Laing, Editor
University of Chicago Press
5750 Ellis Avenue
Chicago, Ill.

Dear Mr. Laing,

The carbon copy of Carnap's *Introduction to Semantics* which I have been reading is on its way to you under separate cover.

The manuscript contains much interesting material, and I urge its publication. An important part of the philosophical world has been expectantly awaiting such a book ever since Carnap abandoned his thesis of syntax several years ago in favor of semantics. During this interval semantics has taken on a peculiar status in philosophy: there has been a growing awareness of its importance, and an awareness that researches were going ahead in this field, and yet no literature but the most fragmentary has been available.

Among professional philosophers and logicians—a limited group, of course—I think the book will rank among the best sellers. It will sell far more widely than Carnap's important and much discussed *Logical Syntax*, because (1) *Logical Syntax* has paved the way and (2) the book will be much less costly (*Syntax* is $7.50). Through this professional group, the book will find its way also into certain college courses; but only into relatively small, advanced courses.

Accidentally, it is likely to sell also to a wide supplementary public because of the popular publicity which has been gained by Count Korzybski's Institute for General Semantics, through the Institute's efficient press-agenting and through Stuart Chase. The circulation secured through this fluke is secured through false pretenses of others, not of yourselves; moreover the public will be rendered a real service in this substitution of science for pseudo-science.

I hazard the guess that you could fairly conservatively print 700 and adjust your get-out at 500. I shouldn't be surprised to see a second edition.

Some minor comments on the MS follow. They are mostly of an editorial kind.

MECHANICAL ERRORS:

P. 8, line 4: "once" should be "one".

P. 36, line 5: The *first* occurrences of inferior "i" and "j" should be interchanged; later occurrences O.K.

P. 39, line 6: "reveals".

P. 54, line 4: insert comma after " 'Pferd' ".

P. 71, line 11: apparently " 'L-implicate' " should be " 'L-equivalent' ".

P. 75, line 25: "S": should be "S_3".

P. 222, fourth from last line: "sentences".

MISSPELLINGS:

P. 48, line 18 "analogously".

P. 126, line 1: "permissible".

P. 201, below mid.: "incompatibility".

Also all occurrences of "interchangeable", "interchangeability"; e.g. p. 126, line 6, also p. 165, lower half, also p. 191, table (twice), also p. 195, table (twice): also there are occurrences in the first 125 pages which I have not noted.

UN-ENGLISH IDIOM:

P. 31, fourth from last line: "But this is in such a way" should be "But it does so in such a way".

P. 32, third from last line: "or both is the case". This intolerable construction could be remedied, without detriment to clarity, simply by deleting "is the case". Same thing recurs on p. 33, lines 1, 6, 20; p. 36, line 12; p. 90, line 2.

P. 36, line 2: this adoption of "embracing" as a technical adjective is bad idiom. An excellent term for the purpose would be "exhaustive"; but I suppose this is unacceptable, because he has used this word for another purpose on pp. 195 ff. Perhaps a satisfactory substitute, either directly for "embracing" or else for "exhaustive" so as to release the latter as a substitute for "embracing", would be "comprehensive". Besides the occurrence of "embracing" mentioned above, there are the following recurrences: p. 40 above mid. (3 times); p. 40b near end; p. 74, fourth from last line; p. 96 near foot (twice); p. 97 (ten times); p. 98 (four times); p. 106, sixth from last line; p. 110, line 5; p. 117, lower half (twice); p. 151 (nine times); p. 152, upper half (five times); p. 154, lower half (three times); p. 156, below mid.; p. 165, line 7; p. 175, lower half (twice); p. 191, table (twice); p. 192, table (twice); p. 195, table (twice).

P. 38, end (and beginning of next), the unidiomatic phrase "at all a false $\dot{T}_i$ in S" could be remedied as "any false $\dot{T}_i$ in S" or perhaps more clearly as "a false $\dot{T}_i$ at all in S".

P. 92, eighth from last line: erroneous use of future in antecedent of a conditional. Correct it by putting "turns" for "will turn". Similarly p. 220, below mid., put "is constructed" for "will be constructed".

P. 188, seventh from last line: Change "The simplest though trivial way" to read "A simple though trivial way"; or, if the author feels it important to preserve the exact sense, "The simplest way (though a trivial one)".

P. 223, last five words would be better thus: "On the basis of the two identifications".

OBSCURITIES:

P. 27, foot, and also p. 29, line 9: "DA" is used to refer to D7-A"; but this usage is not explained until later (p. 34). Hence this explanation should be transferred to an earlier point, or else the two cited occurrences of "DA" should be changed to "D7-A".

P. 42, line 8: omit comma: the antithesis intended in the next sentence then becomes a little clearer.

P. 46, last sentence of double-spaced matter. The obscurity here could be removed by inserting a comma after "purposes", changing "add to" to "supplement", putting parentheses around "as metalanguage", and inserting the words "by adding" right after the latter parenthesis.

P. 149, tenth from last line. Obscurity can be removed by changing "is the following (in ordinary terminology, formulation A)" to read thus: "is, in ordinary terminology, the following (formulation A)".

P. 178: obscurity can be removed by inserting "then" after "K" in line 9 and in line 11 (doing as you like in the matter of using a comma before "then" in both cases).

THEORY

P. 41, D10-1: "for every u" here is intended in the sense "for every sequence u of appropriate degree". The author feels, apparently, that the theory of types automatically provides this restriction; but it does *not* if we construe sequences as the author himself suggests at mid. p. 8.

P. 48, line 19: "regard a proposition as an attribute of degree O" is anticipated (Quine, Journal of Symbolic Logic, vol. 1, p. 2).

Sincerely yours,
W. V. Quine

[94. G. J. LAING TO QUINE   1940-6-27]

THE UNIVERSITY OF CHICAGO PRESS
5750 ELLIS AVENUE   CHICAGO ILLINOIS
1891   1941
FIFTEENTH ANNIVERSARY
June 27, 1940

Dr. W. V. Quine
65 Sparks Street
Cambridge, Massachusetts

Dear Dr. Quine:

Thank you very much for your excellent report on Carnap's *Introduction to Semantics*. On the basis of your review the Board of University Publications at its recent meeting approved the manuscript for publication provided it can be financed. It is not a large book but composition will be expensive.

I am passing on to Carnap your suggestions without, of course, giving your name. We never reveal the names of our special readers to authors for that would inevitably involve the former in correspondence. Your reading fee ($20.00) is being forwarded to you today.

With kind regards
Sincerely yours,
G. J. Laing
Editor

GJL:EEK

[95. QUINE TO MALONE 1941-2-20]

Feb. 20, 1941

Dear Mr. Malone:

The chairman of the department has asked me to write you my opinion regarding Carnap's two little books on semantics, whose publication the department contemplates subsidizing. Both manuscripts contain much interesting material, and I urge their publication. An important part of the philosophical world has been expectantly awaiting these ever since Carnap abandoned his thesis of syntax several years ago in favor of semantics. During this interval semantics has taken on a peculiar status in philosophy: there has been a growing awareness of its importance, and an awareness that researches were going ahead in this field, and yet no literature but the most fragmentary has been available.

Among professional philosophers and logicians, the more general of the two books (INTRODUCTION TO SEMANTICS) will surely rank among the best sellers. It will sell far more widely than Carnap's important and much discussed LOGICAL SYNTAX, because (1) the latter has paved the way and (2) the cost will be far lower. Through this professional group, the book will find its way also into certain college courses. Accidentally, also, it is likely to sell also to a wide supplementary public because of the wide publicity which a less responsible form of so-called semantics has received through Korzybski, Stuart Chase, and others. There can be no question but what that one volume will pay for itself and show a profit. The other volume will sell less widely, surely, being more specialized; but I should expect it also to make a fair showing, and anyway there is the subsidy.

It has perhaps never before happened that I have known simultaneously of three unpublished books which I was anxious to see in print. But this is now the case—the little Tarski book being the third. This book contains really sensational results, and urgently demands release. Tarski ranks with Gödel as one of the two greatest living logicians; and he is a very distinguished mathematician on other counts as well. This book will be a *must* for all who are concerned with mathematical logic or with foundations of mathematics. The book has the effect of palliating, in certain striking ways, Gödel's epoch-making discovery of a decade ago regarding the incompletability of arithmetic. Despite its remarkable content, it is written in a sufficiently elementary style to be available to a fairly wide public; its sale will by no means be limited to experts in the aforementioned fields. And it contains enough general discussion of the background to serve, incidentally, as a much needed survey of the whole array of problems connected with Gödel's discovery. This is the livest part of all present studies in foundations of mathematics: there is real demand for a readable treatment. Herrmenn of Paris had planned, as you may know, on an unsubsidized edition of a thousand copies; and the book was in galleys when the invasion stopped it. So I think the book is capable of paying for itself, at least in a smaller edition; and its publication will be a real service to science.

Sincerely yours,
W. V. Quine

[96.   CARNAP TO QUINE   1941-6-26]

Bethlehem N.H., June 26, 1941.

Dear Van:

Sorry, no bag in the car. Ina remembers that she gave a big straw bag apparently containing bathing suits to Naomi from the car when you stepped out.

We are enjoying it here very much, we wish the same to all of you there and on your further travel.

Yours,
Carnap

⟨This postcard contains (curiously) the following note in Quine's hand:⟩
Write to:

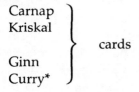

Carnap
Kriskal
⎫
⎬ cards
⎭
Ginn
Curry*

*Mention book & his reprints

[97. QUINE TO CARNAP   1943-1-5]

843 51st St., S.E.
Washington, D.C.
Jan. 5, 1943

Dear Carnap,

In the past year, as you may have heard, my life has diverged a good deal from the usual routine. In May I flew, via the Antilles and Guiana, to Brazil, where I lectured in Portuguese as visiting professor at Sao Paulo. Also, while there, I wrote a book in Portuguese, *O sentido da nova logica*. In September I flew back, via Bolivia and Panama, and became a lieutenant in the Navy. Late in October Naomi and daughters and household goods joined me in Washington and we moved in at the above address. I am being kept very busy here. I look forward to getting back to pure science when the world stops tottering, but meanwhile I find much satisfaction and relief in devoting my energies to the waging of war—if only within the security of the Navy Building.

Such has been the strenuous round that has delayed me in acknowledging your *Introduction to Semantics*. Thank you very much for it. I'm impressed with it as a masterly job of organization and presentation, and much of the theory is decidedly to my liking despite my dissension on certain points. On the other hand I do feel that the points where I dissent are peculiarly crucial to semantics; and my mind has become somewhat clearer on them in the year and a half since we talked.

These points can be considered independently, I think, of the program of finitistic constitution system on which the four of us talked at intervals in 1941. Some such program may indeed be essential to a satisfactory epistemology. The problem of epistemology is far from clear, as you have emphasized; and essential details of the aforementioned program must depend, as we have seen, on some increased clarification as to just what the epistemological problem is. I am more hopeful than you of the eventual possibility of such a clarification; i.e., the possibility of eventually reducing to the form of clear questions the particular type of inarticulate intellectual dissatisfaction that once drove you to work out the theory of the *Aufbau,* and Goodman his related theory. Moreover, I find this an important objective. However, I think the essential semantic issues between us are readily divorced from that finitistic program and from epistemology altogether. In our discussions epistemological matters entered the semantical scene in these ways:

(a) Tarski and I questioned the precise nature of your distinction between analytic and synthetic, and in the course of such discussion it began to appear increasingly that the distinguishing feature of analytic truth, for you, was its epistemological immediacy in some sense. (True by "fiat", perhaps; but then a "subconscious fiat", which is to me as much a metaphor as the Kantian sieve.) Then we urged that the only logic to which we could attach any seeming epistemological immediacy would be some sort of finitistic logic. So here we were in epistemology and envisaging a finitistic constitution system.

(b) I argued, supported by Tarski, that there remains a kernel of technical meaning in the old controversy about reality or irreality of universals, and that in this respect we find ourselves on the side of the Platonists insofar as we hold to the full non-finitistic logic. Such an orientation seems unsatisfactory as an end-point in philosophical analysis, given the hard-headed, anti-mystical philosophical temper which all of us share; and, if this were not enough, evidence against the common-sense admission of universals can be adduced also from the logical paradoxes. So here again we found ourselves envisaging a finitistic constitution system.

How, then, to divorce our essential semantic issues from the questions of epistemology and finitism? As to (b), the answer is immediate: let us *accept,* provisionally, whatever rudimentary Platonism may be embodied in our regular logic and classical mathematics, and so proceed with our semantics, just as we have in the past been proceeding with our regular logic and mathematics. If independent progress should be made sometime in the way of an epistemologically motivated finitistic substructure, so much the better; it would be a case of resolving the Platonic kink without much altering the existing logical, mathematical, and semantical superstructure, perhaps, just as Weierstraß eliminated the nonsense about infinitesimals without wrecking the differential calculus.

If (a) were to be deferred in analogous fashion, we should find ourselves proceeding with semantics using provisionally an ultimate and unexplained notion of "analytic". But this is different from the provisional acceptance of Platonism suggested in the preceding paragraph; for in accepting such Platonism we go no farther than had been done already in our regular logic and mathematics, but in accepting the notion of "analytic" we take on an unexplained notion to which we were not committed hitherto. It remains to explain the notion, but along lines other than those hinted in (a).

I am content to narrow the problem down by supposing our logical notation given. Let us also accept the general notion of truth (restricted in one way or another to avoid the Epimenides). Then we can, of course, define *logical truth,* simply as truth which survives all uniform changes of component expressions other than the enumerated logical signs. For the specified language, thus, there seems to be no difficulty in saying what statements are analytic. However, I do not agree even to this. What I have in mind is our actual scientific language, or something approaching it, with all its virtually unlimited extralogical vocabulary; only the logical vocabulary is narrowed down, and even this need not be narrowed down beyond the point of a long list, provided the list is fully specified. Now there will be statements in this language, e.g. 'No spinster is married,' which we should want to cover by the term 'analytic' despite the fact that they are not logical truths in the defined sense; 'analytic' is broader than 'logically true'. A common answer to this is to say that 'No spinster is married' is a definitional abbreviation of a logical truth, 'No woman not married is married'. Here we come to the root of the difficulty: the assumption of a thoroughgoing constitution system, with fixed primitives and fixed definitions of all other expressions, despite the fact that no such constitution system exists. The question whether 'No spinster is married' is analytic or synthetic would seem to depend on whether we are thinking of a constitution system in which 'spinster' is defined as 'woman not married' or as some other expression which, though in fact denoting the same individuals, might render the context synthetic. Certainly little progress is made toward clarifying the term 'analytic' in any of its preëxisting usage, if in the face of every statement which is not explicitly a logical truth (like 'No woman not married is married') we have to conclude, 'Whether this is analytic or not depends on what constitution system we adopt, and we aren't going in fact to adopt any.'

Thus it is that I feel there is false security in the common appeal to definition, in philosophy. The status of definitions as I use them in logic is, I believe, this: indications of how to paraphrase a rich logical language into a meager logical language, proving that certain metalogical conclusions established more easily in application to the meager language apply equally to the richer, more convenient language. Another function of such indications of how to paraphrase the whole into the part is to show that certain philosophical *Bedenken* once levelled against the whole are groundless, not being applicable to the part; or to show that certain philosophical consequences thought to follow from the whole are groundless, not being implicit in the part. Such, e.g., is a great value of Russell's logical definition of descriptions. But note how this characterization of definition makes no use of the idea of linguistic revision or fiat, nor accords to definition any integral status within a language.

It is clearer, I think, to shortcut the question of definitions in connection with the relation between the analytic and the logically true, and to speak directly, rather, of the relation of *synonymity* or sameness of meaning. Given this notion, along with that of logical truth, we can explain analyticity as follows: a statement is analytic if it can be turned into a logical truth by putting synonyms for synonyms. (Incidentally this enables us also to get along with the specification of fewer logical signs, in the previous formulations—say just those which are "primitive" in my *Mathematical Logic*. We can define a statement as analytic when, by putting synonyms for synonyms, it can be turned into a statement whose truth survives all uniform changes of component expressions other than those very few specified logical signs. The synonymity clause then serves to let in any further expressions of our more abundant logical vocabulary.)

The problem remains, of course, to explain this basic synonymity relation. This is a relation whose full specification, like
that of designation, would be the business of pragmatics (not
that this excuses us from it!). Once thus specified, designation
can be studied within the narrower field of semantics; and the
analogous is true of synonymity, although the field that studies
synonymity is semantics in another sense (or perhaps a more
inclusive sense). The definition of this relation of synonymity,
within pragmatics, would make reference to criteria of behavioristic psychology and empirical linguistics. I have never succeeded in setting up a satisfactory one, but consider that it
would be very useful to do so, both for philosophy and for empirical linguistics itself. It is, for example, because of the lack of
such a definition that Bloomfield's chapter in Semantics is so
weak, in the midst of his otherwise very fine book *Language*. I
find it interesting to have reduced the notion of analytic to this
as yet unanalyzed notion of synonymity because I feel this
shows, more clearly than hitherto, the gap that has to be
bridged. The notion of synonymity in turn is as important and
as needing of analysis as that not only of *analytic,* but of *meaning;* for the three are interdefinable. Synonymity is definable as
sameness of meaning; and the meaning of an expression is definable, conversely, as the class of its synonyms. The definition of
analytic in terms of synonymity (and truth) has been seen; and
conversely, expressions are synonymous if, whenever one is put
for the other within a statement of the form 'p ⊃ p', the result
is analytic. (I couldn't say 'The result of joining the expressions
by '=' is analytic', because '=' attaches only to substantives,
whereas any expression that can occur in a statement is allowed
meaning and synonyms.) Incidentally here is a simpler definition of 'analytic' in terms of synonymity: a statement is analytic
if it is synonymous with '0 = 0'.

Note that meanings do not correspond to designata even in
the case of substantives, having designata. The expressions
'Morning Star' and 'Evening Star' have different meanings, but
they have one and the same sphere of rock as designatum. Both
deserve study, designation and meaning, but they must be kept
distinct. Semantics, in a broad sense, splits off into two parts;
one concerns designation, denotation, and truth, and the other

concerns meaning, synonymity, analyticity. It is right here, in
what seems to me your failure to keep meaning distinct from
designatum, that I find myself in strongest disagreement with
your various writings on semantics. My objection is not terminological; my guess is, in fact, that a sharper distinction on this
point would even have obviated the seeming advantages, for
you, of intensional contexts. I suppose all our semantical disagreements tie up, ultimately, into one.

So I'll be glad when we have a chance to talk some more
about these problems, particularly inasmuch as my views of
intensional contexts have developed and clarified themselves a
good deal of late. In my Portuguese book (whose appearance is
being delayed, to my great discomfort, though the book has lain
in Brazil ready for print since September) I tried, among other
things, to set forth just what the essential restrictions are on our
use of intensional contexts, independently of special dogma or
philosophy on the matter: and some of what comes out of this
is, I think, surprising and rather compelling. Fragments of the
Portuguese book, covering this matter and various semantical
matters closely connected with other parts of this letter, I translated into English last September and sent off to the Journal of
Philosophy, where I expect it to appear in another month or so.
Meanwhile I have been wanting to send you my carbon copy of
that article, but have been delayed, as indicated earlier, by a too
busy life.

Also I have still a packed-up copy of *Logical Syntax*, which
you left with me in case of further requests from students; but
now that I'm out of academic life for the duration I'd better
send it back. Since I'm not sure of your address (hearing you
are on sabbatical or Guggenheim), please drop me a card saying
where you are and I'll thereupon send both the book and the
carbon copy of that article.

I wish we could get together with more leisure than there
was at Harvard—weeks of leisure for scientific talk. I think our
Harvard talks would have yielded some first-order results if to
begin with we had been aware of things that have since gone
into the Portuguese book and the article; so I'm very anxious to
have your reactions to the article.

We are very well, and the children are now both very nearly

human, having reached the advanced ages respectively of seven and six. The other evening Elizabeth and I had our first disputation over religion and first causes, she having been atavized by neighbor children. But I must cut short the personal news, lest I be led to touch upon the delights of flying over the West Indies, the Amazon jungles, and the Andes; for in this event the 2000 words thus far typed would be only a beginning.

With best regards and best wishes 4:2,

Yours,
Van

[98.   CARNAP TO QUINE   1943-1-13]

Rudolf Carnap
Box 307, Route 2
El Paso, Texas.

January 13, 1943.

Dear Van,

Thank you for your long and extremely interesting letter. I shall answer to your discussion of semantics after I get your article.

I have been in bed all the time since last July with back trouble. However, most of the time I have no pain, except when it began again with a very bad attack in July. Thus I could write and work and also look out of the window at the wonderful scenery of Santa Fe. When it became too cold we moved to El Paso. My doctor here thinks an operation might help. He sent my X-rays to the Mayo Clinic in Rochester, Minn. and they advised me to come there—then the final decision will be made whether they will operate or not. We plan to leave in the last days of January. We plan to come back to the South afterwards. I have a Rockefeller-paid leave of absence until June or (more probably) September. I shall be very glad to get your article as soon as possible. I hope to write to you still from here after reading it. As to the copy of "Syntax", could you perhaps keep it until I am in Chicago? If that should be inconvenient for you,

you could sent it to a friend of Ina's in Chicago: Miss Erna Lowenberg, 5735 Harper Ave; in this case write on it that it should be held for me there.

I wonder whether you were able to find good quarters in Wash. The stories about the overcrowding sound appalling. How does Nae like it there? Please give her our love.

I will write more later on, this has to be hurried off to town.

> With warm wishes and regards
> Yours,
> Carnap

Is your house number "843" or "343"? You typed the first and wrote the second.

[99. QUINE TO CARNAP 1943-1-16]

> 843 51st St., S.E.
> Washington, D.C.
> Jan. 16, 1943

Dear Carnap,

Naomi and I were very sorry indeed to hear about the bad time you have been having with your back. Six months in bed— this is a terrible thing. I certainly hope that they decide at the Mayo Clinic that there is an operation that will put an end to these troubles once and for all. We shall be anxious to hear news of the developments.

Too bad you can't enjoy El Paso and Juarez, which Naomi and I liked very much. Also we reminisce often on relatively nearby Chihuahua, where we spent several weeks.

Enclosed is the article. In looking it over just now I am reminded, by lines 9–10 of page 13 ⟨"Notes on Existence and Necessity," perhaps the last sentence of the fourth full paragraph after (15) therein⟩, that lines 6–7 of page 4 of my previous letter ⟨p. 298, Quine's remark that 'a statement is analytic if it is synonymous with '0 = 0' '⟩ are untenable. For the same reason, the footnote of page 13 of the article is itself untenable, as I now discover for the first time. Even if we waive this difficulty and let logical equivalence be a case of synonymity (i.e., even if we waive lines 9–10 of page 13), there remains another difficulty in that footnote; namely, when we speak of "putting the one for the other" (top 2 lines of page 14, within same footnote) we should somehow limit the kinds of occurrence involved, so as to rule out e.g. occurrences within quotes, so as to exclude obviously unintended cases. But how to limit the kinds of occurrence? "Purely designative occurrence" won't do, for I am concerned here with a wider range of expressions than substantives. On account of these considerations I am merely deleting that footnote from the article (incidentally letting lines 9–10 of page 13 stand).

My street number is 843. Incidentally the "S.E." at the end, for "southeast", is theoretically essential, to resolve a four-way ambiguity (though actually the numbers happen to get as high as 51 only on this side of town).

I'll keep that copy of *Syntax* till you are in Chicago again.

I'm much concerned to know your reactions to the article and letters; however, take it easy and give first consideration to your wayward vertebra! Best wishes for a quick and lasting recovery.

Yours,
Van

[100.   CARNAP TO QUINE   1943-1-21]

Rudolf Carnap
Box 307, Route 2,
El Paso, Texas.

January 21, 1943.

Dear Van,

Your article and your letters have interested me very much. Last year I have thought about some problems which are closely related to yours, especially in these last months while working at [III]ˣ. Your discussion is as always very instructive and

---

ˣ'[I]' etc. designates *Semantics*, vol. I etc. [II] will appear very soon (twelve

stimulating, even at points where I cannot fully agree. I have also thought a lot about our earlier talks, your conceptions, system forms etc., and I have accepted some things of yours for my purposes (e.g. I use in [III] and [IV] only systems with closed | a. sentences, and I adopt for them your Axioms of Quantification).

I am going to explain something of my terminology, notation, conceptions etc.; I think that my comments on your article will then be easier understandable.

Comparison of terminology:

	Quine:	Carnap:
1.	meaning	designatum
2.	designated object	--- ('denotatum' could perhaps be taken)
3.	designating the same	synonymous
4.	synonymous	L-synonymous (=having the same meaning, [I] p.75)
5.	designating the same, but not synonymous	F-synonymous
	(e.g. 'morning star' and 'evening star'; '9' and 'the number of planets')	
6.	substitutivity	interchangeability
7.	?	L-interchangeability
8.	logically true	--- (L-true on the basis of a certain part of the semantical rules, excluding the rules of designation)
9.	analytic	L-true (i.e. true on the basis of all semantical rules incl. rs.of des.)

I am not quite clear, not even intuitively, what you mean by 'meaning' and '*synonymous*'. It seems to me that most and per-

---

months after I sent the finished MS to the Harvard Press). I am now working on [III] (Modal Logic) and [IV] (Probability and Degree of Confirmation).

haps all of what you say about 'synonymity' in way of requirements, explanations and examples, is in agreement with my
'L-synonymity' if we take the latter as comprehending the following three relations:
1. L-equivalence of sentences, 2. L-equivalence of predicates,
and perhaps sentential functions ([I] T22-13), 3. L-synonymity
of individual constants and perhaps descriptions (T22-30).

One might perhaps consider to take a still narrower concept;
perhaps your remark p. 13, l. 9 ⟨"Notes on Existence and Necessity," perhaps the last sentence of the fourth full paragraph after
(15) therein⟩ is meant to suggest this. Perhaps something of the
kind of S-equivalence might come into consideration, i.e. sense-
equivalence. (Perhaps you remember that I made some brief indi-

b. | cations about *sense-modalities* once while walking around the
Lost Pond. I believe I indicated that we require more than L-
equivalence for the translation even of a theoretical book.) So far
I have not given much thought to these new concepts. As far as
I can see at present they will probably be definable on the basis
of L-concepts and hence not require new semantical rules. However, I believe that for most applications of your synonymity
and the concepts defined by it, including all examples you give,
L-synonymity and the other L-concepts will do. (E.g. all your
examples of analytic sentences are L-true, see below). And I believe that taking L-synonymity for your synonymity would lead
to a simpler theory than taking S-concepts. It seems to me that
in your last letter ("If we waive. . . .") you are at least consider-

c. | ing the acceptance of L-equivalence and hence L-synonymity.

For the construction of L-semantics I prefer now rules of L-
ranges to rules of truth (as in [I] p.130, but now state-
descriptions as elements of L-ranges, in a similar way as § 19 E).
In this procedure the metalanguage may be extensional. I have
used this method in [II] and I am using it now in [III] and [IV].
It works very well, also in the theory of probability and degree
of confirmation. What would your rules of synonymity look like
(see below)?

Your definition of 'analytic' (p. 13) is, I believe, subject to the
same objection as my definition for 'L-valid' in "Syntax" because
it refers to all expressions of a certain kind instead of to all entities. (Counter example. Let the system S contain 'R' as only

predicate of degree 2. Suppose 'R' happens to be symmetric, i.e.
'(x)(y)(R(x,y) ⊃ R(y,x))' is F-true, not L-true. Since, however, the
sentence is the only instance of its logical form in S, your criterion for 'analytic' is fulfilled, contrary to the intended meaning.)
The concept 'universal logical form' which you need for your
definition should be defined not by referring to the instances
but rather in the way of [I] D11-2 (based on D10-1).

My '*L-true*' does not correspond to your 'logically true', but to
your '*analytic*'. E.g. 'No spinster is married' would be L-true in a
suitable system even if 'spinster' and 'married' are primitive
predicates. (I should raise the question of L-truth only with respect to a given semantical system; see below). In this example
the L-truth would be based not on definitions but on the semantical rules of designation: " 'spinster' designates the property of
being a non-married woman".

On Modal Systems.

I use 'N' as primitive sign for logical necessity.

I use the following abbreviations (I follow you in regarding
them as shorthand not belonging to the system itself):
D1. 'p ⥽ q' for 'N(p ⊃ q)'.
D2. 'p ≌ q' for 'N(p ≡ q)'
D3. 'x ≐ y' for 'N(x=y)'
D4. 'F ⊃ G' for '(x)(F(x) ⊃ G(x))'
Analogously:
D5. 'F ≡ G'.
D6. 'F ⥽ G'.
D7. 'F ≌ G'.

You assume that the principle of interchangeability on the basis of '=' does always hold. But your argumentation is based on
the supposition that an individual constant designates an object;
This supposition, however, must be abandoned at least for
modal languages (see below). In a system with logical modalities
we have instead the following principles: d.
P1. Interchangeability on the basis of '=' holds only in non-
modal contexts.
P2. L-interchangeability on the basis of '=' holds generally, also
in modal contexts.
In a certain system with predicate variables I have expressed
these principles by the following primitive sentences (in a sim-

pler system without predicate variables I use instead primitive sentential schemata):

P1. $(x)(y)(F)[x=y \supset (F(x) \supset F(y))]$

P2. $(x)(y)(\dot{F})\ [x\dot{=}y \supset (\dot{F}(x) \supset \dot{F}(y))]$.

'F' is here a non-modal variable; i.e. only non-modal sential ⟨*sic*⟩ functions may be substituted for 'F(x)'. On the other hand, '$\dot{F}$' is a general (or modal) variable; i.e. any sentential function may be substituted for '$\dot{F}(x)$', also one containing modal signs. (We could do with '$\dot{F}$' alone; the use of two kinds of variables has the advantage that certain formulas of the extensional system may be simply transferred to the modal system, as e.g. P1.)

e. | Connection between identity and synonymity of individual constants:

1. 'a' and 'b' are synonymous if and only if 'a=b' is true.
2. 'a' and 'b' are L-synonymous if and only if 'a$\dot{=}$b' is true (hence 'a=b' L-true).

The customary theorem of the interchangeability of sentences on the basis of '≡' is here replaced by the following two (which

f. | are analogous to P1 and P2):

T1. Interchangeability on the basis of '≡' holds only in non-modal contexts.

T2. L-interchangeability on the basis of '$\dot{\equiv}$' holds generally, also in modal contexts.

Here likewise there are corresponding schemata. I do not take them as primitive sentential schemata but I prove them inductively. T1 and T2 hold also for predicates (applying D4 through D7) and sentential functions.

Designation and denotation.

	(1) Kind of expressions	(2) Designatum	(3) Denotatum (?)
a.	Predicate (degree 1)	Property	Class
b.	Sentence	Proposition	Truth-value
c.	Individual constant	Individual concept (?)	Object

(g. marks rows a–c)

In distinction to [I], it now seems to me that it would be better to say that the designatum of an individual constant is a concept of individual type (I call them tentatively 'individual concepts') rather than an object. As before, I regard properties as designata of predicates and propositions as designata of sentences. It is true, with respect to an extensional language we might say, in consequence of the special conditions of interchangeability, that individuals designate objects, predicates designate classes, and sentences designate truth-values (as Frege said). However, we might consider even here to call the entities (3) not designata but to use another word, perhaps 'denotata'. If so, we could say (with respect to any language): a predicate designates a property and denotes a class. Then we should also say: 'Pegasus' designates something but does not denote anything. (The idea of this use of 'denotation' has occurred to me only now while reading your letters; It needs more careful examination.)

You seem to have got the impression that I do not make the distinction between meaning and designation (in your sense). I believe that this is due to a misunderstanding of my term 'designation'. I do not mean it in your sense but as the relation between an expression and its meaning. (I see now that I am at least partly responsible for this misunderstanding because I was not quite consistent in that use of 'designation'. I believe I was, as far as predicates and sentences are concerned; but I was not when I said in [I] that '2' designates an object. This is perhaps admissible with respect to a non-modal language, but today I should prefer not to say so.) I made the distinction between 'synonymous' (designating (or denoting) the same object) and 'L-synonymous' (having the same meaning) already in "Syntax" (see p.290, examples 6 and 7). Today, of course, I do not regard the syntactical method as adequate here but express the distinction by semantical concepts.

Modalities and quantification. Your assertions (p.18) "It does not admit pronouns . . ." (line 14), "but the. . . ." (line 6 -3 f.p.), and "but such . . ." (last line) seem to me erroneous. Hence also your conclusion (p.19) that a system with modalities and quantification is not possible. I have constructed and examined in detail such systems (semantical and syntactical); in them the difficulties which you expect do not appear. I believe you are committing here a fallacy quite analogous to that in the well-known objection by some philosophers against set-theory: to say that a set has the same cardinal number as a proper sub-set involves a contradiction because x cannot at the same time be smaller and equal to y. The mistake consists, if I see it correctly, in either case, in transferring uncritically certain rules which are familiar to us within a well-known field, to a new field where in fact they do not hold any longer. You presuppose the principle of the interchangeability on the basis of '=' as valid for all languages, and then you procede to construct a contradiction in modal logic. For the latter, however, that principle does not hold but is to be replaced by P1 and P2. You are, of course, free to declare that you do not like to use systems for which the principle mentioned is not valid—just as those philosophers are, of course, entitled to refuse to use the theory of transfinite cardinals. You are, however, not right in saying that a modal system with quantification must lead to contradictions—no more than those philosophers with the assertion of the inconsistency of set-theory. For these reasons it seems to me more advisable if you would express your opinion only in the more cautious form of the last paragraph of §4. — The sentence "But such . . ." implies that (18) and (23) express the same affirmation in different forms. But this is certainly not the case since those sentences are only F-equivalent, not L-equivalent. — For the same reasons I believe that there is an essential difference between the use of variables within an expression in quotes and within the arguments of modal sign. — Similarly, the analogous sentences on p.23 (especially "Expressions of . . .", "It is, in particular, . .", and "The only recourse . . ." seem to me untenable. (Comp. T1 and T2, above, for predicates and sentential functions.)

h.

i.

Remarks on a few other points.

Q.13, footnote, (now omitted). The attempted definition would run in my terminology like this: "L-synonymous = $_{Df}$ L-interchangeable". You are right in rejecting this definition. I have pointed out the difference between those two concepts in the paragraph after T14-112 in [I], see esp. the sentences "If they . . ." and "and if . . .".

To your letter of January 5th, p.1, (a). I do by no means regard epistemological immediacy as the characteristic of 'analytic' (in pragmatics) (I emphasized this against Schlick, I do not remember where), but rather that here the truth is independent of the contingency of facts (this, of course, should be made more precise).

j.

Ibid., p.2, last paragraph. Here is an important methodological point. I believe that we cannot construct an exact and workable theory of concepts like 'true', 'analytic', 'meaning', 'synonymous', 'compatible' etc. if we refer merely to the actually used
language of science. It seems to me that we can use those concepts only if we replace the given language by a system of rules;
in other words, we have to go from pragmatics and descriptive
semantics to *pure semantics* (see [I] §5, esp. example p.14). You
are right in saying that it is the task of linguistics (hence pragmatics) to define 'synonymous'; but this holds likewise for the
other concepts mentioned: 'true', etc. in a certain sense. However, the pragmatical definition cannot be taken as the basis for
the semantical theory. If the concept 'synonymous' is to be used
at all in pure semantics, you have to state rules for it.

    k.

Typing errors. p.4, l.2, write 'on' instead of 'of'. p.9, last line;
p.10, lines 9, 15, 18: 'substantives'. p.10, l.11: 'Pegasus' in
quotes.

My general impression of your article and letters. It seems that
our views on semantics (not those on modal systems) are now
much closer to each other. Especially your requirement of the
bipartition of semantics (letter of Jan.5, top of p.4) is much in
agreement with my views. As I see it, this requirement is fulfilled by my distinction between radical semantics and L-
semantics. (Therefore I do not quite understand what you have
in mind when, immediately afterwards you speak of "strongest
disagreement".) The difference between our views here (i.e. leaving aside all questions concerning modal systems which in my
view are not essentially relevant for the present question) consists, as far as I can see, only in the fact that we propose different ways for the construction of the second part of semantics.
As mentioned earlier, I start with rules of L-ranges; on this basis
all L-concepts including L-synonymity can easily be defined.
This is done in an extensional metalanguage. You want instead
to take your concept of synonymity as basic. The question is
simply: which way is better? Perhaps your way will prove to be
good. At present, however, I have still some doubts. But first
you have to explain how your semantical rules will look; then
only can the question be discussed. Your synonymity—whether
construed as my L-synonymity or as a still stronger concept—is

    l.

extremely strong. In general it has turned out to be more advisable, both in syntax and in semantics, to take as a starting point not such strong concepts (as e.g. 'provable' in syntax, 'L-true' in semantics) but rather simpler concepts (as e.g. 'directly derivable', '(direct) designatum', 'L-range') such that the other concepts are definable on their basis. Furthermore, we want in general the concepts with which we start to be definite (effective), e.g. defined by finite enumeration. This is obviously not possible for your synonymity. Hence the practical question is: on which definite concepts are you going to base it? (Here I am, of course, speaking of the role of that concept in pure semantics, not of its pragmatical definition.) You should give the rules for the concepts on which your synonymity is to be based at least for a simple system, e.g. the logic of quantification. Then we shall find out what are the relative advantages of my and your ways. I believe that both ways will finally lead to the same concepts. If this is so, then the choice between them will be merely a question of technical expediency.

We shall leave here for Rochester on the 1st of February. My address there will be: Hotel Zumbro, Rochester, Minn. I suppose you have another copy of the article; thus I keep this one in case you wish to refer to it in a letter. This half year in bed was not so bad; mostly I had no pain. So I could enjoy working and at the same time look out of the window at a wonderful scenery in Santa Fe. I could see a little cottage half a mile away up on the hill. At the end of our stay it turned out that the painter who owned it and who had built it himself wanted to sell it quickly and reasonably. And now we are buying it (with enormous complications in the legal formalities in New Mexico), and we hope to go there after the Mayo Clinic.

m. | To all of you best regards,

Yours,

n. | Carnap

[MARGINALIA ON QUINE'S COPY:]

a. note Berry's improvement
b. Yes, synonymity is sense - eq.
c. Yes
d. No. But it must between occurrences that refer merely to the entities talked about (Cook up exxs. using classes as the entities in question.)
e. The entities your signs proper names of
f. (*here* is what I mean by designation; and it can't be a "modal rel'n", for the entity is unchanged by the name).
g. When I say "object" I mean entity, not thing.
h. No; I do not object to the "Giorgione" idiom or the "necessarily" idiom.
i. Not denied I said, "However, no need to assimilate . . ."
j. O.K.
k. Just what difference would it make (outside pure semantics book) if in real life one were to say something analogous to a *semantic rule?* Maybe your rules of semantics would be like the rule of truth in Tarski? Axioms fulfilled by any suitable sense of "true" bzw. other semantical terms?
l. No, this is not what I care about. Only that it seems best chance of getting connection eventually with empirical criterion.
m. OVER
n. ⟨on the other side⟩ Think of signs on the one hand entities on the other. We have perhaps predicate

$$\text{des}_1 \bigwedge \text{des}_2$$
$$\text{prop} \diagup \diagdown \text{class}$$

No; here is what my argument refutes; can't be talking *about* the property *in any* such fashion Try to get this down to the sense of bd. vbl. "Whatever entity . . ." (or "Whatever entity, . . .") *Here* is the neutral import of the article.

[101.   QUINE TO CARNAP   1943-2-21]

Feb. 21, 1943.

Dear Carnap,

Many thanks for your long and valuable reply. I am anxious
to study its implications more fully than I just now have had
time to do (what with the great pressing Navy work plus the
house hunting and the impending move to the new address
noted above). I hope to be able to reply more in detail fairly
soon. Already your letter has proved instructive to me on a
number of points. But I also see that in certain respects, I have
been less clear, in my letter and in my paper "Notes on existence & necessity", than might have been desired. Attached,
meanwhile, is a copy of an addendum that I have made to the
proofs of the paper. In particular it emphasizes a certain *tolerance*
(!) of modal contexts, intended in my paper without, I believe,
your having sensed it.

Naomi and I are anxious for word on the results of your trip
to Rochester. With very best wishes,

Yours,
Van

[102.   CARNAP TO QUINE   1943-5-1]

From: R. Carnap
      P. O. B. 1214
      Santa Fe, N.M.

May 1, 1943

Dear Van,

Rumors may have reached you to the effect that the Mayo
trip was not particularly successful. The doctors seemed to be
fairly sure of their diagnosis that two disks (between the verte-
brae) are slipped out of place. It seems that in a number of similar cases they have done successful operations. However, they
said that they felt my case was not serious enough for an imme-

diate operation and that there was still a fair chance for a spontaneous improvement. They bade me wait for "say another six or
twelve months" whence they would reconsider an operation if
the spontaneous improvement has not occurred. Well, after ly-
ing in bed since last July without any improvement taking place,
I am somewhat sceptical about the beneficial effect a few more
months will have, but that seems all that can be done at the
moment. Aside from the fact that my Rockefeller-year is drawing to a close and I am scheduled to teach in the fall, I am not
particularly worried, because I have not much pain and I can do
good work. Since May 14th we have now been in Santa Fe
where we have acquired a cottage high up in the hills and
where life is very enjoyable. True, I am not much out of doors
as yet. But we have hung up a large mirror in such a way that I
can see a good deal of the landscape from my bed. And thus
the days go by quite pleasantly and—in so far as my work is
concerned—also spent in a fruitful way.

I hope you won't be too much shocked about the enclose
questionnaire. I know that you are already overburdened, but,
as you can imagine, your opinion on the questions asked is of
particular value to me. And still more I shall be extremely interested in your reaction to my last letter; it will influence my paper a good deal because, I suppose, it will make me understand
your opinion on modal systems somewhat better, and also, I
hope, it will help me to clear my own ideas e.g. concerning the
relation between individual concepts and individuals.

Do you have to stay in Washington all through the hot summer? I assume Takoma Park is less hot and crowded; but how
much time does the commuting take? The government and the
war offices should be in a more merciful climate, e.g., in Santa
Fe!

Love from us both to all of you,

Yours,
Carnap

[103.   CARNAP TO QUINE   1943-5-1]

Rudolf Carnap
P.O.B. 1214
Santa Fe, N.M.

This copy to go to: Quine
(you may keep it if you wish
to)

May 1, 1943.

Dear Van,

I suppose that, under the present circumstances, all of you are very busy. If in spite of that you could find the time to answer the enclosed questionnaire, I should be very much obliged to you.

Sincerely yours,
Carnap

⟨This was a general cover letter to be sent with the following item. This particular copy was personalized in several ways.⟩

[104.   CARNAP TO QUINE   DATED APRIL 1943 BUT SENT
1943-5-1]

Rudolf Carnap
P.O.B. 1214
Santa Fe, N.M. April 1943.

Questionnaire on Terminology for Expressions and Meanings

The problems of designation and meaning, which are of course of special importance to semantics, have recently been dealt with in two articles by *Quine* ("Notes on Existence and Necessity", J.Phil. 40, p.113–127, No.5 of March 4, 1943) and *Church* (review of my "Semantics", forthcoming in "Phil.Rev."), which I found very stimulating. I am preparing a paper as a contribution to this discussion. And here I am bothered once more by the fact that there is not even a moderately systematic

terminology for expressions and their meanings. I am thinking
of a new terminology; and I should be very grateful to you for
giving me you opinion on both the general principle and the
single terms.

A. *Terminology for Expressions.*

Occasionally, in analogy to 'functor' and 'operator', I have
thought of terms like 'predicator' and 'relator'. Now Morris is
using 'designator', 'stator' and other terms with '-tor' for expressions of certain kinds. I wonder whether we might not apply
this tor-terminology throughout. I enumerate the questions by
'A1', 'A2', etc. In each question I first indicate which kind of
expression I mean with the help of a customary term or an example. Then possible answers are listed, marked by '(a)', '(b)',
etc., mostly in the order of my preference, (a) being my first
choice (provided the tor-principle finds sufficient approval). In
addition to the tor-terms I list others so that you can express
your preference. Please state first those terms which you like,
including, if you want to, any terms not listed here; give them
in the order of your preference (first choice first); then, after a
semicolon, state those terms which you find acceptable without
liking them, likewise in the order of your preference. Reference
by number and letters will suffice (e.g. "A1 : e, f; c, b".) In a
similar way I divide the terms listed by two semicolons in three
classes: those preceding the first semicolon are the ones I like,
those between the two semicolons I find merely acceptable,
those following the second semicolon I dislike. (Some of these
classes may be empty.) In answering questions A, consider also
B and C, because the existence of suitable terms with '-tion' and
'-tum' may influence the choice of a corresponding term with '-tor'.

Even if the newly-coined terms with the endings '-tor', '-tion',
'-tum' are approved, this would not mean discarding the customary old terms. The latter ones would still be preferable in most
non-technical contexts, while the new terms would chiefly be
used in technical discussions.

A1. Declarative sentence. (a) propositor, (b) sentence, (c) state-
   ment; (e) stator (Morris), (f) declarative sentence; . | a.

A2, 3, 4. *Predicate expressions* (a coherent triple of terms is to be
chosen):

		(a)	(b)	(c)	(d)
A2.	Any degree	attributor	predicator	predicator	attributo:
A3.	Degree 1	predicator	qualificator	-----	-----
A4.	Degree >1	relator	relator	-----	-----

	(e)	(f)	(g)
A2.	predicator	relator	(some other
A3.	-----	-----	terms without
A4.	-----	-----	'-tor')

'-----' means that here no special term is used but the term for
A2 together with an adjective indicating degree (see A14 ff.).

A5. functor expression. (a) functor, (b) functor expression; (c)
function expression; . (Here and throughout let us disregard the question whether to use 'expression' or 'sign' or
anything else for linguistic complexes of any length.)

A6. Individual expression (individual constant or description,
see A7). (a) nominator, (b) individual expression; (c)
individuator, (d) descriptor, (e) object expression; (f) individual name, (g) name, (h) object name.

A7. (Individual) description '(ɿx)(. .x. .)'. (a) (individual)
descriptor, (b) (individual) description;;.

A8. Predicate or functor expression (or perhaps only those constructed with an operator for functional abstraction, e.g.
'λx(. .x. .)'). (a) abstractor, (b) abstraction expression;; (c)
conceptor (however, see A13a), (d) concept expression.

A9. Sentential connective. (a) connector (this word, not with
this meaning, is in Oxford Dictionary), (b) connexor (more
correct Latin than (a), but not good in English), (c)
connective;;.

A10. Modal connective of any degree (e.g. a sign for necessity
or for strict implication). (a) modal connector (or
connexor), (b) modal conceptor, (c) modal attributor (or
whatever term is chosen for A2), (d) modal expression (or
sign); (e) modator;.

A10'. Modal connective of degree one (e.g. a sign for necessity).
(a) to (e), as in A10 ((c) with A3).

A11. Operator (e.g. '(x)', '(λx)'). (a) operator;;.

A11'. Quantifier. (a) quantificator, (b) quantor (Bernays), (c)
quantifier;;.

A12. Expression of any of those kinds, of which we want to say that they designate something (some may wish to restrict it to A2, 5 and 6, others might include A1, and perhaps A9 and 10 or even more). (a) designator (Morris), (b) intentor, (c) designative expression; (d) denotor, (e) denotative expression;. | l.

A13. Expression of the kinds A12 but excluding A1. (a) conceptor, (b) concept expression; (c) conceptual expression;.

A14 - 25. In combination with the terms A2, 3, 4 (especially in the cases c, d, e, f), A5, and A9 we need *adjectives indicating degree* (number of arguments):

A14 Predicates, *A15* functors, *A16* connectives, of degree one. (a) singulary, (b) monadic;; (c) unary. | m.

A17 Predicates, *A18* functors, *A19* connectives, of degree two. (a) binary, (b) dyadic;;. | n.

A20, A21, A22. Degree >1. (a) polyadic; (b) multinary, (c) plurinary; (d) --- (no term). | o.

A23, A24, A25. Degree >2. (a) --- (no term); (b) multinary, (c) polyadic;. | p.

A34. What is your *general reaction* to the *tor-terminology*? Does it seem too radical a change or is the uniformity achieved worth the price? Of course, also the question whether other authors would probably accept or reject it has to be taken into account. — (a). In favor of using tor-terms (in addition to customary terms) in all those cases where suitable ones can be found. (b) In favor of using in general only more customary terms (perhaps with the exception of a few special cases). | q.

A35. Is there another ending which might suitably be used instead of '-tor' to achieve uniformity here?

B. *Terminology for Meanings.*

The word 'green' has a certain semantical relation R_1 to a certain property, viz. The color green or greenness, and another relation R_2 to a certain class, viz. the class of green things. In general, R_1 is a relation between an expression and what is usually called its meaning; R_2 is a relation between an expression and what sometimes is called an extension. Then there is a third relation R_3 between a meaning and the corresponding extension, e.g. between a property and the corresponding class. R_3 is not a semantical relation since no expression is involved. Here in B, we consider terms for meanings; in C, terms for extensions. B30, 31 will concern terms for R_1 and its converse, C30 and 31 terms for R_2 and its converse, C32 and 33 terms for R_3 and its converse. Some logicians (e.g. Russell) start with properties and then define classes; others (e.g. Quine) go the other way round; still others take both properties and classes as primitive. I believe that the terminological questions can be dealt with independently of those differences. And I wish to emphasize still more that in my view any choice of terms does not imply a commitment to a metaphysical belief (in my view, a pseudo-belief) concerning the ontological status (e.g. metaphysical reality) of the

r. | entities in question, e.g. properties and classes.

Among the customary terms for meanings there are several with the ending '-tion' (sometimes '-sion'), e.g. 'proposition', 'relation', 'function', 'connection', 'intension'. Also in many other cases the replacement of '-tor' in A by '-tion' seems to give suitable terms for B. While the term 'predicate' has been used by some for certain signs, by others for properties, we should then have the two terms 'predicator' and 'predication', both closely related to the traditional term but indicating by their endings unmistakably (once the tor-tion-principle is established) what is meant. In some cases where we take a tor-term in A, the corresponding tion-term has usually a somewhat different meaning than the one assigned to it here. In some of these cases, the term seems to me to be still suitable for the new use as a technical term (e.g. 'predication', 'attribution'); in other cases (e.g. B13 'conception', B6 'nomination') I have somewhat more hesitation and should perhaps prefer a customary term to the term with '-tion'.

The numbers here correspond to those in A.

In thinking about the questions B and C, Church's articles in the Dictionary of Philosophy are very helpful (see e.g. Description, Designate, Name Relation, Intension and Extension, Propositional Function, Function, Class, Abstraction, Logic, formal).

s. | B1.   Proposition. (a) proposition;;.

B2.   Attribute (of any degree). (a) -tion (this means here and in what follows: the term with the ending '-tion' corresponding to whatever term with '-tor' may be chosen in A; thus here for B2, it means someone of the terms 'attribution', 'predication', 'relation'), (b) attribute; (c) propositional function;.

B3. Property, quality. (a) -tion, (b) property, (c) quality; (d) predicate; (e) class concept, (f) class conception, (g) --- (i.e. no special term).

B4. Relation. (a) relation; (b) ---;.

B5. Function. (a) function; (b) descriptive function;.

B6. Individual concept (there is no customary term because these concepts were usually confused with the individuals, C6). (a) -tion, (b) individual concept;;.

B7. (a) description (Church); (b) descriptional concept, (c) description concept;.

B8. Attribute or function. (a) abstraction; (b) function; (c) concept (see however B13a), (d) conception.
⟨several lines crossed out, apparently by Carnap⟩

B9. Connection (may be regarded as a property or relation of propositions). (a) connection;;. | t.

B10. Modal concept of any degree. (a) modal connection, (b) - tion (e.g. 'modal conception', 'modation', etc.) (c) modal concept;;.

B10'. Modality (modal concept of degree one, e.g. necessity). (a), (b), (c), as in B10.
Most logicians do not regard operators as designators. Let us nevertheless supply terms (B11 and 11') for those who do. | u.

B11. (a) operation, (b) operator concept;; (c) operator conception

B11'. (a) quantification, (b) quantifier concept;;. | v.

B12. Meaning. (These terms, in distinction to B31, are meant for absolute, not for relative use; not as in "x is the meaning (designation, etc.) of y" but as in "x is a meaning (a designation, etc.)". Nevertheless, we may choose the same term for B13 and B31, e.g. 'designation' or 'meaning'. (a) entity, (b) intension, (c) intensional entity; (d) meaning, (e) sense; (f) designation.

B13. Concept, notion. (a) concept; (b) conception, (c) notion;.

B30. 31. Semantical relations:

B30. The expression x has the meaning y (relation R_1). (a) x designates y, (or 'L-designates', if it turns out to be an L-concept; that will be discussed in my paper); (b) x means

w. | y; (c) x connotes y, (d) x denotes y. (If the tion-terminology
            is accepted, then the noun 'designation' should no longer
            be used for the relation R$_1$; instead of "the relation of desig-
            nation" we should say "the relation of designating".

B31. x is the meaning of y (the converse of B30). (a) x is the
            designatum (or L-designatum) of y, (b) x is the designative
            meaning of y; (c) x is the intension of y; (d) x is the mean-
            ing of y, (e) x is the sense of y; (f) x is the connotatum of
x. | y, (g) x is the denotatum of y.

B34. What is your *general reaction* to the *tion-terminology*, pro-
            vided the tor-terminology is accepted? (a) in favor wher-
            ever suitable terms are found, (b) not in favor (perhaps
            with a few exception).

B35. Which other ending could be used instead of '-tion' here
            in B? '-tum' might perhaps be considered if it is not taken
            in C. (B2 'attributum' would even be better than '-tion',
            likewise B13 'conceptum'; however, B1 'propositum', B4
            'relatum', B5 'functum' would be much inferior to the
            terms with '-tion'.)

C. *Terminology for Extensions.*

In my view, the entities listed below (e.g. truth-values,
classes, individuals) belong together; they are possible values of
variables in an extensional language. Here it seems more difficult to construct a uniform terminology than in A or B. The
ending '-tum', to replace the '-tor' in A and the '-tion' in B,
might be considered. In some cases, it gives satisfactory results,
e.g. C6 'nominatum', C7 'descriptum', C8 'abstractum', C13 'conceptum'. However, I do not propose to use it throughout. In
some cases it gives unsatisfactory terms (e.g. C4 'relatum', C3
'predicatum' or 'qualificatum'). [Furthermore, if '-tum' were
used throughout for extensions then it would probably be advisable to restrict it to extensions; this would prevent Morris' term
'designatum' for B31 which seems there most suitable. This rule,
though, can hardly be always followed. We shall violate it by
using 'extension' here in C, although the ending '-sion' or '-tion'
is chiefly used in B.] I do not know of any other ending that
would seriously come into consideration. The ending '-tex'
would well suggest extension; but the resulting terms ('relatex'

etc.) sound rather unnatural, somewhat like commercial names
for a cleansing powder or a building material.

For these reasons I do not try to construct a uniform terminology. In what follows, I list some customary terms—but often
there is no suitable one—then a few with '-tum', further some
of the form '. . . extension' where '. . .' is a term in B. I think,
until somebody finds a good solution, the best way is to forgo
uniformity and just look in each case for the relatively best solution. The numbers here correspond again to those in A and B.
(A semicolon preceding '(a)' indicates, of course, that I do not
like any of the terms listed.)

C1. (a) truth-value;;.

C2. ; (a) . . . extension (with whatever term may be chosen in
      B2); (b) . . . in extension, (c) -tum (attributum,
      predicatum).

C3. (a) class;;.

C4. ; (a) relation extension, (b) relational extension; (c) relation
      in extension, (d) correlation, (e) --- class (with the adjective
      A20, e.g. 'polyadic class').

C5. ; (a) function extension, (b) correlation, (c) value distribu-
      tion (Frege 'Wertverlauf'), (d) value correlation; (e)
      functum.

C6. Element of the universe of discourse of the langauge in
      question; entity of lowest level (a neutral term, to be ap-
      plied no matter whether these entities are physical things
      or space-time-points or numbers or whatever else). (a) indi-
      vidual; (b) object, (c) nominatum, (d) descriptum;.

C7. (a) descriptum, (b) individual; (c) object, (d) nominatum;.

C8. (a) abstractum; (b) abstract extension, (c) function
      extension; (d) concept extension, (e) conception extension.

C9. ; (a) truth-value distribution, (b) connection extension; (c)
      connectum (or connexum).

C10. 10', 11, 11'. These will hardly ever occur. If you think oth-
      erwise, please propose terms.

C12. (a) extension, (b) extensional entity; (c) denotatum (but
      used absolutely, see B13, in distinction to C31); (d) in-
      tentum, (e) extentum.

C13. (a) conceptum, (b) concept extension; (c) conceptual exten-
      sion; (d) conception extension, (e) notum.

y.

z.

aa.

bb.

cc.

dd.

ee.

ff.

gg.

hh.

ii. | C30. 31. Semantical relations:
    | C30. The expression x has the extension (or truth-value) y (relation R_2). (a) x denotes y (relation of denoting); (b) x designates y, (c) --- (no special term);.
    | C31. x is the extension of the expression y (the converse of C30). (a) x is the denotatum of y, (b) x is the extension of y; (c) x is the extension designatum of y, (d) x is the desigjj. | natum of y; (e) ---.
    | C32. 33. Absolute (non-semantical) relations:
    | C32. x is a meaning which has the extension y (relation R_3, e.g. x is a property whose class is y). (a) x is an intension of y; (b) x is a meaning corresponding to y, (c) x is a sense correkk. | sponding to y, (d) ---; .
    | C33. x is the extension of the meaning y (converse of R_3; e.g. x is the class determined by the property y). (a) x is the extension of y (I think this would not interfere too much with the simultaneous use of the same term in C31b);;
ll. | (b) ---.
    | C35. Would you favor a more uniform terminology here in C than is proposed above, by using one form of terms in most, though not necessarily all, cases? ; (a) '-tum', (b) . . . extension (where the blank is filled by whatever noun is
mm. | chosen in B); (c) -tex, (d) any other form?

D. Degree of Confirmation.

Another terminological question, not related to the foregoing. I am working on the problem of the degree of confirmation. I take it (like Hosiasson, JSL 5, 1940, p. 133) as a function of two sentences with numerical values: "the degree of confirmation of S_1 with respect to S_2". However, I find this phrase too long and awkward for frequent use. Could we perhaps coin a new word 'confirmancy' (in analogy to some newly-coined terms in physics)? Or would it sound too strange? 'Confirmation' is also short enough; would the fact that we use it—and, no doubt, will continue to use it—for the procedure of confirming make it unsuitable as a technical term for the numerical function?

    | D1. (a) confirmancy); (b) confirmation, (c) degree of
nn. | confirmation;.

[MARGINALIA ON QUINE'S COPY:]

a. (c)
b. (e)
c. (a)
d. (f) (or: thing name) Objection to (a), (e), (g), (h)
e. (b)
f. (b) (dropping 2nd word when no ambiguity); reserve (a) for the prefix, like 'quantifier'.
g. All of these are rather bad, since (i) idea of connection needn't suggest sentences, & (ii) anyway some of the "sentential connectives" are connectives out of courtesy, viz. the 1-pl. connectives.
h. (c)
i. (c)
j. integrator (Neumann) (inc. qfrs. abstraction, descriptions). Objection to "operator"
k. (c)
l. Depends on sense of 'designate' (see my preceding letter). For 'designation' in the sense of 'meaning' (which your sense of designation approaches) simply 'expression'. Or my sense 'name' might do (broad sense), or 'nominator'.
m. (a)
n. (a)
o. plurary Reserve '-adic' for relations (& classes)
p. (a)
q. (b) (as at top p. 6) ⟨This reference is to the paragraph just before C1.⟩
r. Note that *I* couldn't use "designatum" in conn with R3 either. Rather "extension" as you do and I agree with
s. (a)
t. Disagree, if props. are meanings. They would be rel'ns. bet. the things *named by* sentences. (ind. designata in *my* sense). There aren't any
u. OK if desig is mng
v. Integrator
w. (c), (b)
x. (f), (d)

y. My view elsewhere too.

z. (a)

aa. ?

bb. (a)

cc. (c) & (e) intchbly

dd. function (in extension)

ee. Anything in range of [illegible] of the (bd.) vbls: entity (= object). In ptclr. non-class (where class incl rel'n & functions) individual

ff. (a): as species of (d) provided not limited to (b)

gg. truth value of the compound

hh. When we take functions & relns as classes of pairs (triples etc.) then "clas" covers all this exc. truth-vals

ii. "Determines" was used by Berry thesis for [illegible] D matrices (I disapprove of (b) as much as you do.)

jj. (b)

kk. (b)

ll. Phps (a)

mm. No

nn. Prefer (b) for short with recourse to (c) when ambiguity threatens. 'Confirmancy' has the wrong voice: properly 'confirmingness' rather than 'confirmedness'.

[QUINE'S NOTES ALSO ON THE LAST PAGE:]

In re of B-C:

(α) I don't feel the parallelism bet. the two. For me every expr'n, or nearly every, used in sens. shall be allowed a meaning (a connotation); whereas only predicates and Sentences (which are O-pl. preds.) need extensions. Incidentally, I'd even rather speak of Satzgerüste here than predicates (thus emphasizing a form of context & not requiring notational unity). Matrix does about as well & it implies Satzgerüste ∴ you don't see just in my work.

(β) You may speak also of extns. of functors et al. but their extensions are reducible to those of matrixes. E.g., instead of speaking of ext. of '+' we may speak ext'n of '$x + y = z$'.

(γ) Because of this lack of parallelism I deliberately do not recommend parallel terminology "extension—intension"

And designation in *my* sense doesn't come in at all. "Naming"
but not restricted to individuals (and including descriptions).

[105. QUINE TO CARNAP   1943-5-7]

> 1006 Elm Ave.
> Takoma Park, Md.
> May 7, 1943

Dear Carnap,

Very sorry to hear that your trip to Minnesota wasn't more
immediately successful. But it is encouraging to know that an
operation is possible, and that the operation may not even be
necessary. On the other hand it's pretty awful to be laid up a
year and more this way. The one consolation is that you are able
to work.

We are living in pleasant surroundings, on the edge of a
woods and near a stream. We are seven and a half miles from
my work, but have bought a second-hand car to take the curse
off commuting. The drive is through residential districts and
park, with few stoplights, for the place where I am now working is an annex away from the heart of town; so commuting
takes me only about 20 minutes each way. Life is thus more
pleasant than when we lived on 51st St. and I had to spend two
or three hours a day going and coming.

However, the demands on my time are great, so that I have
been slow in working out my thoughts a propos of your letter
of Jan. 21. Finally, here they are.

1. 'Object'

For the moment I want merely to clarify my use of the term
'object'; fuller terminological discussions will come later. I intend
'object' in the completely general sense of 'entity'; not merely
individual, but class or property (if "properties" be recognized
at all) or anything else, regardless of logical type. This all-

inclusive sense of 'object' can be inferred from various passages of my article (reprint of which is sent under separate cover), e.g. page 126, line 12, and page 116, passim; and perhaps you have been aware of it. But your letter of Jan. 21 departs from it, e.g. in first 4 lines of running text of page 4, in which you say "a concept . . . rather than an object." Concepts, whatever precisely they are (and if such there be), are certainly objects in my sense of the term.

2. *Quantification over intensional contexts*

Away now from terminological questions, for the moment, in favor of a question of theory. I'm going to try to make the essential theoretical point of my article without use either of the term 'designation', on which you have noted a divergence in use (to be discussed later), or of the formal theory of identity. I will appeal to two examples, one of which has to do with an individual (the city of Caracas) and the other with an abstract object (the ninth positive integer), just to emphasize that it is not the distinction between concrete and abstract that is essential.

First example:

Let us agree, for purpose of the example, to regard the following statement as true:

(1) It is impossible that the capital city of Venezuela be outside Venezuela.

From this it would seem natural, by existential generalization, to infer the following:

(2) ∃x it is impossible that x be outside Venezuela (We needn't worry here about the additional "existence" premise that would be needed according to Russell's theory of descriptions. Either suppose this given as further premiss, or adopt the theory of descriptions of my *Mathematical Logic*, under which "existence" is always guaranteed for descriptions.)

Now just what is the object x that is considered, in inferring (2) from (1), to be incapable of being outside Venezuela? Not a capital-city-concept, for the concepts aren't in or out of countries. It is a certain mass of adobe et al., viz. the capital city itself. And it is this mass of adobe that is (apparently) affirmed, in (1), to be incapable of being outside Venezuela. Hence the apparent justice, intuitively, of the inference of (2) from (1).

However, that same mass of adobe et al. is affirmed in the following true statement (apparently) to be *capable* of being outside Venezuela:

(3) It is possible that the native city of Bolivar be outside Venezuela.

Justification of (2) by (1) is thwarted by (3), for (3) has just as much right to consideration as (1) so far as the mass of adobe in question is concerned.

There is obviously a connection between the above considerations and the substitutivity of identity, but I have *not* rested the above argument on conventions of an identity calculus. I have rested it on ordinary meanings of words and bound variables. The last paragraph of printed article shows that I agree with you as to the legitimacy of exempting intensional contexts from the substitutivity requirement; but this is beside the present point, and does not excuse (2).

I have no quarrel with the idioms (1) and (3), nor with their violation of the substitutivity of identity; my only quarrel is with (2). My thesis is (a) that existential generalization is invalid in connection with modal contexts of this type, and (b) that the very notion of quantification, taken in its ordinary sense, therefore becomes meaningless in such contexts as (2).

Nor does it alter matters to adopt a meaning of 'designation' according to which the expressions 'Caracas', 'the capital city of Venezuela', 'the native city of Bolivar' may be said to "designate" individual concepts rather than an individual. For, I have not depended on the word 'designation' anyway, in the above argument; and, however the word 'designation' may be used, it is rather the material city—regardless of its name or description—that figures as instantial value of the bound variable 'x' in (2) when we infer (2) from (1). Whereas actually there is no material city, no mass of adobe, that is logically incapable of being outside Venezuela. Nor does (1), properly construed, say there is; for (1), properly construed, does not have (2) as consequence. (1) might be reconstrued, if you like, as speaking about the concept of the capital city of Venezuela *rather than* (as it appears to do, and as inference of (2) supposed that it did) about the capital city itself.

(In my terminology, the occurrence of 'the capital city of Venezuela' in (1) is not purely designative. I have no objection to indesignative occurrences, either this one or the indesignative occurrence of 'sun' in 'sunder' or of 'Cicero' in ' 'Cicero' '; but I do argue that they resist certain quantificational operations.)

I am speaking of quantification in its ordinary sense, corresponding to the sense of the parallel pronominal constructions of ordinary language. You *can* perhaps preserve the outward form of (2) by somehow reconstruing the meaning of quantification. I have not said that formal contradictions arise; in lines 12–13 of page 5 of your letter of Jan. 21 ⟨p. 308, Carnap's attribution to Quine of the claim that a modal system must lead to contradictions⟩ you misunderstand me. But if you take quantification in some such new sense, you depart from the topic of my article. And of course the properties of the new sense of quantification need to be carefully considered in abstraction from the intuitive meaning of the old. Moreover, since, even if some such new sense of quantification proves to have a certain utility, no doubt the ordinary type of quantification would still be needed in addition, so that a distinguishing notation and terminology would be in order. At present, I repeat, I don't know what the precise sense, the distinguishing properties, or the usefulness of such a variant concept of quantification would be; so the present paragraph is for me of only negative importance.

Not that I consider quantification in the old or ordinary sense to be concerned exclusively with external objects rather than concepts, etc. Values of bound variables in my sense can be objects of any kind, concepts included (supposing I know what concepts are supposed to be). It just happened in the above example that the object relevant to (2), supposedly incapable of being outside Venezuela, was an external object rather than a concept. If instead of (2) we were to write:

(4) ∃x x is incompatible with the concept of externality to Venezuela,

thinking of incompatibility as a relation between concepts, then I should regard (4) as true. To (4), as opposed to (2), the relevant object x would be a concept rather than a mass of adobe. And (4) *is* legitimately to be inferred, by existential generalization, from:

(5) The concept of capital city of Venezuela is incompatible
     with externality to Venezuela.
In fact, I should not object to regarding (5) as a translation of (1)
(assuming I knew what all this concept talk is about). The fact
remains that 'the capital city of Venezuela', in the context (5) no
less than in the context (1) has indesignative occurrence (in my
sense). On the other hand 'the concept of capital city of Venezuela' in (5) has purely designative occurrence, and designates (in
my sense) the concept in question (assuming, again, concepts).
   Second example:
   From the true statement:
   (6) 9 necessarily exceeds 7
it would seem natural, by existential generalization, to infer:
   (7) ∃x   x necessarily exceeds 7.
But what is the object that is considered, in this inference, to
exceed 7 necessarily? It is a certain number; only numbers exceed 7. But that same *number* is apparently denied to be necessarily greater than 7 in the true statement:
   (8) The number of planets does not necessarily exceed 7.
Justification of the inference of (7) from (6) is thwarted by (8),
which has just as much right to consideration as (6) so far as the
number in question (which is at once the number 9 and the number of planets, the one and only integer between 8 and 10) is
concerned. The comments on the first example apply in full,
mutatis mutandis, to the second.
   So I do not agree that I am making the fallacy that the philosophers made who objected to set-theory (your letter of Jan.
21, pp. 4–5). This charge would be justified if I argued merely
that factual identity should be substitutive in all contexts; but I
don't hold this. Independently of any such untenable thesis, I
hold that certain intensional contexts (logical necessity and
impossibility, also belief, etc.) are not amenable to quantification
(barring, of course, unimagined changes of the meaning of
quantification).
   The more cautious form used in the last paragraph of §4 of
my article (noted in your letter of Jan. 21, page 5, line 16) was
not a mollification of earlier claims, but had rather the following
reason: the kind of examples constructed above in this letter for

the modal contexts of logical impossibility and necessity, and likewise in the article, *cannot* be constructed (with similar effect) for *every* intensional context.

3. 'Designation'

If, as suggested on page 4 of your letter of Jan. 21, you make 'moon' designate the lunar concept rather than the moon (i.e. the lunar ball of rock), then you are not using the term 'designation' in the sense in which I have intended it. Let me explain how I intend 'designation'. I can't define it, any more than 'object', but must try to explain it indirectly and through examples.

The lunar concept (if for the sake of argument I assume I know what this is) *can* be designated, in my sense, and so can the moon itself, and so can any other entity (but not *every* entity of course, on account of indenumerability). However, the designatum (in my sense) of 'moon' is not the lunar concept, but the moon itself. The lunar concept, on the other hand, is the designatum (if any) of 'the lunar concept'. Again the Pegasus-concept if ⟨sic⟩ the designatum of 'the Pegasus-concept'; whereas 'Pegasus' has no designatum. Again the class of horses is the designatum of 'the class of horses'; whereas the property of equinity (if for the sake of argument I recognize properties) is the designatum of 'the property of equinity'. Again, the designatum of '9' is the number 9; and the designatum of 'the number of planets' is that same number 9 (for there are no two numbers one of which is 9 and the other the number of planets). In a word, the designatum of an expression (if any) is the entity (of any logical type) that the expression is a name (incl. description) of.

I have chosen the above examples in such a way as to dodge, for the present, any issue of classes vs. properties, and any issue as to the designata of predicates. I have not raised the question of the designatum of 'horse' or 'equine' or 'is equine'—the question whether it be the class of horses, or the property of equinity, or nothing whatever. For, however this may be, it remains clear that the designatum (in my sense) of 'the class of horses' is the class and not the property, and that the designatum (if any) of 'the property of equinity' is the property and not the class. Actually I consider it arbitrary whether *predicates* be regarded as designating classes, or properties, or nothing at all; but I defer this topic to §5, below.

4. *Meaning*

Your version of 'designation', according to which 'moon' designates the lunar concept and 'red' the property of redness, comes closer to what I call *meaning*. I should be willing to agree in general that the *meanings* of expressions *are* concepts; that the meaning of 'moon' is not the moon (which is the designatum) but the lunar concept; and that the meaning of 'the lunar concept' is not the lunar concept (which is the designatum) but the concept of the lunar concept. The expressions 'moon' and 'lunar concept' are so related that the meaning of the first is the designatum (in my sense) of the second. I should agree, further, that statements (though they have no designata) have meanings, and that these meanings are concepts which may be called propositions. In all this you see a close agreement between 'meaning' in my sense and 'designation' in yours.

Also that 'red' or 'is red' means the concept (= property) of redness.

But I should go farther, and allow meanings also to other fragments of statements, perhaps all others. Syncategorematic expressions lack designata, but are meaningful, and have meanings, from my point of view; and these meanings likewise may be considered to be concepts.

But I should want in turn to arrive at a theory as to what sort of entities these meanings, these concepts, are. Here I proceed rather in the spirit of the Russell constructions and your own *Aufbau* constructions. Concepts are meanings; meanings are what is in common among expressions with the same meaning, i.e., among synonymous expressions; but that which is in common among synonymous expressions is (here the spirit of Russell and *Aufbau*) the class of those expressions. So now you see the connection between my above remarks and those in paragraph 2 of page 120 of my article.

As to this underlying relation of synonymity, I agree to everything in lines 4 to 21 of page 2 of your letter of Jan. 21 ⟨p. 304, paragraph beginning 'One might . . .'⟩. To lines 1–3 of that page ⟨p. 304, just before paragraph beginning 'One might . . .'⟩, however, I must add this remark: I should like synonymity to hold not only among statements, predicates, constant terms, and descriptions, but among expressions of any sort, or very nearly so. More thought is wanted on this topic; suitable elaboration of a certain auxiliary notion of "genuine occurrence" of an expression (even a syncategorematic expression) in a statement is wanted; I look forward to thinking about this sometime.

It strikes me as strange to use the term 'designation' as you do. Not to insist on 'meaning', mightn't 'connotation' be suggestive and well in line with tradition? As to my use of 'designation', I don't know how usual it is, but feel sure it checks with Tarski's. 'Denotation' wouldn't do for my sense of 'designation', for it would conflict with the version of denotation as relative product of (my) designation into converse of membership.

Don't misunderstand me as urging upon you a revision of your terminology. I recognize the difficulties in that direction, with two of your semantics books off the press already. What I am trying to do rather is to get to a mutual understanding of ideas. The practical terminological question, which is indeed a knotty one, would have to be ironed out independently. I wish we had reached the present point much earlier, for we are certainly in a fair way to confusing the public!

5. *Designata of predicates. Classes vs. properties.*

If you agree that your "designation" answers more nearly to my "meaning" that ⟨*sic*⟩ to my "designation", then it will seem less strange to you than formerly that I should dismiss as trivial the question whether predicates "designate" properties or classes or whether they are syncategorematic and designate nothing. Actually I consider that the choice among these alternatives is altogether distinct from the question whether to recognize classes and properties (i.e., admit them as values of variables).

This may be clear from the following considerations. Consider the four versions of (roughly speaking) one and the same idea:

(1) x is equine,
(2) x is a horse,
(3) $E(x)$
(4) $x \in H$.

Suppose that the position occupied by 'E' in (3) is a position appropriate also to property variables, bound in the context; and that the position occupied by 'H' in (4) is a position appropriate also to class variables, bound in the context. Then 'E' may (from my point of view) appropriately be said, given the assumed meanings of the above statements, to designate the property of equinity, and 'H' the class of horses. But it does not follow that 'is equine' or 'equine' in (1) is thereby equated to 'E', or 'horse' in (2) to 'H'. If we so choose, 'is equine' and 'equine' and 'horse' can even be regarded as syncategorematic and as designating nothing. We can say that (3) and (4) are part-for-part translations not of (1) and (2), but of:

(5) x has the property of equinity,

(6) x is a member of the class of horses.

'E' answers to 'the property of equinity' and 'H' to 'the class of horses'; the use of parentheses and reverse juxtaposition in (3) answers to the 'has' of (5); and the epsilon of (4) answers to 'is a member of', this connective being syncategorematic like the 'is a horse' of (2). From this point of view the versions (1) and (2) have no part-for-part translations into the language of (3) and (4), but become translated, as wholes, through the mediation of their paraphrases (5) and (6).

Or, conversely, we can set up our artificial language in such a way as to use, even in the artificial language itself, only syncategorematic predicates (like epsilon in (4))—thus writing 'E(x)' but *not* allowing property variables or indeed any variables to occupy the position of 'E'. This is part of what happens when, as in *Mathematical Logic*, all names (all designating expressions, in my sense of 'designation') are avoided in the primitive language, and introduced by contextual definition. Independently of such a change, properties and classes continue to be recognized and still figure as values of the variables; but they are never designated, in the primitive language. (It happens in *Mathematical Logic* that properties, as distinct from classes, are avoided altogether; but this is a separate and independent matter.)

The above remarks may give you a clearer idea of the motivation behind some of my work that has gone before; but so far as immediate purposes of the present letter is concerned, the important point of the present section remains to be added now:

The essential difference between your sense of designation and mine does not turn on the question of classes vs. properties as designata of predicates. I grant that properties (in the sense at least of concepts, in the sense in turn of meanings) stand in a certain important relation to predicates, viz., they stand as their *meanings* or *connotata* or *intentions* and I agree that classes also stand in a certain important relation to predicates, viz., they stand as their *extensions*. Whether, over and above this, we see fit to make predicates stand as names of (i.e. designate, in my sense) their intensions, or make them stand as names rather of their extensions, or take them as non-names having indeed their intensions and extensions but no designata, is an arbitrary question to be decided by minor technical purposes immediately at hand (like Church's making true statements serve as names of the number 2 and false ones as names of the number 1, and like my making them serve respectively as names of universal class and null class for the special purposes of "Toward a calculus of concepts", and as names rather of certain sequences for the special purposes of *A System of Logistic*). Decision of this arbitrary question in one way or another is equivalent to certain decisions regarding use of predicates in positions accessible to variables, as suggested by remarks earlier in the present section. Fact remains that predicates *have* their intensions (meanings), and have their extensions, just as statements have their propositions (meanings) and have their truth values, regardless of whether predicates and statements be used also as names or not.

6. *On some further points of your letter of Jan. 21*

(1) I am pleased that you find my procedure of closed statements and Axioms of Quantification suited to your purposes. But note the following improvement:

(a) Change my definition of 'closure' in such a way as to identify the closure not with the result of prefixing the alphabetically ordered string of all missing quantifiers, but rather the reverse-alphabetical string. In other words, the new closure is the result of applying the missing quantifiers one at a time in alphabetical order (so that they stand in reverse-alphabetical order in the result).

(b) Thereupon 101 can be omitted; can be proved from the

rest. This was established by George Berry, *J.S.L.*, March 1941 (though in a different formulation). I can send you a more elegant proof than his of 101 if you need it.

(c) Of course 101 can also be omitted if we redefine a "closure" of a matrix in the more general sense of *any* (closed) statement formed by prefixing quantifiers to the matrix in any order. I was aware of this from the start (though Fitch pointed it out as a new idea in J.S.L., Mar. 1941), but preferred a unique concept of closure. The revision (a)−(b) above preserves this.

(2) I can agree with page 2 of your letter, last sentence, and with the theoretical background thereof, now that I take your term 'designation' in the sense of my 'meaning', and your 'property' in the sense of 'concept'. My past misgivings over your notion of rule of designation are in a fair way to being cleared up by just this consideration. Rules of designation would encounter difficulties when put to your purposes. (And this is not only because of divergence between the two senses in application to individuals; situation stays the same in connection with abstract objects, e.g. the number 9.)

> Continuation follows,
> Yours,
> Van

[106.   QUINE TO CARNAP   1943-5-10]

> 1006 Elm Av., Tak.Pk.,Md.
> May 10, 1943

Dear Carnap,

Here is the continuation of my letter dated May 7.

6. *On some further points*—continued

(3) Answer to lines 16–19, page 5, of your letter of Jan. 21: No, I recognize that (18) and (23) are not equivalent (however misleading my formulation, in the passage which you cite, may be). My point is rather this:

The particular inference by existential generalization, with which the cited passage is ultimately concerned, turns on the notion of a certain object (viz. the integer between 8 and 10) having a certain property (viz. that of being necessarily-greater-than-7). According to (18), apparently, that integer (which is in fact 9) has that property; whereas according to (23), apparently, that integer (which is in fact the number of planets) does not have the property. This argument does not depend on assuming any necessary connection, and equivalence, between (18) and (23); all is merely factual, rather, with the necessity component squeezed rather into the property necessarily-greater-than-7. My solution of the apparent paradox is to repudiate the two remarks that I have just now qualified with 'apparently', and say that actually (18) does not say that a certain integer has the alleged property, and similarly for (23). (18) amounts rather to saying that a certain *concept* (viz. the 9-concept) has a certain property (viz. that of connoting excess over 7) and that a certain very different concept (viz. the number-of-planets-concept) lacks that property. You will note that I am now trying to formulate this in terms that will mesh with your point of view as closely as possible. But my conclusion is that therefore the proposed inference, by existential generalization, that something (which would have to be a number, not a concept of a number) exceeds 7 necessarily, is unwarranted and in fact meaningless. Here we arrive at an instance of my thesis about quantification of certain modal contexts.

You observe that the above paragraph simply repeats, in miniature and in application to a particular passage of your letter, the theory set forth in §2 of the previous installment of my letter.

(4) In re penult. paragraph of p. 5 of your letter of Jan. 21 ⟨p. 308, paragraph beginning 'To your letter . . .'⟩: My error. As to your phrase 'independent of the contingency of facts', though, this is a phrase which I cannot better clarify to myself, intuitively, than by explaining it as meaning 'analytic'; so it doesn't help. However, you remember my saying this before; anyway it is off the main point.

(5) Concerning last para. of same page 5 ⟨p. 309, paragraph beginning 'Ibid., p.2, . . .'⟩: I agree to the advantages of schematizing natural language for use as object of theoretical dis-

cussion. It is not this that I question on p. 2 of my letter of Jan. 5 ⟨p. 296, paragraph beginning 'I am content . . .'⟩. The point can be made more clearly if we begin, by way of analogy with the notion of sentence. The empirical linguist who goes into the field to study and formulate a language unrelated to any languages hitherto formulated has a working idea, however vague (and it would be interesting to refine it), of *sentence* in general, say in the form of a relation; x (sound pattern) is a sentence for y (person). Then, ideally, he concludes by observation and induction that such and such a class of sound patterns (a class which he specifies in purely phonetic terms) does in fact comprise all and only the sound patterns which stand in the sentence-relation to the people he is studying. His phonetic specification of the class in question will be complex, and will depend, for convenience, on arbitrary introduction of many auxiliary concepts (parts of speech, declensions, etc.) of which, of course, the natives speaking the language have never heard; nor do these auxiliary concepts even need have any clear analogues on other language studies (cf. for example the concept of "*der*-words" often used in German grammar to cover 'dieser', 'jener', 'jeder', 'der', etc.). But the concept of sentence *does* have its analogues in other languages, and it is this concept that the linguist had in mind at the start to guide his research.

Now when for theoretical discussion we specify an artificial language as object, we again specify, in purely phonetic terms (actually *graphic* or syntactical terms, but the essential idea is the same), the class of expressions which are to be regarded as sentences for this language. The idea of "sentence" is the same in both cases; only the languages are different, and the class of expressions constituting sentences for the respective languages. It is only thus that we understand what is intended, what is coming, when you tell us: "the following are to be the sentences of my new language". Otherwise it would be as if you said "The following are to constitute, for my new language, what I shall call the class α". This latter remark would be uninteresting, except insofar as possibly introducing an auxiliary concept whose purpose would be explained afterward; it would be like "*der*-word" in the German grammars.

This is what I mean when I say that whereas the sentences of any given language can be specified in pure syntax, the notion of sentence itself has to be borrowed from pragmatics.

Now my view on the notion of "analytic" (if to simplify the analogy we consider this the central notion of what I called the second part of semantics on p. 4 of my letter of Jan. 5) is similar to my view on the notion of sentence, in this respect: It is only by having some general, pragmatically grounded, essentially behavioristic explanation of what it means in general to say that a given sound- or script-pattern is analytic for a given individual, that we can understand what is intended when you tell us (via semantical rules, say) "the following are to be analytic in my new language". Otherwise your specification of what is analytic for a given language dangles in midair, as the specification of the *der*-words would do in abstraction from the pragmatic notion of sentence.

Thus the requirement which I have in mind isn't met by saying that the analytic statements are those which follow from the semantical rules of the language; any more than the general notion of sentence would be satisfactorily provided by saying that a sentence is anything that is a sentence by virtue of the grammatical rules of a language. The grammatical rules are artifices of the linguist to enable him to specify the class of expressions which are (by observation) in fact sentences for the people in question; and correspondingly for the semantical rules, in relation to "analytic". Artificial languages are in no way different from natural ones in this respect, except that in the case of artificial languages we have a hypothetical construction *as if* there were people speaking it; the question of a behavioristic definition of 'analytic', like that of 'sentence', remains basic—part of the pragmatical substructure of the (more abstract) science of semantics.

Whether such a project can best be effected in direct application to 'analytic', or can best be effected in application rather to 'synonymity', is an open question. It was with the latter alternative in mind that I chose in my article and in my letter of Jan. 5 to think of 'analytic' as derivative from 'synonymity' (a point discussed in p. 6 of your letter of Jan. 21).

(6) Concerning your technical objection of penult. paragraph

p. 2, letter of Jan. 21 ⟨p. 304, paragraph beginning '*Your defini-tion . . .*'⟩:

The type of counter-instance which you propose cannot, pre-sumably, be constructed in a language which contains the ele-mentary logic of statement composition and quantification in the form in which these are developed in my *Mathematical Logic*. Given this logical substructure, and given further (as you say) just one predicate of degree 2, or, to formulate it more clearly in relation to my book, just one atomic matrix in 'x' and 'y', namely 'R(x,y)', it does not follow that the statement:

(1) (x) (y) (R(x,y) ⊃ R(y,x))

is the only instance of its own logical form. For, the logical form of (1) (i.e., the most specific logical form having (1) as an in-stance) is:

(2) (x) (y) (. . .x. . .y. . . ⊃ ---x---y---), | a.

and there are falsehoods of this form, e.g.:

(x) (y) (R(x,y) ⊃ R(x,y) .⊃. R(x,y) .~R(x,y)).

I realize that you would think of (1) as possessing a logical form yet more specific than (2), viz.:

(x) (y) (Pr$_1$(x,y) ⊃ Pr$_1$(y,x));

but this further step of analysis is appropriate, sub voce "logical analysis", only for languages based on a logic which (like yours) has predicate variables usable in contexts similar to the context (1) of the constant predicate 'R'. For such a language, 'R' is ap-propriately regarded as a component (logically) of 'R(x,y)' and 'R(y,x)', logically analyzable out; for mine, not. Relative to a logi-cal foundation of my type, the most that can be said of the logi-cal form of 'R(x,y)' is that the expression is a matrix in 'x' and 'y'; and similarly for 'R(y,x)'. This, in fact, is the reason for my use of metamathematical Greek letters for matrixes, in Ch. II of my book, instead of predicate variables.

Or should we think of the 'R(x,y)' of your example rather as having the form of relational predication which I introduced by contextual definition in §36 of *Mathematical Logic*? But then again I can construct a false statement having the logical form of your true one, as follows:

(x) (y) ([ẑŵ(R(z,w) ⊃ R(z,w))](x,y) ⊃ [ẑŵ(R(z,w) ·~R(z,w)](y,x)).

Here of course I am assuming more than elementary logic; but the same assumption is implicit when we answer affirmatively the initial question of this paragraph. In fact 'R' itself (under the version of the present paragraph) would be an abbreviation of some abstract, according to pp. 151–152 of my book. (Under the version of the preceding paragraphs, on the other hand, 'R' is only a syncategorematic sign like '(' or '∃'.)

I don't mean to impose the idiosyncrasies of my own logic, and accordingly I grant that I would have done better to devise a definition of 'analytic' adaptable to a wider array of theories. On the other hand the above discussion may have the incidental virtue of suggesting the interlocking motivations of several features of my own procedure: the definition of 'analytic', the avoidance of primitive names other than contextually defined abstracts, and the presentation of quantification theory with help of metamathematical variables for matrices.

Also I am not particularly interested in adapting the definition of 'analytic' or similar concepts to a *very* wide range of styles of logical theory. As I urged in our Cambridge talks, I favor the canonical-form approach: translate the language into one having a stereotyped foundation of elementary logic in a stereotyped form (though leaving plenty of scope for variations in strength of added higher logic), and then work out the semantics for the stereotyped scheme once and for all. Can't have a completely general semantics anyway, in any non-trivial sense; and the canonical-form approach is a way of lopping off a lot of elaborate theory. (But the fact remains, as noted in preceding paragraph, that I'd like to make the development less dependent on very special features.)

In urging the canonical-form approach I may at first glance seem to be taking a stand rather opposite to the stand which I take in urging a general pragmatic criterion of 'analytic' or 'synonymous', etc., in application even to natural languages. But this opposition is only apparent, as I think you will agree in view of (5) above.

7. *On your terminological questionnaire of Apr. 1943.*
A1: (c).* A2-4: (e). A5: (a). A6: (f). [Objection to (a), (e), (g),

*For what you call closed sentences. For the broader sense, 'matrix'.

(h): these are suited to names of entities of any logical type, rather than merely to names of individuals.]

A7: (b). The terminology (a) seems better suited for the prefix '(℩x)' itself, on the analogy of 'quantifier', 'operator'. (Avoidable, of course; in my own writing I have said 'description prefix', to avoid coining a term.)

A8: (b). A comment parallel to the foregoing one applies to (a) here. As to (b), I should of course drop the second word, 'expression', when there is no danger of ambiguity. Alternative suggestion for A8: 'abstract' (as a noun, with stress on first syllable). I have used this, but am not sure whether to urge it.

A9: All three are about equally good, it seems to me, and about equally bad. The innapropriateness ⟨*sic*⟩ of the "connection" idea is twofold: (i) too general, in that there is no restriction to statements (and matrices) suggested by the terminology; (ii) too limited, in that it connotes exclusion of singulary cases such as denial (which we actually include, of course, but only to the detriment of the term 'connection'). I have pondered this problem before now, but have no solution.

A10-10': (c).

A-11: Von Neumann's term 'integrator' seems to me much more suggestive than 'operator' for the variable-binding kind of prefix. The connotation of 'operator' seems to me to point in the wrong direction: that of 'functor'. (I realize that your use of the 'operator' has as its historical background the use of that term for such prefixes as 'd/dx' in analysis; but I think that also this usage is analysis is unsuggestive, and stems from the non-logicians' failure to appreciate the peculiarity of bound variables.)

A-11': (c).

A-12: Choice here depends on the sense intended for 'designate' (see my letter of May 7, §3). If we take it in the sense of 'meaning', which your sense of 'designation' approaches (see May 7, §4), then a possible answer to A-12 would be simply 'expression', or perhaps 'significant expression', 'meaningful expression'; far more inclusive, of course, than A1,2,5,6,9. If on the other hand we take 'designation' in my sense, then my answer to A-12 would be 'name' or 'nominator', in a broad sense which includes descriptions and which is not limited to names of individuals as against entities of other logical types. Note, however, that it would not cover *all* descriptions or other substantives; not, e.g., 'the king of France in 1912', nor again 'Pegasus'. Whether a substantive designates (in my sense) or not is in general a factual question, not wholly decidable by semantical rules. The broader category, presumably determinable by semantical rules and including 'the king of France in 1912' and 'Pegasus' as well as names in the above sense, might be called 'substantives' (roughly: potential names, facts permitting). But this category would be far narrower than A2,5,6. See letter of May 7, §5.

A13: no suggestion. A14–19: (a). A20–22: 'plurary' (though I speak without conviction). A23–25: (a). My practice has been to reserve the '-adic' forms to relations (classes of singles, pairs, triples, etc.) as against expressions, but I can't say why.

A34: (b). My feeling here is much the same as that which you express, in another connection, at the top of p. 6 of your questionnaire.

I am inclined to favor the '-tor' terminology only when the expression thereby referred to can be regarded as virtually an agent with respect to the action expressed in the root verb (conformably with the original meaning of this Latin suffix); and the corresponding remark applies to the use of the passive suffix '- tum'. By this standard, 'descriptor' has its place (and indeed even in the sense of A7, despite my foregoing suggestion under A7), and so also have 'nominator', 'abstractor', etc.; so also 'attributor'; on the other hand such a pair as 'relator', 'relatum' would give quite a false suggestion.

A35: No.

B–C: General remarks:

I don't feel the parallelism between B and C. For me every expression used in statements, or nearly every one, should be allowed a meaning (or connotatum); whereas only predicates (including perhaps statements, as 0-place predicates) need extensions.

Incidentally I'd even prefer to speak of Satzgerüste here than predicates, thus emphasizing a type of context rather than insisting on notational continuity. *Matrix* serves about as well, and is simpler to handle than the notion of Satzgerüste. This is why you don't see much reference to "predicates" in my work, but, instead, much about matrices.

You may speak also of extensions of functors et al., as well as extensions of predicates or matrices; but such extensions are reducible to those of matrices. E.g., instead of speaking of the extension of the functor '+', we may speak of the extension of 'x + y = z'.

Because of the aforementioned lack of parallelism, I deliberately avoid, below, any recommendation of parallel terminology of the type "intension vs. extension".

Neither does my own notion of *meaning* seem to correspond *quite* exactly to your "designation" (R_1), nor does my "designation" correspond at all, as you may have supposed, to R_2. (See my letter of May 7, § 3–5.) "Designation" in my sense answers rather to "naming", but in a sense not restricted to individuals.

In Part B, I can't answer many. Insofar as we construe R_1 in the manner of what I call meaning, I'd prefer to use as B-terms simply the corresponding A-term with the word 'meaning' added; for the meaning is from my point of view "epilinguistic", as appears from my letter of May 7. (Not that I'd insist on a cumbersome terminology where frequent reference is necessary.) However, here are the answers in scattered points:

B1: (a). (But I must then retract my remark in *System of Logistic* and elsewhere: "Propositions are those entities, if any, whereof statements are the names." Propositions are now the meanings rather than the nominata, or designata in my sense, of statements. This is as it should be.)

B9: I disagree with your parenthetical remark. This would be the case only if propositions were the entities whereof statements are the names; the nominata rather than connotata of statements. (See B1, above). Nor would I say that "connections" are properties and relations of truth-values; for again truth-values, though they are the extensions of statements, are not for that reason nominata (designata in my sense) thereof.

B30: (c), (b). B31: (f), (d).

C1: (a). C3: (a). C4: (c) and (e) interchangeably; briefly 'relation'

C5: 'function (in extension)'.

C6: For anything in range of the (bound variables, regardless of type *entity* (= *object*). In particular, non-class (counting relations as classes, and functions as relations); *individual*. Apropos of (c) and (d), moreover, note that not all entities are nominata (nor descripta), on account of indenumerability.

C7: See C6. C8: Perhaps (a), or 'abstract' (though I have used the latter for the expression rather than the class). C9: Truth value of the compound.

C12: When we take functions as certain relations, and relations as classes of pairs (and triples etc.), then 'class' covers everything in C12 except truth-values.

C13: See C12

C30: 'Determines' was used by George Berry in his thesis. (He applied it to the relation of a matrix to its extension, but this doesn't matter; see top of my preceding page.)

C31: (b). C32: (b). C33: perhaps (a). C35: No.

D1: (b) for short, with recourse to (c) when ambiguity threatens. 'Confirmancy' has the wrong voice; active in place of passive. It suggests 'confirmingness', whereas the desired direction is 'confirmedness'.

Best wishes for an early recovery. Love to Ina and from Nae.

Yours,
Van

[MARGINALIA ON QUINE'S COPY:]

a. Wrong. See my letter of Sept. 14.

[107. QUINE TO CARNAP 1943-8-23]

1006 Elm Avenue
Takoma Park, Md.
August 23, 1943

Dear Carnap,

Thank you for *Formalization of Logic,* and congratulations on it. I like it very much. It contains a lot that I find interesting, and exceedingly little that I should have preferred to see handled otherwise. I want to write you more at length on it when I get a chance.

Let me know if you didn't get both instalments of my long last letter (ca. 7000 words). The first instalment was dated May 7, and the second was dated May 10 (though mailed a couple of weeks later).

We keep hoping for good news regarding your back. Our best to Ina and yourself.

Yours,

[108.   CARNAP TO QUINE   1943-8-28]

P.O.B. 1214
Santa Fe, N.M.

August 28, 1943.

Dear Van,

I am sorry I have delayed my answer to your long letters of May 7 and May 10 to June 4 so very long. The reason is that I had the illusion that my article would soon be written. And since it deals with the problems discussed in your paper and your letters more systematically and more in detail than I could do in a letter, the article would be a better answer than a letter. Just now, at last, I am finishing the article and Ina is beginning to type it. It has become much longer than I expected; it will have about 250 typed pages, and Ina thinks it will take her many weeks to type it. As soon as it is typed I shall send you a copy. I propose in the article to leave aside the concept of the name-relation (or denotation) because I believe that it is responsible for all the puzzles which you found (e.g. in connection with modal sentences) and likewise, in other respects, Frege, Russell and Church. I propose to use instead only the concept of extension and intension, and I try to show that this leads to a more satisfactory semantical method for the analysis of meaning, and also to a more simple structure of the object language than the methods used by Frege-Church and Russell. I also show how

a.

quantification can be used in modal sentences without the restrictions imposed by your method, without the use of two kinds of variables as in Church's method, and without ascribing to the quantifiers any artificial or Pickwickian sense. Your long letters have been very valuable to me both by making me understand your conception more clearly and by stimulating my thinking about my own conception. In my view, the difference between your conception and mine (and further that of Frege-Church and that of Russell) is not a difference in theoretical assertions but rather in practical procedure. Therefore I discuss these different conception as methods, not as theories, If you can find the time to read the manuscript and make some comments on it, that would be very valuable for me. I should like to have your and Church's reactions before I put it into final form for publication. First I planned to publish it in one or two issues of the JSL; now I see it is much too long (it will be between 120 and 150 printed pages) and thus I have to publish it as a monograph. If you happen to have any suggestion where I might try to have it published, I should be very grateful.

I will answer here only one point in your letters which is not dealt with in my article: your letter of May 10, p.3 item (6). I think the question, which is the most specific logical form having (1) as an instance, can be answer in two ways:

b. | (I) The consequent in your (2) should be replaced by '. .y. .x. .'; in other words, it belongs to the characteristics of this logical form that the consequent is the same matrix as the antecedent but with variables interchanged. (I suppose you will agree to this; otherwise I think your conception of logical form would deviate too much from the ordinary one.)

II. I myself should take a further step (as you presume) in which you probably will not follow me. I should add the specification that the antecedent and therefore the consequent are atomic matrices. I should do this even if 'R' is taken as syncategorematic and is not a value expression of a variable.

Now it seems to me the answer to the question whether there are false instances of the same logical form as (1) is affirmative if we adopt concept I of the logical form, but that it is negative if we take the stronger concept II. Thus the question is: Do you have any reason for not taking the difference between atomic and non-atomic matrices as relevant for the logical form?

My back is still in the same state, so I expect I shall have to undergo an operation perhaps around the end of the year. Fortunately my leave of absence, financed by the Rockefeller Foundation, has been prolonged for the next academic year. Thus we are glad that we do not have to worry for the near future. Now that the article is finished I shall go back to the work on probability and degree of confirmation. We just had news that Feigl will come here for a few weeks and are very pleased about it. Don't you ever get a leave of absence and if so would you not like to come to us? We have a wonderful climate here, a spare bedroom, and a puppy which barks every morning at 6 o'clock. I should be delighted to have an opportunity to talk with you at length about many problems, logical and otherwise.

Many thanks for the reprint, and also for the trouble of answering my questionnaire.

With best regards to all of you from both of us,

Yours,
Carnap

[MARGINALIA ON QUINE'S COPY:]

a. Good! What I urged May 7, mid. p. 7 (Lack of parallelism noted May 10, near top p. 6, operates only when we consider expressions of a wider variety than you would be doing in this connection.) ⟨Quine's references to May 7, p. 7 is to the last paragraph of his section 5. His reference to May 10, p. 6 is apparently to the second and third paragraphs of his "B-C: General Remarks".⟩
b. You are right.

1006 Elm Ave., Takoma Park, Md.
Sept. 14, 1943

Dear Carnap,

I am glad to hear you have decided to use only extension and intension, omitting designation. This is in line with what I urged in my letter of May 7, middle of page 7 ⟨p. 334, paragraph beginning 'The essential difference . . .'⟩.

It is natural that I should hail the elimination of designation in your sense, which has been the object of so much objection and incomprehension on my part. But also, as you know, I favor the ultimate elimination of designation also in my sense (viz. naming, in a sense going beyond individuals), for this is what happens when names (in my sense) are swept away by contextual definition as in my *Math. Logic.*

There remains for me, after the reduction last mentioned, the important relation between variables and their values (not their substituenda, but values in the semantic sense). This also remains a crucial relation for you, I should think; and it is the one channel, according to my theory, through which language makes ontological demands on *re*[with your kind indulgence]*ality.*

My remarks near the top of page 6 of my letter of May 10 ⟨p. 342 f., first three paragraphs of 'B–C: General Remarks'⟩, directed against supposed parallelism of extension and intension, are no objection to the course on which you have decided, for they operate only when we consider "expressions" in a broader sense than you would be considering in this connection (thus including those fragmentary expressions concerning which it is senseless to speak of an extension).

I think I must concede the point at foot of first page of your letter (Aug. 28) ⟨p. 346, subparagraph I ('The consequent . . .') in paragraph beginning 'I will answer . . .''⟩. Further, this concession affects the argument of page 3 of my letter of May 10 ⟨p. 339, passage surrounding (2)⟩ in an essential way. Suppose we correct (2) of that page as you suggest. Can I find a falsehood in the new form (2)? So long as two objects are distinguish-

able of the language—(i.e., so long as there is a matrix, simple
or complex, say '==x==', which is satisfied by some values of
the variable and not by all—I *can* find a falsehood of the new
form (2). One such falsehood is:

(x) (y) (==x== ⊃ ==y== .⊃. ==y== ⊃ ==x==).

Thus my original argument in question (page 3, May 10) ⟨p. 339,
passage surrounding (2)⟩ can be revised, conformably to your
correction, in such a way as still to serve its purpose in relation
to all but very trivial languages: languages whose variables need
only one value, so that quantification theory becomes vacuous.

As to your second step (near top of page 2, Aug. 28) ⟨p. 346,
subparagraph II ('I myself should take . . .') in paragraph beginning 'I will answer . . .'⟩, you are right in presuming that I do
not agree. My reasons for not taking the difference between
atomic and non-atomic matrices as relevant for the logical form:

(a) (the less important reason): It seems natural to say that all
statements got by substitution for letters in a schema share the
logical form depicted by the schema (along with the logical
forms of any more complex schemata from which the several
statements are derivable by substitution).

(b) (the more important reason): To make logical form depend
on idea of atomicity is to presuppose completion and adoption
of one specific constitution system for the empirical language in
which the logic is applied; for it is only in terms of such a constitution system that we can distinguish between the truly atomic
and the apparently (via definitional abbreviations) atomic. I have
regarded it as important to avoid such a presupposition, and to
shun the notion "the definition of . . .". (I do appeal to definition only in certain very special cases where my intent could be
conveyed in other ways, e.g. correlations between a specific re-
dundant language and a specific more economical language.)

In fact, it was also to avoid that presupposition that I have
declined to define "analytic" merely as "logical truth (defined in
turn) or definitional abbreviation of logical truth", and defined it
rather as "logical truth or reducibility thereto by putting synonyms for synonyms". So doing, I presupposed (instead of a
constitution system) the whole idea of synonymity, sameness of
meaning. (I consider, as you know, that this latter should ulti-

mately be defined in turn in pragmatics, behavioristically; but it is primitive, for me, relatively to pure semantics).

We were extremely sorry to hear that your back has not improved. What a delight it will be to have the operation over with and to be on your feet again!

The idea of spending some days with you in Santa Fe is a Schönheit erster Klasse, ersten Ranges und höchster Stufe. The scientific value of it, the pleasure of your company, and the appeal which that part of the world has for me, are all very strong attractions indeed. But I don't see how it can be managed, at least not for a long time. It was with some difficulty that I got a week's leave last June (which I spent in Ohio), and there are no near prospects of more. However, I'll let no opportunity slip by. Best to Ina and self.

> Yours,
> Van

[110. QUINE TO CARNAP 1943-11-9]

> 1006 Elm Avenue
> Tacoma Park, Md.
> Nov. 9, 1943

Dear Carnap,

The typescript of "Extension and Intension" came yesterday. I found it very interesting. By this I mean that I sat down with it on coming home from work and didn't let go of it, except for a brief meal, until after proper bedtime. By that time I had read two thirds of it: it had a grip on me like a mystery thriller. This evening I finished it. For me—I speak admittedly from biassed interests—it is your most interesting work in nine years.

Over the fundamental issues, I am not yet altogether sure how far my agreements and disagreements go. The stuff is going to have to ferment in me a while. Meanwhile I have some specific critical remarks to make. I'll start with the most trivial and least questionable, and work up bzw. down.

I. PHYSICAL:

Pp. 158–161 occur twice in this copy. Probably missing from another copy.

Pp. 230–231 missing from this copy.

II. EDITORIAL:

P. 29, line 5: "within" here should be "with in", and "some" should be "one". (Note that the proper idiom is "for one . . . for another", or "for some [systems] . . . for others".)

P. 33 refers twice to Frege's method, which is taken up only later. If this is an intentional anticipation, I think a remark is needed.

P. 76, line 16: "subsequent" should be "following" or "ensuing", to avoid inappropriate shade of meaning. | a.

P. 77 below middle: "implicitely," "tacitely": omit "e".

P. 107, line 5: "belongs the class Human" should read "does the class Human belong".

P. 122, 5th from last line: "would" should read "were to".

P. 146, 6th from last line: "of" here gives wrong sense: I suggest "between".

P. 147: smoother to omit "of" from beginnning of 7th from last line and "them" from beginning of the line next thereafter.

P. 161, 1st sentence of new paragraph: transpose "at all" to follow "names". In next line, delete 'in".

P. 170, line 9: delete comma. 2 lines later, suffix "ly" to "independent".

P. 172, line 7: for "as if we were" put "of".

P. 177, 8th from last line: for "Just the" put "The very".

P. 181, beginning: for "speak not" put "do not speak".

P. 183, lines 4–5: "an analogous . . . and (11)" must be expanded, e.g. as follows: "a way analogous to that in which (5) was obtained from (20-1) and (20-2), and (12) from (10) and (11)".

P. 202, 16th from last line: delete comma after "that", or insert comma after "premisses". (But do not do both. No commas or two.)

P. 211, line 12: for "as if our method presupposed" put "of presupposition, by our method, of"—or recast sentence.

III. LOGICAL (NON-SEMANTIC):

P. 204: The virtual contradiction which you derive from PM is new to me, and significant; but I think it wants putting in a different light. Note to begin with that the whole thing is a question of "scope" (on the analogy of "scope of a description" in PM). By determining scope one way, we can construe (24-12) as short for (24-14) as you do; by determining scope in another way, we can construe (24-12) rather as the denial of (24-11) and hence as short for the denial of (24-13). The two are not equivalent. But Whitehead and Russell were familiar with such nonequivalence in the case of scopes of descriptions, and hence adopted a convention (clumsy, I confess) to fix the scope uniquely. *And here is what saves them, technically from your charge of (virtual) contradiction: They explicitly announce adoption of analogous conventions for scopes of class expressions,* on p. 188, lines 12–14.

Were it not for this saving provision, your argument would have shown (not that PM was strictly contradictory, as you properly have emphasized yourself, but) that the principle of extensionality was provable for properties in PM, contrary to intention of authors, and hence that their elaborate gesture of starting with properties and deriving classes was wholly empty.

Though this charge cannot be levelled, in view of above citation, still it is clear from lines 14–16 of p. 188 of PM that the authors were quite unaware of the situation which you have uncovered. In fact you *have* proved that the correspondence which they allege in the lines last cited is lacking.

It occurs to me that perhaps you also should examine your own contextual definitions, scattered through your essay, on the score of similar ambiguities of scope. Even ambiguities of scope which do not issue in contradiction should be avoided on formal grounds, in my opinion. I have not studied your constructions from this point of view.

P. 188: Last sentence, in parentheses, is too strong. There are other ways not depending on stratification. One is the revision of my ML itself occasioned by Rosser's discovery of the deducibility of Burali-Forti's Paradox; see the Corrigendum slip to ML, and also (and especially) "Element and number". The whole reference to stratification is swept away by the revision. Also the systems of Fraenkel, Neumann, Bernays, Zermelo are independent of stratification, and yet readily modified so as to use variables of a single homogeneous type.

P. 85: Suggest you insert "non-logical" at beginning of 9th from last line, in conformity with end of 6th line, or else put "these" for "the" at end of 10th from last line.

IV. SEMANTIC: IN RE A COUPLE OF YOUR COMMENTS ON MY IDEAS:

Reply to your questions on p. 247: Yes, I *would* say that (29-3A) and (29-3B) are meaningless, precisely like (29-3C) or my own example (30-1). Moreover, you seem substantially to share my uniform disapproval of (29-3) yourself, though you use the milder phrase "better avoided" (p. 240). But I would *not* infer from the alleged meaninglessness of (29-3) that your (29-1aA) or (29-1aB) or even (29-1aC) is meaningless, any more than you do, since you hold in reserve another reading for the symbols of your (29-1a), viz. (29-2), (which may still be assumed to have meaning).

So you see that my attitude is quite symmetrical, in this respect, as among columns A, B, and C. The line which you take in §30, in attributing my rejection of (30-1) to a failure to regard individuals in the same light as classes etc., is therefore a wrong diagnosis so far as I can see. In fact, I never intended the 7 of my example (30-1) as an individual, but as Frege's class of all sevenfold classes! (If all classes are for my ML themselves "individuals" in the sense of your p. 29, that is merely because I pool types and get on with homogeneous variables, which hardly seems relevant to present matters: fact remains that they are designata or denotata, for me, of abstraction expressions.)

Thus I feel in particular that the sentence beginning at foot of p. 243 is off the point and that lines 14–16 of p. 244 are wrong. In contradistinction to the lines last mentioned, I believe that a sentence of the form 'there is something which . . .' can and should be interpreted in terms of any and every entity whatever, and is verified by any entity that fulfills the condition '. . .'. It was to emphasize this very indifference of mine as between kinds of entities (for purposes of the problems at hand) that I varied my examples as I did, appealing now to the Evening Star and now to the class 7.

My rejection of (30-1) depends neither on a predilection for individuals, in any restrictive sense, nor even on my predilection for classes as against properties, concepts, or whatnot; but merely on the view that the particular context 'greater than' calls for reference to a number (be it class or whatever) and not to a number-concept. You grasped this, p. 245, lines 5–7, and I think the argument which comes after those lines is a bit shaky and inconclusive; witness the artificiality of (30-3)—reminiscent, don't you think, of the tours-de-force of the subject-predicate logicians? I think that *compatibly with your own general point of view and theory* you could equally well have taken an opposite stand, considered (30-1) as analogous to (29-3) rather than to (29-4), and hence rejected (30-1) precisely as I did.* Note that the first occurrence of 'class' in (29-3A) is unnecessary in view of the ensuing context and could be omitted, and similarly for (29-3B) and (29-3C); hence [I would regard (30-4), despite absence of 'individual' or 'number' before] 'x', as quite a just rendering of (30-1) and as quite parallel to (29-3); and I regard it as meaningless or "to be avoided" along with (30-1) and (29-3). Granted you *can* get a parallel of (29-4) related to (30-1); thus you might define '$>$' in obvious fashion and say:

(i) There is an x such that x $>$ 7.

Again you could get a parallel of (29-2) thus:

(ii) There is a concept (number-concept, property, as you like) which $>$ the 7-concept.

Your less direct (30-3) is to the same purpose. I could agree to the Zulaessigkeit of (i), (ii), or (30-3), along with (29-4) and (29-2), without thereby admitting (30-4) or (30-1) any more than (29-3).

You could do that within your theory, and I could admit it within my own theory even as the latter has been described by you (apart from discrepant details already contested above). For, from the point of view of the theory of my [Notes], I would say that the name '7' occurred non-designatively in (i), (ii), and (30-3), and similarly for the name 'Walter Scott' in (29-2C) and (29-4C), and the name 'Scott' in (29-2B), without my therefore having to *reject* (i), (ii), (30-3), (29-2), or (29-4).

Note incidentally that I don't even have to go that far in the

---

*Or precisely as you did (29-3).

case of 'Human' in (29-2A) or 'human' in (29-2B), for I have nowhere regarded predicates (in the grammatical sense) as naming or denoting or designating classes or anything else. No need to; clearer not to, I have felt; better to regard them as having extensions and intensions but not as naming or designating or denoting at all. Abstraction expressions, of course, I *have* regularly regarded as naming, and in fact as naming classes; but '$\hat{x}$(x is human)' is for me synonymous with 'the class of humans' and not with 'human'. (It follows also that I haven't regarded epsilon as synonymous with the 'is' of 'is human', but only with 'is-a-member-of'.)

One more look at (30-4), by way of putting my point in another light: this is analogous to:

(iii) There is something which necessarily Scott, which, in contrast to:

(iv) There is something which is L-equivalent to Scott, amounts to:

(v) $(\exists x)$ $(N(x = \text{Scott}))$

and is to be rejected like (29-3) etc. One could conceivably construe 'is necessarily' in (iii) rather as a single expression tantamount to 'is L-equivalent to', in which case (iii) would indeed converge with (iv) rather than (v); and similarly one could construe the 'is necessarily greater than' of (30-4) as a single expression tantamount to '$>$', instead of taking the 'necessarily' as an 'N' governing the clause; but if this type of reinterpretation had occurred to me in writing [Notes], I would have rephrased (30-1) in the first place so as to avoid it and make my intended point. ⟨following handwritten:⟩ I meant (30-1) as an example of variable occurring, in effect, in an immediate extensional context '$x > 7$' governed by 'N'.

I can see why you hesitated to introduce the very special symbol '$>$', resorting rather to the type of paraphrase seen in (30-3). It was because it seemed unfortunate to have to introduce a new analogue of the very fundamental-seeming '$\equiv$' in connection with so special a matter as '$>$'. But other no less special examples could be constructed presenting a similar problem and calling, seemingly, for similar special analogues of '$\equiv$'. Thus, suppose we were to start with 'Scott' instead of '7', and 'contemporary with' instead of '$>$'.

Now some minor points on other passages. Pp. 82–85 accord with my own views, and in fact it was such considerations that have led me to withhold designata, or denotata, from predicates proper (see paragraph just above middle of preceding page of this letter: also section 5 of my letter of May 7). Your page 86 is different, though, for here you are speaking of abstraction expressions, which for me *do* denote classes. Furthermore, I find your argument here very telling.

Pp. 76 ff. sound as if I held to P12-3, whereas I countenance exceptions to it and call such exceptional occurrences not purely designative (as you properly explain elsewhere in your essay). Note further that the expressions, as opposed to occurrences, designate as always under my theory, despite indesignativity of occurrences.

P. 253: Here you quote two passages from [Notes] in such a way that one seems a partial retraction of the other, whereas the two passages can be seen to represent a single point of view when examined in their different contexts. The first quotation is apropos of not-purely-designative contexts, and is meant with its full strength within that scope. The second quotation relates to non-extensional modes of statement composition in general, and is accordingly put in the less categorical, more cautious form because I have nowhere proved that all possible non-extensional modes of statement composition involve not purely designative occurrences of names. (Rather, I have claimed to prove this only for very special kinds of context,* including necessity in the special sense of logical necessity as defined by you.)

V. SEMANTIC: IN RE YOUR THEORY PER SE:

The idea which you develop at foot of p. 103 and pp. 104f comes to me as a decided novelty and surprise. I think you are right and that I must accept the thesis which you put forward in those pages, alien though you know it to be to my customary orientation.

Your notion of "conceptual composition", pp. 67 ff, strikes me as an interesting and valuable idea for handling the notion of

---

*See especially middle of p. 124. [Notes].

meaning or synonymy in the narrower-than-logical sense. Very neat indeed.

Over the absence of a (to me) satisfactory analysis of 'L-true', I remain as disturbed as in the days of our Cambridge talks—your intervening books notwithstanding. In terms of (1-3) of p. 7 of your present essay, the locus of my dissatisfaction is of course the phrase 'can be established on the basis of the semantical rules of S alone'; for my familiar question is, 'can be established using what auxiliaries of the metalanguage?' One auxiliary appears to be such as to tell us that 'human being' and 'rational animal' in the metalanguage mean the same (see p. 5, lines 1–3); on the other hand these auxiliaries must not be strong enough to enable us to establish 'H(s)' on the basis of the semantical rules of the object language, for 'H(s)' is to remain synthetic (cf. p. 59). Where to draw the line? Honestly I don't know whether 'Scott is human' is for me analytic or synthetic, nor whether 'human being' means the same as 'rational animal'. Sameness of meaning is indeed as bad, for me, as analytic⟨;⟩ the two are pretty satisfactorily interdefinable, so that, if I knew the intuitive or metalinguistic sameness of meaning appealed to on your p. 5, I wouldn't be worrying about "analytic". However, I agree to the importance of sameness of meaning and (necessarily, in view of the interdefinability) of "analytic", so I am not for dismissing the whole business, but am very anxious to see the problem solved.

Now to your main idea, as of this essay. It interests me greatly; I find it even has certain allurements. The thing strikes at fundamentals, and it has an unmistakeable aura of importance. But, as I said at the beginning of this letter, I can't be sure yet how far I agree. Meanwhile, the following observations:

(a) Your theory appears to solve the problem, raised in second paragraph of p. 3 of my letter of May 7 ⟨p. 328, paragraph beginning 'I am speaking . . .'⟩, of a new interpretation of quantification capable of applying to variables in the modal contexts under discussion. Moreover, so far as I can see at present you accomplish this end without running into complications of the sort suggested in 4th and 5th sentences of that paragraph. (My own statements about quantification remain unrefuted as regards the original sense of quantification which I was discussing, but this is beside the point.) Your new theory of quantification (better, of interpretation of variables) retains the restrictions of the old so far as concerns extensional immediate contexts within intensional broader contexts, as you have pointed out in eschewing (29-3), but your theory does cover, as the old did not, the homogeneously intensional contexts.

(b) Your claim of telescoping our ontology (as I call it) by avoiding duplication of entities (pp. 211 f, et al.) is dubious, in the following curious way: This coalescence of entities takes place, if I understand correctly, only under the sort of metalanguage which does not speak of identity. Once identity is brought in, the neutral entities split again into classes vs. properties (and the rest). But the coalescence of entities, the elimination of duplication, is a question of identity and diversity, and hence can hardly be claimed at the one place where we abandon all notion of identity or diversity, coalescence or duplication.

I can see, though, that a certain elegance or conceptual economy very analogous to reduction of entities is accomplished by that scheme—albeit that the very notion of entity in the ordinary sense goes by the board, I suppose, when we abandon identity. The theory can be used, I imagine, as an interesting argument for the abandonment of identity. An odd convergence with Korzybski here!—but of course the argument is very different.

I suppose I better hold the copy of your essay for possible references in your next letter; let me know if you need it, meanwhile, or if I should forward it to someone. Enclosed are the duplicate pages mentioned in I above; perhaps you need them so as to complete another copy.

Hope there is some encouragement about your disability. Otherwise I suppose you will soon return to Rochester. With best regards to you both,

Yours,
Van

[MARGINALIA ON QUINE'S COPY:]

a. 75

[111.   CARNAP TO QUINE AND INA C. TO QUINE
1943-11-17]

11-17-43

Dear Van,

I am delighted that you found my discussions interesting (Ina
thought them the dullest* I had written since years), & I am
very glad to have your detailed comments. I shall study them
very carefully & shall write you later.
Here the missing pages.
Please keep the ms. for the time being.

Yours, Carnap

over

Dear Van, are there no Navy planes on which you can hike free
rides going to Santa Fe?? It would be swell having you here!

Love to Naomi & you
i.

[112.   CARNAP TO QUINE   1943-11-25]

Rudolf Carnap
P.O.B. 1214
Santa Fe, N.M.

November 25, 1943.

Dear Van,

Many thanks for your letters, that of September 14th, and the
long one of November 9th with very interesting comments on

*=Df hairsplitting

my manuscript. I have sent you pp. 230f. I follow all your editorial suggestions (except one, see below); furthermore, I intend to ask somebody, probably Singer, to revise the ms. with respect to language. Then I make of course changes in all points where you show me that I misunderstand your views. And your general discussions interest me very much. I am very glad to see that in some essential points our views seem to come closer to each other.

Here my replies to some of your points. ⟨The following page references are to Carnap's own manuscript that became *Meaning and Necessity*. Apparently the manuscript has not survived.⟩

p. 146, 1.6.f.b. I meant "of" (i.e. "of the two names (and espec. the first)"), not "between". Is the formulation misleading?

p. 204, *Contradiction in PM*. You probably overlooked the six lines in parentheses immediately following (24-14), explaining the situation with respect to scope. After reading this, do you agree? — Why is the convention concerning scope in [P.M.] clumsy? I intended a similar one for my contextual definitions (the smallest sentence or matrix is the scope). Is there a simpler one?

a.

p. 76ff (your letter p.5) ⟨p. 356, paragraph beginning 'Pp. 76ff. . . .'⟩ *on P12-3*. Your present formulation, viz. that you countenance exceptions to P12-3, is certainly possible. But another formulation of your method is possible, I think, and, if so, I should prefer it in my essay, because, it seems to me, it makes clearer to the reader the relation between your method and the other variants of the method of denotation. This formulation says: the occurrences in question are non-designative, i.e. have no denotata; therefore P12-3 does not apply to them (and hence they are no exceptions to it). (See p. 154f.)

b.

p. 253 (your letter p. 5) ⟨p. 356, paragraph beginning 'P. 253: . . .'⟩. I thought indeed that you made here a retraction. But I see now that I misunderstood you, so I shall change this. Your letter p.3, third and fourth paragraph ⟨p. 353, paragraphs beginning 'So you see . . .' and 'Thus I feel . . .'⟩. I understand now that you regarded 7 as a class, and hence that my interpretation p. 244 of your views was wrong. Therefore I shall change it. Since, however, I still do not understand clearly your views (see below), I shall say less about them and try to make more

clear my views and the reasons why I cannot accept your results, without trying to say what reasons you have for them.
Even so, I should like you to check later my changed formulations to make sure that there is no misrepresentation of your
views in any point.

Your explanation of your view, p.3 and 4 ⟨p. 354, paragraphs beginning 'My rejection . . .' and 'You could do . . .'⟩. I haver read
these pages more than ten times and pondered over every sentence but still I cannot say that I quite understand your view. I
understand your results: you admit certain sentences while rejecting others; but I do not yet understand your reasons for doing so. You take (i), (ii), and (iv) as admissible, but not (30-1),
(iii) and (v). You give as reason that only a number, not a
number-concept, can be an argument for 'greater than'; but in
(ii) you put "the 7 - concept" as argument expression to '>' and
hence in the expansion of (ii) it becomes an argument expression to '>'. Similarly with (iii), (iv), and (v). In several cases,
you seem to make a difference in the interpretation of two sentences, one abbreviated, the other its expansion; I say "you
seem", I can hardly believe that you really do; hence I suppose
that I have misunderstood you but I cannot discover where.
Any way, I do not make that difference; therefore I do not see
any reason why I should hesitate to use '>' as you expect. I
cannot see what difference there is for you between (iii), (iv),
and (v), which seem to me three formulations for the same
thing; likewise with (i) and (30-1) or (30-4), which seem to me
merely expansions of (i). You seem to make (bottom of p.4)
⟨p. 355, lines 19–24⟩ a related distinction whether or not something "is construed as a single expression"; you refer to my 'L-
equivalent', but I do not make that distinction and find it hard
to understand it. (29-1a) and (29-1b), e.g., have for me the same
meaning; do they not for you?

   You think (p.3) ⟨p. 354, paragraph beginning 'My rejection . . .'⟩ that from my point of view I could reject (30-1) as
analogous to (29-3) rather than to (29-4). But I do not see how I
could. I reject (29-3) because it contains a reference to an extension in a modal context while the neutral formulation (29-4)
does not. Now, (30-1) seems to me as neutral as (29-4) (and as
(i), which you surprisingly admit).

(A few days later.)

Reconsidering the whole, a new idea occurs to me (unfortunately only after I spent a good deal of time in writing a draft of a changed version of §30). It seems to me that we now are in agreement in the main point, viz. the admissibility of quantification in modal sentences as in (29-1) and (29-4). The remaining disagreement (still inexplicable to me) with respect to (30-1) and (30-4) seems less important in comparison. I hope still that we shall come at least to an understanding and perhaps even to an agreement in this second point. However, I wonder whether it would be wise for us to discuss this remaining divergence publicly. Perhaps the best would be for me to drop §30 altogether. However, I could not entirely omit any mention of your objections against quantification in modal sentences, because the reader would ask after §29: "What about Quine's objections?" Now this is what occurred to me as a possibility: could you perhaps formulate your view concerning my position in §29, and permit me to quote you at the end of §29? I suppose that the chief points would be to the effect that your objections were meant only on the basis of such and such an interpretation of the variables, that, however, on the basis of the interpretation of variables in my method, these objections do not hold and that you regard modal sentences with variables, as e.g., (29-1a), (29-1b) and (29-4) as here interpreted, as admissible. I think you could find a formulation which would not involve any commitment to a definitice judgment about the method of extension and intension in general. If we find a way of doing something of this kind, then it will be much more helpful for the reader than a discussion of secondary points of divergence, in which we ourselves are not yet entirely clear. I think in general that it is better to straighten out differences privately as far as possible before discussing them publicly. If, however, you think that our agreement in this point does not yet go as far as I assume, then my suggestion is of course not feasible.

Cordially,
Carnap

[MARGINALIA ON QUINE'S COPY:]

a. a) Preliminary use of prefixes.
   b) Not lifting defined abbreviations to get smallest context.

[113.   QUINE TO CARNAP   1943-12-8]

1006 Elm Av., Tak.Pk., Md.
Dec. 8, 1943

Dear Carnap,

I question the need of having Singer revise the language. It seems to me very straightforward already, except for the points I mentioned.

As to the third reply in your letter of Nov. 25: einverstanden! Now to various other points.

I.

Concerning p. 146, line 6 f.b. (see your letter Nov. 25, 1st reply):

"CHOICE OF" BEZW. "BETWEEN"

I don't see how your choosing the *two* names would be motivated by the view that the method of denotation is responsible for the antinomy; this would motivate only the first name ('antinomy of denotation') to my mind. Wouldn't it be enough to say "My choice of the name 'antinomy of denotation' is motivated . . ."?

If for some reason you do still want to speak of choosing the *two* names in this particular connection, then on editorial grounds I advise avoiding the phrase 'choice of the two'; for, the reader has already been prepared, by the alternation of two proposed names, for a choice *between* them, and will consequently misread you and even try to change your word, as I did. Better: "I have hit upon these two names for the antinomy because, from my point of view, . . ."

II.

Concerning p. 204 (see your letter Nov. 25, 2nd reply):

INCONSISTENCY BEZW. CLUMSINESS OF P.M.

You are right: I overlooked your parenthetical remark following (24-14). But my defense of the consistency of P.M. persists, and can now be given the following form: (24-11) and (24-12) are not really mutual contradictories, nor even mutually inconsistent!—(24-12) being, as you rightly insist yourself in the cited parenthetical remark, an abbreviation of (24-14) rather than of the denial of (24-13).

Nor, in general, could we hope to find a contradiction depending irreducibly on definitions, so long as there are directives (e.g. the scope conventions) for unique expansion of abbreviations.

But your example does illustrate very vividly one of my reasons for calling the P.M. scope conventions clumsy (a point which you ask about, Nov. 25). The conventions are clumsy in that they let one expression seem to be the denial of another when it is not really even materially equivalent to that denial. The above is one example, and a parallel example could be constructed from descriptions.

More generally, the conventions are clumsy in that they seriously obstruct the simple interchange of definiens and definiendum. We cannot put '$\sim(y = (\imath x)\ \phi x)$' for '$y \neq (\imath x)\ \phi x$' or vice versa, because scope is changed; and similarly for other definitions.

(Another clumsy feature, though superficial, is the use of scope prefixes. I say "superficial" because these are got rid of by the scope conventions; really an expository device. The previous objection is the serious one.)

My own procedure departs from P.M. in that I take as scope the minimum context from the standpoint of primitive notation. This overcomes the awkwardness and the near-paradox noted above. I do have to pay for this gain by imagining all overlying definitional abbreviations expanded before eliminating a description (or abstraction expression); but I have found this to be no obstacle in practice. In fact it actually expedites recursive proofs of interchangeability etc. in connection with descriptions (or abstracts), because the primitive forms of atomic context are exhaustible. My own practice is to exhaust these forms explicitly in the contextual definition of descriptions (or abstracts); see *Math. Logic*, pp. 133, 140 f.; also "New foundations for mathematical logic," (1936), pp. 74 f.

III.

A propos of your letter Nov. 25, 2nd page:

MY VIEW ON (30-1) ETC.
A.

Extraordinary, the difficulty of communication on these funda-mental semantic matters; but I'm sure I can do better than I did. Let us disregard my letter of Nov. 9 for the moment (I will recur to it in C) and go back to "Notes on existence and necessity", where I objected to (30-1); but instead of using (30-1) itself let us now use this symbolic version of it, which is the sort of version I had in mind:

(a) $(\exists x) N(x > 7)$.

(I will return to the verbal form (30-1) later, in B.) My objection was as follows ("Notes", p. 124):

(a) is meaningless. For, would 9, that is, the number of plan-ets, be one of the numbers x such that $N(x > 7)$? But $N(9 > 7)$ whereas $\sim N(\text{number of planets} > 7)$.

You supposed (§ 30) that my argument depended on a theory of numbers as individuals plus a theory restricting quantification to individuals. Actually I had no intention to withhold any en-tities from quantification, and no intention to construe numbers as individuals. The version of number uppermost in my mind happened to be the class version, but I intended my argument to be independent of any particular version of number.

It was immaterial to my argument whether numbers be con-strued as individuals or as classes or even as some manner of "concepts", if this is possible, so long as the following condi-tions were fulfilled:

(I) No two so-called numbers are arithmetically equal.

(II) The matrix '$x > 7$' is fulfilled only by values of 'x' which are numbers, in the unspecified sense in question.

Granted (I) and (II), my objection to (a) can be defended as follows: If in an effort to overcome the objection you take x as a 9-concept in contradistinction to a number-of-planets concept, then x is not a *number*, by (I); hence it violates '$x > 7$', by (II), and is irrelevant to the problem (a).

In short I think you should attribute my rejection of (a) not to a theory of numbers as individuals *or* as classes, but to my assuming that the satisfiers of 'x > 7' (so-called numbers, in some sense) are incapable, severally, of arithmetical equality with anything but themselves. This assumption was implicit in the phrasing of "Notes", p. 124: ". . . 9, that is, the number of planets . . ."; and the very choice of my example (a), or (30-1), depended on my belief that this assumption would be contested by none concerned.

So long as this assumption is adhered to, we cannot regard the context 'x > 7' as a neutral context like your 'H(s)' or 'Scott is human'; rather we have to regard it as prejudiced to one side like your 's ∈ H' or 'Scott is a member of mankind'. By this I *don't* mean that x and 7 should be classes, like H. I *do* mean that 'x > 7' fixes x as one of a set of entities among which *arithmetical equality* implies identity, just as 'y∈α' fixes α as one of a set of entities among which *extensional equivalence* implies identity. Thus it is that I have felt you should ban (a) in the same spirit in which you banned (29-3). *Not* because (a) contains a reference to a class or truth-value or individual in a modal context (see your Nov. 25, p. 2, next to last paragraph) ⟨p. 361, paragraph beginning 'You think . . .'⟩, *but* because the precisely *parallel* objection holds for *number* under any theory of number fulfilling my assumption about arithmetical equality.

B.

Now what of (30-1) itself, as opposed to (a)? My objection to a neutral reading of (a), or of its fragment 'x > 7', does not hold as a objection to a neutral reading of (30-1). For, suppose we symbolize 'connotes the exceeding of 7' as '⊘ 7'. Then (30-1) becomes:

(b) (∃x) (x ⊘ 7).

Now (b) *can* be defended as meaningful, on the ground that the entities x fulfilling 'x ⊘ 7' *aren't* actual numbers, in the sense which forbids arithmetical equality between one and another, but rather are *concepts* other than numbers, and variously related to numbers. One such is a certain 9-concept; *another* is the number-of-planets concept. Thus (b) remains true, and immune to the objection which I levelled against (a).

A point I overlooked in my letter of 9 November, with the result of making you think I was interpreting a sentence differently from its abbreviation, is this: 'x $\ominus$ 7' *cannot* from my point of view, be regarded as an abbreviation of 'N(x > 7)'. Reason: the values of 'x' fulfilling 'x $\ominus$ 7' are non-numbers (as just explained), whereas the values of 'x' fulfilling 'x > 7' (and hence, *a fortiori*, the values fulfilling 'N(x > 7)', if the latter were meaningful) are the numbers proper. It is to emphasize this divergence of '$\ominus$' from the analogy of your '$\equiv$' that I am now using the circle instead of a dot.

You may point out that my distinction between satisfiers of 'x $\ominus$ 7' and satisfiers of 'x > 7' should apply equally to the '7' in the two cases, so that a different sign—say '$\oslash$'—should be used in the second case. My reply: Yes, that would be clearer, but not necessary, since I can condone the old '7' in 'x $\ominus$ y' as a non-designative occurrence. It is only the variable that raises difficulties relevant to the present discussion.

In view of the very different fates of (a) and (b), we may wonder: Was I not wrong in condemning (30-1) as such, when prepared only to condemn the special reading (a)? In answer, two points are relevant:

(i) Explicitly, what I was trying to prove in "Notes" by use of my example (30-1) was that 'necessarily', governing a matrix and preceded by a quantifier, makes trouble. Hence the only relevant version of (30-1) as I used it would be (a), which exhibits 'necessarily' ('N') governing a matrix.

(ii) Nor is it much comfort to a reader to be able to keep his (30-1) and forego the analysis (a), since his rules of 'N' and '>' become useless in dealing with forms like (b) taken as irreducible to 'N' and '>'.

C.

What puzzled you in pp. 3–4 of my letter of Nov. 9 ⟨pp. 353–354, paragraphs beginning 'Thus I feel . . .' and 'My rejection . . .'⟩ is probably explained in B above. For one thing, I have explained away my appearance of distinguishing in interpretation between a sentence and its abbreviation. Again, you see now what I meant by "is construed as a single expression": I had no technical concept of "single expression" in mind, but was referring merely to my refusal, in (b), to analyze the 'is-necessarily-greater-than' of (30-1) into 'N' and '>'.

However, I think you can now regard A and B above, rather than pp. 3–4 of my letter of Nov. 9 ⟨pp. 353–354, paragraphs beginning 'Thus I feel . . .' and 'My rejection . . .'⟩, as my basic answer to §30. Said pp. 3–4 now merely offer supplementary remarks on some points.

In all the above I have been merely explaining my point of view as of "Notes", without taking into consideration your subsequent invention of two-way variables having both extensional and intensional values. Thus A and B are intended to be relevant to your revision of § 30, in case you find after all that § 30, in a revised form, may satisfactorily be retained in the book. Now we can turn to—

IV.
MY VIEWS ON YOUR THEORY

I have thought more about your theory meanwhile, and feel now that I see its status clearly. What I am about to write is not intended as the formulation which you requested (Nov. 25, p. 3) ⟨p. 362, paragraph beginning 'Reconsidering the whole, . . .'⟩ for possible quotation at end of § 29 (though I shall be glad to undertake such a formulation afterward if you still so wish), but is intended rather as a plea for a revision of your book! A revision which promises, to my mind, to obviate much public confusion and fruitless discussion, without detracting from the positive contribution made in your book. On the contrary, setting that contribution off in clearer relief than before.

The revision which I urge is this: Use '=' instead of '≡'; restore your term 'designation', and let the designata of your designators and the values of your variables be *intensions* and intensions only; drop all reference to "neutrality", and supplant all "neutral" interpretations by interpretations referring explicitly to intensions; let the "overcoming of duplication of entities" (p. 189) consist solely in contextual definition of extensions by intensions (using essentially the methods of pp. 174, 201).

For, I now consider that your so-called neutralism is a pure intensionalism in disguise; and that by presenting it as an outright intensionalism you would facilitate understanding, appraisal, and comparison with other systems. The structure would stay unchanged, and likewise its efficacy in dealing with the antinomy of denotation and my "quasi-antinomy" of variables.

The following are the considerations which lead me to call your neutralism a pure intensionalism in disguise:

(i) Your neutralism, as achieved under your metalanguage M', does *not* fuse the entities of extension and intension, because, instead of identifying the entities, you extrude the very notion of identity (cf. pp. 178 f.) and thus eliminate any question of identity or diversity. If we ask what *entities* (thinking of entities in the usual way as self-identical and mutually distinct) your language treats of, apparently we have to go back to the point of view of M (which admits identity and diversity) and thus regard your language as involving the duplication of entities (via systematically ambiguous use of designators and variables) which you have been trying to avoid.

(ii) But this is not necessary. We can analyze your language from another point of view and come out with the result that your only entities are intensions. Thus, suppose I am given your object language, described as you describe it in M', so that there is no stipulation of identity conditions. Then I (thinking in my own regular identity language) ask myself, what *are* in fact the distinct entities whereof your language treats? I decide naturally to take, as translation of identity into your object language, that designator connective which holds between all and only the designators that are interchangeable in all contexts. It turns out to be '$\equiv$'. I decode that '$\equiv$' ' means '$=$', and consequently that your entities are the *intensions;* there are, over and above these, no extensions (apart from possible subsequent contextual definitions), and there is no duplication of entities. Under this analysis your 'F1.B' and 'H' designate properties, not classes, *wherever* they turn up—both in 'F1.B H' and in '~(F1.B '$\equiv$ H'. It seems evident equally that intensions are adequate as sole values of your variables, without any complication of "extensional and intensional values", much less "neutral values".

In particular the point of view which I urge toward your language would clarify your own ban of extensional contexts within intensional contexts. The procedure which I'd prefer now is the following: *allow* extensional contexts within intensional contexts,* but restrict the rule of interchangeability (with respect to ' ') so as not to get the antinomy of denotation. There is nothing unnatural here, for your entities are intensions (see above), and '≡' is not identity of intensions, so that there is no intuitive presumption, in '≡,' of interchangeability in all contexts. When you go on to introduce extensions by contextual definition, and allow '≡' to serve *as if* it were identity between certain introduced fictitious quasi-entities which serve the purpose of extensions, we remain quite prepared for the failure of interchangeability within intensional contexts—simply as a technically necessary restriction on these artificially introduced quasi-entities. Just as we were prepared for the exceptional behavior, in certain cases, of Russell's contextually introduced descriptions. In both cases the anomaly of the behavior is explicable by expansion of contextual definitions.

I venture to say that the reinterpretation I have been urging is the very one you had in mind in the first place, before neutralism occurred to you. In any case I think it far better.

I suppose also that the suggested revision would enable you to get along with a good deal less discussion of the mechanics of metalanguages. And your criticism of the "method of denotation" would drop out, for your own language now becomes a case of the method, sub voce 'designation'. (It just happens in your system that the denotata, or designata, are concepts rather than individuals, classes, etc.) Incidentally I think the word 'denotation' could now be dropped in favor of 'designation' everywhere.

Your theory, thus revised, comes to look more like P.M. than it did. But it differs from the latter in a crucial point: it takes as its entities *properties, propositions,* and *individual concepts,* instead of properties, propositions, and individuals. This *is* a revolutionary departure. For you an individual comes to be "a mere manner of speaking" (via contextual definitions), just as a class is for P.M. (and you). This departure is what is needed to take the kinks out of the old intensional theories of P.M. and Lewis, as well as your own old ones. Your book thus assumes importance,

---

*Except when special connectives of extension-designators are introduced, if any; see below, last 3 scientific sentences of letter.

to my mind, despite my own anti-intensional tendencies. But all this is obscured when, as in the existing draft of your book, you veil your intensionalism in a professed neutralism.

When this revision is assumed, I can answer as follows regarding my views in "Notes" on the inadmissibility of variables in certain modal contexts quantified from outside.

I had argued that certain modalities, notably the 'N' of necessity in the specified sense, could not govern matrices whose variables were quantified in a wider context. Naturally I did not hold that trouble would always arise, regardless of what matrix followed 'N'; for, trivial and harmless cases could readily be got by letting the matrix contain its variable merely in such a manner as 'x = x'. The matrices causing trouble are in fact just those such that, when 'N' is prefixed, the whole is seemingly satisfied by a certain value of the variable or not according as we think of that value in terms of one or another of the expressions which designate it. The existence of such matrices depends on there being an object designated by two non-synonymous expressions. You accordingly have overcome the difficulty by abolishing such objects and retaining only objects such that any two designators of any one of them are synonymous. These retained objects are concepts, intensions.

I see no fallacy in your solution, and would merely set the advantages over against the price: adoption of an ontology of intensions to the exclusion of individuals, classes, etc. (except as "manners of speaking" introduced by contextual definition). The following suggests itself as a plausible principle: modal contexts (of the contemplated kind) can be permitted (in the usual unrestricted way) only in a language which countenances no individuals or other extensions as values of its variables.

In particular, as to (30-1), or better III(a) above, there are two procedures open to you compatibly with the revision of your book which I have just been urging:

(i) Numbers may be conceived as entities proper (rather than quasi-entities introduced by contextual definition), hence as intensions. But if 9 and the number of planets are taken as numbers in this sense, then despite their arithmetical equality they must be regarded as distinct numbers; for, as observed a paragraph or two above, no one entity can be designated by two non-synonyms. So my argument against (a) in III is dodged by not admitting III(I). Or,

(ii) Numbers may be conceived as quasi-entities, say classes, introduced by contextual definition. This is probably better, for the anomaly of having to deny III(I) is avoided. (The anomaly, that is, of having to say that 9 and *the* number of planets are *two* numbers.) But then the contextual definitions should be framed in such a way that the sign '>', *if* construed as having to do solely with *numbers* (my III(II) above), is prevented from turning up after an 'N' as in III(a). Naturally the same precaution would have to be taken in introducing *any* connective for use between "names" solely of extensions and not intensions. Note that '≡' is not a connective of this kind, but rather an *ex*tensional connective of names of *in*tensions.

It would be a delight to hop a Navy plane for Santa Fe. Thanks to Ina for adding her urging to yours. However, there are no prospects. I have in fact done a little hopping of Navy planes on days off—seven planes all told; but never beyond a 400-mile radius, since my maximum periods off duty (apart from leave) vary from 24 to 48 hours. One *could* fly a long way in 48 hours if it weren't for the necessity of allowing time for return by train in case the hitch-hiking by plane peters out. As to leave, I wangled a week last June only with difficulty, and can't hope for more for a long time.

With best wishes, christmatic and passim, 4:2,

Yours,

[114.   CARNAP TO QUINE   1943-12-17]

Santa Fe, N.M., Dec. 17, 1943.
P.O.B. 1214

Dear Van,

Thank you very much for your detailed and extremely interesting letter of Dec. 8. I shall write more later in detail, after digesting your proposal somewhat more. Now I wish only to tell you briefly, (1) that I am very glad now to understand *your* view much better, and (2) that your suggestions as to a modification of *my* set-up have something very attractive in them, especially the idea of giving up the (apparent) neutrality in M'. I have to think still more about what to do with the obj.-lang. The introduction of extension expressions (e.g. '$\hat{x}$ (H(x))' by contextual definition as in P.M. would perhaps still be an unnecessary duplication, as I tried to show with respect to P.M.

With cordial Xmas greetings to all of you from both of us,

Yours
Carnap

[115.   INA (AND R.) CARNAP TO QUINE   1944-5-23]

Carnap, P.O.B.1214,
Santa Fe, N.M.

May 23, 1944.

Dear Van,

No sign of Naomi. On receiving your message I left a message at General Delivery for her since we have no phone. But she may have come through before your card reached me (I only fetch mail twice a week) or she may not have come through at all. However, if *you* could manage to come, will you?? Can't you wangle another two weeks this year? And if so, can't you spend them here? Your parents can come to Washington but the Carnaps can't. We expect Hempel for August and Feigl may come some time during the summer. But even if our house should be full, I could get a room for you at a neighbor's. We both should love to have you here—not to mention Carnap's need for masculine company and minds after having been cooped up with a female for such a terribly long period.

Carnap: "As you see from the sheet enclosed I do not yet know when and in which form to publish the Extension article. If you have any suggestion about it I should be grateful. After thinking over your suggestions I am inclined at the present moment to make some thoroughgoing changes in the direction suggested by you; but I am not yet clear about the details. Since there seems no early prospect of publication I shall probably postpone the working out of the changes. Perhaps in the mean time there might be opportunities for talking over these problems with you and other friends. Will you please send now the Extension ms. together with the sheet enclosed to Prof. Herbert Feigl, Dept. of Phil., Univ. of Minnesota, Minneapolis, Minn. In the mean time I have worked much on probability and the matter is progressing well."

Carnap's back is much better—he is now up an average of six hours a day (not consecutively); and thus we expect to return to Chicago in September when his Rockefeller year expires. Isn't it maddening to think that if we had had the right doctors in time there would not have been any need for his staying in bed so long? On the other hand, Rockefeller would not have come through with a second year if it had not been for his illness.

How do you stand being separated from your work proper for such a long time? Are you in any way confident that the consequences of the war i.e. the peace will be such that you will find it was worth devoting your time for whatever it is you are doing now?? We never heard: was there any pressure exerted on you from the Harvard authorities to join up or did you expect that your special abilities would be useful? And if the latter, do you find that they are really made use of?? Well, that's enough soul searching questions for one day. I am enclosing a snapshot of Carnap with my puppy which at least shows him on his feet again (I mean C., the puppy is a she).

> Love from us both,
> Yours,
> i.

[116. ENCLOSURE IN 115   1944-5-?]

R. Carnap   May 1944

Remarks to my ms. "Extension and Intension".

Quine suggests a revision in my method: "Use '=' instead of '≡'; restore your term 'designation', and let the designata of your designators and the values of your variables be *intensions* and intensions only; drop all reference to "neutrality", and supplant all "neutral" interpretations by interpretations referring explicitly to intensions; let the "overcoming of duplication of entities" (p. 189) consist solely in contextual definition of extensions by intensions (using essentially the methods of pp. 174, 201). For, I now consider that your so-called neutralism is a pure intensionalism in disguise . . . . .".

Church writes: "The entire discussion in your paper must be regarded as preliminary to the construction of a formalized system of logic which shall take account of intension as well as extension, and of a formalized semantical meta-language of this system. . . . judgment must be suspended on all the issues which are debated, until we have one or more successful formal constructions of this kind . . . Some preliminary discussion of methods and desiderata is certainly necessary before undertaking the construction of the projected logistic systems. But, granted the point that I am making, I would raise the question whether the actual work of construction might not profitably begin sooner than is the case in your manuscript as it stands. . . . I appreciate that a treatment sufficiently formal to be accurate would simply not be read by many. But I believe that the work of popularization should follow rather than precede the accurate technical treatment."

My practical problem is this: I agree with Church, that it is only a preliminary discussion; therefore not suitable as a book; on the other hand, it is too long for a periodical. I might perhaps try a way of publication less pretentious than a book and for a smaller distribution, e.g. mimeographing. Or I could leave it for the time being in the form of a typescript only and ask only a few friends for their reactions; then I should work it out much later into the planned volume on modal logic, utilizing the results of the present discussions. (I am at present working chiefly on probability and therefore I have decided to postpone writing the volume on modal logic, probably for quite a number of years.)

[117.   CARNAP TO QUINE   1945-3-20]

Chic., March 20, 1945.

Dear Van,

Thank you very much for your book "O Sentido . . .". I was astonished to see that Portuguese is easily understandable (to some extent). But you should publish an English version too.

The book came via Santa Fe. But we have been in Chicago since last September. The improvement of my back progressed so well since about the beginning of 1944 that I was able to resume my teaching, as expected in Sept. Now I have given my courses for 2 Quarters, and everything went o.k.. I get tired quicker than in former times, but I can give 2 consecutive hours; and at home I alternate between desk and couch. There are not many students here now, but I was satisfied to have about 10 in each course; I had expected fewer. And there are a few intelligent ones among them. I have just given a course on "Concept, Theories, and Methods of the Phys. Sciences", at the suggestion of the Dept. of Physics. While in Prague my chief field of teaching was "Naturphilosophie", I did not teach it in this country before. Therefore I had to build up this course anew, & I spent much time in preparing it, reading books, etc. I found again that physics is a fascinating topic. On the other hand, it did not leave me much time for work on probability. Of the planned book on probab., ca. 550 pp. are typed; but this is only about half of the whole, & although I have most of the theorems with proofs for the remaining chapters, I realize now that it will take me years to complete it. Well, I ought not to complain, seeing how much of your time you are sacrificing without being able to continue your own work. Or do you still work at logic around midnight? Will V-E-day or only V-day return you to normal life?

Since my book is still so far from completion, I have written two papers on probability, to appear perhaps in a few months. I shall send you reprints and I shall be very interested to get your reactions.

If you still have my ms. "Extension", keep it for the time

being. (You probably overlooked my request last May to send it to Feigl; never mind!)

We should be glad to hear about you, Naomi, and the children, your life, and your logic work (if any).

Cordially 2:2,
Yours,
Carnap.

[118.   QUINE TO CARNAP   1945-5-10]

2391 N. Danville St.
Arlington, Va.

May 10, 1945

Dear Carnap,

We were delighted to hear that you are well again and have long been back at your teaching.

Somehow I completely overlooked your request that I send your MS on "Extension" to Feigl. I'm very sorry. I'll hold it now pending further instructions.

Lately I've sent a couple of papers to the Journal of Symbolic Logic. One due to appear in the belated March number, gives an Entscheidungsverfahren for monadic theory of quantification (monadic functional calculus) which I think is more practical and more feasible pedagogically than those previously known; also a proof that the rest of quantification theory can be derived from the monadic theory by an easy rule. I think of the whole as an improvement over the old deductive way of presenting quantification theory (just as I prefer truth-tables to deduction in the case of truth-function theory). The method of deduction from a minimum of schemata retains value, though, as an aid to simple metamathematical formalizations of logic (e.g. for Gödel).

The other paper, yet more recent, is a brief novelty on ordered pairs: I show how to define x:y so as to make it homogeneous in type with x and y. Sequences, built up by iteration of the pair, thus turn out likewise to be of the same type. Relations of all degrees thus turn out to be homogeneous in type with classes.

But my latest article is on Peano, for the Encyclopaedia Britannica.

Otherwise, such desultory work as I've done in leisure hours has gone toward planning one or another book, maybe yet another logic book and maybe a more philosophical venture, but with little tangible effect. My latest tendency is to think of the two ventures as combined into one big book, with certain section-headings in brackets to indicate that they are of purely technical interest and can be omitted by the general or philosophical reader, and certain other section headings in braces to indicate that they may be omitted by the reader who is primarily interested in technical theory and indifferent to philosophical controversy. This book would make a translation of the Portuguese book unnecessary, by including or improving upon the novelties of that book and going farther. Maybe a magnum opus superseding all four of my previous books and carrying over into semantics and ontology. But virtually none of it is done.

Maybe I go to Rio for a year as cultural attache, returning to Harvard in Sept. 1946. Or maybe I stay on in the Navy and return to Harvard after the defeat of Japan. I won't know for weeks. Family is well. Very best to you and Ina from Naomi and

⟨presumably Quine just signed the letter at this point.⟩

[119.   CARNAP TO QUINE   1945-9-22]

Santa Fe, N.M., Sept. 22, 1945

Dear Van:

Thanks for your letter of May 10. I shall be very interested to read your papers; I didn't see yet the March issue of J.S.L., it is probably in Chicago. Still more am I looking forward to your future magnum opus, especially if it deals also with semantics & ontology (I hope, the latter only in the Quinean private sense of the word, not in the generally accepted sense; I think your use of the word is awfully misleading). Too bad that I don't have the time to write the entirely revised edition of "Semantics" which I have in my head and in notes and have already taught last year in a class.

The Univ. of Chic. Press will publish my "Extension . . .". Thus I plan to work it over during October. I have thought very seriously about your suggestion for a complete change of the whole scheme but have finally come to the conclusion that it would be better not to make it. Not that I regard my scheme as the final solution; very far from it; it is quite tentative. And it may be that finally we shall find a way somewhere between my method & the method of denotation in its customary form. However, your proposal just as it now stands is not quite acceptable to me; it seems to me it would have some of the disadvantages of P.M. especially the unnecessary duplication of expressions (if not of entities). And at the present time I do not see a solution which would appear clearly preferable to my present scheme. Thus I shall publish it in about its old form, but emphasize its tentative character.

Now, how about my suggestion to omit § 30 and instead add something formulated by yourself at the end of § 29? (see my letter of Nov. 25, 1943). If you are willing to write something I shall be glad to insert it, perhaps or a quotation from a letter of yours.

I suppose the copy of "Extension" you have is the original (not a carbon copy). If so, I should be glad to get it back perhaps about the middle of October, or when you do not need it any longer.

My work on the book on Probability is progressing but it is still far from the end. Some days ago I sent you reprints of the paper on probab.; I am anxious to hear whether you will be as dismayed about my conception of probab. as Reichenbach & some others.

Since this probab. stuff will keep me busy for quite some time still, I shall not have time to work the book on modal logic, working out the modal systems which I constructed in 1942 & 43 and which are mentioned in "Extension" pp. 250 f. Therefore I have decided to publish at least a few of the results without proofs. I have written a paper in June. It will probably appear in J.S.L. March or June 1946, maybe in two parts. It contains only technical stuff, no discussions of interpretations as in

"Extension"; I use your axioms of quantification, with Berry's modification.

What are your plans, now the war is ended?

We shall drive back to Chic. in the next days. Classes begin on Oct. 2. We had again a pleasant summer here; but I was not much outside because I spent all my time on the probab. book, which grows more and more.

Cordial regards to you and Naomi from both of us.

yours,
Carnap

(Thanks for returning the copy of "Syntax".)

[120.   QUINE TO CARNAP   1945-9-30]

604 A St., S.E.
Wash. 3, D. C.
Sept. 30, 1945

Dear Carnap,

A terrible thing happened. You remember in December 1943 you and Ina urged me to hitch-hike to Santa Fe sometime on Army planes. I very much wanted to but couldn't get away. Finally, however, seven weeks ago, I did it. Army plane to Roswell, N.M.; thence by bus through Santa Fe to Taos.

The terrible thing is that I had no idea you were there. After you had been confined there on your back so long, it never occurred to me you might be back there again or anywhere away from Chicago so soon. I looked at the hills as I passed and wondered which of them your place might have been on, and regretted not having been able to get there while you were still there. And then after returning to Washington I learned by letter from Peter Hempel that you were at Santa Fe!

Enclosed is something which I have written in criticism of the idea of your § 29, in response to your suggestion. I'll be glad to change it to suit your needs or in the light of future discussion.

The copy of "Extension and Intension" in my hands is a carbon copy. Let me know whenever you want it.

In returning to this topic after long interruption, I suddenly see what I did not see before: that it is very unfortunate to use the term "antinomy of denotation" as you do! When I re-discovered this phrase in your pages yesterday, what it meant for me was the basic form of Grelling's paradox:

'Not denoting self' denotes itself.

In fact, I had recently used precisely the same phrase in some writing which I recently did on the semantic paradoxes. This writing was not for publication, so I am not concerned on that score, but it does seem to me that the phrase is much more appropriate in the present connection. (Note that 'denote' in the above paradox has the sense which you and Morris used to give it: relative product of designation and converse of membership.) Why not adhere to the alternative phrase which you also put forward, 'antinomy of identity'?

Incidentally, I think it unfortunate that you have departed from the former sense of 'denote' defined parenthetically above. To avoid confusion on that score mightn't it be better in "Extension and Intension" to say 'naming' where you say 'denotation'? I appreciate your reasons for not saying 'designation' in this connection.

Thanks for the reprints. I read the discussion concerning Hall and Bergmann with interest and sympathy, recalling when I had a similar task regarding Ushenko in Journal of Philosophy. I've just begun reading one of the probability papers, and look forward with pleasure to continuing.

I'll return to Harvard as soon as released. I don't know when this will be; possibly around midyears. At present I lack 3 points. I cancelled arrangements with the State Dept. after VJ-day, since I then knew I could soon return to my proper job.

[121.   QUINE TO CARNAP   1945-9-30]

Washington, D. C., Sept. 30, 1945

ON § 29 OF CARNAP'S MS. "EXTENSION AND INTENTION"

In appraising the bearing of (29-4) on the problems involved in quantifying modal contexts, perhaps I am not warranted in reading the phrase 'There is an x (or F or p) such that' in the fashion 'There is an entity x (or F or p) such that'; or perhaps I am.

Case 1: I am not. Then let me call these phrases "quasi-quantifiers", for certainly they must differ radically in meaning from quantifiers ordinarily so-called. You may be said then not to have reconciled genuine quantification with modality, but to have abandoned quantification in favor of a new device of "quasi-quantification". What this new device means, in terms of explicit translation into standard English (as explicit say as the rejected 'There is an entity such that'), would have yet to be explained. Perhaps no such translation is possible, and the best you can do is to provide some incomplete semantic rules establishing certain connections of logical consequence between your quasi-quantifications and standard English sentences. In this event your quasi-quantifier is an irreducible enrichment of ordinary language, like Hilbert's selector function $\in$; so that, from a point of view of economy as well perhaps as of clarity, a considerable price will have been paid for circumvent⟨ing⟩ the problems involved in quantifying modal contexts.

Case 2: I am. Then I ask, "What *are* the entities in question, and under what circumstances are they identical?" In M' there is no talk of identity, but I can still conduct an indirect inquiry. I observe that

(x)(x is L-equivalent to x),

and hence that x and y must be distinct whenever x is not L-equivalent to y. Therefore they are not extensions but intensions. (I neglect the further possibility of distinctness among L-equivalent entities, which would compel the entities to be somehow "ultra-intensional"; for it is evident that you have no cause in the present connection to go so far.) So I see in (29-4) only a repetition of (29-2), and in M' only a copy of the intensional part of M with extrusion of all extensional entities.

I agree that such adherence to an intensional ontology *is* an effective way of reconciling quantification and modality. All the bad combinations depend, like (29-3), on extensional values of variables: when on the other hand extensions are extruded, we can proceed to quantify modalities without restriction.

And the price of this freedom? Repudiation of, among other things, the concrete world; for even individuals have disappeared, leaving only their concepts behind them.

Lest comparison of (29-3) with (29-2) seem to suggest that the repudiation of the concrete and the extensional is little more than a stylistic matter, let us note some different examples:

(I) There is a number (class of classes) F which necessarily exceeds 7.

(II) There is an individual x which necessarily eats whatever Scott eats.

These, which proceed by existential generalization respectively from 'N(9 > 7)' and 'N(Scott eats whatever Scott eats)', are subject to the same sort of criticism as (29-3). Briefly the criticism is this: The alleged number F in (I) does or does not necessarily exceed 7 according as F is 9 or the number of planets, yet these are one and the same number; again the alleged individual x in (II) does or does not necessarily eat whatever Scott eats according as x is Scott or the author of Waverly, yet these are one and the same individual.

Repudiation of extensions throws (I)–(II), like (29-3), into the discard. But a shadow of (29-3) seemed in effect to be preserved in (29-2), wherein sameness and necessary sameness of extensions gave way to equivalence and sameness of intensions. Can we correspondingly preserve a shadow of (I) and of (II)? Yes. Just as equivalence of intensions parallels sameness of extensions, so we may introduce a relation of number-intensions which parallels the > of a number-extensions; and we may introduce a relation of individual concepts which parallels eating on the part of individuals. The required relation of number-intensions will differ markedly from the > of arithmetic, for it will not be serial; and the required relation of individual concepts will differ markedly from eating. But an ontology of pure intension may indeed be expected to differ markedly from one which countenances concrete things or classes.

Regular quantification of modalities conflicts with there being classes or even concrete things. In M', if reinterpreted intensionally instead of "neutrally", you have outlined a language whose ontology is exclusively intensional. This I find valuable, for it enables us to picture what it would be like to be able to give the modalities free rein.

W. V. Q.

[122. QUINE TO CARNAP 1945-10-9]

604 A St. S.E., Wash. 3, D.C.
Oct. 9, 1945

Dear Carnap,

Since my letter of last week, I have read "On inductive logic" and "2 concepts of probability" with much pleasure and appreciation. I am much instructed by them, and am glad you are bringing your powers to bear on this problem. I look forward to your book with much interest, and am struck with the idea that I'd like to make a course of it at Harvard. (Though there is some danger that Williams has preempted the subject there.)

One problem occurred to me on reading page 87 of "On inductive logic". The reasoning at the middle of the page, leading to (1), presupposes that there be no "property" of "identity with b"; for, if there were, it would be a known property of b, and hence the whole question of c having all known properties of b would be vacuous (supposing c distinct from b). Now since identity is expressible in L, the lack of any property of "identity with b" seems a very special and even unnatural assumption. What worries me at the moment is the question just how far this assumption invests other portions of your theory. More generally, the question just how far your theory depends on restricting "property of b in L" beyond "what can be said about b in L". I haven't studied this through; you of course have.

Typographical: op. cit., p. 91: I urge use of roman type instead of italic for the subscript 'qi', to avoid connoting the italic 'q' and 'i' which are used as variables elsewhere.

Linguistic: I think somebody told you the story about the pedant whose cuckold, walking in on him and the lady of the piece, expressed surprise. "No," said the pedant, "you are astonished. It is I who am surprised." I regret the story because I'd much prefer 'surprising', 'surprised', etc. in places where you have written 'astonishing', 'astonished', etc. Reasons: 'Astonish' is too strong, too open-eyed. 'Surprise' is common currency. And the story is no good, unless with heavy underlining of 'pedant'!

> Yours
> Van

[123. CARNAP TO QUINE   1945-10-12]

> Chicago, Oct. 12, 1945

Dear Van,

Best thanks for your two letters of Sept. 30 and Oct. 9, and your formulation for my § 29. I regret all the more that we missed each other in Santa Fe, since your formulations cause a good deal of doubts and headache (metaphorical only) to me, which could be dissolved so much more easily by a talk. Both for myself and the readers, it would be highly desirable if you could clarify some points by insertions and reformulation.

    1. To your p. 1. Certainly Case 2 holds: I mean genuine quantification, not quasi-quant. (Perhaps the paragraph "Case 1" might be shortened or omitted, unless you think, it will clarify the situation for the reader.

    2. My main trouble: how are your formulations "extensions of all ext. entities", "intensional ontology", "repudiation of the concrete world", "individuals have disappeared", etc. to be understood? They might mean:

I. Whoever accepts my modal system S_2 (or a similar language for the whole of science) as described in M' (or also in M ?) shows thereby, that he believes that extensions (concr. world, indiv.) do not exist.

I. a. 'to exist' is here meant in its ordinary, scientific sense, as it can be expressed in a scient. lang. (e.g. "there are no unicorns", "There is no natural number such that . . .").

I. b. It is meant in a non-scientific, metaphorical sense (e.g. in the sense in which an idealist might say that the horses,

which exist (in distinction to unicorns) in the sense (1a),
are nevertheless not real in a metaphys. sense.)

II. A much weaker assertion: in S_2, we cannot talk about extensions, i.e. a sentence in the ordinary lang. about extensions
(concr. world, etc.) can in general not be translated into an
(L-equivalent) sentence of S_2.

Taken literally, your statements mean I. Since this seems to me
obviously absurd, I presume that you mean II or something
else. (I regard II likewise as wrong; but I will not now discuss
our difference of opinion but merely obtain a clear formulation
of your opinions.)

Your word 'ontology' definitely suggests Ib. If you do not
mean this, I should advise strongly against its use. Or, as the
least, you should add a remark to the effect that it is meant in
the sense of Ia (or perhaps something else) and not Ib.

Following your suggestion, I shall abandon the term "antinomy of denotation". ". . . of identity" is perhaps not clear
enough; ". . of identical extensions" might be better.

I thought that the earlier sense of 'denote' was rather useless
(see p 74 footnote), & that the present sense is now more &
more accepted (ibid., references to Russell and Church). Is this
not the case? But I will consider saying 'naming'. Your p.1, 1.2
a. f.b. "ultra-*extensional*"; is this correct?

To your letter of Oct. 9; the property of "identity with b".
Properties like this one are not excluded; but in my book on
probab. (and in my paper "Modalities & Quantification" for
J.S.L.) they are not factual properties, because '$a = b$' is here
taken as L-false. My theory on prob. is hereby not restricted in
general, but some theorems are. Some theorems refer to sentences of all kinds, others only to those without '$=$'; as it is
customary in deductive logic. (I have no variables for properties.) — I have also studied alternative forms of modal systems
(not of inductive logic) where '$a = b$' is factual. They are more
complicated because the state-descriptions cannot have the simple form. In modal logic there are some reasons in favor of this
more complicated form. But for a simple, extensional system of
inductive logic the simpler form seems to me preferable.

Keep the copy of "Extension" for the time being.

What is your general opinion, leaving aside details: is there a useful concept of degree of confirmation and an inductive logic. With best regards to you and Naomi from both of us,

Yours,
Carnap

[MARGINALIA ON QUINE'S COPY:]

a. No, *"in-"*.

[124.   QUINE TO CARNAP   1945-10-24]

604 A St. Southeast
Washington 3, D. C.

October 24, 1945

Dear Carnap,

I enclose a new draft designed to meet the questions raised in your letter of October 13. But I consider it in no sense final, and will be happy to continue trying further revisions until we seem to be in a fair state of equilibrium on the issue; because I consider the issue important and all effort upon it well spent.

Yes, "ultra-extensional" should have been "ultra-intensional".

On inductive logic: Yes, I think there is a useful concept of degree of confirmation and an inductive logic. This hopeful view is mainly due to my reading your work and Hempel's.

Yours
Van

[125.   ENCLOSURE IN 124   1945-10-23]

Washington, D.C., Oct. 23, 1945

ON §29 OF CARNAP'S MS. "EXTENSION AND INTENSION"

Every language system, insofar at least as it uses quantifiers, assumes one or another realm of entities which it talks about.

[*387*]

The determination of this realm is not contingent upon varying metalinguistic usage of the term 'designation' or 'denotation', since the entities are simply the values of the variables of quantification. This is evident from the meaning of the quantifiers '(x)', '(F)', '(p)', '($\exists$x)', '($\exists$F)', '($\exists$p)' themselves: 'Every (or, Some) entity x (or F or p) is such that'. The question *what there is* from the point of view of a given language—the question of the *ontology* of the language—is the question of the range of values of its variables.

Usually the question will turn out to be in part an a priori question regarding the nature and intended interpretation of the language itself, and in part an empirical question about the world. The general question whether for example individuals, or classes, or properties, etc., are admitted among the values of the variables of a given language, will be an a priori question regarding the nature and intended interpretation of the language itself. On the other hand, supposing individuals admitted among the values, the further question whether the values comprise any unicorns will be empirical. It is the former type of inquiry— ontology in a philosophical rather than an empirical sense—that interests me here. Let us turn our attention to the ontology, in this sense, of your object language.

An apparent complication confronts us in the so-called duality of M' as between intensional and extensional values of variables; for it would appear then that we must inquire into two alternative ontologies of the object language. This, however, I consider to be illusory; since the duality in question is a peculiarity only of a special metalinguistic idiom and not of the object language itself, there is nothing to prevent our examining the object language from the old point of view and asking what the values of its variables are in the old-fashioned non-dual sense of the term.

It is now readily seen that those values are merely intensions, rather than extensions or both. For, we have:

a.   (x) (x is L-equivalent to x),

i.e., every entity is L-equivalent to itself. This is the same as saying that entities between which L-equivalence fails are distinct entities—a clear indication that the *values* (in the ordinary non-dual sense of the term) of the variables are properties rather than classes, propositions rather than truth-values, individual concepts rather than individuals. (I neglect the further possibility of distinctness among L-equivalent entities themselves, which would compel the entities to be somehow "ultra-intensional"; for it is evident that you have no cause in the present connection to go so far.

I agree that such adherence to an intensional ontology, with extrusion of extensional entities altogether from the range of values of the variables, is indeed an effective way of reconciling quantification and modality. The cases of conflict between quantification and modality depend on extensions as values of variables. In your object language we may unhesitatingly quantify modalities because extensions have been dropped from among the values of the variables; even the individuals of the concrete world have disappeared, leaving only their concepts behind them.

I find this intensional language interesting, for it illustrates what it would be like to be able to give the modalities free rein. But this repudiation of the concrete and extensional is a more radical move, in general, than a mere comparison of (29-3) with (29-2) might

⟨What follows from here until the next editor's note is a page through which a line is drawn. The page is marked at the top: "Superseded Jan. 1, 1946".⟩

suggest. Passages from (29-3) to (29-2) looks like a minor stylistic change; but let us note some different examples:

(I) There is a number (class of classes) F which necessarily exceeds 7.

(II) There is an individual x which necessarily eats whatever Scott eats.

These proceed by existential generalization respectively from 'N(9 > 7)' and 'N(Scott eats whatever Scott eats)'. (I) and (II) are, like your (29-3), examples of the insusceptibility of modal contexts to quantification with respect to extensional entities. Briefly, the predicament in (I) is this: the alleged number F does or does not necessarily exceed 7 according as F is 9 or the number of planets, yet these are one and the same number. And in (II): the alleged individual x does or does not necessarily eat whatever Scott eats according as x is Scott or the author of Waverly, yet these are one and the same individual.

Repudiation of extensions throws (I) and (II), like (29-3), into the discard. But a shadow of (29-3) seemed in effect to be preserved in (29-2), wherein sameness and necessary sameness of extensions gave way to equivalence and sameness of intensions. Can we correspondingly preserve a shadow of (I) and of (II)? Yes. Just as the equivalence of intensions parallels sameness of extensions, so we may introduce a relation of number-intensions which parallels the $>$ of number-extensions; and we may introduce a relation of individual concepts which parallels eating on the part of individuals. This is, however, no minor stylistic change. The required relation of number-intensions will differ markedly from the $>$ of arithmetic, for it will not be serial; and the required relation of individual concepts will differ markedly from eating. But it is not surprising that an ontology of pure intension should differ markedly from one which countenances concrete things or classes.

⟨This is the end of the superseded page. The top of the next page is marked "[substituted Jan. 1, 1946]". ⟩

suggest. The strangeness of the intensional language becomes more evident when we try to reformulate statements such as these:

    (1) The number of planets is a power of three,
    (2) The wives of two of the directors are deaf.

In familiar logic, (1) and (2) would be analyzed in part as follows:

    (3) ($\exists$n) (n is a natural number $\cdot$ the number of planets = 3^n)
    (4) ($\exists$x) ($\exists$y) ($\exists$z) ($\exists$w) [x is a director $\cdot$ y is a director $\cdot$ ~(x = y) $\cdot$ z is wife of x $\cdot$ w is wife of y $\cdot$ z is deaf $\cdot$ w is deaf].

But the formulation (3) depends on there being numbers (extensions, presumably classes of classes) as values of the bound variable; and the formulation (4) depends on there being persons (extensions, individuals) as values of the four bound variables. Failing such values, (3) and (4) would have to be reformulated in terms of number concepts and individual concepts. The logical predicate '=' of identity in (3) and (4) would thereupon have to give way to a logical predicate of extensional equivalence of concepts. The logical predicate 'is a natural number' in (3) would have to give way to a logical predicate having the sense 'is a natural-number-concept'. The empirical predicates 'is a director', 'is wife of', and 'is deaf', in (4), would have to give way to some new predicates whose senses are more readily imagined than put into words. These examples do not prove your language-structure inadequate, but they give some hint of the unusual character which a development of it adequate to general purposes would have to assume.

[MARGINALIA ON QUINE'S COPY:]

a. ⟨Quine circles 'is L-equivalent to' on this line and writes '≡' in the margin, circles that mark and connects the two circled expressions. Also in the margin at this point is the note: "[Revision of Jan. 1, 1946]".⟩

[126. CARNAP TO QUINE   1945-12-3]

Chicago, Dec. 3, 1945.

Dear Van!

First my cordial congratulations to your return to civilian life. I suppose you will now enjoy a few months of well deserved vacations before you begin teaching again. Did you keep your house? or do you have to hunt for a new one? That would be an awful problem now, I suppose.

Many thanks for your new formulation of Oct. 23, & for your willingness to consider further changes. If I actually have not yet exhausted your patience, I should indeed like to mention some points where your position might perhaps be made more clear.

To p. 2. You intend to analyze my object language itself, independently of any particular metalanguage. Then, however, you take as example (x) (x is L-equ. to x)", which is in M', not in the object language. Would it suit your purpose to take instead a

a. sentence in S_2, e.g. "(x) (x≟ x)"? This might then be translated into words, e.g. with "necessarily equ." or "L-equ.".

To p. 1. end of first paragraph. It will help the reader (& myself) if you would add here an explicit remark either (a) to the effect that the range of values of the variables of a language

b. contains all entities about which one can speak in that language (at least for a language which contains variables for all kinds of designators occurring), or (b) that not. Then you might make, for greater clarity, a corresponding addition on p. 2 in the par. beginning "I agree" to the phrase "extrusion . . . from the range of values", e.g. either (a) "and hence from the range of entities about which one can speak", or (b) "although not from the range . . ." .

To p. 3, top. It might help the reader if you said explicitly that

c. the sentences (I) & (II) are rejected by *both* of us.

To p. 5, 2nd par., "Repudiation . . discard". This sounds as if it were desirable to have the sentences (I) & (II), which my repudiation eliminates from the language, back in the language; or at least to "preserve a shadow" of them. Is this actually your opinion? If not, it might be good to say what is your purpose of the

d. discussion on this point.

In your letter of Sept. 30, you suggest *"naming", instead of "denotation"*. I see the advantage of avoiding the ambiguity of "denot.". On the other hand, the disadvantage would be that "named entity" would be more awkward than my "denotatum", which occurs frequently; "nominatum" seems rather artificial; what else might be considered? Please look again at my footnote p. 74. Is not the fact that both Russell & Church have used "to

e. denote" in my sense a good reason for keeping this term?

Church writes* that the printer does not have '⊃' but he has '⊃'; he advises against using '⊃' combined from two types because the dot often drops out. '⊃' does not seem nice. What do you think about putting some sign behind '⊃' instead of above

---

*This concerns my paper "Modalities & Quantification". I think I should use the same symbol in this paper and in the "Extension" booklet, although the latter will probably be planographed and hence I could easily write in the dots by hand along with German and Greek letters.

it, e.g. '⊃*' (& '≡*')? It does not give quite the impression of one symbol; but the advantage would be that it can easily be set (I suppose).

To you, Naomi, & the whole family our best wishes for a happy return and a good solution of all problems connected with it.

Cordially
Carnap

f.

g.

[MARGINALIA ON QUINE'S COPY:]

a. *Yes*
b. No. Not the point. If I (from the point of view of my own language, e.g.) think there is another entity, I may be able to say that a certain sentence of your language *is* about that entity without being able to convict *you* of considering that there is such an entity. So I prefer not to speak in terms of "what your language can talk about" but only "what your language presupposes that there is and is not". (What is C. trying to pull?)
c. Yes
d. (Important & fix this.)
e. Too bad you feel 'designation' is spoiled. (You spoiled it, you bastard.) I used to say "denote" & changed to "designate" because of *your* then use of "denote". "Denote" isn't (as in your note p. 74) unnecessary. It is important in contexts where we avoid universal entities but talk still about relations between predicates (or predicate-inscriptions) and things. Useful because in this context we can avoid going beyond nominalism. E.g. in heterological paradox: showing it is not a result of Platonism.
f. Recommend '⊋', also inverting '≡' to conform.
g. Sep'n

[127.   QUINE TO CARNAP   1946-1-1]

25 Ware St., Cambridge 38
Jan. 1, 1946

Dear Carnap,

Enclosed is a new page 3, which please substitute for page 3
of my last previous draft. This substitution disposes of the questions raised in your letter of Dec. 3 with regard to page 3. It
may of course raise further questions in your mind. I shall be
very glad to go on with our discussions and concomitant revisions of my comments just as long as you like, feeling as I do
that all possible progress toward a mutual understanding on
these points is important. And the more we can accomplish privately before publication the better.

I agree with your emendation of my page 2: in line 7, please
change 'is L-equivalent to' to read '$\equiv$'.

As for your remarks concerning page 1, on the other hand, I
think it is simpler to avoid the formulation 'entities about which
one can speak in that language'. The following illustrates my
reason. Suppose I believe in a certain entity (suppose e.g. it figures as a value of variables in my own language), and that you
do not believe in it (thus excluding it from the range of your
variables). Suppose further that a certain sentence of your language has, as its most natural translation into my language, a
sentence which is about the entity in question. Then it would be
quite natural for *me* (who accept the entity) to speak of your
sentence as speaking about the entity, though without being
able to convict *you* of presupposing that there is such an entity.
Rather than resolve this ambivalence by arbitrary convention, it
seems clearer in the present context not to ask "what your language can talk about" but only "what your language presupposes that there is and is not".

On the question of 'naming' vs. 'denotation', I don't know
quite what to urge. I also used to say 'denotation' for this purpose (in the days of System of Logistic), but switched to 'designation' because of the other sense of 'denotation' which you
adopted at that time. I can't agree with your view (footnote

[394]

p. 74) that this sense of 'denotation' is insufficiently important to need a name. Its importance is in relating predicates (or predicate-inscriptions) directly to things, yielding a province of semantics—"nominalistic semantics"*—which can be treated without assuming classes or properties. One specific product of nominalistic semantics is the demonstration that the heterological paradox is constructible without help of abstract entities and is hence not attributable (like the logical paradoxes) to Platonism.

Of course my own term for naming is 'designation' and it is only in latter years that I've learned that I wasn't merely copying your usage in this regard.

I suppose if there is one among this complex of notions that *I* feel could well be left unnamed, it is the notion which you have come to call designation!—insofar as it diverges from my designation, naming. But at this point I strike to the very center of our semantic divergences, and I should be guilty of a petitio principi in urging a terminological reform upon you along this line.

It might have been well for you to have used 'signification' instead of 'designation' in your sense, reserving the latter word for the sense of 'naming'. But probably confusion would arise from your switching now.

I *don't* think 'signification' is good for the sense of 'naming'.

Maybe simply the word 'naming' is best. Saying 'naming' always in preference to 'nomination', but resorting to 'nominatum' in the relatively few places where you need the participle. But whatever your decision, perhaps the above remarks will influence your remarks (to the extent e.g. of modifying your disparaging attitude toward the old sense of 'denotation' in footnote to p. 74).

As to the typographical question, I think '⊃' is much better than putting a sign after '⊃'. Your sign '≡', which presumably *is* available in type, could then be inverted in the fashion '≡' for the sake of uniformity.

Sive "elementary semantics", on the analogy of "elementary arithmetic": no class variables.

I should tell you that Naomi and I have been separated since last June. She and the children are living at 93 Mt. Vernon St., Boston.

Very best wishes to you and Ina for the new year.

Yours

[128.   CARNAP TO QUINE   1946-2-23]

RUDOLF CARNAP
Department of Philosophy
University of Chicago

Chicago, Illinois   February 23, 1946

Dear Quine:

Thank you very much for your letter of January 1 and the new page three. As you see from the enclosed copy of my letter to the Harvard Press, the work in finishing my m.s. has taken much longer time than I had planned and now the whole has become much longer and, I hope, thereby clearer and better. Following your suggestion, I have discarded the use of the term "denotation" (and deleted the disparaging remark about the old sense of this term in footnote page 74); instead I use now "name relation". Following Church's suggestion, I have adopted "sense" instead of "meaning". Instead of a dot above the symbols of conditional and biconditional, I used now a dash above them. I am sure that your new formulation will contribute to greater clarity of your position. I am still not entirely clear about all points of your position, as you will probably see from my discussion (which is not yet written); but I think that further correspondence could hardly clear them up entirely. I suppose that more thinking on these points by both of us will be necessary. And I hope that you will publish soon a systematic treatment of these questions which will make your position clearer than these short formulations. Since your planned book on logic and ontology will probably still take quite some time, I hope you will soon write a paper about these things.

In case the Harvard Press asks you for my ms. and for your opinion about it, would you be so kind to give them?

I read with great interest your paper on the "Logic of Quantification". I think you have achieved here a very interesting and
important simplification of the of the ⟨*sic*⟩ logic of quantification.
I wonder whether the table method for monadic schemata could
not perhaps be simplified still more. That would be greatly desirable. I have some vague ideas in this respect, but no time now
to pursue them.

I plan to attend the meeting of the A.A.A.S. at St. Louis
(March 27 to 30). I hear that Hempel, Nagel and others will
come. It would be excellent if you too would come, and also
Nelson Goodman. Then we could have some private discussions
about our problems. I shall perhaps stay in St. Louis until Saturday night or, if some of you stay longer, even until Sunday
night. For the official program, get in contact with Morris (c/o
New School for Social Research, New York City); for our private
program with Hempel; we must decide very soon how long to
stay there because of reservations for room and return trip.

Hoping to see you soon,

Cordially yours,
Carnap

[129. CARNAP TO HARVARD UNIVERSITY PRESS
1946-2-21]

RUDOLF CARNAP
Department of Philosophy
University of Chicago

Febr. 21, 1946

Harvard University Press
Cambridge, Mass.

Gentlemen,

In the preface to vol. II of my "Studies in Semantics" (*Formalization of Logic*, 1944) I announced that the next volume would
deal with modal logic. At present I have on hand a manuscript
on this subject; it is not quite as comprehensive as the system I

envisaged at the time of the announcement but it fulfills at least the greater part of what was then promised. I should like to ask you whether you are interested in publishing it as vol. III of the series since it would fit in very well with the first two volumes.

The basis for the present manuscript on "Extension, Intension, and the Logic of Modalities" is a treatise which I have written two years ago. Since it set forth very new ideas I wished to see the reactions to it by other men in the field whose opinion I value. I am enclosing quotation from letters about it by Prof. W. V. Quine (Harvard) and Prof. Ernest Nagel (Columbia). It was a rather small manuscript (261 small typewritten pages of about 240 words each, hence roughly 60,000 words), and therefore I did not consider it suitable for publication as a volume in the series. I was thinking of publishing it as a small monograph, perhaps planographed, and I asked the University of Chicago Press for an estimate on production costs; to my surprise they expressed interest and willingness to publish it as a small book (because of the paper shortage they did not mind the shortness of the manuscript). A few months ago I began to work it over in order to bring it into final shape for publication. In the process of remolding the manuscript, its size and character have been changed considerably. Extensive parts have been added, and the old parts completely reshaped. The whole constitutes now a systematic development, and the necessary explanation especially in the first chapter, have been added to make the whole now a self-sufficient unit. According to my rough estimate, the final version will be longer than the first by about one fourth or one third.

Since its content is so closely related to the previous volumes of my "Studies in Semantics", I should prefer its publication as the third volume of this series. However, there is the question of financing it. You may remember that the publication of the first two volumes was subsidized with $2000.—($1000.—from the Harvard Department of Philosophy—where at that time I was an exchange professor—, $1000.—from the A.C.L.S.). This time I do not wish to undergo all the trouble and delay (it took twelve months until the grant from the A.C.L.S. came through) which the begging of a grant-in-aid of publication always involves. Since the University of Chicago Press has not requested a subsidy when they offered to publish it, I wonder whether

you might be willing to undertake the publication as a third volume without a subsidy. After all, the first volume sold relatively
well and I believe that the present book will have a considerably
better sale than the second volume because it deals with problems which interest a wider circle of philosophy students and
offers new solutions, which, I think, will stimulate a lively discussion though certainly not always agreement. I have not yet
published anything about this subject.

I expect to have the manuscript in final shape within a few
weeks. If you would care to see in the meantime the ms. in the
earlier version, I am sure that Prof. Quine will be glad to give
you the copy which is in his hands now. And I suppose that he
also would be willing to give you his opinion about it, if you
wish. You will see that the ms. contains some formulas of symbolic logic. However, their number is much smaller than in the
first two volumes. The same holds for the present version. This
fact will decrease the cost of composition; it also will give to the
book a less technical character and thereby make it more attractive for many philosophers.

I should be glad to hear your opinion on the matter fairly
soon since I wish to wait for it before I take any further steps
with the University of Chicago Press.

Sincerely yours,

⟨This is the enclosure in 128.⟩

[130. QUINE TO UNIVERSITY OF CHICAGO PRESS
1946-10-29]

to Univ. of Chi. Press   Oct. 29, 1946

UNIVERSITY OF CHICAGO PRESS—MANUSCRIPT REPORT

Author: Rudolf Carnap

Title: Probability and Induction

Reader: W. V. Quine

TO THE READER: Please be completely frank. Your report is
solely for the guidance of the Press, and your name will not be

revealed to the author of this manuscript without your permission. If the manuscript is not publishable in its present form but could be successfully revised, you will help immensely by suggesting such revisions.

What does the author set out to do?
To devise, in explicit terms, a general measure of the degree to which a statement of evidence may be said to confirm a hypothesis.

Since what is sought is a numerical function of pairs of *statements*, the formulation must be relative to the language in which the statements are couched. The author chooses a simple language, poor in power of expression, thereby reducing the proportions of his problem. The larger problem of defining degree of confirmation for a language adequate to the general purposes of science is not embarked upon. But the author feels that the solution of the lesser problem may, in the quality of a model, illuminate the more general problem in essential ways.

How well does he accomplish his purpose?
Very well. Enhances generality, (a) by parallel treatment of model languages with finite and infinite ranges of variables, and (b) by leaving the most arbitrary details of his construction unsettled till after deriving such portions of inductive theory as can be kept independent of those details.

Nevertheless, extension to a language of serious proportions involves problems concerning which there is no glimmering of hope. The author's solution of the simpler problem is to be viewed less as a partial solution of the general problem than as an instructive analogy.

Incidental achievements: Clarifies nature of philosophical explication in general. Formulates and resolves the major controversy over probability with great clarity. Good criticism of specific views. Much new light on general nature of probability.

Is the manuscript an original contribution to its field?
Highly.

Is the author's scholarship sound?
Thoroughly. And his criticisms show temperance and sympathetic understanding.

Is his style ponderous, straightforward, or dynamic?
Straightforward. High standard of rigor of clarity. But I think
more effort might have been made to weed out technical details
in cases where they are neither particularly illuminating for their
own sake nor needed for other purposes. (But hard to judge
without painstaking analysis and also access to the sequel.)

What audience is the manuscript designed for, and what part of
this audience will actually buy the book?
For a professional audience with a little background in modern
logic, primarily. But the book can be used selectively by a wider
group; portions could advantageously be assigned to students in
a first course.

Everyone professionally concerned with foundations of probability theory must reckon with it, for surely it is the most serious
work ever produced on this topic, and the first book in which a
real command of modern logic has been brought to bear on it.

Are there competing books in the field?
No.

My final reaction is that I would—would not—publish the
manuscript.
Would.

Have you any suggestions for improving the manuscript, or any
additional remarks? (Use the back of this sheet if necessary)
Page 51: Under (ii), where Keynes and Jeffreys are mentioned,
    perhaps also Peirce should be included, on the score of priority.
Page 127: For elegance I advise dropping 't' from the language
    in favor of '$a_1 = a_1$'. The syntactical sign 't' can be kept, but
    becomes an abbreviation of '$in_1 = in_1$'; thus virtually no
    changes would have to be made later in the book. On the
    very rare occasions where 't' itself appears, '$a_1 = a_1$' is brief
    enough to use instead.
Page 144: The ideal of logical independence will mystify many
    readers, when applied as here to primitive predicates. Maybe
    more should be said.
Page 155: T19-8: Simplify statement of the theorem by changing
    "Let R_i" to read "Then R_i" and deleting the short sentence next
    following. The star notation can then be defined inside the

proof itself, which is long anyway and in small print. Better to keep the statement of the actual theorem as simple as possible.
Page 216: T26-2a: Treat similarly.
Page 391: mathematical terminology: "monotonously" should read "monotonically", I believe. (Middle of page, right side.)

OVER

Date _____ October 29, 1946 _____ Signed _____ W. V. Quine _____

Page 585: It should be pointed out that T4 here is just another way of writing the "general division theorem" of page 520. Also Bayes' theorem should be correlated with the present development: and the terminology of page 515 ("ratio of increase of confirmation") should be equated to the present terminology("relevance quotient"). In fact it might be neater to transplant this whole discussion of relevance quotients so as to make it precede p. 515, and then use the relevance-quotient notation and terminology in §60 (pp. 515 ff).
Page 779: Simplify T83-6 and T83-7 by dropping the first sentence of each ("Let e and e' be L-equivalent') and simply writing "e" instead of "e'" (thus "MC(h,e,h',e)"). Simplify proofs correspondingly.
Pages 780–784: Similar simplifications.
Page 841: Perhaps the author should explore the correspondence of his "principle of invariance" with the traditional postulate of the uniformity of nature. (I advance this suggestion with little assurance.)
Stylistic: There are traces of a German accent here and there. I have assumed these will be smoothed out in a final draft, but occasionally I have pencilled in a correction of idiom, as on p. 620. Also I have pencilled occasional suggestions of revisions of obscure formulations, as at the top of page 619.

⟨This is obviously a referee report on what became *Logical Foundations of Probability*. Fred Wieck, associate editor for the University of Chicago Press, had written to Quine on September 14, 1946, indicating that Quine had agreed to read Carnap's "Probability and Induction" for that purpose. No doubt this is what became *Logical Foundations of Probability*.⟩

[131. QUINE TO CARNAP   1946-12-4]

Emerson Hall
Harvard University
Cambridge 38, Mass.
Dec. 4, 1946

Dear Carnap,

This letter is of a rare kind for me, in that it is prompted solely by inclination; no business.

I read the MS of your book on modalities, and the vol. 1 on probability, with much pleasure and admiration. Always seems odd being called on to referee your books for U. of C. Press, but I'm always glad to, for I want to read them anyway, and may as well collect a fee in the process. And I managed in both cases to give them a little something in return by way of suggestions to you for emendations.

The issue between us over extension and intension, though still unresolved, seems to me to have reached a plateau. I think we did accomplish a good deal toward ironing out misunderstandings in the preliminary correspondence, and that it is all right to let the public in.

A little paper of mine on the same subject, "On interpreting modal logic", is at press with J.S.L. It was written before your J.S.L. article on modalities appeared, so the systems of modal quantification explicitly considered are Barcan's and Church's.

The question of bringing out your modality book here at the Harvard Press turned out to reduce to the question of a subsidy by the Philosophy Department. This was finally decided in the negative because of U. Ch. was already willing to bring the book out without subsidy. If publication of the book had depended upon it, I'm sure the department would have rallied around.

I'm finishing a new logic book, elementary but broader and better than *Elementary Logic,* and altogether different from the latter. I'll use a mimeogram of most of it in Phil 1 this spring. Also a second printing of *Mathematical Logic* (with small corrections only) is in process at Harvard Press, to be ready for Math 19 this spring.

I've discovered an extension of Gödel's theorem which surprises me. See enclosed abstract.

I hope to spend five weeks in Mexico right after Christmas. Regards to Ina. Best wishes for a merry Christmas.

Yours
Van

[132. CARNAP TO QUINE   1946-12-21]

a. | RUDOLF CARNAP
    | DEPARTMENT OF PHILOSOPHY   December 21, 1946
    | UNIVERSITY OF CHICAGO   CHICAGO, ILLINOIS

Dear Van;

Thank you for your letter of December 4 and the abstract on "Incompletability". The latter result is indeed surprising and extremely interesting. I am looking forward to the full explanation which, I hope, you will publish soon.

My book "Meaning and Necessity" (the earlier "Extension and Intension", now greatly changed and extended) will probably appear in February. I just finished reading the page proofs. I shall send you a copy as soon as it comes out. Your suggestions for emendations were helpful; I did not know that they came from you. It was, of course, an advantage that the Press here was willing to publish the book without subsidies. On the other hand, that compelled them to put the price at $5.00; awfully high, I think, for a book of only 220 pages.

I am enclosing a list of directions for your "Math. Log."; but perhaps it will be too late. Probably you found these errors by yourself.

If you should come through Chicago on your trip to or from Mexico, we should be delighted to see you. But if you drive a car, you will probably choose the more Southern route.

Best wishes from both of us, for good holydays and a nice trip,

Yours
Carnap

⟨The enclosure is a half page as follows:⟩

R. Carnap   Dec. 21, 1946

Corrections to Quine's Math. Logic

p. 47 1.5: symbol
p. 85, 1.5 f.b.: "Ponential".
p. 120, 1.3; "A man".
p. 142, 1.7 and 10: circumflexes.
p. 206, 1. 19: dot above "V".
p. 251, 1. 4 f.b.: delete "of".
p. 272, 1.5: insert "to".
p. 301, 1. 5 f.b.: (and 302): "2" instead of "?"?
p. 320, 1. 15: dot above "o"?
p. 340, 1.4: "Formalization".

[MARGINALIA ON QUINE'S COPY:]

a. Ans'd. Guadalajara, Jan. 8

[133.   CARNAP TO QUINE   1947-4-13]

RUDOLF CARNAP
Department of Philosophy
  University of Chicago

Chicago, Illinois,   April 13, 1947.

Dear Van,

My "Meaning" has appeared, at last. The delay was chiefly
due to the fact that the factory did not supply the mats for the
symbols in time. Thus I had to read the proofs without the symbols in. I do not like the too thick dot for conjunction; but it was
too late to change it. You will get your copy one of these days.
You will see many new things in it, among them the whole second chapter. I simplified the discussion of the metalanguages by
throwing out M". You will also be interested in pp. 115 ff, card.
numbers as properties of properties; I think Russell was not
right in saying that they *must* be *classes*.

Many thanks for your "Short Course in Logic", which I studied with great interest. This treatment of quantification seems indeed a great simplification. I am, of course, intensely interested in Ch. VII, & eagerly looking forward to VIII. I am now inclined to agree with you in regarding 'Socrates', 'Pegasus', etc., as abbreviations for descriptions, so that all primitive non-log. constants are predicates. I feel somewhat uneasy when entities like Socrates, kindness, & 7 are grouped together as "objects". Frege did so, and it was his undoing. You can, of course, avoid contradictions by suitable restrictions. But the question is whether the contradictions are not symptoms for a fundamental unsoundness. — Here is an important question which you must answer in order to make your conception clearly understandable: What is the nature of questions like: "Are there classes (properties, propositions, real numbers, etc.)?" and of the true answers to them? You call them ontological & even frankly metaphysical. I suppose that this means that you regard them neither as analytic (purely logical) nor as empirical. Are they then synthetic apriori, so that you abandon empiricism? Or what else? More specifically, what is the method of establishing their truth? Supposedly neither purely log. analysis nor the scientific method of confirmation by observation. Perhaps Kant's transcendental analysis or Husserl's "Wesensschau"? Clarification of this point will greatly help further discussion, & indeed be indispensible for it. (I regard those statements as analytic; see "Meaning" pp. 43 f.; but the corresponding metaphys. questions & statements as devoid of cognitive meaning.)

I think your judgments on Wittgenstein (p. 119) are not quite correct. He uses 'name' in a narrower sense. He does not make the confusion you mention; he merely proposes a different language form. This can be arrived at consistently, but causes complications (see my "Syntax" p. 50); Therefore I reject it like you. W's language does not have two diff. synonymous names like 'Cicero'-'Tully' (see his 5.53; for his reasons, see 4.243). But it can still express that Scott is *the* author of Wav. (see 5.5321). See also 4.241; this might seem incompatible with his rejection of '='; but it not, since he does not take 'a = b' as genuine sentence (4.242 & third par. of 4.243).

a. |
b. |
c. |
. |

To p. 119. Does Leibniz actually say "two *terms*"? Not simply "eadem"?

To p. 127. Is "x socratizes" meant as expressing a qualitative property ("x has a long nose, etc.") or a positional pr. ("x is the thing at such and such a space-time-point"). I regard this distinction ("Meaning" pp. 84, 111) as of great log. importance. If you agree, you should explain & discuss it from your point of view.

I regard the customary synonymous use of 'proof' & 'derivation' as very unfortunate, because it (e.g. in Cooley's book, which I use in my courses) makes it so much more difficult for the students to learn the difference between the properly ". . . is provable" & the relation ". . . is derivable from . . .".

I am now putting the finishing touches on the ms. of vol. I of "Probability". I suppose, you have now or will soon get from the U. of C. Press the remainder of vol. I, chiefly the chapter "Estimation". Your remarks (& those of another, unnamed, reader) are very helpful. Did the suggestion to drop 't' come from you? I like to keep it because it simplifies construction of normal forms (also in other systems; comp. "Modalities & Qu." pp. 39 f., 58f.).

I just learned that I shall have the next Autumn Quarter off. Thus we shall be in *Santa Fe (P.O.B. 1214)* from the middle of June till Xmas. I shall then work at the second volume of "Probability", containing the theory of c*. (By the way, do you have suggestions for volume titles? The whole work will be called "Probab. & Induction. But how vol. I (perhaps "General Theory of Probab."?) & vol. II (perhaps "A System of Inductive Logic")?)

If your way leads you again S or W this summer, we would be delighted to see you with us.

With best regards from both of us,

Yours,
Carnap

[MARGINALIA ON QUINE'S COPY:]

e.

f.

g.

h.

a. 1
b. 2

c. 3
d. 4
e. 5
f. 6
g. 7
h. ⟨With line to e. above⟩ Gerhardt, Phil. Schr. von G. W. L.,
   vol 7, Scientia Generalis. Characteristica, XIX. Def. 1
   Eadem sunt quorum unum potest substitui alteri salva
   veritate. Si sint A et B et A ingrediatur aliquam proposi-
   tionem veram, et ibi in aliquo loco ipsius A pro ipso
   substituendo B fiat nova propositione eaque itidem vera,
   idque semper succedat in quancunque tali propositione, A et
   B dicuntur esse Eadem;

[134.   QUINE TO FRED WIECK   1947-4-22]

Emerson Hall
Harvard University
Cambridge 38, Mass.
April 22, 1947

Mr. Fred Wieck, Associate Editor
University of Chicago Press
5750 Ellis Avenue
Chicago 37, Ill.

Dear Mr. Wieck:

I am decidedly in favor of publication of Carnap's volume 1
without waiting for volume 2. The subject is timely, and the
book is needed.

As for a new edition of Carnap's LOGICAL SYNTAX, I
should expect you could sell well over a thousand copies in the
first couple of years. I imagine, moreover, that the author will
want to make some substantial revisions. If so, the sales expectation would be increased; many persons and institutions holding
the old edition would still want the new one.

Sincerely yours,
W. V. Quine

⟨In Fred Wieck's letter (mentioned above in connection with letter 130) *Probability and Induction* was described as the first of two

volumes on probability. On March 10, 1947, Wieck asked Quine
for an opinion on a revised version and on April 4, 1947, in-
quired about the merits of publishing an American edition of
Carnap's *The Logical Syntax of Language*. This (134) is evidently
Quine's reply.)

[135.   QUINE TO CARNAP   1947-5-1]

Emerson Hall
Cambridge 38
May 1, 1947

Dear Carnap,

Thanks very much for MEANING AND NECESSITY. I like
the looks of it, and the additions. I agree that if we are to admit
properties we may as well identify numbers with them as with
classes; and indeed one must if modalities are to be applied to
contexts containing variables whose values are numbers (and
quantified beyond the modal operators).

And many thanks for the careful comments on my SHORT
COURSE IN LOGIC. I shall answer them in order.

1. "I feel somewhat uneasy when entities like Socrates, kindness, and 7 are grouped together as 'objects' . . . ."

By 'object' I mean merely 'entity'. I agree that the logical antinomies are symptoms of a fundamental unsoundness somewhere, but I suspect that this unsoundness lies in platonism
itself—i.e., in the admission of abstract values of bindable variables. The contradictions which issue from platonism can indeed
be staved off by various artificial devices, and in my view the
theory of types is merely one among various such devices.

2. "What is the nature of questions like 'Are there
   classes' . . . analytic . . . synthetic apriori . . ."

As you know, I am not satisfied that a clear general distinction has yet been drawn between analytic and synthetic. I am
even more in the dark on the Kantian distinction between analytic and apriori. This much, nevertheless, I can say: If the statements of the usual higher mathematical logic are analytic, then
so are such platonistic statements as 'There are classes', 'There

are numbers'; for, these statements are not to be distinguished from the theorems '(∃α)(∃χ)(χ∈α)' and '(∃γ)(γ∈NC)' of Principia. [Exception: If foundations for logic should be somehow so devised that these latter formulas and others like them became abbreviations of formulas involving bound variables for concrete objects only (and without resorting to such devices as combinators for escaping variables), then indeed the platonistic content which I have alleged would be lacking.]

a.

That such platonistic statements should be analytic (if true at all) is no more surprising than that the statement that there are infinitely many individuals should be analytic (if true at all). Yet you must hold that this latter statement is analytic (or contradictory), since it contains only logical signs.

Perhaps a typical feature of ontological truths is that they are analytic statements of a kind which would be too trivial to invite assertion or dispute except for doubt or disagreement as to adoption or retention of special features of the language on which their truth depends. And such disagreements are hard to settle simply because the basic features of the language or languages in which the dispute takes place are themselves at stake, depriving the disputants of a fixed medium of discussion.

The thought I have just expressed is vague because of the word "analytic', among other things. Also, I should hesitate to extend the above conjecture to all metaphysics; most metaphysical statements simply mean nothing to me.

Moreover, there are statements which we should commonly call non-metaphysical but which share the described status: analytic (if true), but commonly disputed, and turning on questions of how to frame our language. Typical: '(∃χ)(χ∈χ)', '(∃χ)(y)(y∈χ)'. Maybe these *should* be called metaphysical also; anyway I think the similarity is important. I am not ready to say, though, that when we so fix the basic features of our language as to decide such statements in one way or another our guiding consideration is normally convenience exclusively. In my own predilection for an exclusively concrete ontology there is something which does not reduce in any obvious way to considerations of mere convenience; viz., some vague but seemingly ultimate standard of intelligibility or clarity.

b.

3. I am glad for your correction regarding Wittgenstein. I'll

avoid that example in the final book. I had indeed remembered p. 50 of Syntax, but supposed merely you had trod too lightly on old W.

4. I'm glad also for your questioning the Leibniz passage. My basis had been the translation in Lewis' Survey of S.L., but I've now gone to the original. I see I must drop Lewis' translation and annotate the point a bit in the final book. Leibniz says "*Eadem* sunt quorum unum potest substitui alteri etc., and goes on to say that the substitution takes place in a proposition. If by "propositio" he means a statement, my objection still holds. And in any case his phrasing "Eadem . . . unum . . . alteri" shows he is confusing *same* with *different*; the objects should be *eadem* while the names are *alteri*.

5. Whether 'x socratizes' is qualitative or positional in meaning will depend, for me, on whether 'Socrates' is qualitative or positional in meaning; i.e., whether synonymous with 'the snub-nosed philosopher who drank hemlock' or with 'the thing at such-and-such point'. For everyone nowadays, probably, 'Socrates' is qualitative; but some other examples would for many or most persons be positional. It is a question in each case of empirical semantics, presupposing a behavioristic definition of synonymy. But in any case I intend 'socratizes' to be synonymous with 'is Socrates', whatever the semantics of 'Socrates' may be. (Note that synonymy does not, for me, imply similarity of internal grammatical structure; no part of 'socratizes' need match 'is' alone and no part need match 'Socrates' alone.)

In a language in which all the names of individuals are construed as positional, all the predicates by which I propose to eliminate such names would indeed likewise be positional in meaning.

6. I shall amend my use of 'Proof' as you have urged; I think it is important to do so. But I'd rather say 'deducible' than 'derivable', allowing the latter word a broader significance independent of consequence relations. Thus I should like to speak of deriving an instance from an existential quantification, though the instance cannot be inferred; deriving a statement from a matrix by prefixing quantifiers; deriving a truth-table from a statement; or deriving, from a statement, a schema which depicts its logical form. 'Derive' would mean 'make from', 'construct from'; 'deduce' would mean 'Derive that which is logically implied by'.

Yes, I have since seen the rest of Vol. 1 of Probability. This is a vast opus, and will begin a new era in inductive logic.

The suggestion to drop 't' did come from me. I meant drop it from the object language, keeping the convenient designation in the metalanguage but letting it name the compound equivalent of 't'. I see, though, that it can be convenient in other uses—as in my own "Completeness of the propositional calculus".

I like your titles 'Probab. and Ind.', 'Gen. Thy. of Probab.', and 'A System of Ind. Logic'. I think of no improvements.

Glad to hear you'll be off this summer and fall. I'll be off this summer, but staying here preparing my fall course on Philosophy of Language (and, I hope, working on Short Course in Logic). I wish it were possible to visit you in Santa Fe. I am still very sad about having passed you that time, a couple of years ago, thinking you were in Chicago.

In closing let me try to be the first to pass along to you the most appalling scandal of the year. For a week at the end of this month Korzybski is to lecture at Harvard, in Harvard. The senior common room of Adams House will be his temple. He will put on his regulation 40-hour show.

With best regards to Ina and yourself,

Yours
Van

[(SHORTHAND) MARGINALIA ON CARNAP'S COPY:]

a. Certainly not surprising; I consider them so for analytic!
b. Is this not also a question of "engineering"?

[136. CARNAP TO QUINE   1949-1-23]

RUDOLF CARNAP
Department of Philosophy
University of Chicago
Chicago 37, Illinois   Chicago, Jan. 23, 1949.
Dear Van,

A week ago Nagel, Black, Feigl, Ph. Frank were here (on their way back from a meeting in Madison, Wis.) and we had a nice

discussion together. We all missed you. And I came to realize
how very long we have not seen you and talked to you. And I
remembered with a guilty conscience that we had not even written you when we learned about your marriage; will you belat-
edly accept our warmest wishes? And then you even sent us a
Xmas-card and we, in all our 13 years of life in America, have
never accepted this friendly habit (and I often think that friends
who do not know that this is a general failing may think that
we only neglect them, and then I ask Ina to take it up but she
refuses!).

Ernest Nagel told us the reason for your continued stay in
New Hampshire—it sounds fantastic! We hope that you are
very happy. From my own experience I am a great believer in
second marriages. Ernest also told us that you had a Sabbatical
leave coming and that you will spend it in Mexico. Chicago will
not be on your way going there, but if by any chance you
should be coming back while we are in Santa Fe (end of June to
the end of September), perhaps that is not too much out of the
way. We should love to see you again and to meet your wife. If
ever you do come to Santa Fe, let us know beforehand; it's almost impossible to find us without having detailed directions.
True, we have a telefon in the house, but usually our first act
after arrival there is to have it disconnected since we are on a
party line and our phone rings each time somebody else on the
line is called. This time we want to make sure that we won't
miss each other in Santa Fe!

You may have heard that Hempel was with us in S.F. in August for about three weeks. I also did a good deal on the Probability last summer. The first volume—the manuscript of which is
in the hands of U. of C. Press since last Spring—is not any
nearer publication; the Press has applied for a grant from the
ACLS and does not touch the ms unless and until they get outside money.

My back has not given me any trouble since last June which
we both think a wonderfully long period. Otherwise there are
no news to report. As usual, there are a few bright students
who make teaching enjoyable; but I infinitely more enjoy doing
my own work, particularly when I can do it in ideal surroundings like Santa Fe.

With warnest ⟨*sic*⟩ regards and wishes from us both to the
two of you,

Yours,
Carnap

[137.   CARNAP TO QUINE   1949-7-21]

RUDOLF CARNAP
a. | Department of Philosophy
b. | University of Chicago
   Chicago 37, Illinois   Santa Fe, N.M., July 21, 1949.

Dear Van,

I wonder whether you are still in Mexico and whether on
your way back you might come through here. If so, please write
a few days in advance because we do not pick up our mail every day—then I shall send you a description (to Gen. Delivery,
Santa Fe) how to find us. We do not have a phone, but you
might call up our neighbor (Mrs. Paxton, tel. 0216-R3), if you
should arrive unannounced; she can tell you whether we are at
home (which is the case most of the time), and how to get here.

I have just written the first version of a paper "Empiricism,
Semantics, and Ontology" (which deals with the problem of the
admissibility of abstract entities, especially in semantics.) I discuss here also your nominalistic views together with those of
Nagel and Ryle. I heard that you had recently published a paper
"On What There Is", which presumably deals with the same
problem. If your paper contains anything new in comparison
with your earlier papers, I should like very much to take it into
consideration for my discussion. Could you perhaps send me a
reprint? Or, if they are not yet available, could you send me for
a short time proofs or a copy of the ms. itself? If you are not yet
back at Harvard, I suppose you would now have neither inclination nor time to read my ms. (30 pages) and make some comments on it. But if you have, I should be very glad to sent it to
you, and your remarks (just scribbled on the margin with soft
pencil) would be most welcome. Especially, I should like to hear

whether you think that I did or did not do justice to your position and that of the other nominalists. What I want to avoid above all is, of course, complicating the discussion by misrepresenting your views.

We are again enjoying our life here very much. We should be delighted if you could come. We shall be here until about the 18th of September.

The U. of C. Press has at last begun the printing of my probability book; it is expected to come out by next spring.

We hope that you are having a wonderful time for pleasure and for work. Our best regards to you and your wife,

Yours,
Carnap

[MARGINALIA ON QUINE'S COPY:]

a. Gen'l Del.
b. Ans'd July 27 & sent reprint

[138.   CARNAP TO QUINE 1949-8-15]

Santa Fe, August 15, 1949.
General Delivery

Dear Van,

Was there a telepathic connection which made us think simultaneously of the possibility of meeting? I am so glad that after eight years it will at last be possible. Herewith I am sending you a map which shows the way to our house. You write that you will come "briefly". But don't make it too short, we have to catch up on many things and there is a lot to see around Santa Fe. We would like you two to stay with us, if you are satisfied with a (not very good) double bed in the living room. The hotels and tourist courts in town probably will be overcrowded in the early days of September since just then the fiesta is going on, which we think is much overrated but which attracts large crowds of tourists nevertheless.

Here I am sending you my paper: I don't need it back before you come. You also may give me your comments then orally. I read with great interest your paper "On What There Is". I was very glad to find at the end your plea for "tolerance and experimental spirit". This is exactly the same attitude for which I plead in my paper (and which I expressed almost in the same terms, even before having read yours). Much in your discussion is illuminating: but it seems to me that there is still an underlying basic ambiguity. To formulate it in the terminology of my present paper, there seems to me to be a lack of distinction between two questions: the question of existence *within* a framework and the question of the existence of the framework itself. Well, we shall then discuss these things and many others when you are here. I shall likewise be very much interested in hearing your views and perhaps objections concerning my views on probability and inductive logic.

What you say about the contents of your new book "Foundations of Logic" makes my mouth water. I hope to hear more about it when you come, and I hope that the book will appear soon. This will really be an important achievement.

Would you perhaps like to make a trip to Los Alamos? If so let us know the approximate date of your coming (passes are good for two weeks, I believe), and the exact dates of birth, place of birth, given names, etc. for you and your wife, as they appear in your passports (which you can use for identification). Of course, we shall see only the residential section and not the technical area which is inaccessible to ordinary mortals. This trip could be combined with a side trip to old Indian cave dwellings and such like—perhaps that might interest you too.

Since you cannot predict just when you will arrive by car, it would be good if you phoned our neighbor (Mrs. Paxton, 0216-R3) when you arrive in town: but if it is hard to get her line (it is one of those country lines with a large number of gossippy participants) just strike out for yourself: you should not find it too difficult to find us. We are greatly looking forward to your coming and to making the acquaintance of your wife!

Cordially yours,
Carnap

[QUINE'S NOTES ON THE BACK OF CARNAP'S LETTER:]

When are rules really adopted? Ever? Then what application of your theory to what I am concerned with (language now)?

Why *reserve* "platonism", "ontology", etc. when you deny you are reserving them for any meaning? Why not say "platonistic" (or "realistic") math. & physics? (Plato's full metaphysics irrelevant, say "realistic" if you don't mind the ambiguity) Say frameworkhood is a matter of degree, & reconciliation ensues.

[139.   CARNAP TO QUINE   1949-11-30]

PROF. DR. RUDOLF CARNAP
    Prag XVII.
Pod Homolkou 146

November 30, 1949. | a.

Dear Van:

Do you remember good old "Pod Homolkou"?

I compared your bibliography in the report of the Society of Fellows with my card index in order to see whether the latter was complete. It was. But, not finding "A Unified Calculus . . ." in the bibliography and not noticing that it was merely in abstract, I thought you had forgotten it and I therefore wrote to you to remind you. The use of the preprinted card was merely a joke. Sure, I have a reprint.

Hempel just wrote about the interesting discussion he had with you and the other friends. I should have liked very much to be present (though not until 2 A.M.!)

I have an invitation from Urbana to teach there during their Spring semester. Since the teaching load is very little and the pay very good, and we have a chance for the sublease of an apartment, I probably shall be there from February 12th on until the beginning of June.

I always meant to ask you—but there was no time for it in Santa Fe—what you think of Haskell and his work. On the one hand he seems to be very intelligent, on the other hand, the results of which he is so proud that he thinks they will shake the world, are so extremely obvious and simple, that it made us wonder how come he does not see it too.

Our best to you and Marge from both of us,

Yours,
Carnap

[MARGINALIA ON QUINE'S COPY:]

a. Ans'd Jan. 2

[140.   QUINE TO CARNAP   1950-1-3]

January 3, 1950

Professor Rudolf Carnap
Department of Philosophy
University of Chicago
Chicago, Illinois

Dear Carnap:

I remember Pod Homolkou well. You had a nice brick house, and across the road there were clear slopes where you used to ski.

When Ed Haskell was in college he was very much a rebel. He had an independent mind, and a good one; but his independence, coupled with a conviction of his own intellectual importance, stood in the way of his accomplishing the full drudgery of technical science. With the passing of time he has kept his enthusiasms without growing as a technical scientist. He doesn't know what it is like to devise, or master, a serious mathematical theory; and consequently, impressed as he nevertheless is with the role of such theory in modern science, he has exaggerated notions of the possible efficacy of little theoretical devices of his own which are simple minded to you and me.

As an observer Ed is keen, thoughtful, and imaginative. He is at his best when he is closest to fact. I wish he would devote himself to the concrete, and even to poetry, where he has shown ability. But his determination to create an epoch-making theory, or to believe that he has created one, is bound up with his persistent need to think of himself as achieving what he himself deems most important.

We had a jolly time at the Worcester meeting. I thought the morning session in logic the most stimulating one in my experience.

I was shocked to hear, I think from Peter, that you had further trouble with your back. I hope this has passed.

Best wishes to you and Ina for a good final year of the half century (for that, you know, is what this year really is), and for a pleasant term at Urbana.

Yours,

[141. CARNAP TO QUINE   1950-2-?]

Rudolf Carnap
Faculty Exchange
University of Chicago
Chicago 37, Illinois   February 1950

My address will be as follows:
From February 12 to June 9:
    208 W. High Street, Urbana, Illinois
From June 10 to September 25:
    P.O. Box 1401, Santa Fe, New Mexico
From September 26:
    Chicago, as above.

[142. QUINE TO CARNAP   1950-2-10]

WILLARD VAN ORMAN QUINE

Professor of Philosophy   Emerson Hall
Harvard University   Cambridge 38, Massachusetts
                                             Feb. 10, 1950

Dear Carnap,

Harvard is unable to help Bar-Hillel for the same reason as Chicago: because he is a Ph.D. Hence I am working on Rockefel-

ler Foundation for him. It would be a great help if you would
write there in his behalf, addressing your letter to Dr.
Chadbourne Gilpatric, Rockefeller Fdtn., 49 W. 49 St., N.Y.C.
Thanks very much for recommending me for the Fulbright.
Best wishes for a pleasant time in Urbana.

> Yours cordially,
> Van

[143. CARNAP TO QUINE 1950-11-26]

RUDOLF CARNAP
Department of Philosophy
University of Chicago
Chicago 37, Illinois   Nov. 26, 1950

Dear Van:

Thank you for your letter of September 16th. Yes, I too would
call yours a vigorous program of travel! Did you and Marge enjoy it? Our travel days are over, I think, at least as long as my
back behaves so unpredictably.

Of course, I have taken up immediately with the department
the matter of your availability for the spring as a visiting professor. There was great interest for it, but after long soul searching
on the part of the administration, the final answer was negative
because they have no more funds available in this budget year
(just as it seems that Harvard has not enough free funds to
have you and Goodman simultaneously, odd though it seems;
by the way, how come the invitation of Goodman was not postponed for another year when you or someone else would be off
for a Sabbatical or so? Or was his substitute already engaged
and he would have been unemployed in that case??). We all
were very sorry about it; since I am off in the spring quarter,
they would have had good use for a logician! I had an inquiry
from Reichenbach whether I would wish to be invited there for
the spring semester as a visiting professor. I turned it down, but
wrote him about your availability. But perhaps you have heard
from him directly about the matter. I share your feelings about

the Fulbright terms; to have to teach at Oxford instead of at Harvard should not require a heavy financial sacrifice, and it would seem far more tempting and worthwhile to spend the time writing if you could not find a visiting professorship for the time. I feel that it is Oxford's loss not yours, though, because they definitely would have profited more from your presence than you from being there. In general, I am inclined to think writing more important than teaching for people who have ideas to write about! If I should hear about another opening, I shall write there immediately on your behalf.

Thank you for having sent to me your *Methods of Logic* which I have read with great interest. Especially the development of new methods of deduction, useful for finding a way to an intended conclusion, seems to me very valuable. Our exchange of terminological positions is really funny. Let's try to come to an agreement one way or the other, and then apply that in the future. Your argument against "matrix" is a good one; for the same reason I did not feel quite happy in adopting the term. But no other term seems quite satisfactory. The term "statement form" (Cooley, following you I believe) is in conflict with occasional phrases like "the form of this statement". I should like to take "sentence" and "statement" as synonymous. Therefore I should not like to use the term "open sentence" with respect to those systems which admit only closed statements. Which other term might come into consideration?

a.

Your suggestion to identify a state description with the class of its (positive) atomic sentences would be in conflict with my other uses of terms referring to classes of sentences, e.g. "true", "L-implication", etc.

I am, of course, looking forward with great interest to your article "Two dogmas of empiricism".

I have written (last summer) an article "The continuum of inductive methods". It explains the λ-system (as indicated in the preface of the probability book). It has just been typed and is much longer than I thought: 140 typed pages, ca. 38.000 words. Do you have any idea where such a long thing might be published? An additional difficulty is that I want to use this material, though in a somewhat changed form, in the second volume. Therefore, a publisher would probably not like to bring it as a separate little book. Professor Starck wrote to me that the Proceedings of the Academy would require a considerable subsidy.

Enclosed three films, reminiscences of your fleeting stay in Santa Fe; don't return.

Our best to you and Marge,

> Cordially yours,
> Carnap

P.S. The Graduate Philosophy Club at Yale (c/o Mr. Abner Shimony⟨,⟩ 2707 Yale Station, New Haven, Conn.) has reprinted my "Testability and Meaning" which was unavailable otherwise for a long time. If some of your students might want it, it could be ordered from him, at $1.— a copy if 10 copies are taken at one time, I understand (or presumably a little higher if less than 10 are ordered).

The following parts of the prob. book were written later:
Ch. VIII & IX in 1946 (They were probably in the ms which you read)

§§41 & 42 in 1947.

[MARGINALIA ON QUINE'S COPY:]

a. clause

[144. QUINE TO CARNAP 1950-12-1]

December 1, 1950

Dear Carnap:

Many thanks for your good letter and for your very kind efforts to help me out for next spring. I hasten to tell you that the matter is now settled; the Harvard administration has generously put me back on the spring program *with* Goodman.

Now some further historical clarification. It was already after July first, with our budget settled and Goodman obtained, that the actual documents of my Fulbright award arrived (though we had previously learned by 'phone that the award had been granted). Only on getting the documents did I learn that the terms of the award were inferior to the original assurances. When I finally decided to reject the Fulbright, I was still very anxious to keep Goodman from feeling he should withdraw; for I was particularly glad he was to be here, and didn't want the event to be postponed and perhaps lost altogether. My own lot really was not desperate; I could have coasted through the spring getting some writing done, and then recovered part of my financial loss by teaching in the Harvard Summer School. But it was a good free time for me to take a visiting professorship somewhere.

The offer did come through from Reichenbach, and I declined it in much the same terms that you did. Both of us have now helped them, possibly, in their struggle with their Regents.

It is good that we are staying on in Cambridge at this particular time, and that I am back on the payroll for the full year, for Marge is expecting a baby in a few weeks, and we are now in the midst of buying a house.

Now to 'open sentence'. I thought this a rather ingenious way of making use of the fact that the word 'sentence' is central to your vocabulary and 'statement' to mine; for, by coincidence, you have in the past often allowed your "sentences" to be open or closed, while I have always reserved 'statements' to closed cases. It seemed to me that in calling matrices "open sentences," and statements "closed sentences" (and "statements" for short), I had effected a neat reconciliation of our terminology, at the same time as getting rid of 'matrix'. (We can still, for literary continuity, *recognize* 'matrix' as short for 'open sentence', but just let it fall into disuse.) Is it really so desirable to take 'sentence' and 'statement' as synonymous? This means wasting one of two 'good' words, and I think your past usage and mine would fit in with my suggested distinction fully as well as it would with the synonymy.

I'd be glad if you could be persuaded to the above. But if not, another thought occurs to me: 'open clause' and 'closed clause', closed clauses also being called statements.

Tarski wisely remarked long ago that it is well to let a general term include its degenerate cases (thus including lines among curves, and circles among ellipses). Under this maxim, 'open clause' (or 'open sentence') is better than a single word like 'matrix'; for, the basic term 'clause' (or 'sentence') then comes, unlike 'matrix', to include the case of 0 free variables.

A big advantage of 'sentence' over 'clause', if your feeling in favor of synonymizing 'sentence' with 'statement' is not too strong, is that it would minimize future novelty of terminology in a matter where the terminology has already been vexatious. Why not simply treat some systems as having valid sentences (open and closed) as theorems while other systems have just true sentences (hence closed sentences, hence true statements) as theorems? This fits well with your past terminology, and still it enables us to speak of open sentences (for *all* languages).

For "The Continuum of Inductive Methods" my first thought also would have been the American Academy. But I hadn't known about the subsidy requirement. I have now checked with Starck, who assures me that it is the rule.

Certainly there is an obstacle to publishing it as a book, in the fact that you will need the material again in the second volume on probability. I wonder if it would be suitable for Trans. Amer. Math. Soc., in two installments? They publish rather long articles. Or how about Herrmann in Paris? Or E. W. Beth's series of monographs?

Thanks very much for the negatives; we are delighted to have them.

Our best regards to Ina and yourself.

Cordially,

Professor Rudolf Carnap
Department of Philosophy, University of Chicago
Chicago 37, Illinois

[145. QUINE TO CARNAP   1951-3-29]

Emerson Hall
Harvard University
Cambridge 38, Massachusetts
March 29, 1951

Dear Carnap:

Enclosed is my publication version of the paper which I read at Chicago. I have done virtually nothing to it except (a) lop off the part which duplicated parts of "Two dogmas of empiricism," (b) append a few concluding paragraphs in place of the dropped material, and (c) make small readjustments with a view to print as distinct from talk.

The main illumination for me, in our joint performance at Chicago, was that your "analytic-in-L_0", and "analytic-in-L_1," etc., which I have represented as mutually irrelevant and irrelevant to "analytic-in-L" (for variable 'L'), do have a principle of unification precisely in the sameness of the explicandum. The issue therefore becomes: is it a reasonable explicandum?

The reason I haven't revised my paper to cover the above important point is that this point comes in answer precisely to the part of my talk which duplicated "Two dogmas of empiricism" and is hence deleted. My proposal is that in your paper, conceived as an answer both to my enclosed *and* to "Two dogmas," *you* impart the context of the preceding paragraph above.

Another point I learned in the seminar at Chicago was your attitude toward the difficulties I represent in your notion of "internal" vs. "external." But I think this matter can be covered equally effectively in your printed reply, and that it will be useful for the public for you to present it in that manner, without my withdrawing any of my remarks in advance.

But I may have forgotten some point which could be accommodated better by a change in my paper. If so, please let me know (returning my paper, of which I have no complete carbon, having sent you the carbon of the first draft before going to Chicago). If on the other hand you think the enclosed is right for Feigl and Sellars, then please just sent it on to them along with your own paper.

I enjoyed my short time in Chicago, especially the time, all too short, with you and Ina. I forgot to mention two things: our delight over Ina's very successful snapshots, and the fact that I have assigned the reprint edition of *Testability and Meaning* (as well as part of *Meaning and Necessity*) in my course on the Philosophy of Language.

Douglas is healthy and very crescent. Marge and I envy you your present habitat. Warm regards to you and Ina from us both.

Yours,

[QUINE ON ANALYTICITY]
Rudolf Carnap

a.

3.2.52 ⟨February 3, 1952⟩

IT MUST be emphasized that the concept of analyticity has an exact definition only in the case of a language system, namely a system of semantical rules, not in the case of an ordinary language, because in the latter the words have no clearly defined meaning. Quine advocates the thesis that the difficulty lies in the concept of analyticity itself, not in the ambiguity of the words of ordinary language. He says: "I do ⟨not know whether the statement 'Everything green is extended' is analytic. Now does my indecision over this example really betray an incomplete understanding, and incomplete grasp of the "meanings", of 'green' and 'extended'? I think not. The trouble is not with 'green' or 'extended', but with⟩ 'analytic'."[X] It seems completely clear to me, however, that the

⟨This is a transcription and translation of item [102-62-04] in the Rudolf Carnap Collection at the University of Pittsburgh. The manuscript is in German shorthand and was transcribed in German by Richard Nollan and translated into English by Richard Creath. Because the paper was not prepared for publication, the quotations and references were left incomplete. For ease of reading, however, the ellipses have been filled, and this has been indicated in the text by enclosing the added material within angle brackets: ⟨ ⟩. Small additions to the text to make the translation smoother are also enclosed in angle brackets.⟩

[X] W. V. Quine, "Two Dogmas ⟨of Empiricism)," ⟨Philosophical Review 60 (January 1951)⟩, p. 31

difficulty here lies in the unclarity of the word 'green', namely in an indecision over whether one should use the word for something unextended, i.e., for a single space-time point. In daily life it is never so used, and one scarcely ever speaks of space-time points. For that reason this special unclarity plays as small a role as the unclarity over whether the term 'mouse' should also be used for animals which, apart from their greenness, are completely similar to the mice we know, but are as large as cats. Because there are no such animals, one ordinarily never considers the question of whether one would use the term for them or not. That, however, means an unclarity in the meaning of the term. This unclarity of 'green' in ordinary language is not important.

Naturally, in laying down a language system, however, it cannot be tolerated. If one takes space-time regions as individuals of the system (so that each individual corresponds to a non-empty class of space-time points), we want to leave it open here whether every such class corresponds to an individual or whether further limiting conditions will be made perhaps with respect to connection and continuity. That is a matter of postulation. Which postulates will be chosen is a matter of indifference for the present discussion. Suppose someone introduces 'G' as a one-place predicate of individuals and declares that it shall have the same meaning as the word 'green' in customary usage. We cannot be satisfied with that; he must make more exact postulates. Here we want the postulate about the boundary of 'G' in the color system set aside, because it is irrelevant for the present discussion. We ask the person laying down the language system what his intention is with respect to the application of 'G' to single space-time points. Suppose we use the predicate 'E' in the sense of 'extended', and indeed the more exact sense of 'comprising more than one space-time point' (or even the still much stronger sense of 'containing at least a two-dimensional continuous region of positive area'). (It may be noted, by the way, that 'E' is not a descriptive predicate, but rather a logical one; it denotes not a qualitative but a positional property; see Meaning & Nec⟨essity (Chicago: University of Chicago Press, 1947)⟩; but that need not trouble us here.) Also suppose that the architect of the language system tells us that 'G' is not applicable to single space-time points because he takes the

statement '(x)(Gx ⊃ Ex)' as true, from which '(x)(Ux ⊃ ~Gx)' follows, where 'U' stands for 'unextended' in the sense of 'region
consisting of a single space-time point' (perhaps defined as 'region
of which no other region is a part'), but that does not satisfy us. We
require that he decide whether the latter formula is meant in the
same sense as say 'all mice are non-green'. In other words, he might
so intend 'G' that the discovery of a U-individual (i.e., of a space-
time point) that is G is conceivable but unexpected, because he
believes that that will not occur. That occurrence would be per-
ceived as surprising. ⟨Alternatively, he might decide⟩ that this case
is thereby impossible. That is, he might so intend 'G' that it may not
be applied to a space-time point. He can reach his conclusion by one
or the other method; he is free to choose. (The question of which of
the two conclusions with respect to 'G' more usually gives the meaning of a predicate of the ordinary word 'green' is an empirico-
linguistic question which is not relevant for the present discussion;
it seems to me that I myself connect the word 'green' with a meaning which excludes its application to a single point; but that may
vary with other people.) In any case, one thing is clear: so long as he
has made no decision on this, he has still not given 'G' a completely
clear meaning. As soon as he makes a decision, however, Quine's
question is unequivocally answered. If he takes the second option,
then '(x)(Gx ⊃ ~ Gx)' is analytic; an obvious form of stipulating this
decision via a rule consists precisely in laying down that sentence as
a postulate. And thereby the sentence '(x)(Gx ⊃ Ex)' is also analytic.
That is the sentence discussed by Quine, or rather the sentence of
the language system which is one of the ordinary translations of the
sentence that Quine is talking about from ordinary language. Because of the ambiguity of this later sentence, one cannot even raise
the question of whether it is analytic.

In connection with the question under discussion Quine ad-
vances the following argument in order to show that the problem
of analyticity cannot be resolved by ⟨an appeal to⟩ the semantical
rules of an artificial language system (op. cit., p. 32). Suppose the
semantical rules of a language system Lo determine a certain class
of sentences as analytic in Lo. Now Quine distinguishes two cases
with respect to the question of how these rules are to be understood. (1) They may be meant as assertions or as information that
such and such sentences are analytic in Lo. That, however, helps

us not at all, Quine says, because we do not understand the word 'analytic'. (2) The rules are meant merely as a convention, as a definition of a new, presumably not previously understood expression 'analytic in Lo'. In this case, so he says, it would be better, less misleading, to take not an expression already in current use, but rather a new symbol, perhaps 'K', "so as not to seem to throw light on the interesting word 'analytic'." Our rules are meant neither in the first nor in the second sense, neither as an assertion nor as a mere nominal definition, which serves as an abbreviation. Their purpose is, rather, the explication of an inexact concept already in current use. The rules denote a certain class (or, as I would prefer to say, a property) of sentences in Lo. This definition, however, is not arbitrary; we advance the claim that the defined concept embraces what philosophers have meant, intuitively but not exactly, when they speak of "analytic sentences" or, more specifically, of "sentences whose truth depends on their meanings alone and is thus independent of the contingency of facts".

Quine's discussion at this point is somewhat obscure, since it is not clear whether he is asking about the elucidation explicandum, "analytic," or about an explicatum. If he means the latter, then it is given in the rules of a semantical system. (For a system with independent primitive predicates ⟨it is given⟩ by the rules which I treated in earlier publications as L-true; for systems with dependencies between the primitive predicates ⟨it is given⟩ by meaning postulates, as explained in another paper.) That at least some of these rules must be set up for each separate language system is surely obvious; that holds for every semantical and syntactic concept. In case Quine's remarks are meant as a demand to be given one definition applicable to all systems, then such a demand is manifestly unreasonable; it is certainly neither fulfilled nor fulfillable for semantic and syntactic concepts, as Quine knows.[x] I conjecture that Quine means the first, an elucidation of the explicandum "analytic". Naturally, such an elucidation can be rendered only in terms that are themselves not yet exact.[xx] In this case

[x]This is clearly emphasized by Richard Martin in ⟨"On 'Analytic'," *Philosophical Studies* 3 (1952): 42–47⟩.
[xx]Compare (Prob.) 2 "On the clarification of an explicandum". ⟨Rudolf Carnap, "On the Clarification of an Explication," § 2 of *Logical Foundation of Probability* (Chicago: University of Chicago Press, 1950), pp. 3–5.⟩

the answer to Quine's question is provided by the formulation at the end of the previous paragraph, by our earlier distinction between a surprising, unexpected case and a case impossible on grounds of meaning, and by various examples, including those through which Quine himself illustrated the problem (whose legitimacy, to be sure, he suspects).

Later Quine says: "Semantical rules ⟨determining the analytic statements of an artificial language are of interest only insofar as we already understand the notion of analyticity; they are of no help in gaining this⟩ understanding" (op. cit., p. 34). This is the same obscurity again. The answer is the same too: we have an understanding of the notion of analyticity, in practice clear enough for application in many cases, but not exact enough for other cases or for theoretical purposes. The semantical rules give us an exact concept; we accept it as an explicatum if we find by comparison with the explicandum that it is sufficiently in accord with this. It seems to me that this demand is fulfilled for the two concepts under consideration here with respect to the simple, limited language systems treated thus far: (1) for the concept of L-truth as an explication for logical truth in the narrower sense, (2) for the concept, based on meaning postulates, of L-truths as an explicatum for analyticity, truth in virtue of meaning (in the broader sense).

Quine has emphasized that in revising the total system of science no statement and no rule is immune or sacrosanct. Empirical laws in terms of the observation language we revise readily; we revise the principles of theoretical physics with greater hesitation; still more seldom and hesitantly do we make changes in logic and mathematics. But under some circumstances they will be made or suggested or at least brought up for consideration. Thus far I agree with Quine. One can consider replacing the usual form of logic by an intuitionistic one or a three-valued one or whatever. However, I cannot agree with Quine when he concludes about this that there is no sharp boundary between physics and logic. In my view it is not a feature of the explicandum "analyticity" that these statements are sacrosanct, that they never should nor can be revoked in the revision of science. The difference between analytic and synthetic is a difference internal to two kinds of statements inside a given language structure; it has nothing to do with the transition from one language to another. "Analytic" means rather much the same as true in virtue of meaning. Since in changing the logical structure of language everything can be changed, even the meaning assigned to the '.' sign, naturally the same sentence (i.e., the same sequence of words or symbols) can be analytic in one system and synthetic in another, which replaces the first at some time. Since the truth of an analytic sentence depends on the meaning, and is determined by the language rules and not the observed facts, then an analytic sentence is indeed "unrevisable" in another sense: it remains true and analytic as long as the language rules are not changed. The attribution of truth values to synthetic sentences changes continually, induced by new observations, even during a period in which the logical structure of language remains unchanged. A revision of this sort is not possible for the analytic sentences.

It follows from this clarification that the analytic-synthetic distinction can be drawn always and only with respect to a language system, i.e., a language organized according to explicitly formulated rules, not with respect to a historically given natural language. The language of science lies between the two. Often, certain definitions, rules, and basic assumptions ("axiomatic method") will explicitly be made for it; but perhaps even today there remain ⟨many rules that are⟩ implicit, or so to speak based on the tacit agreement of the people who work in a specific discipline. Explication for "analytic" as for all other concepts of logical analysis can be given exactly, of course, only for a system of rules, thus with respect to the language of science only to the extent and with the degree of exactitude which corresponds to the current degree of explicitness of the rules of the language. (Today in the practice of the most exact discipline of empirical science, namely physics, this degree ⟨of explicitness⟩ is still very small; but of course its development is very recent. There is no doubt that scientists even in the immediate future and especially in the exact disciplines will standardize and codify more and more of the rules of the logical structure of language that today are implicitly presupposed.)

Marginal note:

a. (Perhaps as a separate paper.)

RUDOLF CARNAP
Department of Philosophy
University of Chicago
Chicago 37, Illinois   19 June 1952

Dear Van, | a.

We are at the point of leaving. This summer we shall be in
the East; we should be delighted if you came to see us in West
Dover, Vt. near Wilmington. (House of v. Laue).

Congratulations to the invitation to Berkeley? Did you accept?
When will you go to Oxford?

Many thanks for "Methods of Logic" (very valuable with the
interesting new methods), the new edition of "Math. Logic" (I
am very glad to have it with the modifications all nicely worked
out), & several reprints (most interesting, as always). Frank
plans to have you at the Oct. meeting in N.Y., but some private
talks would be much better still. Best greetings to you & Marge
from both of us,

Yours,
Carnap

[MARGINALIA ON QUINE'S COPY:]

a. Ans'd June 21

[147.   INA CARNAP TO QUINE AND MARJORIE Q.
1952-8-25]

Rudolf Carnap
West Dover, Vt.   August 25, 1952

Dear Van and Marge:

High time to write to you if this is still to reach you in Mexico. Hope you are having a very good time there! How we envy

you the (presumably) dry climate; here we are shivering and actually are heating the house practically all day! We do hope, you will be able to see us here on your way back. The immediate cause for this letter is to give you directions on how to find us.

In Wilmington turn north onto Route 8 under the traffic light; go 2.3 miles until you come to a side road on the left, Coldbrook Road (on Route 8 there is a sign shortly before which says "pavement ends"); follow that dirt road for 3.7 miles, keeping to the right when in doubt, i.e. follow the brook and the valley (you will pass by the Goodman house which you may know), until you come to a dark red house behind two maples on your left. Another dark red house just a little beyond on the right is not it. For possible inquiries: our house belongs to Prof. von Laue. We also have a phone: Wilmington 196, ring 13—but I hear it only when I am in the kitchen.

A few days ago we received a big batch of mail from Santa Fe which they had failed to forward since June. Among it various communications from Marcus Dick, trying to get in touch with us. Since he gave no future addresses, we are unable to clear up the muddle.

The Goodmans expect to be back here around Sept. 2; Stevenson arrived a few days ago—haven't seen him yet. They have a new house and he is building cupboards etc., cannot yet waste time on philosophy. Perhaps they all could come together here when you come.

Unfortunately, Carnap's back is not good—he has been in bed for the past five weeks, and the great dampness and cold are not conducive for the improvement.

For a couple with a small baby you are most enterprising! I am willing to bet that this is Marge's doing who is firmly decided that her having a baby should not mean any interference with the kind of life you like. Correct??

So you are staying at Harvard! This is what I had expected, whereas Carnap was inclined to think you would go to Berkeley! We are looking forward to your coming with great pleasure!

Yours,
ina

[434]

Looking forward to seeing you both soon,

Cordially, Carnap

[148. CARNAP TO QUINE 1954-7-15]

July 15, 1954. | a. | b.

Dear Van:

I have read your essay for the Schilpp volume with very great
interest, and I am now thinking about my reply. Because of the
importance of your discussion, I plan to reply in greater detail | c.
than to most of the others. Now there is a point where I should
like some clarification of what you mean so that my reply can be
more specific. It might even be advisable to insert remarks into
the manuscript at some places; but this is of course for you to
decide. The question is, which of your discussions are meant to
refer to (a) natural languages, and which to (b) codified languages (i.e., language systems based on explicitly formulated
rules). I should like to have these clarifications especially for sections VIII–X, because my REPLY will chiefly concern sections.
The distinction is of great importance for my discussion, because from my point of view the problems of analyticity in the
two cases are quite different in their character (see "Meaning
Postulates" p. 66). At the beginning of section VIII I assumed
that you meant (b), because my semantical discussions applied
to (b), except for occasional informal examples. But then I was
startled by your reference to "analogy with . . . artificial languages". You do not say analogy of what. But the only plausible
interpretation seems that you meant "analogy of natural languages". Therefore my guess is now that on p. 32 you had (a)
in mind. Here an insertion would seem desirable for the reader.
Similarly on p. 35 in connection with truth and the logical vocabulary with technical notation. At both points you probably
mean (b); if you should mean (a) for truth, could you give me a
reference for an author you have in mind who has given a definition of truth for (a)? P. 36 seems puzzling; you have given a
definition of "logical truth" only for (b), but then you suddenly
refer to White whose discussion deals only with (a). On pp. 37

[435]

and 38 clarification is desirable, especially for the assertion of p.
38, l. 4–6. I guess that here you mean mostly (a) but then your
remarks on my conception are not quite clear because this conception concerns chiefly (b). Further, the second paragraph on
p. 38 ("logical truth . . . definable . . . ") could only be meant
for (b)? On p. 39, in the last sentence, the standards are presumably meant as standards for the choice of rules in constructing a
system (b); on the other hand, the clause "if there were one"
seems to suggest that the rules are meant to be already given.
Since section X is a discussion of my paper "Meaning Postulates", which is explicitly restricted to (b) (p.66), I presume that
your discussion is also meant in this way. However, in some
places this seems doubtful and in a few places it seems more
probable that you meant (a). Thus, for section X, it would be
especially desirable to indicate at each place which of the two
cases you have in mind.

A minor point. Your footnote 18 refers to "p. 32n". There are
two footnotes on p. 32. And from the context I guess that you
mean none of them but something like "pp. 31f.". However,
since this paper has been repeatedly reprinted with different
pagination, it might be best to write instead "§3". Similarly in
your footnote 19: "§2" or "§2, fifth paragraph".

I am just reading your "From a logical . . ." with great interest. My new version of the "Abriss" has appeared and will be
sent you.

You know of course that I have accepted UCLA—we will go
there about Sept. 1. Will we see you before we go away so far?
Hope, you had a good and fruitful time in Europe! Our best to
all of you,

Carnap

⟨This appears in Carnap's hand on Quine's copy in the margin of the letter's first page:⟩ There's no hurry with your answer. I shall be working on the Reply for months still.

[MARGINALIA ON QUINE'S COPY:]

a. Ans'd 9 Aug. Copy lost by stenog.

[MARGINALIA (IN SHORTHAND) ON CARNAP'S COPY:]

a. (to Oxford and Harvard)
b. *No rush* with your answer. I shall work for months yet on the Reply.

[149.   QUINE TO CARNAP   1954-8-9]

8 Logic Lane,
Oxford.
August 9th, 1954.

Professor Rudolf Carnap,
Institute for Advanced Study,
Princeton,
N.J.,
U.S.A.

Dear Carnap,

We lately returned from several good weeks in Germany and Austria. In Münster I finally met Scholz, as well as Hermes and Hasenjaeger. Despite the torrential rains it was a pleasant occasion. Then we flew to Berlin for four stimulating and exciting days. Finally the Rheingau, Rothenburg, and some walking in the Lechtaler and Oetztaler Alps. I remember that the Oetztal is an old haunt of yours. On returning, I found your letter of 15 July.

You ask whether I mean "(a) natural languages" or "(b) codified languages . . . based on explicitly formulated rules." Now here I suppose you mean codified languages to carry explicit 'semantical rules" with them—i.e., outright specification of the so-called analytic sentences. If so, then (b) is not what I am talking about, as stressed in "two dogmas" (foot p. 35 and top p. 36, in *From a Logical Point of View*). But I do not mean to limit myself to (a) either. It is indifferent to my purpose whether the notation be traditional or artificial, so long as the artificiality is

a. not made to exceed the scope of "language" ordinarily so-called, and beg the analyticity question itself.

If you intend (b) to include thus a packaged formulation of analyticity, then your dichotomy into (a) and (b) is a false dichotomy, acceptance of which would precisely omit my point. The languages I am talking about comprise natural languages and any (used, or interpreted) artificial notations you like, e.g. that of my *Mathematical Logic* plus extra-logical predicates. They are not uninterpreted notations. Each predicate has its unique extension, and correspondingly for the logical signs (except in so far as extensions may fail to exist because of gaps in the universe of classes, as needed to avoid paradox). But they are not of kind (b) if, as I suspect, "languages" of kind (b) are conceived as embodying a complement of transformation rules—a ready-made stipulation of a boundary between analytic and synthetic.

In view of "Two dogmas" and our years of discussion, I think the above brief remark will suffice to convey my meaning. In my essay for Schilpp, I have of course been reluctant to repeat much of "Two dogmas"; but I have cited it.

In connection with p. 35 you ask for "a reference for an author . . . who has given a definition of truth for (a)." This puzzles me. I assume the notion of truth *without* definition, and in a footnote I cite *From a Logical Point of View*, pp. 137f., in defense of such a course. But let me repeat that I am not talking only of (a); see above.

You say in connection with p. 36 that I have (previously) "given a definition of 'logical truth' only for (b)." On p. 35 I have myself stressed the limitations of my treatment of logical truth. But it would be mistaken to view the matter as limited to (b) if you mean (b) in the manner queried earlier in this letter.

Your query regarding the last sentence of p. 39 is answered by the early part of this letter; "if there were one" relates to there being an artificial universal notation for saying everything we care to say in science, but it does *not* relate to there being an assumed set of rules of analyticity. See particularly p. 34, last 5 lines.

The point on p. 66 of "Meaning postulates" to which you refer several times is taken up in p. 40 of my paper, and more at length in the part of "Two dogmas" cited above (though this antedated "Meaning postulates"), as well as in our past discussions. I had thought we finally achieved successful communication on this point, when last we talked (so long ago, alas) in Santa Fe and Chicago.

My footnote 18, which you query, seems to me to be in order. It is intended to refer to the second footnote of p. 32 of your "Empiricism, semantics, and ontology." Specifically, what I had in mind was lines 4–9 of that second footnote. The brief reference "p. 32n" was deliberate, despite there being two footnotes on p. 32; in general what the bibliographical suffix "n" means to me is "among the footnotes of." In the present instance the other footnote on p. 32, a bibliographical reference to Feigl, would of course not be taken as the intended one.

Linsky's reprint of "Empiricism, semantics, and ontology" preserves the original pagination. But I see from your letter that there are other reprints of it which do not. So, following your suggestion, I am changing my references, in my footnotes 18 and 19, to read respectively "§3, longest footnote" and "§2, fifth paragraph."

I have had only a look at the new and much enlarged version of the *Abriss,* in the bookstore. I am very glad it is being sent to me. Many thanks.

b.

I was delighted to hear the good news that you are going to U.C.L.A. It is a very favored corner of the world, and relatively handy to Santa Fe; and perhaps you will now change Santa Fe for something further west. I do hope your health is well recovered again and that your years in L.A. will be happy ones.

My daughter Elizabeth is now married (Mrs. Charles O'Brien) and living in Los Angeles. My daughter Norma may be entering U.C.L.A. this fall. Marge and I now have, besides our three-year-old Douglas, and Oxford-born daughter, Margaret.

We do not sail till 8 September, so there is no saying when and where we shall be able to see you next.

Marge joins me in warm greetings to Ina and yourself.

Yours
Van
W. V. Quine

[MARGINALIA (IN SHORTHAND) ON CARNAP'S COPY:]

a. (That is, of course, trivial)
b. Thus, not yet received. (This is a free copy from me; to Harvard)

[150.   CARNAP TO QUINE   1955-9-22]

UNIVERSITY OF CALIFORNIA

Los Angeles 24, California   Sept. 22, 1955.

Dear Van:

   I do not even find a carbon of a letter to you during the past years. Whether we have been so remiss in writing or in filing is unclear. In any case, we have not had a good talk for a long time. What a pity that you were not in the East when we were there, and now we are far away again. However, you two are the great travellers and a trip to the West coast should not be out of the question. Are we just dreaming or is it correct that you have a second child now? One really gets out of touch far too much with one's friends!

   A few weeks ago we refound an old friend, Arne Naess, whom we had known long ago, but especially enjoyed this time when he was here for a few weeks with his newly married wife. We liked them both so much and felt again what a pity it is that friends live so far apart and meet only for such brief times; in this respect, the world is still too large. Arne is here on a Fulbright grant, and is now slowly on the way East and then back to Norway. He is going to give some lectures before returning, offhand I remember Cincinnati, Chicago, Michigan. I offered to ask you whether it would be possible for you to arrange a lecture for him at Harvard, not only would he very much like to do it, but it would also look good on his Fulbright report if he had been asked from such an important place. Of course, a paid lecture is always welcome, but I know that he would already be happy to speak in a seminar or before the Philosophy Club, if there is such a group. The lectures he gives at the other places deal with Gandhian political ethics as a normative system, and

with the role of wmperical ⟨*sic*⟩ research in solving problems of
so-called logical analysis (this, I believe, is a presentation of the
material in his latest book, *Interpretation and Preciseness*, to which
I referred in Note (6) to my paper "Meaning and Synonymy in
Natural Languages" of which I sent you a copy). If you find it
possible to arrange something for him (between Oct. 20 and
Nov. 15), the best would be to communicate with him directly:
c/o Dept. of Philos., Univ. of Cincinnati, Campus Station, Cincinnati, Ohio.

Although Arne Naess was the immediate cause for my writing to you today, it was not the sole reason: I regret that we
have now so little contact, and I know that it is largely my own
fault, since the two of you were much better in writing occasionally and also sending fotos.

We are glad that we took the plunge and transferred from Chicago to here. The department is here more congenial to my work
(due to Reichenbach's influence over the years, no doubt), and the
landscape is, of course, incomparably more attractive to Chicago.
We live in a tiny rented house with a patio for the dog—all our
Chicago belongings are still in storage.

With best regards and wishes for you and Marge, Cordially,

Carnap

P.S. I saw very little of Morton White in Princeton. These were
two somewhat difficult years for me, and I did not look eagerly
for new contacts. Now I am much better than I have been for
many years.

[QUINE'S NOTE IN HIS HAND ON THE BACK OF CARNAP'S
LETTER:]

Good to hear, indeed been long. Mnwhile had got good news
indirectly of recovery of good health.

[151. QUINE TO CARNAP 1957-12-30]

AMERICAN PHILOSOPHICAL ASSOCIATION

Office of the President

Dec. 30, '57

Dear Carnap,

The enclosed should have gone back to you long ago. Somehow it got covered up.

We were all disappointed that you don't feel you can come on to Harvard this spring or next. But Marge and I are hoping to see something of you and Ina next year, for we shall be at the Behavioral Center at Palo Alto.

Last year I was at the Institute for Advanced Study, and we lived in what had been the guest house, in Maxwell Lane across from where you once were. The book on which I was working, *Things and Words*, is still in process; meanwhile I uttered a condensation of part of it as my presidential address, evening before last.

With fond greetings to Ina and yourself,

Yours,
Van

[152. CARNAP TO QUINE 1958-6-24]

Rudolf Carnap
11645 Chenault St.
Los Angeles 49, Cal.

a. | June 24, 1958.

Dear Van:

Thank you for your letter of December 30. I suppose, I also owe to you the repeated invitations to give the Santayana lecture; I hope, you understood the reasons for which I declined.

I waited so long with my reply, because I did not know for certain where I was going to be for the coming year. I knew, of courese, that my department had asked the administration for my reappointment (I am reaching official retirement age this month), and we all knew that in theory such reappointments on an annual basis are possible until age 70, but we did not know whether it would be granted in my case, since only a very small fraction of the retiring professors are kept on after age 67. But now it has just become certain, which means that I will be here all summer and also all the next academic year. Thus I hope we shall really see something of you and Marge since you will be at Stanford. We have not seen each other since your visit to Santa Fe! How nice it would have been to be at the Princeton Institute at the same time, with a chance for detailed and leisurely discussions!

We live about 10 minutes driving from UCLA in an area which is called Brentwood. Our telephone is: GRanite 2-9964. Los Angeles has several telephone books for the different areas; we are listed in the Western directory.

I am still at work on the Schilpp volume; the first draft needs a good deal of overhauling and cutting (I had dictated the text into a tape recorder on the basis of a German shorthand ms.). I expect to be able to deliver the ms to Schilpp on his return from Europe in September.

With best regards to both of you, and also many thanks for the unusually nice Christmas cards which Marge has been sending us so faithfully,

Yours,
Carnap

P.S. The English translation of my 1954 Einführung in die symbolische Logik has just appeared at Dover. I suggested that they send you a copy; if they should not take up my suggestion, of course, I will send you one myself.

[MARGINALIA ON QUINE'S COPY:]

a. Ans'd ca. July 22

[153. QUINE TO CARNAP 1958-7-17]

HARVARD UNIVERSITY
DEPARTMENT OF PHILOSOPHY

Emerson Hall
Cambridge 38, Massachusetts
July 17, 1958

Dear Carnap,

I was glad to have your good letter of June 24 and, last week, the Dover edition of your logic text. It will be a boon to American and English readers to have this translation and the more so for its compactness and its low price. I guess it's the first time a substantial introduction to the subject has appeared in English in this form—a pocket book. I think it could have an enormous sale and be a major influence in spreading knowledge of the subject.

I wonder if you remember Beacon Hill, a picturesque quarter of downtown Boston built with brick row houses of about 1805-1825. We bought one, improved the inside, and moved in last March. We are delighted. Also we have a cabin in a woods by a lake 30 miles out, where we are now. Ironically we are reluctant to leave for a year. Yet it is a year to look forward to, and not only for the splendid freedom from duties.

We sail eight days hence, from New York, on a freighter for Vera Cruz—complete with Douglas (7), Margaret (4), and car. At Mexico City my daughter Norma, who just graduated from U.C.L.A., will meet us by plane. We will drive slowly via the west coast of Mexico to Arizona and California, reaching Stanford in time for public schools. I hope we may manage a glimpse of you and Ina on the way through, and show you the children. But also we are counting on seeing you under easier conditions during the year.

Yours,
Van

[154. CARNAP TO QUINE   1959-1-29]

January 29, 1959.

Dear Van:

We hope very much that you are well enough to be able to
enjoy life and to work, even though you are restricted in your
activities. I understand that there is much leeway at the Stanford Center (as there was at the Princeton Institute) with respect
to their expectations of how members will spend their time, so
at least you have no pressure on you from that side. That is
very good. I happened to have a miserable period with my back
while I was at Princeton, and it was a great comfort to me to
know that I could afford to stay at home, and work in bed
when necessary, without being considered remiss in my duties.
Of course, we would very much like to see you both before you
return East, if that is possible. I am very well, and my back has
improved remarkably; but from the miserable period I have retained a certain reluctance to travel (also one of the reasons why
I declined the Whitehead lectures) unless there is a very compelling reason. I am officially retired here as of last June, but I have
been reappointed to the same job on a yearly basis (this is University of California procedure from age 67 on). You will have
received my recent letter re my contributions to the Schilpp volume; from his reply to me I myself only learned that the book
will not go into production until the Broad volume is completed;
thus even "1960" would seem optimistic.

The immediate reason for my letter today is the following.
You may already have received a direct letter by a Prof. Roman
Susko, Asst. Prof. at Warsaw, who would like to talk to you
some time during the next months if you are well enough. He
has asked me to write you about him, since he has spent the
last two months here, and has talked to me and shown me several manuscripts.

He has good training in formal logic and in metatheory (according to Tarski's method), and seems to have a good knowledge and understanding of Tarski's, your and my work. He is
skillful and exact in constructing formalized systems, is eager,

intelligent and productive, but I cannot yet judge whether his ideas will show great originality. He is a very pleasant person. There is some communication difficulty—his German is definitely better than his English—but he is improving rapidly.

With best wishes and regards for both of you,

Yours,

C.

[155.   QUINE TO CARNAP   1959-2-14]

CENTER FOR ADVANCED STUDY IN THE BEHAVIORAL
SCIENCES

a.

202 Junipero Serra Boulevard   •
Stanford, California   DAvenport 5-0026

February 14, 1959

Professor Rudolf Carnap
University of California
Los Angeles 24, California

Dear Carnap:

Thanks for your good letter. My recovery seems to proceed at the canonical rate, and meanwhile I have been getting on well with my work. I now believe that this book that I have been stewing over for so many years may be ready for the publisher in a couple of months. The tentative title is *Terms and Objects*. Early and late your influence on it has been strong, even where

b. | negative. May I dedicate it to you?

Enclosed is a copy of a letter I have written to Schilpp. I will hold the original for a week before mailing it to him, so as to give you a chance meanwhile to let me know if for any reason you dislike the idea.

Davidson determined today that the Stanford University Press could bring out the Schilpp volume within a year of delivery of manuscript, and that they would almost certainly be willing to do so without subsidy. If Schilpp feels that the uncooperative line adopted by Tudor gives him no ground for considering their contract unbinding, still as unpaid contributors we all remain free to withdraw our manuscripts and submit them to Stanford for editing and publishing without the Living Philosophers imprint. This

is strong language, and I have not used it in this opening letter to
Schilpp; but, if things get sticky, the mere mention of the alternative might suffice to precipitate constructive activity at Tudor.

I have written Suszko and hope to see him next week.

I do hope it proves possible to see you and Ina sometime this
spring. Since arriving here last September, I have never ven-
tured as far afield even as Berkeley (though once I went to a
meeting a few miles short of there). But I propose to modify this
pattern abruptly in June, when I am to give the Gavin David
Young Lectures in Australia. Thence to Japan for further lecturing, and back to Harvard for the fall. Marge will skip Australia
but is counting on Japan.

With fond greetings to Ina and yourself.

Yours,

Van

W. V. Quine

WVQ:act

[MARGINALIA ON CARNAP'S COPY:]

a. Confidential! Please return!
b. ⟨in shorthand:⟩ yes

[156. QUINE TO PAUL A. SCHILPP   1959-2-14]

CENTER FOR ADVANCED STUDY IN THE BEHAVIORAL
SCIENCES | a.

202 Junipero Serra Boulevard •
Stanford, California   DAvenport 5-0026

February 14, 1959

Dr. Paul A. Schilpp
The Library of Living Philosophers
Northwestern University
Evanston, Illinois

Dear Schilpp:

I interpret your circular letter of January 26 as predicting a
substantial further interval of delay of the Carnap volume, be-

tween the date when the material can be made ready for the printer and the date when manufacture will begin. I feel I must protest this.

I think I can assume that when you obtained essays against a deadline five years ago for this volume, you deflected every contributor's creative energy, for a period of one or several months, into channels that the contributor would not have chosen on his own initiative. What enabled you to succeed in this was the contributors' good will toward Carnap and yourself, together with their expectation that the effort thus diverted would still be productive enough in a scholarly way.

Five years of delay have detracted from the value that was reasonably to be expected under the latter head, since thought has meanwhile had to progress as best it might without benefit of the waiting essays. Contributors have had much reason to feel imposed upon, however insuperable your obstacles.

But if a further obstacle now threatens at the level of mere convenience to the publisher, I do not see how a contributor can reasonably react otherwise than with a sense of outrage. Surely it is your responsibility to seek another publisher who will produce the book without delay, and to contest any contract that purports to bind you to a publisher so unmindful of a moral debt to his unpaid contributors or so ill equipped to meet his responsibilities.

Sincerely yours,
W. V. Quine

WVQ:act

⟨This is obviously an enclosure in 155.⟩

[MARGINALIA ON CARNAP'S COPY:]

a. ⟨in Quine's hand:⟩ Advance Copy ⟨in Carnap's hand:⟩ Please return.

[157. CARNAP TO QUINE 1959-2-21]

Dept. of Philosophy
UNIVERSITY OF CALIFORNIA

a.

Los Angeles 24, California

February 21, 1959

Dear Van:

Thank you very much for your letter of Feb. 14, which reached me late since I do not pick up my mail at the office, except when I go there on business. If ever you want to reach me quickly, you had better use my private address:

11645 Chenault St., L.A. 49. (Phone: GRanite 2-9964).

That you think of dedicating your next book to me pleases and touches me greatly.

Your letter to Schilpp of Feb. 14 seems to me quite appropriate. I myself have not yet replied to his circular letter, but I have pondered also how the publication could be speeded up (at some point in my thinking I even had considered putting some money of my own into it, not as a subsidy, but repayable from sales, if that would induce the publisher to go ahead right away, perhaps with an other printer. But, of course, I know nothing about Tudor Publishing Co., and their business methods, and would rather not risk my money.) By the way, the arrangement with the Library (or with Schilpp, who is the Library) is such that I too am an unpaid author, the Library does not pay royalties or give reprints, I think 2 free copies is all I have to expect— and somehow or other I put the larger part of four years into the writing. On the other hand, I am not entitled to the same degree of moral indignation as the other contributors, since the delay up to last October was entirely my fault. But I will write to Schilpp and also urge him to the same course of action as you do. I foresee that he will reply that he has an agreement with this publisher for the whole Library, and that he cannot induce Tudor to print two volumes at the same time nor seek another publisher—but that is surmise. What puzzles me somewhat is what caused the delay in sending the Broad volume to the publisher: he wrote me in February '57 that he has had Broad's Autobiogr. in his hands for 2 years, and that a month ago Broad had sent him his completed "Reply", and at that time he was dreaming that it might be nice if the Broad vol. came out in time for B.'s 70th birthday in December 57 (which causes me to think that he also had all the other contributions for this volume at that time, in addition, they must have been in before Broad could reply to them). One reason for the delay might have been that the publisher refused to start it before the Jaspers volume was out (it came out in Feb. 58, according to Schilpp). But then the puzzle begins, why Schilpp did not send the Broad mss. to the publisher in Feb. '58? The simple answer seems to be that the editorial work was not finished, since he writes that he finished it after his return from Europe, end of Sept. 58, and sent it in end of Dec. '58. Well, but that is water over the dam by now, and since I am the culprit on the Carnap volume, I cannot well reproach Schilpp for having delayed his work on the Broad volume.

Aside from Schilpp's feelings in the matter, the possibility of having the volume appear e.g. at Stanford U. Press within a year, sounds very attractive. Although it has its advantages of having a volume in a series such as the Living Philosophers, I think the book can stand on its own.

Of course, there always is the possibility that Tudor may not be too eager to bring the Carnap volume at all because of its size. Sch. wrote me on Jan. 21: "I still have the tremendous job of selling the publisher on what—in all probability—will have to be published as a 2-volumes work ahead of me". And before he used expressions like "I dread the reaction of our publishers when they see the overall size of the Carnap volume. I am afraid they will hit the ceiling". All this makes me think that Schilpp will not have the courage to tell the publishers what their "moral responsibilities" toward the contributors are. I presume that the whole enterprise is making money—at least some of the volumes make more than others loose ⟨*sic*⟩, or no publisher would keep on with it. Therefore I do not quite understand why Schilpp is playing scared.

We are surprised about your major travel plans, and hope that they indicate that you expect to be completely well by then.

Of course, we would like very much to see you at some time or other before you disappear again from this part of the country.

It seems that the Stanford Center is broadening their conception of the "behavioral sciences": you are there this year, and I hear that Nagel will be there in the next, and also Hempel unless he receives a Fulbright for England. But then, the Princeton Institute too had finally succumbed to the (rare) infiltration of philosophers; Stanford has the additional attractions of more money and better climate than Princeton.

Our best to you both,

Yours,
Carnap

[MARGINALIA ON CARNAP'S COPY:]

a. Please return

[158. CARNAP TO QUINE   1959-9-29]

Rudolf Carnap
Department of Philosophy
University of California
Los Angeles 24, Cal.   Sept. 29, 1959

Dear Colleague:

You may have heard that Arthur Pap of the Department of Philosophy at Yale University died on September 7.

He is survived by his wife and four young children who are of course now in straitened circumstances. His department has established a fund to receive contributions for their benefit. Checks should be made payable to the Arthur Pap Fund, and sent to Miss Mabel Weld, Secretary, Depart. of Philosophy, Yale University, New Haven, Conn. Miss Weld is handling the whole matter, and deposits checks (anonymously) in the Fund's account.

The Yale Philosophy Department does not intend to make a general appeal, and I heard about the establishment of the Fund only in reply to my own inquiry. They intend to let the appeal go around by word of mouth. Since I think that word of mouth might not go around sufficiently, I am taking it upon myself to inform some of my colleagues directly, in the hope that they might spread the word further and especially in their own departments.

It does not happen too often that one of our colleagues dies so tragically early and leaves a large family without having had the time to provide for them adequately. Our contributions to the Fund cannot do that either, but they will be a useful way of expressing our sorrow over the loss of a gifted colleague and friend and our concern for his family.

Sincerely yours,
Rudolf Carnap

⟨Quine's copy of this letter is variously marked in different handwritings (neither Quine's nor Carnap's). These indicate that the full text of the letter was reproduced and distributed to Quine's colleagues at Harvard.⟩

[159. INA CARNAP TO QUINE   1960-5-3]

May 3, 1960

Dear Van:

Carnap was so pleased about your dedicating your new book to him and the dedication itself sounded so very nice. He will write you later when he has had more time to read in it.

Unfortunately the last two weeks were taken up with other concerns: he had a small accident, fell over a step and wrenched his back. Nothing is broken, but it's a painful sprain and—what's even more important—it's just in the area where he has had so much trouble for decades and therefore it will take him longer to get over it. He is working again, right now on his promised paper for the Fraenkel Festschrift which is due right now. But when that is out of the way he can get to immersing himself in your book to which he is looking forward.

Ernest Nagel just was here for a weekend from Stanford—

what a pity that Van could not come. But maybe there will be a meeting in August at Stanford? Carnap has promised to give a talk there.

With best regards, wishes and thanks,

Yours,

[160.   ROBERT Y. ZACHARY TO QUINE   1961-3-28]

UNIVERSITY OF CALIFORNIA PRESS
~~BERKELEY AND~~ LOS ANGELES

LOS ANGELES OFFICE   214 Royce Hall
405 HILGARD AVENUE   Los Angeles 24

28 March 1961

Mr. Willard V. Quine
Department of Philosophy
Harvard University
Cambridge, Massachusetts

Dear Mr. Quine:

The Press is considering the publication of a translation of Rudolf Carnap's *Der Logische Aufbau der Welt*. It would be extremely helpful to us if you would provide us with a statement as to the value of the work, whether at this late date it should be translated and published. Also, do you feel it necessary that any such translation should incorporate commentary (footnotes, etc.) that would bring the original text into some harmony with Carnap's present thought? It is doubtful to me whether he could afford the time to do this work. At any rate, your judgment about the work will be kept entirely confidential.

Sincerely,
Robert Y. Zachary
Los Angeles Editor

RZY:dd

[161. QUINE TO ZACHARY   1961-3-31]

March 31, 1961

Mr. Robert Y. Zachary, Editor
University of California Press
214 Royce Hall
405 Hilgard Avenue
Los Angeles 24, California

Dear Mr. Zachary:

Carnap's *Aufbau* is one of the most interesting and stimulating philosophical writings I know. Yet at important points it is simply wrong: objectively so, quite apart from questions of philosophical party. These errors are ones that presumably cannot be corrected in such a way as to attain the original goal of the book. Perhaps the best course would be to translate the text without essential modification but add a long critical preface. If Carnap cannot undertake this, perhaps you could persuade Professor Nelson Goodman, of the Department of Philosophy at the University of Pennsylvania. He is at once the book's staunchest admirer and minutest critic, and his sense of its importance might induce him to accept. His own *Structure of Appearance* (Harvard Press) contains a critical analysis of early portions of the *Aufbau*, so the task might not be a forbidding one for him; he might even take excerpts from *Structure of Appearance* and just round them out with a moderate amount of new writing.

Sincerely yours,
W. V. Quine

[162.   CARNAP TO RODERICK FIRTH   1962-11-4]

Department of Philosophy
UNIVERSITY OF CALIFORNIA   a.

Los Angeles 24, California   November 4, 1962

Professor Roderick Firth
Chairman, Department of Philosophy
Harvard University

Dear Professor Firth:

Thank you very much for inviting me again to give the Alfred North Whitehead lecture at Harvard. Although I feel honored by the renewed invitation and I appreciate your kind letter, I do not think that I shall be able to make a trip to the East during the second half of the academic year. As a matter of fact, I am just preparing to leave Los Angeles for a place even further West: I have been invited to be a Fellow at the Center for Advanced Study in the Behavioral Sciences at Stanford for this year and I would already be there if I had not been prevented by special circumstances from arriving there in time. I expect to move there at the end of November.

I have retired from UCLA last June in order to be able to give most of my time to my writing and I feel that a trip East would take up too much of my time. I do not believe that single lectures at various places are of sufficient benefit to listeners to make it worth my time, whereas my writings will reach larger numbers and present my views in necessary detail. I am not completely averse to giving single lectures if they do not involve too much travelling time but I trust that you will understand my reluctance where long trips are involved.

Please give my best wishes and regards to the Department and express to them my appreciation for the invitation and my regret that I cannot accept it.

Sincerely yours,
Rudolf Carnap

[MARGINALIA ON QUINE'S COPY:]

a. Copy for W. Q.

⟨While this letter is neither to nor from Quine, it is included here in part because a copy of it is included in Quine's "Carnap" file, in part because Carnap must have foreseen that Quine would receive such a copy, and in part because the letter is informative both about Carnap and about his continuing friendship with Quine.⟩

[163.   QUINE TO ERNEST A. MOODY   1963-1-21]

January 21, 1963

Professor Ernest A. Moody
Department of Philosophy
University of California
Los Angeles 24, California

Dear Professor Moody:

Russell had talked of deriving the world from experience by logical construction, but his constructions were sketchy and slight. Carnap, in *Der logische Aufbau der Welt* (1928), set himself to the task in earnest. The conception was a grand one, yet the project, at a time when so few philosophers understood technical logic, was self-effacing. Much ingenuity went into the constructions, much philosophical imagination, much understanding of psychology and physics. If the book did not achieve its exalted purpose, it did achieve a great deal. It afforded for the first time an example of what a scientific philosopher might aspire to in the way of rigor and explicitness. It afforded detailed glimpses also, and philosophically exciting ones, of how our knowledge of the external world could in considerable part turn out to be, in Eddington's phrase, a put-up job. And it provided techniques of construction that can be put to continued use, as they notably have been in Goodman's *Structure of Appearance*.

Carnap's next great contribution was his *Logical Syntax of Lan-*

guage (1934), with its doctrine that philosophy is the syntax of the language of science. Here again the resources of modern logic were vigorously exploited for philosophical ends. The book is a mine of proof and opinion on the philosophy of logic as well as the logic of philosophy. During a critical decade it was the main inspiration of young scientific philosophers. It was the definitive work at the center, from which the waves of tracts and popularizations issued in ever widening circles. Carnap more than anyone else, more than Wittgenstein, was the individual embodiment of logical positivism, logical empiricism, the Vienna Circle.

True, Carnap found his thesis of syntax untenable in the end. There consequently supervened his *Introduction to Semantics* (1942) and substantial subsequent writings, which have given Carnap his present central position in the controversial subject of modal logic and its philosophy.

Alongside all this Carnap's *Logical Foundations of Probability* (1950) continued to develop, a monument to his unwavering concern with the logic of scientific evidence. I gather that a sequel to it is in the works.

I find much to disagree with in Carnap. A lot of my work has been motivated by this disagreement. This was one reason why I dedicated *Word and Object* to him; the other reason was that I had learned so much from him. I think that in the past 35 years of philosophy no figure has loomed larger than Carnap, and only Wittgenstein as large.

Sincerely yours,
W. V. Quine

On January 10, 1963, Ernest Moody wrote to Quine as part of an effort to have UCLA honor Carnap. He asked for "a letter giving your estimate of Carnap's life achievement as a philosopher, and of the significance of his work as an influence on the work done in philosophy during the past thirty years."

Item 163 is Quine's reply. On January 24, 1963, Moody responded, saying "This was exactly what I needed, and was magnificently done—as if I had asked Grant for his estimate of Lee as a general.")

[164. QUINE TO CARNAP 1964-6-3]

HARVARD UNIVERSITY
DEPARTMENT OF PHILOSOPHY

Emerson Hall
Cambridge 38, Massachusetts
June 3, 1964

Dear Carnap,

Just as I was thinking congratulations on your great volume in the Living Philosophers, I received word from Diane of Ina's tragic end. You have my deep sympathy, and Marge's too, in this awful time.

Yours ever
Van

[165. QUINE TO CARNAP 1966-5-13]

HARVARD UNIVERSITY
DEPARTMENT OF PHILOSOPHY

Emerson Hall
Cambridge, Massachusetts 02138
May 13, 1966

Dear Carnap,

At intervals this year I have discussed the philosophy of mathematics and logic with a young Japanese professor named Natuhiko Yosida. Also he has attended my graduate course in axiomatic set theory, and has made a contribution there which will modify the next edition of my Set Theory & Its Logic. He is very intelligent; by far the most rewarding of my rather numerous Japanese contacts, here and in Japan. If he seeks an audience I would urge you to talk with him.

It was splendid seeing you in London. I wonder if I'll see you next week in Denver.

Yours,
Van

[MARGINALIA ON CARNAP'S COPY:]

a. Quine (about Yosida) (See K! He was in LA 19 July 66)

[166.   CARNAP TO QUINE   1970-7-24]

RUDOLF CARNAP
11728 Dorothy St., Apt. 304
  Los Angeles, Cal. 90049
    Phone 826-6377

July 24, 1970

Professor W. V. Quine
38 Chestnut St.
Boston, Mass. 02108

Dear Van,

Thank you very much for sending me your book *Ontological Relativity and Other Essays.* I like very much to have these papers together, and I find especially your discussions in Chapters 5 and 6 very illuminating. Today I will only make a few comments on Chapter 5. [On Chapter 6 I just wish to make the remark that in my work on inductive logic I have used at least since 1960 instead of the earlier state-descriptions (as in my probability book of 1950) rather the corresponding truth-sets, called "events" by statisticians and "propositions" by me (see p. 42, Example (33)); they are classes of models and therefore extensional.]
    Your discussions of natural kinds are clearly of great importance for inductive logic. I shall send you soon* sections 1–5 of my treatise "A Basic System of Inductive Logic", Part I. Part I contains sections 1–13. If you should be interested in further sections (whose subject matter you can see from the table of contents) please drop me a line, then I shall be glad to send them to you. This Part I together with Articles by Richard Jeffrey and others is now in the hands of the University of Califor-

*In the meantime, you might borrow it from Putnam, ⟨This footnote is in German shorthand on Carnap's copy of this letter.⟩

nia Press as vol. I of *Studies in Probability and Inductive Logic*, edited by me together with Richard Jeffrey. We hope that the book will appear early in 1971. Maybe sections 4B and 5 will be of special interest for you. In section 4B I have tried to give an explication (I hope improved in comparison to my earlier attempts) of "natural kìnds" in such a way that Goodman's predicates "grue" and "bleen" are excluded.

On pages 31f. you will find that I agree with you in the view that the transition from everyday concepts (e.g., for colors) to scientific concept systems leads at some places to an abrupt change in the similarity relations.

Another point which might interest you is my new explication of the concept "the proposition A *is about* the individual a_5 (or the attribute P_1)"; in my present terminology: "A *involves* a_5 (or P_1)". See pages 46 to 48.

It is regrettable that we are so far apart. I would often like very much to talk with you. Do you not come some time to the West Coast? For me traveling is rather bothersome because of my eyes. (But the operations a year ago were successful so that a few months later I was again able to read and write, though not to type.)

A few days ago your pupil Mondadori visited me. He is really intelligent and has a lively interest in problems; and, what is more, he is a nice person. We had an enjoyable talk together.

With cordial regards,

yours,
Carnap

RC:jbc

[167.   QUINE TO CARNAP   1970-8-17]

HARVARD UNIVERSITY

Department of Philosophy   Cambridge, Massachusetts 02138
Emerson Hall   (607) 495-3913
                                                      August 17, 1970

Professor Rudolf Carnap
11728 Dorothy Street, Apt. 304
Los Angeles, California 90049

Dear Carnap:

A few days ago I returned with my family from equatorial
Africa. We had been gone nearly ten weeks, ranging from
Isnesstoften, Norway, in 70°7′ N. lat, to Dar-es-Salaam, 7° S. I
came back to a great accumulation of mail. I was particularly
glad to find in it your good letter of July 24, and now I look
forward to seeing sections 1–5 of your "Basic System of Inductive Logic."* It is cheering to hear that we have been thinking
about the same things. Your material promises to be decidedly
relevant to my continuing efforts, a few weeks hence (when I
shall have finished my new revised edition of *Methods of Logic*).

I was much relieved to learn from Peter Hempel that your
cataract operations were successful. Now Peter faces similar
ones.

I have promised to come to Irvine for three weeks of the Summer Institute next August, on the philosophy of language. I
shall count on getting over to see you.

With all good wishes,

Yours,
Van
W. V. Quine

WVQ:aw

*It just came.

[168.   HANNA THOST TO QUINE   1970-9-15]

Dear Professor Quine,

After a sudden brief illness my father, Rudolf Carnap, died peacefully in the morning of September 14th.

Instead of funeral services now, there will be a memorial gathering for him in a few weeks.

Yours, Hanna Thost.

Los Angeles, September 15, 1970

[169.   QUINE TO MRS. THOST-CARNAP   1970-9-18]

Sept. 18, 1970

Dear Mrs. Thost-Carnap,

I deeply sympathize with you over the death of your father. Carnap was my old and valued friend, besides being the greatest of my teachers. So I very much share your personal sense of loss, as well as the sense of an overwhelming loss to philosophy.

He was a towering figure—surely the most significant philosopher throughout the middle third, and more, of this century. His tragic death, while still at the height of his intellectual powers, marks a sad date in the history of philosophy.

Sincerely yours,

HOMAGE TO RUDOLF CARNAP

W. V. Quine

CARNAP IS a towering figure. I see him as the dominant figure in philosophy from the 1930's onward, as Russell had been in the decades before. Russell's well-earned glory went on mounting afterward, as the evidence of his historical importance continued to pile up; but the leader of the continuing developments was Carnap. Some philosophers would assign this role rather to Wittgenstein; but many see the scene as I do.

Russell had talked of deriving the world from experience by logical construction. Carnap, in his *Aufbau*, undertook the task in earnest. It was a grand project, and yet a self-effacing one, when so few philosophers understood technical logic. Much ingenuity went into the constructions, much philosophical imagination, much understanding of psychology and physics. If the book did not achieve its exalted purpose, it did afford for the first time an example of what a scientific philosopher might aspire to in the way of rigor and explicitness. It afforded detailed glimpses also, and philosophically exciting ones, of how our knowledge of the external world could in considerable part turn out to be, in Eddington's phrase, a put-up job. And it provided techniques of construction that continue to be useful.

In his *Logical Syntax* Carnap again vigorously exploited the resources of modern logic for philosophical ends. The book is a

Reprinted from *PSA 1970: In Memory of Rudolf Carnap: Proceedings of the 1970 Biennial Meeting, Philosophy of Science Association*, ed. Roger C. Buck and Robert S. Cohen, Boston Studies in the Philosophy of Science, vol. 8 (Dordrecht and Boston: D. Reidel Publishing Co., 1971).

mine of proof and opinion on the philosophy of logic and the logic of philosophy. During a critical decade it was the main inspiration of young scientific philosophers. It was the definitive work at the center, from which the waves of tracts and popularizations issued in ever widening circles. Carnap more than anyone else was the embodiment of logical positivism, logical empiricism, the Vienna Circle.

Ultimately Carnap saw limitations in his thesis of syntax. Thus came his third phase: books and papers on semantics, which have given Carnap a central place in the controversies over modal logic.

Meanwhile Carnap's *Logical Foundations of Probability* continued to develop, a monument to his unwavering concern with the logic of science. Two months ago I had a lively letter from him about some supplementary work that he was doing on this subject. Also he sent me a sheaf of material from the new work in progress.

Carnap was my greatest teacher. I got to him in Prague 38 years ago, just a few months after I had finished my formal studies and received my Ph.D. I was very much his disciple for six years. In later years his views went on evolving and so did mine, in divergent ways. But even where we disagreed he was still setting the theme; the line of my thought was largely determined by problems that I felt his position presented.

I first heard about Carnap and his *Aufbau* from John Cooley in 1931, when we were graduate students at Harvard. Herbert Feigl was then at Harvard as an International Rockefeller Fellow. He encouraged me to go to Vienna and to Carnap the following year if I got a traveling fellowship.

Carnap moved from Vienna to Prague that year, and I followed him. I attended his lectures and read his *Logische Syntax* page by page as it issued from Ina Carnap's typewriter. Carnap and Ina were a happy pair. He was 41, she even younger. Along with their intense productivity there was an almost gay informality. If you combine strong intellectual stimulation, easy laughter, and warm friendliness, you have an unbeatable recipe for good company; and such were the Carnaps. On a day when Carnap didn't have to come into the city to lecture, my wife and I would ride the trolley to the end of the line and walk the remaining few blocks to their little house in a suburb called Pod Homolkou. As the name implies, the place is at the foot of something; and Carnap and Ina would have just come in, likely as not, from an hour on skis on that very slope. Carnap and I would discuss logic and philosophy by the hour. My wife and I would stay to lunch, or maybe dinner; but, if dinner, that was the end of philosophy and logic until another meeting. Carnap's habits were already austere: no science after dinner, on pain of a sleepless night. No alcohol ever. No coffee.

I was then an unknown young foreigner of 23, with thirteen inconsequential pages in print and sixteen at press. It was extraordinary of anyone, and characteristic of Carnap, to have been so generous of his time and energy. It was a handsome gift. It was my first experience of sustained intellectual engagement with anyone of an older generation, let alone a great man. It was my first really considerable experience of being intellectually fired by a living teacher rather than by a dead book. I had not been aware of the lack. One goes on listening respectfully to one's elders, learning things, hearing things with varying degrees of approval, and expecting as a matter of course to have to fall back on one's own resources and those of the library for the main motive power. One recognizes that his professor has his own work to do, and that the problems and the approaches that appeal to him need not coincide in any very fruitful way with those that are exercising oneself. I could see myself in the professor's place, and I sought nothing different. I suppose most of us go through life with no brighter view than this of the groves of Academe. So might I have done, but for the graciousness of Carnap.

At Harvard the following year, I lectured on Carnap's philosophy. Our correspondence was voluminous. He would write in English, practicing up for a visit to America, and I in German; and we would enclose copies for correction. By Christmas 1935 he was with us in our Cambridge flat. Four of us drove with him from Cambridge to the Philosophical Association meeting in Baltimore. The others were David Prall, Mason Gross, and Nelson Goodman. We moved with Carnap as henchmen through the metaphysicians' camp. We beamed with partisan pride when he countered a diatribe of Arthur Lovejoy's in his characteristically reasonable way, explaining that if Lovejoy means *A* then *p*, and if he means *B* then *q*. I had yet to learn how unsatisfying this way of Carnap's could sometimes be.

Soon Carnap settled at Chicago. Two years later I took him to task for flirting with modal logic. His answer was characteristic:

I do not indulge in this vice generally and thoroughly. . . . Although we do not like to apply intensional languages, nevertheless I think we cannot help analyzing them. What would you think of an entomologist who refuses to investigate fleas and lice because he dislikes them?

In 1939 Carnap came to Harvard as visiting professor. Those were historic months: Russell, Carnap, and Tarski were here together. Then it was that Tarski and I argued long with Carnap against his idea of analyticity.

Because of distances our later meetings were regrettably few. In 1949 my new and present wife and I spent some memorable days at the Carnaps' in New Mexico. In 1951 he and I held a symposium on ontology in Chicago. In 1958 a reunion in California was prevented by an illness of mine. Finally in 1965, to my delight, I saw him at Popper's colloquium in London. He looked well and was vigorous and alert. When Popper confronted him on induction his defense was masterly. It carried me back to his confrontation of Lovejoy thirty years before. It was the same old Carnap. His tragic death, while still at the height of his powers, marks a sad date in the history of philosophy.

Harvard University   W. V. QUINE

[INDEX]

Printed in the United Kingdom
by Lightning Source UK Ltd.
134939UK00002B/148-153/A